Care in Practice
for Higher Still

Edited by **Janet Miller**

Susan Gibb, George Baker, Doris Graham
Ellen Lancaster and Sadie Hollis

Hodder & Stoughton

A MEMBER OF THE HODDER HEADLINE GROUP

To Donna and Jacqui

Orders: please contact Bookpoint Ltd, 130 Milton Park, Abingdon, Oxon OX14 4SB. Telephone: (44) 01235 827720, Fax: (44) 01235 400454. Lines are open from 9.00–6.00, Monday to Saturday, with a 24 hour message answering service. You can also order through our website: www.hodderheadline.co.uk.

British Library Cataloguing in Publication Data
A catalogue record for this title is available from The British Library

ISBN 0 340 738065

First published 2000
Impression number   10   9   8   7   6
Year   2005   2004   2003   2002

Typeset by Wearset, Boldon, Tyne and Wear.
Printed in Great Britain for Hodder & Stoughton Educational, a division of Hodder Headline Plc, 338 Euston Road, London NW1 3BH by J.W. Arrowsmith Ltd, Bristol.

Contents

Acknowledgements vii

Introduction viii

CHAPTER 1   **The care context**.................................George Baker   1
The nature of care 1
What do we mean by care?... 2
What makes a good care worker?... 2
Formal and informal care.. 3
Care work in different fields 4
Care work in the past... 5
Care work today.. 6
Institutionalisation... 7
Who are the service users?.. 11
The power of the carer 11
The nature of work in care 12
The growth in demand for care... 14
The concepts of social exclusion and inclusion 22
Zeitgeists and cohorts... 23
The political context 23
The providers of care.. 27
Summary 30

CHAPTER 2   **Equality of opportunity and
anti-discriminatory practice** ....Susan Gibb   34
Introduction 34
The nature of discrimination 35
Types of discrimination 41
Levels at which discrimination takes place........................... 47
Effects of discrimination 52
Anti-discriminatory practice 57
Summary 81

CHAPTER 3 **An introduction to human development and behaviour** ....Janet Miller 83

Introduction 83

Influences on development and behaviour 84

Socialisation 90

Development at different ages and stages 97

   birth to two years old 97

   two to five 102

   childhood 106

   adolescence 108

   adulthood 116

   older adulthood 122

CHAPTER 4 **The contribution of developmental psychology and its applications** ....Doris Graham 132

Introduction 132

Using the tools of developmental psychology – theories and perspectives .. 134

Maslow's Hierarchy of Needs 136

Lifespan theory 140

Behavioural theory 142

Social learning theory 145

Attachment and separation 149

Development of self concept 155

Transition and loss 158

CHAPTER 5 **The sociological contribution and its applications** .....Janet Miller 172

Introduction 172

Sociology 173

Some sociological background and concepts 174

Sociological perspectives 180

   – A functionalist perspective 181

   – A conflict perspective 183

   – An interactionist perspective 184

   – A feminist perspective 187

Aspects of society 190

   – The family 190

   – Education 199

   – Deviance 205

   – Institutionalisation 212

CHAPTER 6 **Interpersonal skills** ....Ellen Lancaster 219

Introduction 219

The value base 220

Effective communication.. 230
Personal qualities required by the care worker............................... 241
Qualities and attributes – a note on the Higher syllabus......................... 245
The many roles of the care worker 245

CHAPTER 7 **Care planning and the helping process**....................Janet Miller 253
Introduction 253
Introduction to care planning 254
The planning process in health promotion 255
Assessment.. 256
Needs 257
Tools of assessment 264
The care plan 267
The helping process 273
Health promotion and the helping process 294
Evaluation – monitoring and reviewing 294

CHAPTER 8 **Health promotion**..Sadie Hollis 296
Introduction 296

Part 1 – An introduction to health promotion...................................... 298
What is health? 298
Factors which can influence health 300
Factors which influence access to health provision......................... 306
Factors which may influence an individual's concept of health 312
Health promotion 314
Core values and principles of good practice 315
Legislation, policies and charters... 316
Elements of health promotion... 321
– Health education 321
– Prevention.. 323
– Health protection 325
A model of health promotion (Tannahill) 325

Part 2 Introduction... 327
Models of health promotion.. 327
– Medical... 328
– Educational.. 329
– Community development.. 330
– Marketing.. 330
– Political 332
– Client-centred 333
Strategies for analysing the effectiveness of health promotion campaigns.. 333
Skills to promote health and well-being to others 335

CHAPTER 9   **Research and gathering evidence** ....Janet Miller 345
Introduction 345
The research process 346
Choosing a sample 349
Questionnaires 352
Epidemiology and health promotion 355
Qualitative research 357
Longitudinal research 359
Some ethical considerations 363
Using secondary sources.. 363
Combining several research methods 369
Presenting research findings 370
Research and health promotion... 370

CHAPTER 10   **Integration and conclusions** ....Janet Miller 373
Introduction 373
Case study – A tale of two families: The MacDonalds and the Ahmeds 373
Links 378
The strands of human development and behaviour 378
• promoting equal opportunities in a care context 382
• interpersonal skills for care 385
• health promotion 387
Conclusion 388

Glossary 389

Appendix: The Social Care Association and Heatherbank Museum of
Social Care... 401

Index... 402

Acknowledgements

Many people helped us to put this book together. The following list hardly does justice to all of the people who gave us assistance. If we didn't mention you by name we apologise and say thank you anyway. Thanks to service users and staff of Sense Scotland, Crookfur Cottage Homes and East Dunbartonshire Social work Department; to Lorna Trainer, Section Leader, and our colleagues at Cardonald College, who had to keep the team going whilst we were busy writing; to Rachel Ball and Laura Smith at Outlook, Kirkintilloch, and to SHS, Edinburgh for information on person-centred planning; to Rev. Alastair Ramage of the Heatherbank Museum of Social Work, Glasgow Caledonian University; to the Social Care Association in Scotland and in Surbiton; to Mary Cartledge and Sharon McBean of the Graphics Department, Michael Gaughan, art student, library staff and HNC Social Care students at Cardonald College; to Margaret and Roseanne Miller for diagrams and Marion Miller for her writings; to Mike, Siobhan and Martin Hollis; to Alexis Horsfield and John Hamilton of Greater Glasgow Health Board and to Steven Ryecroft of Eastbank Health Promotion Centre; to Dr. Andy Furlong of the Department of Sociology, University of Glasgow; to Elisabeth Tribe at Hodder and Stoughton; to Tom Stannage of the Higher Still Development Unit; to Robin Maclean and Andrew Parry for cartoons; The Scottish Office Department of Health; Blackwell's Publishers; Health Education Library, Scotland; SHEPS; Care Sector Consortium; HarperCollins; Waheeda Parveen; Bob Holman; and to our families, friends and colleagues.

Introduction

Every dance, every lifetime, is unique, and that infinity of dances from every race and from every era is of incalculable value, and comprehends the great ceremonial dance of mankind.

(George Mackay Brown, 1995)

Care in Practice aims to open doors for you, so that you can open others for the people with whom you work now or in the future. It emphasises that you **can** make a positive difference to people's lives if you gain a value base, knowledge and skills which relate to care practice. Although the book won't make you an expert it does offer signposts, suggestions and opportunities to begin the process of becoming as good as you can be in the helping process. The chapters have been written for those who are setting out on a career or course in 'care' or who wish to further their knowledge in this and related areas. The subjects and format of the book do, however, specifically cover the syllabuses of the **Scottish Higher Still** in Care at **Intermediate II** and **Higher** levels.

The work is a group effort written by people with varied and extensive practice experience and academic expertise. As such, there may be some areas of repetition, even occasional contradictions which represent some of the different viewpoints current in this field. We are all aware of the rewards and difficulties of care practice and wish to emphasise that for the people you work with it is often the small things which really matter: how you address people, your manner, the little things you do to make a difference to someone's life. It helps if you also have brilliant, original, creative ideas but, if you do, it is still the **ways** in which they are put into practice which make a difference to the quality of life of those with whom you work.

We have attempted to reach some agreements about terminology, emphasising that the language used by care workers is extremely important in avoiding confusion, discrimination and patronisation. In general we have used the term **service user** to refer to people who use care services. This is the term adopted by the Social Care Association and is the term which is most in evidence in much of the current care and social work literature. It is a term which avoids stigma, implications of possession, dependence or patronising overtones. It places an emphasis firmly upon people being worked with as users of a service, and this comes with the expectation that this service will meet need in ways which respect the worth and dignity of individuals. The term **client** is also in current usage and possesses similar advantages to those of 'service user'. As long as the implication of possession, as in 'my client', is avoided, this term is perfectly acceptable. 'Client' is currently used in counselling and some social work literature and on some occasions in this book. The term **Care Worker** is used to refer to anyone working in the care field. It is an all-embracing term, though it is recognised that in practice such workers have many different titles.

Care practice is essentially a practical subject and no amount of reading and study can replace the value of actually doing the job. It is the **combination** of learning and practice, the application of knowledge and skills to practice situations, which determine the quality of the service provided. Although a practice placement is not an absolute requirement of the Scottish Higher courses, it is recommended that participants should try to gain as much experience as possible through voluntary work, a voluntary placement, visits to care agencies or employment in order to complement the rather more academic content of the syllabus.

The aims of this book and those of the national specifications for the Intermediate II and Higher courses coincide to emphasise the provision of the following opportunities:

- to acquire useful knowledge and understanding;
- to consider the needs of self and others;
- to develop the ability to analyse and evaluate;
- to apply theories and concepts to a range of care contexts.

The book is divided into ten chapters. This division is somewhat arbitrary since the chapters are all related to one another and in the end come back to providing the value base, knowledge and skills which are needed to work with service users. The relationships among disciplines are frequently emphasised and it is hoped that the reader will be able to appreciate these relationships to gain an integrated and 'holistic' approach to care practice. This approach stresses not only that disciplines are related to one another but that the whole person in a social situation should be seen as possessing inter-related needs which are physical, intellectual/cognitive, emotional, cultural and social. This theme of interconnectedness and integration is returned to in the final chapter which attempts to pull together the various threads of the book into a coherent whole. A summary of each of the chapters follows, which also gives an idea of which aspects of the Intermediate II and Higher syllabuses are being dealt with. A table which summarises this information is provided at the end of the introduction (page xii).

Chapter 1, **The Care Context**, is essentially an introductory chapter which sets the scene for caring, examining the concept of care and the contexts in which it takes place. It looks at formal and informal care, the nature of care work and reasons for the growth in demand for formal care in British, and especially Scottish, society. Some sociological concepts are introduced, whilst leaving a more detailed consideration of these to future chapters. There is an examination of the providers of formal care, placing this provision within the context of the development, and partial demise, of the Welfare State. The concepts of institutionalisation and community care are also introduced. Examples from practice are provided where relevant, as they are throughout the book. This chapter provides an introduction to all units of both the Intermediate II and the Higher in care and also provides information about institutionalisation, relevant to **Outcome 2** of the Intermediate II Unit, **Social Influences on Behaviour**.

Equality of opportunity and anti-discriminatory practice are the subjects of Chapter 2. The chapter begins with an examination of the relationships among prejudice, stereotyping and discrimination, including how prejudice is learned. It goes on to look at the meaning of equality of opportunity and anti-discriminatory practice. The nature of discrimination and the levels at which it takes place are examined, together with forms of discrimination and how discrimination may be manifested in care settings. The remainder of the chapter looks at strategies for promoting equal opportunities and anti-discriminatory practice which have the four strands of personal, work place, group, and legislative. This chapter provides material for **Outcome 3** of the Intermediate II Unit, **Social influences on Behaviour** (prejudice, stereotyping, discrimination) and for **all Outcomes** of the Higher Unit, *Promoting Equality in a Care Context*.

Chapter 3 provides **An Introduction to Human Development and Behaviour**, examining the concepts of development and behaviour, the strands of behaviour (physical, intellectual/cognitive, emotional and social) and the influences upon development and behaviour, including consideration of the Nature/Nurture debate and socialisation. Human development is then examined from birth to old age. This section is full of generalisations, though it is emphasised that the changes outlined differ from person to person and a multi-cultural approach is promoted. This chapter covers **Outcome 3** of the Intermediate II Unit, **Social Influences on Behaviour** (socialisation) and **all Outcomes** of the Intermediate II Unit, **Human Development**. It also provides an introduction to the Higher Unit, Human Development and Behaviour.

Chapter 4 is entitled **The Contribution of Developmental Psychology and its Applications**. Initially the chapter considers what is meant by developmental psychology and goes on to look at how this can help to explain human development and behaviour. Among the topics considered in this chapter are the following: attachment and separation; development of the self-concept; loss and transition; Maslow's hierarchy of need; social learning theory; Erikson's eight ages of man; Skinner's behavioural perspective. This chapter is of relevance to **Outcomes 1 and 3** of the Higher Unit, **Human Development and Behaviour**.

The Sociological Contribution and its Applications is the subject of Chapter 5. Included in this chapter is a consideration of what is meant by sociology and how this can help to explain human development and behaviour. The chapter proceeds to look at four different sociological perspectives: functionalist; conflict; interactionist; feminist. It then goes on to look at four aspects of society (the family, education, deviance and institutionalisation) from these four sociological perspectives. Illustration is provided through case study material, and activities relate to a case study presented in the final chapter of the book. This chapter relates to **Outcomes 2 and 3** of the Higher Unit, **Human Development and Behaviour** and provides some additional material for the Intermediate II Unit, Human Development.

Chapter 6, **Interpersonal Skills**, aims to provide an understanding of the constituent parts of these skills through an examination of a value base for care, communication, personal qualities and attributes of the care worker and the many roles which care workers play. The value base emphasises respect for the worth of all individuals, their rights as citizens and the principles which result from these core values, including the promotion of choice, privacy and confidentiality. The section which discusses communication emphasises the importance of effective listening and the establishment of relationships based upon empathy, genuineness, unconditional positive regard and reliability. The concept of Oomph is also introduced. Personal qualities (Intermediate II) and attributes (Higher) are the subject of the next section and finally the interplay of the many roles of the care worker are considered, including consideration of the role of keyworker. This chapter covers **all Outcomes** for the Intermediate II Unit, **Understanding Care Skills** and **Outcomes 1 and part of 2** for the Higher Unit, **Interpersonal Skills for Care**. It is also relevant to the Intermediate II Unit **Health Promotion**.

Chapter 7, **Care Planning and the Helping Process**, aims to present a model of care practice based upon assessment, care planning, establishing contracts, the helping process and evaluation. Two models of care planning are presented: the exchange model and person centred planning. There is a detailed examination of the concept of need and of several ways of helping people including on-the-spot counselling, teamwork and group work A short discussion of boundary issues is also presented. This chapter covers **most of Outcome 2 and all of Outcome 3** for the Higher Unit, **Interpersonal Skills for Care**. It is also of relevance to the Higher Unit **Health Promotion**.

Chapter 8, **Health Promotion**, is divided into two parts. Part 1 provides an introduction to Health Promotion and Part 2 presents models and strategies of health promotion. In part 1 the topics covered include definitions of health, the dimensions of health and factors which influence health. There is an examination of rights and entitlements to health and an explanation of the concept of health promotion. Consideration is also given to some of the legislation and policy which relates to health and health promotion such as the Patient's Charter and the NHS and Community Care Act (1990). Part 2 presents some theoretical models of health promotion and evaluates these models. Some examples are given of the application of these models, together with strategies for analysing the effectiveness of health promotion campaigns. Part 1 of this chapter covers **all Outcomes** of the Intermediate II Unit, **Health Promotion** and provides an introduction for the Higher Health Promotion Unit. Part 2 covers **Outcomes 1 and 2** of the **Higher Health promotion** Unit with some material also relevant to outcome 3.

Research and Gathering Evidence is the subject of Chapter 9. This chapter aims to enable the reader to understand techniques for gathering evidence in sociology, psychology, care provision and health promotion. It also aims to enable the reader to set up a research project and write up a research report. Consideration is given to some of the ethical issues which surround research. This chapter especially relevant to **Outcome 3** of the Higher Unit **Health Promotion** and as supporting material for the higher unit **Human Development and Behaviour**.

The final chapter, **Integration and Conclusions**, aims to make connections among the different sections of the book, especially through the use of case study materials. Connections are made, for example, between Human Development and Behaviour and Promoting Equality in a Care Context, with an account of the meaning of ethnocentrism and its avoidance. The concluding section attempts to pull together the various threads of the book, pointing the way forward for further study and reemphasising the importance of an holistic approach to care practice.

CHAPTERS AND THE SYLLABUS

	Social Influences on Behaviour	Human Development	Understanding Care Skills	Health Promotion
INTERMEDIATE II	**Chapter 1** (Outcome 2 – Institutionalisation + introductory material – all units) **Chapter 2** (Outcome 3 – prejudice, stereotyping, discrimination) **Chapter 3** (Outcome 1 – socialisation) **Chapter 5** (Additional materials, O1 & 2)	**Chapter 3** (all outcomes)	**Chapter 6** (all outcomes)	**Chapter 8** Part 1 (all outcomes)

	Promoting Equal Opportunities in a Care Context	Human Development and Behaviour	Interpersonal Skills for Care	Health Promotion
HIGHER	**Chapter 2** (all outcomes) **Chapter 1** (provides general introductory material for all units)	**Chapter 3** (provides introductory material) **Chapter 4** (outcomes 1 & 3) **Chapter 5** (outcomes 2 & 3) **Chapter 9** (Research methods)	**Chapter 6** (outcomes 1 & 2) **Chapter 7** (outcomes 2 & 3)	**Chapter 8** Part 1 (Introductory material) **Chapter 8** Part 2 (all outcomes) **Chapter 9** (Research Methods)

CHAPTER 1
The care context

George Baker

Every day, social work services make a crucial difference to people's lives, whether it is providing the necessary support for people to remain in their own homes and in touch with friends and family, protecting children at risk, or helping offenders to change their offending behaviour. The workforce that provides these services should be recognised as providing a key professional service . . .

(Donald Dewar in his Foreword to *Aiming for Excellence*, HMSO 1999)

THE NATURE OF CARE

The purpose of this chapter is to examine the concept of care and the varied contexts in which it takes place. In doing so it is necessary to ask some fundamental questions about the nature of society today, and why there seems to be an ever-growing number of people who require the services of others to care for them. In order to help clarify some of the complex issues involved, some ideas and theories from sociology, politics and psychology are considered. These concepts will be further explored in later chapters, but it is necessary at this stage at least to dip our toes in the water. This will be combined with illustrations of the points being covered by reference to the real-life experiences and dilemmas of people in care situations. This is in order to emphasise the important fact that study in this area is not confined merely to improving academic understanding, but ultimately to developing the quality of your intervention in the lives of real people. All names and identifying features have, of course, been changed in order to preserve confidentiality.

This chapter provides a general introduction to all units of the Higher Still in Care, both at Intermediate II and Higher level. It is especially relevant to Outcome 2 of the Intermediate II Syllabus, 'Social Influences on Behaviour'.

It is assumed that you are reading this chapter because you are embarking on a course designed to build or enhance your career opportunities in the field of care. You have chosen an interesting and meaningful career that is sure to stretch and challenge you in many ways. You will be doing important work, helping to address social injustices and making significant contributions to the lives of other people.

WHAT DO WE MEAN BY CARE?

Work in the field of care encompasses a wide range of activities. It covers particular areas such as social care, child care, social work and nursing, each of which involves a range of specialised tasks requiring a variety of different services. The word 'care' itself has a number of different connotations, but essentially means 'to look after or provide for'. You have to be careful, because an unfortunate implication of the word can sometimes denote a degree of dependency or powerlessness. This can serve to exaggerate further the predicament in which people might find themselves.

Activity

Consider the images created by the use of the word 'care' in the following phrases:

- 'Terminal Care'
- 'The Care Services'
- 'Care for the Disabled'
- 'Care Professional'
- 'Community Care'
- 'Acute Psychiatric Care'

WHAT MAKES A GOOD CARE WORKER?

There are a number of factors that contribute to making a good care worker and most, if not all, of these can be learned. The starting point is probably an interest in, and concern for, other people. Like all professions, however, you have to start at the bottom of the ladder and as your knowledge, skills and experience grow, there will be opportunities for you to advance your career. It is often the case that people move around to work with different client groups as they build up experience, and this is something you should be prepared to do. You will find that a broad base of experience is better to start with than a number of years spent working in one particular establishment, or with only one client group. As time goes on, however, you may find yourself beginning to specialise in an area that particularly interests you.

The attributes of a good care worker are outlined in the following chart. It may of course take some time before you feel competent or confident in all these areas. Remember that in this area of work you never really stop learning. If you should reach a point in the future where you begin to feel you know it all, then it's time for a change, because you may have become infected with a degree of cynicism or arrogance, which are not very desirable qualities in any care worker.

Attributes of a good care worker

Knowledge
Awareness of Psychological Theory
Understanding of Social Issues
Awareness of Sociological Theory
Understanding of Needs of Clients
Awareness of how Organisation Works
Specialised Technical Subjects

Skills
Good Communication (verbal & written)
Ability to be Analytical
Able to use Counselling Methods
Good at Building Relationships
Able to work as part of a team
Able to work with initiative

Values
Commitment to Social Justice
Appreciation of Worth of Individuals
Maintains Confidentiality
Promotes Anti-Discriminatory Practice
Supports Rights and Choices
Acknowledges Differences

Personal Qualities
Confidence
Sensitivity
Warmth
Able to project competence
Enthusiasm
Imaginative & Adaptable
Dependable & Reliable
Sense of Humour

Activity

You might want to consider your own current stage of development in relation to the Attributes of a Good Care Worker list. On a separate sheet of paper write down each of the attributes and award yourself a mark for each on a scale of one to five. Add up the total. The maximum possible score is 130. If you are anywhere near this then you are either reading the wrong book, too arrogant for your own good or you cheated! Keep a note of this figure and check yourself out again as you progress in your studies and experience.

FORMAL AND INFORMAL CARE

An important distinction exists between what is known as **formal** care, which is care provided by people generally on a paid basis, and **informal** care, which is usually provided by relatives for no material reward whatsoever. In Scotland today there are a significant number of people who act as carers for someone. They may be parents who care for a child with a disability, a wife caring for her husband with Alzheimer's Disease or a woman who has given up her own life to look after her frail, elderly mother. Although many people willingly take on this role the lot of such carers is not always a happy one. They may be left to get on with things, with little or no support from professional services, necessitating sacrifices socially and economically. For example, they may be unable to work, have little social contact with others or be forced to rely on benefits in order to live, which generally means existing close to poverty. Sadly too, the professionals who come in and take over when they are no longer able to cope have often disrespected them. It can be a twenty-four hour a day, seven days a week job for some carers, hours which no professional would even contemplate. Who cares for the carers?

Many people who undertake the role of informal carer have not had much choice in the matter, but have been forced by circumstances. There is also a great gender imbalance here as this role tends to be undertaken by women rather than men. An interesting fact is that there are more women who stay at home to care for a dependent relative than there are women who stay at home to look after children.

Formal care, on the other hand, refers to care which is received by people in a wide variety of settings, but always with support given by people who are paid to do work with them. Formal care may be defined as caring for people in society, other than self or family, in an agency whose codes of practice are dictated to and guided by legislation, policy and professional ethics. The different types of provider of formal care and the areas in which they operate are examined later (see page 27).

Care work in different fields

In the past care work tended to be carried out in a wide number of different settings which operated very much in isolation from each other, separated by practice, agency and professional boundaries. A significant change, which is occurring in the field of care work at the present time, is a realisation that the work carried out in different fields actually shares many common factors. This is leading to a recognition that boundaries have to be much more flexible and that much can be achieved by closer worker practices. This realisation of common factors may be illustrated by the formation of UNISON, which is the biggest public sector workers' trade union, and was formed by an amalgamation of a number of local government and health service unions. This reflects a dismantling of traditional barriers which previously existed between such professions as nursing and social work. There is now a greater understanding of the commonality of the caring task, and less demarcation between the various professions involved.

This has very positive implications for people entering the field of care work because it means that the opportunities for moving around and gaining skills and experience in a number of fields have greatly increased. It also has significant implications for the people on the receiving end of care services because inter-disciplinary and collaborative work between agencies can only be improved by this approach, which will have positive effects in terms of the quality of services.

One particular area, which is worth examining because of the changes which are occurring, as outlined above, was the degree of rivalry which existed between people engaged in care work and those whose profession was social work. In order to examine the difference between the two tasks we need to go back to a time not that long ago, when there were clear distinctions made between what were seen as *social work* and *care* roles. Sadly there was sometimes a degree of snobbery and elitism around what was seen as the more important role of social worker. These were the professionals who carried out the important functions of assessment and developing intervention strategies. Care staff, on the other hand, were seen as basic grade and relatively unskilled workers in residential homes, day centres and home support services. Despite the fact that these people tended to do most of the direct work with clients, their role was often undervalued in terms of low status, low wages and restricted training opportunities. There was also a significant gender inequality in this set-up – up to 95 per cent of basic grade care staff were women and yet their senior management teams were composed of up to 95 per cent men (who were generally social workers). To add to the confusion, most care services in Scotland came under the jurisdiction of Social Work Departments and Health Boards, and could claim, with some justification, that they were treated as the Cinderella sectors of the agencies.

CARE WORK IN THE PAST

One of the unfortunate features about the nature of care work carried out in the past is that much of the work was carried out in institutions, such as large hospitals for people with learning disabilities (known in the 1970s as 'the mentally defective'), old-fashioned children's homes (or even entire children's villages) or in 'old folks' homes', where people were sent to live before they died. In these kinds of institutions people were not treated with much respect as hardly anybody really knew, or cared, what went on in them. The role of workers in such locations tended to be that of containment and control more than anything else – resources were always short and staff were generally overworked and underpaid and subject to the same sort of institutional rules and regulations as the inmates of the institution. We are only now beginning to recognise the damage these institutions inflicted on people. We are also becoming aware of how many people became the victims of different forms of abuse behind the protective walls of institutions. The following story serves as an example.

CARE IN THE 1970s – JULIE'S STORY

It was a summer day in the early 1970s and Julie's first shift on the ward in the local hospital for 'mental defectives', where she had been offered a summer job as an assistant nurse during her break from university. The ward she had been assigned to was called a villa but she could see little resemblance between the dilapidated red brick building she now stood in and her uncle's holiday home in Spain. Sixty people appeared to spend every minute of their lives confined to this ward where they were looked after by three or four nurses. The worst thing was the smell – a heady mixture of sweat, urine, stale food and disinfectant.

She felt ill at ease and self conscious in her new nurses uniform. She wasn't a nurse so why was she dressed like one. She also felt uncomfortable at being locked in this place, even though she had a bunch of keys securely attached to her belt. She was, if truth be told, even a little scared of the patients, some of whom looked quite frightening and were behaving in strange ways, pacing up and down like caged animals or sitting rocking on the floor.

So far today she had helped to bath twenty of the patients in the ward, ticking off their names in a big bath book as they were processed two at a time in the white walled bathroom with its two baths sitting in the middle of the floor. Each patient was bathed and received a change of underwear twice weekly. She had been amused to see the communal underwear at first, all marked with the hospital name and ward number until she thought what it must be like not even owning your own pants.

Now it was dinner time and she had been asked to help with the two dozen patients in wheelchairs who were unable to feed themselves. 'You can do the feeders', she had been told by the kindly old charge nurse. As she looked at the two rows of patients lined up against each side of the wall and away from the others sitting at tables, a big trolley with steaming hot steel cans of food was wheeled in by Bessie, the other assistant nurse on the shift.

'What do I do here?', she asked Bessie.

'Just fill the bowls and feed them,' replied Bessie, 'and watch out for chokers'.

She watched as Bessie spooned food from the steel containers into the large plastic bowls. Three half slices of buttered bread were dropped in each first, followed by a ladleful of soup, brown mince, mashed potato and then a couple of splashes of milky tea from a huge battered teapot. The resulting mixture was mixed to a runny consistency.

'That's how you do the soft diets love' said Bessie. 'Sometimes if you're in a hurry you can put the custard in as well. All goes down the same way you know. Now you do that side and I'll do this.'

CARE WORK TODAY

As the focus of work moved from institutional settings to smaller units within the community, so the nature of the job changed and the demand grew for care workers to become increasingly skilled in a new range of demanding tasks. There was a gradual recognition that the nature of work carried out by care workers was beginning to reflect a degree of sophistication which at least matched that required by other workers such as nurses or social workers. A further problem existed in that many traditionally trained workers in allied professions had little knowledge and few skills to offer in some of the new areas. Their training did not equip them in terms of specialist knowledge and skills in working with people with multiple disabilities, challenging behaviour or communication disorders for example

A definition of the care task today would need to include the following:

■ direct work with individuals which provides support to them in overcoming the effects of temporary or permanent disabilities
■ empowerment
■ promotion of social inclusion.

This involves the worker in a range of processes and supportive interventions working in partnerships with individuals in a structured way. This accords with the Social Care Association's definition of care, which describes it as essentially improving the quality of people's lives. This goes some way towards answering the question of what care workers do and the following examples may give an idea of the range of work they are involved in.

> Harry is 25 and works for a 'not for profit' organisation which provides social care services for people with learning disabilities who have recently moved out of a large institution. He works directly with John, who lives in his own house now and is gradually being helped to build a meaningful life for himself, despite the fact that he has been labelled as having challenging behaviour and limited communication skills.

> Janet is 32 and employed as a home support services organiser for a local authority social work department. Part of her job is to assess the needs of vulnerable older people living in the locality and ensure they receive the support they need to continue living in their own homes. Such people, she reflects sometimes, would previously have been automatically admitted to one of the dreary and dismal old folks homes in the town, both of which are now closed.

> Gina is 22 and works for a voluntary organisation providing support for children with autistic spectrum disorders who attend the local mainstream school. This enables the two children she works with to continue to receive schooling and the same sort of normal experiences as other kids. Five years ago they would have been sent to a special school and effectively excluded from normal educational opportunities. Nothing impresses her more in her job than the support offered by other children.

INSTITUTIONALISATION

The two previous sections contrasted aspects of care work in the past and present and also highlighted the fact that a lot of care work in the past took place within institutional settings. Such institutions may have been places such as hospitals for people with learning disabilities or mental health problems, or homes or even entire villages for children or older adults.

Very often such institutions were located in out of the way places away from centres of population and in country locations where people would enjoy the benefits of plenty of fresh air. Many institutions were characterised by having large numbers of people living in them, who were cared for by small numbers of poorly trained and poorly paid staff.

Institutions developed for a number of different reasons and were very much the product of dominant thinking of the day about what to do with people who were different. Many institutions for people with learning disabilities, for example, were built in order to provide safe refuge as well as an alternative, less challenging and safe lifestyle for people. There was another agenda though, which was concerned with removing such people from society and placing them in locations where they would not be allowed to have any children of their own because it was felt, quite wrongly, that the moral fabric of society was threatened by a growth in the population of people with such disabilities.

It wasn't until the 1960s in the USA that anyone really started to check out the effects of institutions on people and some of the first to do so were sociologists who began to recognise and research the phenomenon which became known as institutionalisation.

Institutionalisation describes a process by which the needs of the people for whom the institution exists to serve become secondary to the needs of the institution. Individuals start to lose their identity and everything becomes secondary to the smooth and efficient running of the institution. Order and routine become the dominant factors. Both staff and people for whom the institution is providing a service become depersonalised.

The following characteristics are also usually present:
- large numbers of people being cared for by small numbers of staff;
- little contact with the outside world;
- few meaningful activities, lots of empty time and enforced idleness;
- large social distance between staff and service users, with staff in uniforms to emphasise differences;
- staff behaving in an authoritarian manner;
- working to a medical model with emphasis on treatment and attention to physical needs;
- little chance of leaving the establishment either temporarily or permanently;
- lack of respect for dignity of individuals, demonstrated through pejorative language or lack of regard for privacy;
- an almost total preoccupation among staff with the practical, task oriented aspects of the job (mealtimes, bathtimes etc.) with little thought or effort ever applied to imaginative ways of improving quality of life for service users;
- staff pre-occupied with their own affairs and communicating with one another as if service users weren't there.

People who spend a significant amount of time in such institutions will eventually become institutionalised. Common features of this are as follows.
- They become indifferent to their surroundings, other people, the world, the future, anything in fact.
- They lose any motivation to do new things or sometimes anything at all.

- They lose the ability to make choices, decisions or plans of any sort. They expect others to do this for them.
- They become obedient to what people tell then to do.
- Standards of personal habits and cleanliness may go down, as they have little sense of pride in themselves.
- Expectations are that little will change and that today, tomorrow and the next day will all be the same.
- Every now and then there is an outburst of temper or aggression which is quickly dealt with.
- There can be a complete lack of enthusiasm.

The end result of this process is the individual comes to depend on the institution for everything and finds it difficult to cope independently away from it. An interesting point is that many of the people with learning disabilities who have been moving out of institutions after many years are finding adaptation to life in the community very difficult. This is often as a direct result not of their learning disability, but of the effects of institutionalisation.

An important factor to recognise is that many of the establishments which offer care to service users continue to have elements of institutions about them. One of the major tasks of care workers is to recognise the effects of institutionalisation and take measures to reduce or minimise the effects of this on individuals.

Activity

1. If you look back at Julie's story (page 5) what characteristics of the hospital do you see as contributing to institutionalisation?

You may have mentioned:
- 60 people to the ward;
- staff in a uniform, emphasising distinctions between staff and 'patients';
- promoting a medical model of care, with people regarded as 'ill' and needing others to treat their illness and assist with physical (not social, psychological or emotional) needs;
- locked doors and staff carrying keys;
- lack of privacy when bathing;
- emphasis on ticking names off in a bath book (no choice);
- communal underwear;
- applying labels to people ('feeders' and 'chokers');
- everyone getting the same food (no choice again);
- a general lack of respect for the worth and dignity of individuals.

Counteracting institutionalisation

People do not necessarily become institutionalised just because they live in or attend an institution which provides care. It all depends upon how the service is delivered. Some ways of counteracting institutionalisation are:

- providing choices;
- not sticking to strict routines but being flexible according to need;
- staff wearing casual clothes, not uniforms;
- plenty of stimulating activities on offer for those who wish to participate;
- showing respect for the worth and needs of all individuals;
- the privacy of single rooms;
- privacy when bathing, dressing etc.;
- staff trained in the values and skills of care work;
- being as 'homely' as possible;
- wherever possible, using/adapting services which are available to everyone rather than specialised services;
- wherever possible, supporting people in their own homes rather than in institutional settings.

Activity

Look at the descriptions of the care workers Harry, Janet and Gina on page 7 and suggest aspects of their work which counteract institutionalisation.

Your suggestions may have included the following:

- John, with whom Harry works, lives in his own house. This means that **he** can make decisions about how he leads his life;
- John is being helped to lead a meaningful life;
- Janet assesses people's needs in order to provide the support needed to enable them to liver in their own homes;
- the children with whom Gina works attend mainstream schools;
- other children provide support, not just staff.

A further activity relating to institutionalisation and counteracting it is presented at the end of this chapter. You will also find that much of the rest of this book relates to ways of avoiding or counteracting institutionalisation. Chapter 6 Interpersonal Skills looks in a lot more detail at the value base, at communication and the qualities and attributes of effective care workers, all of which are important in ensuring that service users receive the best possible quality of care which is as free from institutionalising influences as possible. Institutionalisation is returned to in Chapter 5, where it is examined from four different sociological perspectives. The case study there of Lilybank (page 212) can also be looked at in terms of identifying factors which may contribute to institutionalisation. You could then suggest ways in which Lilybank could be improved to counteract institutionalisation. As you read through the rest of this chapter you could think of how the topics discussed relate to **this** discussion of institutionalisation.

Who are the service users?

A good description, which illustrates the range of people who may need care, is given below in an extract from 'Caring for People' (1989), the White Paper which preceded the National Health Service and Community Care Act (1990) and which identified those in need of community care.

> *Many people need some extra help and support at some stage in their lives, as a result of illness or temporary disability. Some people as a result of old age, mental illness including dementia, or learning disability of physical or sensory impairment have a continuing need for care on a longer term basis. People with drug or alcohol related disorders, people with progressive illnesses such as AIDS or multiple sclerosis may also need community care at some time.*

(HMSO, 1989)

As you can see from the above description, the range of people who may require care is extensive. It is also important to realise that while all the above may need care the actual type and degree of care they require will also vary enormously. Compare the different range of care needs of someone who has a drug dependency which is ruining their lives with those of someone who has sustained a severe spinal injury in a road traffic accident, who no longer has the ability to manage even their basic physical movements. It is because the range of care needs is so wide that there is an increasing need for carers to develop specialised skills.

Below are some examples of people who receive care.

> Jimmy is 85 now and lives on the fourteenth floor in a high rise building. From his window he can look down on what remains of the street he grew up in and in the distance he can see the tall cranes in the shipyard where he worked. He spends a lot of his time at that window, sitting at the table drinking tea from a flask his home help prepares in the morning.

> Ben doesn't know what age he is. Neither does he know what time or even day of the week it is. He was born deaf and blind and with severe learning difficulties. He does know however the smell and touch of each of the care workers who tend to him. He also knows where to find his own clothes, the ones with the little fur label than he can feel. Ben knows too when it is dinnertime, he can smell the food from the kitchen. He doesn't like some of the food and knows that if he makes a fuss some of the staff will give him something else.

The power of the carer

As a care worker, it is important to realise the extent of the power and influence that you exercise over the individuals and groups of people with whom you work. This may be very obvious in some cases where you may, for example, be speaking on behalf of individual service users who have limited communication abilities. You will be, literally, speaking for them. In other cases, by simply carrying out your assigned duties, you may be perpetuating an element of disempowerment. This may happen, for example, every time you help to 'manage' someone's challenging behaviour. (The term 'serving people who are difficult to serve' is much more respectful and indicative of what we should be trying to achieve, rather than 'managing challenging behaviour'.)

Good intentions and well-meaning actions are often not enough to ensure that your practice is really acting the best interests of the people you are paid to serve. The black civil rights leader Martin Luther King (Oates, S., 1982) once said,

Shallow understanding from people of good will is more frustrating than absolute misunderstanding from people of ill-will.

This was said in relation to racism, but also expresses a sentiment which may be felt by many people receiving social care services. You need a degree of vigilance at all times to ensure that your actions do not serve simply to continue any forms of institutional discrimination or oppression.

This caution is added not without reason for at various times in the history of care, a number of agencies charged with the care of different client groups have acted more as a force for social control than anything else. Examples here are children's services, which colluded in the forced resettlement of 'orphans' to Australia; home helps who locked confused older people in their homes for their own safety; nurses who assisted in giving massive doses of sedatives and tranquillisers to difficult patients or helped remove the teeth of 'biters' – the list is long and does not make comfortable reading.

These are extreme examples but should act as a reminder of the responsibilities of care workers not to collude, unconsciously or otherwise, in systems which treat people badly or disrespectfully while purporting to care for them. If you are ever faced with such a dilemma you should not hesitate to seek advice, preferably outside the agency and in confidence. If you base your practice on the care values outlined elsewhere in this book however, you should not go too far wrong.

An important point is that you will develop the ability to act as an agent of change. You will develop skills and confidence in promoting good practice. You will be able to challenge practices which you feel are not in the best interests of clients and thereby help to ensure that practice continues to be improved,

THE NATURE OF WORK IN CARE

It is important that you realise the nature of work in care. Certainly there are many rewards, but sometimes the work itself is tough and at times stressful. You are dealing with people others may not want to know. You will often work long and sometimes anti-social hours for a low salary. The job does not carry much in the way of social status. Very often it involves work which is physically hard – moving and handling, assisting people to carry out private and intimate tasks which they would much rather be doing for themselves and maybe even working with people who have difficult and anti-social behaviour. Something like one in five social care workers is suffering from stress to a degree that affects their ability to do their job and is having an impact on their personal lives. The demands of the job are continuing to rise as the nature of clients has changed and the expectations of quality of service that is required also rises.

Gone are the days, for example, when 'working with the handicapped' was a soft option. This phrase, with its overtones of paternalism and images of 'do-gooders', reflects a time when many people with disabilities were forced by circumstances to live in institutions. Many were trapped in their homes and looked after only by carrying relatives and a relatively small number received a token service by placement in junior or senior occupational centres. In such places 'the handicapped' were 'occupied' and cared for, very often by quasi-teachers who had never made the grade in proper educational establishments and for whom 'working with the handicapped' was a second option. Without meaning to disrespect such people too much, for their heart was certainly in it, there was also a class and gender issue involved. Many of the workers were middle-aged and middle-class women often with stern Victorian values. I remember visiting one such place many years ago where I was given tea in a bone china cup and saucer. The 'trainees', all fully-grown adults, received their tea, already milked and sugared, in blue or pink plastic mugs dependent on whether they were a 'boy' or 'girl'. After dinner they spent an hour of every day with heads on folded arms on the table 'resting'.

Such practices are thankfully not common today. There is much more attention paid to work practices which serve to empower people and help them lead independent lives as far as possible. There is also great emphasis on providing services which enable people to live normal and ordinary lives. This is one of the great challenges in care work and calls for skilled and knowledgeable workers who understand and can respond sensitively to the needs of people.

Work in care, despite its challenges and demands, can be extremely rewarding and satisfying. Very often, rather than working with people in groups which was a prevailing pattern in the past, the work is carried out on an individual one to one basis. The relationships which sometimes develop can be rewarding in themselves as a mutual respect and understanding develops between those involved.

We are also beginning to build a much better understanding of how people are affected by various disabilities. A good example of this in recent times is the growth in understanding about autism. Most of the knowledge we now have about this condition, which causes difficulties in communication, rigid adherence to routines which may seem bizarre and the apparent inability to form relationships, comes from people who have themselves been diagnosed as having autism.

Work in care sometimes follows a pattern of long periods of work during which you may feel that you are getting nowhere followed by sudden and unexpected breakthroughs. The following story illustrates one such case.

CASE STUDY

John had worked for many months with young Ben and was beginning to feel that he was getting nowhere. Ben lived in a world of his own. He had autism and there just didn't seem any way that John was able to break down the wall that Ben had built around himself. It seems almost that Ben had made a deliberate choice not to communicate with anyone else. He sat at the desk on the other side of the room playing with a toy truck. But not playing with it in the way that other kids would. Ben had placed it upside down on the desk and had been spinning one wheel for about an hour now, all the while making noises which John could only describe as gentle screams. Now and then he had stopped, placed his hands over his ears, and let out a series of blood curdling yells.

He had some other strange quirks as well. He only ate things which were round. Small pizzas, potato fritters, hamburgers and Smarties were fine but chips, sausages and chocolate bars were thrown across the room. His mother cut his toast with a round pastry cutter.

Autism was a condition which John, who was an experienced practitioner in his field, was only beginning to learn about and had started to work with Ben and other children like him in order to gain more experience in this specialised field. For months now he had tried every way he could think of to establish some type of communication or connection with Ben but always to no avail. He didn't even show any signs of recognising him or acknowledging his presence (despite all the Smarties!), turning away and covering his face when John came too close.

Ben had stopped playing with the truck at last and had now picked up the phone on the desk and was holding it to his ear. Without thinking too much, John picked up the phone on his own desk, flicked the connection, and spoke into it.

'Hi Ben, when you going to speak to me?' he said.

'Hi John', replied Ben.

After he had picked himself up from the floor, John built on this indirect method of communication with Ben and they went on to work very closely together. They learned from each other about ways in which they could communicate in other indirect ways.

THE GROWTH IN DEMAND FOR CARE

In examining the need for formal care in society today the following factors will be examined:

1. Demographic changes.
2. Changes in the nature of family and community life.

3. Different lifestyle expectations.
4. Changes in political and personal ideologies and values.
5. Concepts of social exclusion and inclusion.

1. Demographic changes

The major demographic change in relation to the increasing need for care is the growing number of people who are living longer. This is linked with other changes occurring in society which means that an increasing number of people are no longer able to care for themselves.

Demography is the study of populations, in particular the way in which individual characteristics may be distributed throughout the population. It comes from the combination of two Greek words – *demos* meaning the people and *graphein* meaning to write – thus literally 'writing about the people'. Information is gathered and analysed to examine changes in patterns between the past and the present and to try to identify and predict present and future trends.

In this way changes in a range of matters such as family size, life expectancy, divorce rates and ethnic distribution can be examined. Figure 1.1 below identifies a significant change which has occurred this century in Scotland, namely the fact that people are living far longer, while Figure 1.2 illustrates percentage growth in the number of older people in the last thirty years. These figures highlight a challenge facing our society today – who is going to look after the growing elderly population? This has been seen as a major task for those working in the field of care provision.

Why are people living longer?

There are a number of reasons why people are now living longer. Over the last hundred years or so the rise in life expectancy has been quite dramatic. Men born in the 1890s could expect to live

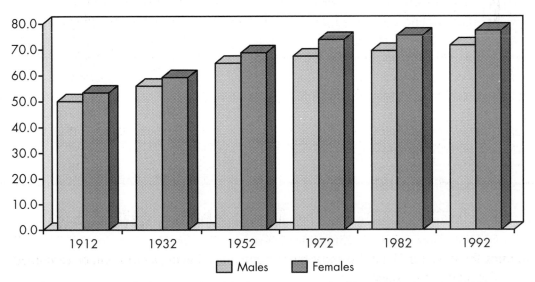

Figure 1.1 Expectation of life in Scotland (Information supplied by General Registry Office, Scotland)

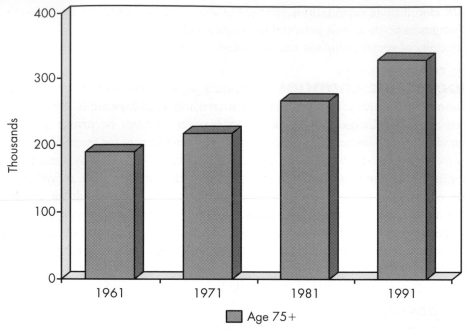

Figure 1.2 Scotland's older adults (Information supplied by General Registry Office, Scotland)

only into their forties. Listed below are some of the factors, which are thought to have contributed to this increase in longevity.

Improved health care

The general availability of free, or at least relatively inexpensive, health care for everyone has made a significant contribution towards people living longer. The most important event in this regard was the introduction of the National Health Service (Scotland) Act 1947, which promised free health care to everyone at the point of delivery. This meant that no longer did people have to pay for the services of a doctor or for hospital treatment or medicines. The National Health Service remains one of the institutions in this country of which we can be justly proud, although it has come under threat a number of times in its history, and costs and charges are now made for different services such as prescriptions. It is argued that the existence of free health services has also created a growing demand which can never really be completely satisfied and which continues to incur ever increasing costs.

Improved public health

Just as vital as the provision of medical and health services is the supply of basic necessities such as clean safe water and sewage disposal facilities. Scotland has so far managed to avoid turning over the supply of water to private companies whose aim is to make profits for their directors and shareholders from the supply of this most basic commodity. Clean water and the safe disposal of sewage have helped to eradicate a number of diseases such as cholera, which used to wipe out significant numbers of the population in epidemics which regularly swept the country. Public health services also monitor and help maintain the quality of the food we eat through environmental health agencies.

Technological advances

Certain technological advances have also contributed significantly towards increasing our lifespan. Most homes now have a fridge freezer which keeps food safe and fresh for longer. Modern methods of storing and transporting foodstuffs by freezing, chilling or canning also mean the general availability of safe food. Other inventions have also played their part. Scotsman Alexander Fleming invented penicillin in 1927 although it did not come into general use for some twenty years. Antibiotics have played a huge role in combating diseases and infections. So much have they been used that there are now great fears that new 'superbugs' are evolving which are resistant to a large number of antibiotics. One such bug which is being increasingly encountered in care establishments is MRSA (Methicillin Resistant Staphylococcus Areus), which although probably not much of a threat to healthy care workers can prove fatal to people whose ability to resist infection is lowered by other factors.

Absence of poverty

This is an area where a certain amount of controversy exists. Some people take the view that poverty has been eliminated from this country. Such people are usually rich and not too aware of the circumstances in which others may be forced to live. While few people in Scotland actually starve to death for want of food, it cannot be denied that for many their lifestyle and chances are affected by the fact that they don't have a lot of cash to throw around. The nature of the society in which we live determines that those with money will tend to get richer and those without will get poorer. (Evidence for this can be found in 'Social Justice – The Report of the Commission on Social Justice' (1933), which states '. . . the poor have become poorer. Between 1979 and 1992 the poorest 10% saw their real incomes fall by 17% while the richest 10% saw their real income rise by just over 60%.)

There are clear links between poverty, ill health and life expectancy as was clearly demonstrated by Carstairs and Morris in their study 'Deprivation and Health in Scotland' (1991). There are certain groups in society, for example working-class males in inner city areas, for whom life expectancy is falling rather than rising. Strong evidence for this can be seen in Figure 1.3 on page 18 which illustrates the situation in the Greater Glasgow area. While we may view the absence of acute and absolute poverty as contributing to the increase in life expectancy, we must also be aware of the areas where this is not occurring.

Figure 1.3 illustrates the changes in mortality rates in Glasgow between the years 1982 and 1992. It examines the differences in mortality rates for two age bands, and by sex over a ten year period between identified 'Affluent' areas of the city (Aff) and 'Deprived' areas.

Significant points

The standard mortality ratios are considerably **higher** for those in the most deprived areas than for both sexes, for the two age bands and for both periods.

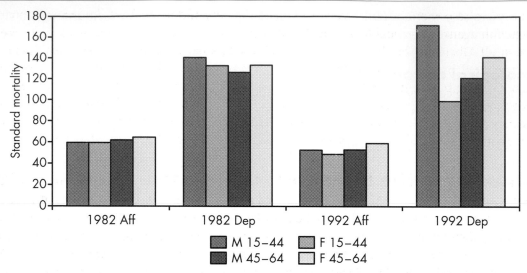

Figure 1.3 Mortality in Glasgow 1982–1992 (Reproduced from Greater Glasgow Draft Community Care Plan, 1995–8)

Between 1982 and 1992 the mortality rate for the 15–44 male population increased for those living in the deprived areas, while the reverse was true for those in this age group in the affluent areas.

For men aged 15–44 in deprived areas **mortality increased by 9%**.

Protective legislation

In the last century there has been a steady increase in the amount of legislation designed to protect people in their work and living situations. Laws exist to safeguard people from exposure to hazardous substances such as asbestos or toxic chemicals in their work environments. Clean air laws have reduced the hazardous emissions from factory and domestic chimneys, which used to cause life-threatening smogs in the big cities. Legislation to reduce emissions from motor vehicles by removing lead additives from petrol should also be of benefit. Health and Safety at Work legislation has forced employers and employees alike to take steps to reduce industrial risks and hazards. A major area still to be worked on is the reduction of road accidents which, with our totally absurd obsession for faster and more powerful cars, continue to kill and maim a huge number of people each year. They also provide care services with a large number of clients with serious head injuries, for many of whom there is little which can be done other than to provide palliative care.

Healthier lifestyles

Some people may consider that we are living much healthier lifestyles today than perhaps our grandparents did, which is contributing to us living longer. Certainly there has been a huge growth in the health and fitness industry. Many people go to health clubs to work out and keep themselves in shape and others have healthy outdoor hobbies such as cycling or hill walking.

Many people also pay a lot of attention to the food they eat and avoid foods known to contribute to things that cause poor health, although many people have sedentary lifestyles and take no exercise at all. Obesity is on the increase although the link between this and poor health is probably exaggerated by the diet industry. Don't let the recent 'revision' of dress sizes fool you – people are getting bigger, probably because we are eating too much and not taking enough exercise. Smoking remains a killer and major contributor to reducing your lifespan. Overuse of and dependency on alcohol and other drugs remains high for some individuals and this often has a particularly nasty series of consequences not only for them but for the people they live with.

2. Changes in the nature of family and community life

Until fairly recently in historical terms people tended to assume that when they became old and reached a stage where they might need help to look after themselves that this role would be carried out by the children they had brought into the world. Indeed, in some cultures this role was ascribed and it was the assumed duty of the eldest daughter to forsake marriage and instead look after her parents until they died. Parents might therefore have had an interest in having as many children as possible in order to ease the future burdens of old age.

This is certainly not the case now. The structure of the family appears to have altered and older relatives are sadly often seen as a burden, rather than occupying positions of esteem and privilege due to them by their years and experience. The days of the close knit, supportive extended family living close by each other seem to have gone. People are living substantially longer and some people don't seem keen on taking on the burden of care for their elderly relatives. They don't have the time or the space and have often moved some distance away. A fortnightly visit to make sure the home help is doing their duty is about as far as some can stretch.

The concept of 'community' is a controversial one in sociology, and is a term which has many uses but no agreed definition. While recognising that there has been a great deal of debate and discussion on the matter, it can be observed that the nature of the community has also changed. People no longer tend to live in communities in the sense of neighbourhoods, where everyone looks out for everyone else. Sadly, there have even been cases of old people found dead and decomposing in their homes after weeks when no one noticed they weren't around.

There is an examination of the nature of changes which have occurred in families elsewhere in the book (see Chapter 5), but a few points might be considered here in terms of this apparent fragmentation. Some argue that the traditional extended family, where the family lived in close proximity and looked after each other, with Granny watching the kids and the kids watching Granny, has become replaced by smaller nuclear families with 2.4 children living on their own as self-supporting independent family units, who moved away from where they had been brought up as part of the process of being seen to be successful. While this may reflect the situation to an extent, it is perhaps more accurate to think of these families as part of a dispersed extended family because they will tend to maintain regular contact using means of communication not available to their forbears. However, you can't help your elderly parents to cook and clean by phone so just as you now employ a childminder to look after the children while you work, which was one of the traditional roles taken on by grandparents, it is now necessary for someone to be employed to look after them. What was a task previously carried out without charge by relatives out of a sense of duty or obligation or love has now become a job which someone needs to be paid to do.

3. Different lifestyle expectations

The nature of society is one of constant change. We live in a different sort of world from our parents. We have different expectations, new technologies, changed beliefs and values and want different things. We are perhaps fortunate in many senses that we have not had some of their experiences such as living through war or enduring rationing. We live in a more materialist society. We want more. We are in danger of becoming obsessed with having rather than being. We don't want new shoes, we want the latest designer trainers. We are victims of conspicuous consumerism. Not only do we want, we need to let others see we've got it and so we wear our labels on the outside. We drive cars built for Himalayan mountain tracks down to the supermarket car park because we are the outdoor type. We look out for ourselves. This is the 'Me First' generation. In order to examine possible reasons why this has happened we need to look at some of the changes in political and personal ideologies which have occurred.

4. Changing political and personal ideologies

Societies throughout history may be seen as originally evolving according to collectivist principles as people saw the benefits of working together and looking after each other's interests. People formed tribal units, clans and eventually nations because of strength in numbers and the ability of large groups to protect themselves. Individuals subordinated their own selfish interests for the good of the larger society. It may be the case that there are some societies today which still function with this set of aims. Japanese culture, for example, is often perceived as operating along these lines. Pictures of people in Tokyo going to work show them with face masks on, not to protect themselves from pollution but to prevent them passing on their colds and flu to others. Only recently, it may be argued, has the trend emerged for all members of particular societies to put their own selfish interests first, a tendency which is sometimes referred to as individualism. Historically, this tendency may have been seen to start with the onset of the Reformation and later the industrial and other revolutions, but we need to look back only at the last few decades in this country to see how individualism has taken off, especially in the sense of how it might be tied up with the other factors mentioned above.

In the 1960s the government told people that they'd never had it so good. It was an age of emancipation and liberation, civil rights movements, the growth of feminism, introduction of the contraceptive pill, even revolution in some places. Everyone got tired with the feeling of being pushed around and bullied by people in power and set out to enjoy themselves. There was also the threat of total nuclear self-destruction hanging over everyone – but what better excuse to have fun! This extended into the 1970s, reinforced by the perceived successes of the protest generation.

In this country we underwent several changes of government during these times and also saw the introduction of important anti discriminatory legislation attempting to iron out some of the injustices built into the fabric of our society.

Things proceeded with no great fundamental alterations until May 1979, when a new Conservative government under the leadership of Margaret Thatcher was elected to power. The following decade and a half saw a time of radical change to many of the country's institutions and the lifestyles of its citizens. This new government possessed a set of political ideas mainly driven by the ideologies of the 'New Right', which were pursued with zeal. This government openly promoted the idea of self-responsibility and individualism. It tried to create opportunities for people to 'get ahead', to make a success of their lives. Individual effort was what counted and what would be rewarded.

The cult of individualism seemed to say it all. Look after number one first. Make money. Get rich. Buy your house. Have a career. Get ahead in life. Be successful and show it. Wear designer suits, designer labels and designer stubble to show you're too busy to shave. This was the message of the 1980s. The 'Me First' generation. Yuppies and Dinkies. The Porsche in the driveway. Conspicuous consumerism. Holidays abroad. Crime rates soared as those who didn't have it decided they weren't doing without. The introduction of market forces, privatisation, the selling of state interests, public ownership bad, private good, soaring divorce rates and falling church

Figure 1.4 The cult of individualism

attendance were all part of it. It is perhaps only now that we can look back and see the scope of the changes which took place during the following years. In the 1980s and 1990s it appeared that greed was acceptable. The cult of the individual, looking after number one, came to the fore.

5. Concepts of social exclusion and inclusion

Many of the people who have traditionally been seen as needing care of some sort have also been the victims of various forms of social exclusion. They have been excluded from mainstream life for reasons of disability or age. This happened in a number of ways, such as people with learning or other disabilities being sent to large institutions to live, because they were seen as threats to society, or later because nobody really knew what to do with them. It has now been recognised that such institutions are essentially bad for people, but similar processes continue.

Children may be diagnosed as having 'special needs'[1] and are therefore sent to 'special schools', where they are excluded from the full range of social and educational experiences that other children learn from at school. Older adults may be encouraged to move from their homes into specialist residential facilities, where they find it difficult to maintain contact with neighbours and friends.

Another way in which some people experienced exclusion was through the fact that their disabilities made it difficult for them to earn an income and compelled them to rely on often inadequate welfare benefits, which served to force them into poverty. In this way they were thrust to the margins of society, a process which was known as **marginalisation**.

Politicians have taken up the concepts of social exclusion in its widest sense and social policy initiatives have been promoted to combat social exclusion and its effects. In a sense 'social exclusion' has become a new buzzword and is sometimes used as a simple euphemism for poverty, but if any of these initiatives serves to reduce the broad effects of such exclusion then they are worthwhile.

The notion of social inclusion describes the attempt to include people who have traditionally been excluded from the benefits of society back into full participation in the life of the community. With regard to specific instances, it has been taken up by people with learning disabilities as a philosophy to replace the concept of normalisation, which no-one ever really understood. Campaigning groups of people with learning disability state inclusion, advocacy and empowerment as their essential goals.

If you consider your own experiences of exclusion, of being left out of things, such as not being picked for the team, not being invited to the party, then you will get some sense of how it must feel to be the victim of this insidious form of denying people the chance of taking part in everyday life.

---

[1] This is a misnomer – they have the same needs as everybody else.

Zeitgeists and cohorts

An important notion to be aware of when working in care is that the people you will be working with will have had very different life experiences from those which you have had. All people are shaped in important ways by the life events which they have lived through and this may be an important consideration when it comes to working with service users who are considerably older than you are. People who were born in the late 1970s have been referred to as 'Thatcher's Children' and have been accused by their elders of having adopted some of the values related to the sort of political principles which were discussed above, together with a predisposition towards a certain political naivety because they had grown up at a time when there were few changes of government or even effective opposition.

The German word 'zeitgeist' literally means 'spirit of the age' and is used to describe the prevailing social and political trends of an age. It includes such things as fashions in dress and music, conventional wisdom, political beliefs and lifestyle expectations. Consider how differently you may view such things as body piercing or tattooing from your grandparents. The importance of zeitgeist is how it illustrates the degree of influence exerted over people living through particular times.

The word 'cohort' is used to refer to a group of people who were born at the same time and therefore shared the same set of experiences and influences. These influences are particularly strong early in life when we experience peer pressure. Remember when you wanted to be different, the same as everyone else!

Someone born in 1975, for example, can expect to live at least 75 years, which means that they will still be around in the year 2050. It is difficult to envisage what the world may be like then, especially if the rate of technological change continues to be as rapid as it is now.

Consider the changes over time experienced by the people in the chart below and also the different influences which are illustrated in the following timeline illustrated in Figure 1.6 on page 25. You might also want to speak to some older people and get them to share some of their experiences with you.

Activity

Have a look at the timeline in Figure 1.6 page 25. Find the year you were born and consider the experiences you have lived through. Then look at people who were born many years before you and speak to them about their memories and experiences.

The political context

You may or may not profess to an interest in politics. Many people, especially those growing up in the 1980s, express an active disinterest in the subject. However, if you are going to work in the field of care it is necessary that you develop an awareness of the political issues as they may

Changes over time

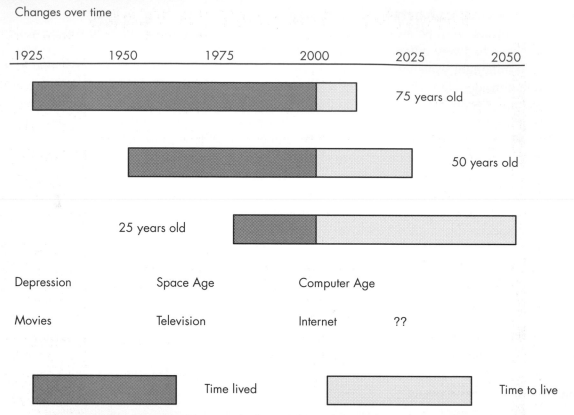

Figure 1.5 Changes over time (Adapted from *Psychology: Making Sense* by David Statt)

affect the lives of the people you will be working with. Politics is the business of life and you should at least have a basic understanding of the processes involved. A brief overview of the general political position in Scotland follows, together with an examination of the recent historical context.

At the time of writing there are four main political parties in Scotland – (New) Labour, Scottish Nationalist, Conservative and Liberal Democrat. They currently have the following number of Members of Parliament in the UK Parliament at Westminster.

Labour	56
Scottish Nationalist	6
Liberal Democrat	10
Conservative	0

Political parties are traditionally allocated a place on a left to right continuum, which gives a rough idea of their overall philosophy and ideology. This originated in the French Parliament in

TIMELINE – THE LAST 75 YEARS

Year	World	UK/Scotland	Social Legislation	Spirit of the Age
2000				
99		Scottish Assembly		**The Nineties**
98	Peace in Ireland			
97	Princess Diana dies	Tony Blair new PM		Age of Computer
96		Dunblane Massacre	Scottish Local Govt Reform	Collapse of Communism
95	OJ Simpson trial			Globalisation
94	Rwandan Civil War			
93	Bill Clinton US President	James Bulger murder	Poll Tax abolished	
92				
91	Gulf War		NHS Patients Charter	
1990	Nelson Mandela released	John Major becomes PM	NHS and Community Care Act	
89	Berlin Wall comes down		Children Act	
88	George Bush is president	Lockerbie Disaster		**The Eighties**
87		Zeebrugge Disaster	Poll Tax introduced	
86	Chernobyl nuclear accident		Disabled Persons Act	Individualism
85	Live Aid Concert			Privatisation
84	Aids virus identified	Miners strike	Mental Health(Scotland) Act	The New Right
83				Market Forces
82	Falklands War	Greenham Common		
81	Ronald Reagan US President	Inner city riots	Education Act	
1980	John Lennon shot			
79		Margaret Thatcher new PM		
78			Homeless Persons Act	**The Seventies**
77	Jimmy Carter US President			
76		James Callaghan new PM	Race Relations Act	'Me First' Generation
75	Vietnam War ends	Regional Authorities formed	Sex Discrimination Act	Energy Crisis
74	World Oil Price hike	Harold Wilson new PM	Rehabilitation Offenders Act	Terrorism
73		3 day working week		Recession
72	Bloody Sunday			
71		Decimalisation	Divorce Reform Act	
1970		Edward Heath new PM	Equal Pay Act	
69	First Man on the Moon	British troops sent to N. Ireland		
68			Social Work(Scotland) Act	**The Sixties**
67	First Heart Transplant	Celtic win European Cup		
66		Aberfan Disaster		Economic Boom
65			Death penalty abolished	Technological Growth
64	Vietnam War escalates	Harold Wilson new PM		Youth and Optimism
63	John F Kennedy assassinated	Alec Doulas-Home new PM		Feminism
62				Protest Generation
61	First man in space (Gargarin)			
1960				
59		First motorway opened (M1)		
58		First CND march		**The Fifties**
57		Harold MacMillan new PM		
56				Economic Recovery
55		Anthony Eden new PM		The Cold War
54		Food rationing ends		The Atomic Age
53	End of Korean War			Rock and Roll
52		Queen Elizabeth II throned		
51		Winston Churchill new PM		
1950	Start of Korean War			
49		Clothes rationing ends		
48	UN Declaration of Rights		National Health Service formed	**The Forties**
47		Coal industry nationalised	School leaving age now 15	
46				Total War
45	World War II ends	Clement Atlee new PM		Universal Conscription
44	D Day Landings			Women in War
43				Industry
42				Rationing
41		Rationing introduced		
1940	Battle of Britain	Winston Churchill becomes PM		
39	World War II starts			
38				
37		Neville Chamberlain is PM		**The Thirties**
36		Abdication of Edward VIII		
35		Stanley Baldwin becomes PM		Economic Depression
34				Inflation
33	Hitler takes power			Unemployment
32				International Tension
31	R101 explodes			Growth of Fascism
1930				
29	Great Depression starts	Ramsay McDonald is PM		
28	Penicillin discovered		Women over 21 get vote	
27	First talking picture			
26		General Strike		
25				

Political Party in Government — Labour — Conservative — Coalition/National

Figure 1.6 Timeline – The last 75 years

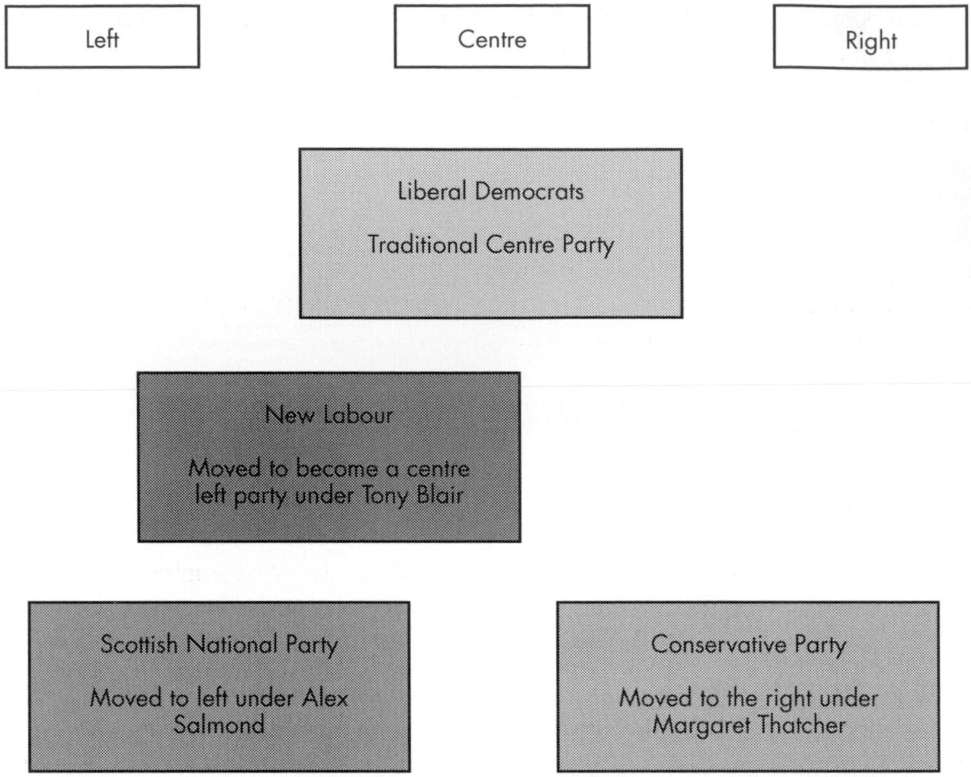

Left		Centre		Right

Liberal Democrats

Traditional Centre Party

New Labour

Moved to become a centre
left party under Tony Blair

Scottish National Party

Moved to left under Alex
Salmond

Conservative Party

Moved to the right under
Margaret Thatcher

Figure 1.7 The political spectrum in Scotland

the eighteenth century when the supporters of the king sat on his right and the supporters of the people on his left. Because of this, political parties are described as being left or right wing. Also individual politicians are labelled in the same way. It is possible to have a politician described as left wing within a right wing party. Political parties also tend to move around this spectrum quite a bit as they change their ideas in order to seek popular support.

Three major political events are shaping the current state of play in Scottish politics. The most significant is the creation of a new Scottish Parliament, which is due to start work in the year 2000. The second is the election to power in June 1997 of a New Labour government under the leadership of Tony Blair in the UK elections. This brought to an end eighteen years of Conservative government which had been dominated by the social and economic policies of the 'New Right'. The third was the dissolution of the previous system of local government, which had become dominated by big, left wing councils such as Strathclyde and Lothian by the Local Government (Scotland) Act (1994) which created the new smaller unitary authorities.

Politics and care

The ideology of a government has a major impact on people who are the clients of care services. Policy decisions on welfare, taxation, employment issues, laws on discrimination and so on exert significant influences. An example to consider may be the last government's policy on community care (as enacted in the National Health Service and Community Care Act 1990) which introduced market forces into a mixed economy of care services, in order to maximise consumer choice and ensure value for money.

We live in a democratic society which gives us the opportunity to get involved. You may not want to live in a treehouse or in a muddy tunnel in order to make your point or protest, but you have a duty to be well informed of the political process and to exercise your right to vote for the party or individual whom you believe will best represent the interest of yourself and the people who concern you. There is no excuse for naivety.

THE PROVIDERS OF CARE

There are a large number of organisations who provide formal care in a wide variety of settings and for a wide variety of client groups. These organisations can be classified as belonging to the **statutory**, **voluntary** or **private** sector, although sometimes those belonging to the last two categories prefer to be known as 'independent' sector providers.

Statutory services
This sector contains organisations such as Health, Social Work and, to a lesser extent, in terms of care provision, Education services. They are known as statutory services because they perform some of their functions, or have been set up under Acts of Parliament. Every Scottish local authority must by law provide a range of certain social work services. In some cases it may not be the direct provider of these services, but acts as the purchasing agency, which buys in services from provider agencies from the private or voluntary sectors. It used to be the case that Scottish local authorities were the direct providers of services themselves – they had big Social Work Departments which ran a whole range of care provision such as home helps, day centres for people with learning disabilities, intermediate treatment services for offenders, adoption services and fieldwork services. Since the National Health Service and Community Care Act (1990), such departments have been forced to slim down their own provision and many services have been transferred to the independent sector. In Scotland it has been possible so far to avoid the wholesale selling off of services to private agencies as has happened in some areas south of the border.

The main agencies in the statutory sector and the main roles they continue to perform are outlined below.

The voluntary sector
The voluntary sector was traditionally seen as the area where new services tended to be developed in order to fill the gaps that statutory services didn't cover. The first services for people with learning disabilities for example were provided on a local level by groups of volunteers such as parents who, in the absence of any provision, grouped together and ran their own services. At the same time such groups lobbied to get the statutory services to take notice of the plight of the people they were caring for and create pressure for proper services to be provided. Some of these

Special Work Departments	Health Boards	Education Departments
Assessment and Care Management Services for Individuals.	Traditional Hospital Services	Special Schools for children with special educational needs.
Homes and Day Centres for Older Adults	Community Support Teams Health Visitors and Visiting Nurses	Support Services to children with special educational needs in normal schools.
Home Support Services		
	Specialist therapies	Educational Psychologists
Day Centres for People with Learning Disabilities.	Psychologists Psychiatrists	Some residential schools for people with special needs or gifts
Monitoring of Qualities and Standards	Speech Therapists Occupational Therapists Physiotherapists	
Support to individuals and families	Community Psychiatric Nursing Services	
Counselling Services	Addiction Services	
Homes for 'looked after' children		

groups grew up to become service providers themselves. One example is Enable, which was formerly known as the 'Scottish Society for the Mentally Handicapped' and was comprised of an amalgamation of local groups of parents all of whom worked very hard for the benefit of their sons and daughters. They opened and ran their own day centres and respite care units, some of which were eventually taken over and managed by local authority services. Enable continues as a campaigning group for this client group and also functions as a direct provider of quality services through a number of affiliated service provision agencies.

Many innovative services continue to be developed by the voluntary sector, often now working in partnership with local authorities. In some cases there were problems in the sort of services run by some voluntary agencies. Because of their paternalistic nature, some of the agencies looked after service users in ways which have now become unacceptable. They were sometimes kept in isolated institutions or villages in some cases, cut off from the rest of the community and subject to inflexible and less than compassionate routines. Unfortunately many parents and local authorities, in the mistaken belief that they were doing their best for people, colluded in sending young people to some places which were very often hundreds of miles away from home. All this was done in the belief that such environments were therapeutic in nature.

Sometimes, but not always, voluntary organisations will also be registered charities and depend on voluntary giving for part of their income. This has proved a problem in the past, for in order to gain the sympathy of the public and encourage them to make donations, they often portrayed the people they cared for in a very negative way, with images of dependency and helplessness. One woman I met, who was a wheelchair user, recounts the story of waiting outside a major department store drinking from a can of cola, when suddenly a man approached her and absent mindedly tried to put some coins in her can. Many service users were extremely angry at being portrayed as objects of sympathy and having to rely on people's charity.

Associated with, and sometimes confused with, the voluntary sector is a new breed of service provider which call themselves 'not for profit' organisations. Many of these are run essentially on models borrowed from commercial undertakings, and can often outperform traditional voluntary organisations, especially in terms of flexibility and responsiveness to peoples' needs.

The private sector

In Scotland this sector has always been and continues to be the smallest sector of providers. The reasons for this might have something to do with the tradition of local authorities being the main providers of services. The NHS and Community Care Act of 1990 promoted a 'mixed economy' of care and the introduction of 'market forces' into the provision of social care which resulted in some growth in this area in Scotland. As long as the aims and actions of private sector organisations are those of any others providing care and accord with a care value base, they have an equal and valuable part to play in the provision of care. Many private agencies do achieve a quality service meeting the needs of their client group. There is a danger though that some private agencies may be driven more by the desire to make profit for individuals, shareholders and directors, than by the desire to provide innovative quality services. The problem can be that in order to maximise profit, such agencies are driven by 'economy of scale'. There is no great profit in running a small group home for three people living in the community. You need to run a unit with at least 30 or 40 people living in it in order to see a handsome return on investment. This has meant that while some agencies in the statutory and voluntary sector were reducing the sizes of places where people lived in an attempt to make them more homely and less institutional, some private sector organisations started building comparatively large units in order to maximise income.

It would, however, be an injustice to portray all care providers in the private sector as concerned only with profit. As stated above, many do provide high quality services at good value for money. In the same way it would be wrong to portray all those in the voluntary sector as pioneering and driven only by altruism. (Paradoxically, some of the highest paid jobs are to be found in the voluntary sector.) In a similar vein, services run by statutory agencies have sometimes been unfairly portrayed as inefficient and wasteful of resources. In reality, there are good and bad services spread across the whole spectrum of providers.

CONCLUSION

As both this century and chapter draw to a conclusion and we head towards the new millennium, there are some major changes being proposed in the way that care in Scotland is delivered. In March 1999 a White Paper was presented to the UK Parliament entitled 'Aiming for Excellence', which will serve as a blueprint for the modernisation of social work services in Scotland. Although directed principally at the area of social care, it will have knock-on effects on all areas of care delivery. The task of enacting this legislation will be one of the first responsibilities of the new Scottish parliament.

The paper recognises that over 100 000 people are employed in social care settings in Scotland and that in the year 1998–99, the government provided a total of £1050 million towards the cost of such services.

Included in the main recommendations in the proposed legislation are that a 'Scottish Commission for the Regulation of Care Services' will be created, which will be a statutory body with responsibility for the regulation of services. In addition a 'Scottish Social Services Council' will also be created which will be responsible for the registration of staff working in this area.

In some ways, this might be said to represent a 'coming of age' of care services, an acknowledgement and recognition of the value of the care tasks carried out daily by a huge number of people, often in a quiet, undemonstrative manner and sometimes in difficult and demanding circumstances.

If you are, or aspire to be, one of the people involved in the important task referred to, then it is hoped you will be encouraged to become a confident and competent practitioner and that the contents of this book may be of assistance or inspiration.

SUMMARY

This chapter has provided an examination of the context of care, in order that you can see where and how care practice fits into a societal and developmental context. The nature and meaning of care were examined with an emphasis upon improving the quality of peoples' lives. The distinction was made between formal care, generally provided by people on a paid basis, and informal care, generally provided by relatives for no material reward. Care work in different fields and the factors common to all of these were examined. Examples both of care workers and service users were provided. Consideration was given to the power of the care worker and empowerment of the service user in order that practice is always in the best interests of service users.

Five reasons for the growth in demand for care were examined. These are: demographic changes; changes in the nature of the family and community life; changes in lifestyle expectations; changing political and personal ideologies and values; concepts of social exclusion. Care was placed in the context of other historical and political processes in the last 75 years. The

High this is fine

Figure 1.8 The Community Care balancing act

providers of care were considered as belonging to one of three main categories: statutory, voluntary or private. Two activities encourage you to explain the meaning of care and changes in provision, and institutionalisation.

Activity

(This activity relates to Outcome 2, all performance criteria, of the Intermediate 2 Unit 'Social Influences on Behaviour'.)

Read the two descriptions below of respite units for children with a disability and then answer the questions which follow.

The Mannering Unit was purpose-built a few years ago in pleasant surroundings within an area of tenements, near to a park, shops and a regular bus service. Ten children at a time attend for respite care and the respite is planned so that the children get to know one another over a period of time. The older children are encouraged to help with preparing lunch and even enter the kitchen to get drinks or make toast, as long as there is a member of staff there. All of the children are given a choice of two or three different dishes at all meals. Breakfast and lunch are fairly flexible. Breakfast can be taken any time between 8 and 9 and lunch is usually a buffet, so that groups don't have to stop suddenly because it's lunch time. The evening meal is almost always at a set time and gives everyone a chance to discuss their day. Bed time varies according to age, the needs of the child and whether or not there is school the next day. At weekends children are allowed to stay up later and older children can choose when to switch off their light.

There are a lot of activities on offer to encourage the children to have an enjoyable and fulfilling stay at the unit. There are four lounges, which sometimes get quite untidy, where children can choose to do different activities. There is also a quiet room for those who need a bit of peace. Staff like to get to know parents so that they can ask them about their children's likes and dislikes if the children are not able to communicate very well themselves. Usually there is one member of staff on duty for every two children and more than half of the staff have a qualification in care work. Staff wear casual clothes for work. All of the children have single rooms all of which are different from one another. The teenagers who attend regularly helped to choose the colour schemes.

The Stuart Unit is located just outside the city boundaries and caters for 24 children at a time in respite care. There are lovely views out over countryside from the windows but for most of the children there's a long journey to get there. A bus passes the entrance every two hours. Staff are rushed off their feet with a staff ratio of one staff to five children, but they do their best for the children who come. They make sure that they are always clean, their rooms are tidy and that the children get their medication if they need it. Staff look very smart in their blue and white uniforms. Children share rooms, usually four to a room. The rooms are all nicely decorated in blue and white, all with the same matching bedding.

Once they are up and dressed and have had their 8 a.m. breakfast, the children are left largely to their own devices while the staff get on with their domestic duties. There is an occasional outing but the children sit in their wheelchairs or on chairs set out around the edge of the lounge with the TV on for long periods of the day. Lunch is at 12 noon and dinner at 5 p.m. The children, whatever their ages, are all in bed by 9 p.m. with lights out. This gives staff a chance to complete the daily log and catch up on gossip before the night shift takes over at 10. Staff have little time to speak to parents and lack the training to be able to be very creative in their practice. They do care for the children, though they don't stand any nonsense from those who want to do something different from the others. They think that these children should realise how difficult it is for staff and should join in with whatever is on offer, even if it's only TV.

Questions

1. Identify four aspects of 'care' in either of the studies which may contribute to institutionalisation.

2. Identify four aspects of care in either of the studies which could counteract institutionalisation.

3. Which unit would you recommend to a friend whose child has a disability? Give four reasons for your choice.

4. You are collecting a child at the end of his or her stay in Mannering Unit. Identify three possible differences in the reaction of this child from a child who has just had a stay in the Stuart Unit.

CHAPTER 2

Equality of opportunity and anti-discriminatory practice

Susan Gibb

Anti-discriminatory practice challenges people's values and their taken-for-granted assumptions in constructing their own sense of reality. Such a challenge can prove to be very threatening and desta-bilising. If not handled sensitively, exposure to anti-discriminatory ideas and values can be so alien and threatening as to arouse considerable resistance and barriers to change ... The focus needs to be on educating and convincing, not bullying

(Thomson, 1997, page 159)

INTRODUCTION

As a worker in a care setting, it is essential to develop a clear understanding of prejudice and discrimination and to learn a variety of methods to combat them. Few people would deny that discrimination exists, but there is still disagreement and confusion about exactly what it is, why it exists and what can be done to change things. Discrimination is a complex subject, and one that is prone to a hostile response because people feel threatened when their views are challenged. This chapter attempts to deal with these issues.

Relationship of chapter to Higher Still The first sections of the chapter present material at **Intermediate II level** for the unit **Social Influences on Behaviour**. This relates to the nature of **discrimination, prejudice and stereotyping**. There is consideration of how prejudice is learned. This covers pages 35–46. The material on the **effects of discrimination and discrimination in a care setting** (pages 52–57) can be used at both Intermediate II and Higher levels. The remainder of the chapter presents material for the **Higher** unit, **Promoting Equal Opportunities in a Care Context**.

THE NATURE OF DISCRIMINATION

What is discrimination?

- Discrimination is the unequal and unfair treatment of an individual or group.
- Discrimination is based on prejudice towards people who are seen as being different.
- Prejudice is learned from picking up negative attitudes from our families and society.
- Discrimination is built in to the way we run our social, political and economic institutions.

What is prejudice?

A prejudice is an attitude about an individual or a group, based on judgements which are often founded on ignorance, fear or speculation, rather than fact. Prejudice – the pre-judging of someone – can be either positive or negative. You can be prejudiced in favour of, or prejudiced against, a person. Everyone has some prejudices: once we become aware of what they are for us, we can begin to do something about them.

The way prejudice works in discrimination is that a negative, biased and intolerant attitude against someone is maintained, even in the face of contradictory evidence. These prejudices are often based on negative **stereotypes** of a group. A stereotype is a label which is applied to all members of a group. A quality or characteristic of the group is taken as always applying to all members of the group, e.g. people with Down's Syndrome like music, girls don't like playing football. People within that group are not seen as individuals with unique needs and interests. They are treated as if they are the same as everyone else in that group, e.g. all gay men are promiscuous, all Aberdonians are mean.

Apart from being based on a lack of correct information, stereotypes like these disadvantage people because negative assumptions are made about them based on one aspect of their identity. People are not seen as a 'whole person', but are categorised according to one feature – being black, disabled, homeless – and related to only on that basis. That one aspect of their identity defines them in the eyes of the prejudiced. Assumptions are made about their abilities and interests based on these stereotypes and prejudices. This limits their opportunity to construct their own feeling of positive self esteem, because they so often meet with negative or misinformed reactions, and this limits their opportunities to participate equally in society.

CASE STUDY: STUDY PAINTS PICTURE OF ISOLATION

Disabled people feel abandoned, patronised and that they are treated as an inconvenience, according to a new study. Their feelings of social exclusion were revealed during discussions organised by disability care charity Leonard Cheshire as part of a survey of attitudes to disability in Britain.

More than half of the 1000 members of the public interviewed in the survey supported Leonard Cheshire's view that disabled people are prevented from being useful members of society. The charity has concluded that ignorance and prejudice about disability contribute to social exclusion as much as poverty. It is urging the government to include disability in the Social Exclusion Unit's remit.

Almost one third of respondents agreed with the statement 'Some people assume that a person in a wheelchair cannot be intelligent.'

The survey report stated: 'The way that people think others might respond can give a clue to their own views . . . a sizeable minority of the public underestimate disabled peoples abilities.
(Source: Community Care 28 May–3 June 1998 p.3)

Questions:
1. What effect does prejudice have on people with disabilities according to the article?
2. What stereotypes about people with disabilities are mentioned in the article?

Prejudice and stereotypes don't occur randomly. They reflect the divisions within any society, whereby those who have power are able to define what is good or bad and what is acceptable or not. Power is the ability to control or to influence other people. Prejudice reflects the power that the dominant group has over other groups. When one group is disadvantaged, another group is advantaged.

Where do we develop our prejudices? The process of socialisation – the way in which we develop our values, attitudes and ideas – will be dealt with in more detail in Chapters 3 and 5, but we touch on it here because it is central to the process of developing prejudice. The messages we pick up, firstly from our family (primary Socialisation) and later from friends, school and the media (secondary Socialisation), influence the way we see the world.

One way in which prejudice can flourish is the limited range of positive identities of certain groups in the media, and an almost non-existent model for other groups, e,g, disabled people in

Figure 2.1 When one group is disadvantaged, another is advantaged

mainstream TV and advertising. There is a deafening silence when it comes to the experience of certain groups, whose experience is omitted from our popular consciousness.

Where do these attitudes and values come from? Historically, the Christian churches have exerted a strong influence on British society and helped define what was seen as being right and wrong. The limited position of women and perceived sinfulness of homosexuality stemmed

---

CASE STUDY: MEDIA IMAGES OF AIDS

Within the media and in public discussion, frightening images have been used to represent AIDS, and stigmatising metaphors have been used to describe people with HIV infection. AIDS has been represented as a condition which marks its 'victims' as socially different, and people with AIDS have sometimes been represented as a source of moral and social contamination and danger . . . Some of the distress or discomfort faced by an HIV positive individual, may derive from the ways in which HIV and AIDS have been socially constructed and from the images and metaphors which have been used to represent AIDS.

(Source: Anderson and Wilkie, 1992, p. 21, *Reflective Helping in HIV and AIDS*)

Questions

This was written in 1992. Do you think media coverage of people with AIDS has improved since then? What picture is portrayed in recent newspapers?

---

directly from interpretations of the Bible. The church was part of the 'Establishment', along with aristocratic men who served in Parliament, and it was their views which were enshrined in laws. Married women couldn't own property in their own right until 1882. Women couldn't vote until 1918 and it was not until 1946 that the civil service dropped its rule against employing married women in certain jobs. Britain's colonial past and role in maintaining the slave trade, provides the basis for many of the negative stereotypes of black people still current today.

Prejudice exists because we are brought up with negative pictures of certain groups which are often based on views developed many generations ago. The negative message still exists today because it is ingrained in legal, political, educational and other structures in society. However, not everyone brought up with these negative images agrees with them or acts on them. Once people are able to make up their minds about issues, they can reject the attitudes and behaviour they have been socialised to accept. Some people, however, even if they can see that the values they have learnt are wrong, still continue to hold them. This may be due to pressure from friends or family to 'fit in with the crowd'. People who have low self esteem, and an intense need for acceptance by others are more likely to conform with values they don't hold, in order to remain part of the crowd. People who have a higher self esteem are able to disagree and not fear the consequences of disapproval, because they have a stronger sense of their own identity.

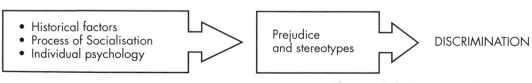

Figure 2.2 Causes of discrimination

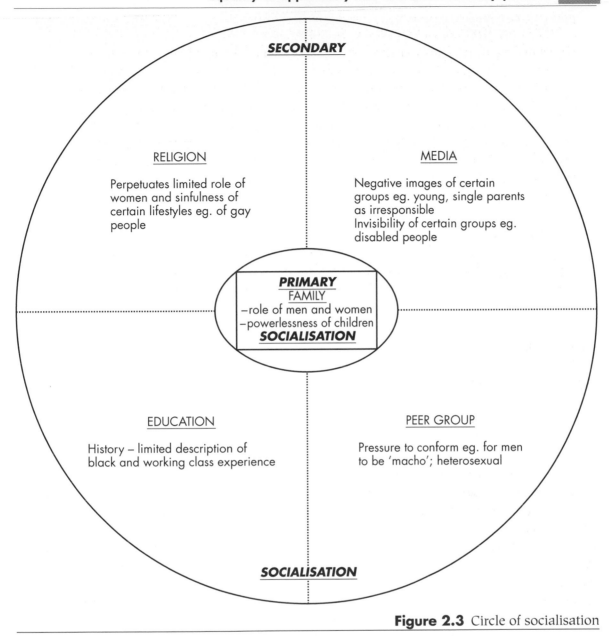

Figure 2.3 Circle of socialisation

Prejudice is ingrained into the process of developing our identity and we tend unconsciously to accept that this is 'just the way things are'. However, it is important as care workers that we don't assume that it is only gay people who have to think about their sexuality, or black people who develop a sense of belonging to a racial group. We have all had to construct our own sense of what being a member of a certain racial group means to us. Some people who belong to the 'mainstream' may not have had to give much active thought to how their identity has been created – it just seemed 'normal'. Anyone who is outside the 'mainstream' will have had to give more active thought to aspects of their identity because it has been stigmatised or is devalued in our society.

Activity: Lifeline

On a piece of paper, write down, 'Who am I' at the top. Answer this question 20 times with as wide a range of responses as you wish: I am female, I am small, I have brown hair, I'm a joker, I am a grandfather, I have a hearing impairment, I help out at the youth club, I am Chinese, I am fat. The list might contain descriptions of what you look like, what you do or an aspect of your personality.

Place a large piece of paper sideways and draw a line with your date of birth at the left hand side and today's date at the right hand side. For each of the 20 responses to the question 'Who am I', write or draw onto the paper WHEN you first became aware of that part of your identity. Things like 'I am a grandfather' will be easy to date, but you might need to think about exactly when you first became aware of your colour or your gender. The purposes of this exercise is to reflect on exactly when you developed your sense of what makes up your individual identity. Discovering and creating an identity is an active process for everyone.

Challenging prejudice

Our attitudes and values are not cast in stone: just as they have been influenced by our background, they can also be influenced by new information and experiences we encounter. Socialisation is a lifelong process, so there is always the opportunity to reconsider our attitudes and behaviour. We don't need continually to react in old ways. We can actively seek to change the way we behave and the way we think.

One way of tackling prejudice is through advertising campaigns. There have been some high profile advertising campaigns which confront public perceptions of disadvantaged groups. The Commission for Racial Equality ran a highly controversial campaign showing advertisements of black people in stereotyped roles (as a potential rapist and as being as athletic as an orang utan) masquerading as bona fide adverts for rape alarms and sportswear. The point of their campaign was to see whether members of the public complained about the racist stereotypes in the adverts, but very few people did. The second part of their campaign was then to point out this apathy and complacency, and comment on the fact that people just don't feel strongly enough about racism to complain.

Age Concern ran another provocative billboard campaign, with a head and shoulders picture of a 56 year-old woman wearing a bra with the caption: 'The first thing some people notice about her is her age – let's make age discrimination a thing of the past'.

Both campaigns succeeded in stimulating debate and challenged peoples' perceptions, but there was concern with both that their point could be missed. They could also be seen to confirm stereotypes – the CRE campaign could be seen as confirming racist stereotypes if people weren't aware of the second part of their campaign and the Age Concern campaign, although trying to promote a positive image of older women, could be seen as being sexist because it links a woman's worth with her attractiveness, her body shape and her availability to men.

The Zero Tolerance campaign was another large-scale public advertising campaign developed by the Women's Unit of Edinburgh District Council. The target was male violence against women and children, through challenging stereotypical views of violence and the excuses men make for their violence. The campaign is now being used throughout Britain, and other countries are showing an interest because it has been so effective in tackling the silence about male violence against women.

Breitenbach (1995) reports that research into the impact of the poster campaign indicated that it was extremely successful in both attracting the attention of and gaining a positive reaction from, members of the public. The campaign achieved its initial aim of generating debate and high-lighting the prevalence of male violence, sending out a clear message that this should not be tolerated. The campaign has also led to a change in the perceptions of women who experience male violence. There is evidence that the campaign has enabled women to come forward in greater numbers to seek advice and assistance in relation to domestic violence, child sexual abuse, rape and sexual assault.

Activity: Challenging prejudice and stereotypes

What do you think? Have your ideas ever been changed by a poster or an advertising campaign? If not, what HAS led you to change your views? Are prejudices and stereotypes best challenged by this direct, uncompromising and sometimes confrontational approach? Many of the Health Promotion initiatives in Chapter 8 look at this way of influencing our attitudes and behaviour. What would you say are the advantages and disadvantages of this approach?

Types of discrimination

There are many types of discrimination from the obvious, direct, intentional act to the unintentional discrimination that is so much part of our daily way of life that we don't know it is negative until it is pointed out. In this section we will look at three types of discrimination: **direct**, **indirect** and **unconscious** discrimination.

Direct discrimination

Discrimination is direct if the unfair and unequal treatment of a person is obvious and open. According to the Sex Discrimination Act (1975), a person directly discriminates against a woman if 'on the ground of her sex he treats her less favourably than he treats or would treat a man'. In determining whether an offence has been committed the motivation and intention of the person who discriminates is irrelevant. So, for instance, sexual harassment is a form of direct discrimination even though it is often minimised by the perpetrator with statements such as 'It's only a joke', 'I didn't mean any harm', or 'They just can't take a bit of banter'. It is not a defence to say that you didn't intend to cause any harm or hurt. What needs to be proved, legally, is simply that the woman concerned was treated less favourably than a man would have been in the same situation. In British law, it is also illegal to discriminate against men, or on the basis of marital status, racial origin or disability.

Many other people who experience direct discrimination, because of their age or sexuality for instance, are not protected by law. Often the discrimination they experience is active and intentional. The perpetrator knows they are discriminating, and intends to disadvantage someone. Due to a prejudice they have, they dislike or disapprove of the person and act negatively towards them.

> **CASE STUDY: DIRECT DISCRIMINATION**
> Coming to terms with the fact that their children have a sex life is difficult for many parents, and the transition to adulthood is a time of friction in most families. But for gay teenagers, it can be the beginning of a lifelong battle against prejudice. And it can leave them homeless.
>
> Some find themselves 'out' in the streets, rejected by their family. Others can be forced to move away from their homes when hostility from neighbours becomes too much. People who contact the Gay and Lesbian Switchboard have had horrible objects put through their letterbox, or received nasty letters telling them to leave. Some have been threatened, some have had windows broken. But the problem of homelessness amongst gay people is underestimated since many are reluctant to talk about the real reasons for their homelessness.
>
> A national survey by Social and Community Planning Research confirms that people who are openly gay are likely to face discrimination by landlords. 90 per cent of gays and lesbians thought landlords wouldn't rent to homosexuals. 61 per cent of heterosexual landlords confirmed their fears, by admitting they would be less likely to rent a room to a homosexual couple, while 58 per cent would avoid taking lesbians. (Extracts from: 'Out in the Cold' by Stephen Naysmith *The Big Issue*, June 1994, pp. 22–3)
>
> **Questions**
> 1. What kind of direct discrimination do young gay people face according to the article?
> 2. What impact might this have on their lives?

Other examples of direct discrimination

■ An Asian woman was prevented from viewing a house in an affluent suburb by a Glasgow estate agent, because of her ethnic origin. She won her case of racial discrimination and received £2000 damages. The Estate Agent was ordered to pay £100 000 in costs.

- A 32 year-old man refused work by a security firm and a 33 year-old women applying for job as a PA to a company director were told they were too old for the posts.
- Save the Children carried out a survey into the treatment of travelling families in Scotland and found that many caravan parks refused the travellers a pitch, with some displaying signs such as 'We don't take gypsies' and 'No Travellers'. Scotland has between 10 000 and 15 000 travellers and if they are not allowed to stop, the children don't have the opportunity to exercise basic rights such as going to school and gaining access to a doctor.
- The West of Scotland Community Relations Council has dealt with the following cases: young Asian women abused in the streets, their children spat at and punched; doors set alight while families sleep in their beds; excrement and rubbish pushed through their letterboxes. In some areas, where there are fewer Asians, residents have sent petitions to the local authority demanding the removal of a particular family on the grounds of their colour.

2. Indirect discrimination

It is possible to describe many examples of direct discrimination where there has been some obvious wrong done to someone and where an injustice has occurred. However, discrimination also occurs on another level where the injustice is less obvious and may not even be intended, but it is discrimination nonetheless. Indirect discrimination occurs when a condition is applied that limits the opportunity for a group to comply. This is quite a complicated idea to understand, therefore a number of different examples will be given to illustrate how indirect discrimination works.

- If a job advert stated that only people aged under 28 can apply then this obviously *directly* discriminates against people over 28. However, it has also been legally proved to *indirectly* discriminate against women, because a very substantial number of mothers return to work after the age of 28. Although the advert did not intend to stop women as mothers applying, in reality it was more difficult for women returning to work after having children to comply with this part of the job requirement, and therefore it was indirect discrimination under the Sex Discrimination Act 1975.
- If a job advert asks for a driving licence, it could be indirectly discriminating against physically disabled people. The intention is not necessarily to bar disabled people from applying, but many disabled people don't drive. The forms of transport disabled people use mean they cannot comply with that condition in the advert, and so are deemed not suitable, even though driving may not actually be an essential requirement of the job. Indirectly, they have been discriminated against, because they do not have the opportunity of applying for that job, even if they fulfil all the other criteria.
- One way in which indirect discrimination might occur in a social care setting would be if an organisation did not provide publicity and information about the service it provides in all the languages spoken by people in its catchment area. The intention is not to bar people from ethnic groups from attending, but in reality if they do not read

English, they will find it more difficult to discover whether any of the services are relevant to them.

■ Many buildings do not have disabled access, or have limited opportunity for disabled people to use all their services. This again is indirect discrimination: no-one has put a notice up saying 'Disabled people not welcome', but in practice, disabled people are less able to take advantage of the service that is apparently open equally to everyone.

CASE STUDY: INDIRECT DISCRIMINATION

Mr Hussain complained to Leeds Racial Equality Council that he was unable to become a member of Streamline taxis because of the rule that he had to first buy a taxi from a proprietor member and then be sponsored by that member and two others – 195 of Streamline's 196 members were white.

Leeds Industrial Tribunal found the sponsorship arrangements to be indirectly racially discriminatory. Of the 631 people with Leeds Hackney licences, 32 per cent were of Asian ethnic origin. As Streamline Taxis was well aware of the consequences of the membership rule, the tribunal awarded £1000 in damages for intentional injury to feelings. The tribunal also pointed out that its decision had immediate implications for two other Leeds taxi associations with exclusively white membership and the same membership rules, and gave notice that, if there was a next time, the tribunal might well award much higher damages.
(Source: Commission for Racial Equality (1997) Annual Report p. 36)

Questions
1. What changes would the taxi firm have to make to avoid indirect discrimination?
2. What rules or procedures might there be in a care setting which could lead to indirect discrimination?

---

3. Unconscious discrimination

Conscious discrimination occurs when a person knows they are acting negatively and wants to disadvantage someone. Unconscious discrimination occurs when a person discriminates against someone without realising that they are discriminating. It could be direct or indirect, and can be seen in everyday behaviour and language.

Many actions disadvantage people because they perpetuate stereotypes of people being weak and helpless. This is the 'Does he take sugar?' syndrome, where people talk to the person who is pushing a wheelchair and not the person using the wheelchair. The unconscious prejudice is that because the person is physically disabled, they are somehow also not able to think or talk on their own behalf.

As a social care worker, it is possible to fall into another version of this patronising behaviour. Under the guise of 'helping' someone, you do things for them that they could do independently. This creates a dependency on the worker and keeps a power imbalance in their favour. As Thomson (1997, p. 104) notes:

One significant aspect of ageist ideology is the process of infantilisation – treating older people as if they were children . . . In recognising this, we must also recognise that the more protective we become the more we challenge older people's rights to make their own decisions and be responsible for themselves.

The language we use is one of the most obvious ways of unconsciously showing our prejudice. Many of the words, phrases and expressions we use are insulting to, or undermining of others, without us being aware of it. For instance, shortening the 'difficult to pronounce' name of an Indian to a Western nickname, can be seen as an attempt to make the person part of the group, but underlying this assumption is the fact that people can't be bothered to find out and use the proper pronunciation. Examining and changing the words you use is more than just window dressing. Although it is apparently a small step, it is something you as an individual can start thinking about, and acting on, immediately. It is a symbolic step, because you notice it and so do others around you.

Language is an important representation of our thoughts and feelings, therefore it is important to consider what message is given by the words we use. Changing the term 'disabled

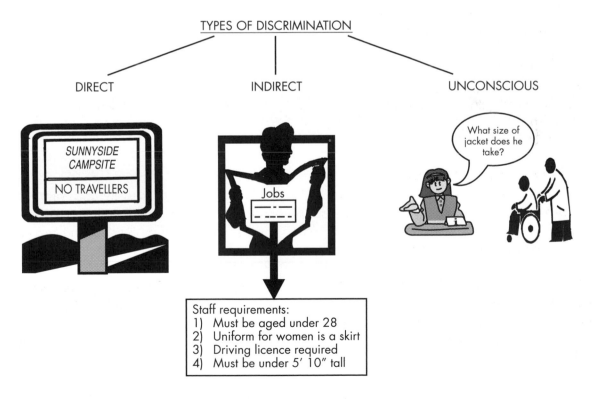

Figure 2.4 Types of discrimination

toilets' to 'accessible toilets' gives a different message to everyone. It emphasises the attributes of a building, not of a person. A number of organisations for disabled people have changed their name because they wanted to portray a more positive and modern picture of their work – The Spastics Society renamed themselves Capability Scotland and The Scottish Society for Mental Handicap changed their name to Enable.

Our use of language changes all the time and terms that were once commonplace are now rarely used. Most people would agree that it is unacceptable to call someone who is mentally ill a moron, or someone with learning disabilities an imbecile, but they were once the normal medical term. This is not about political correctness, but about being aware of the effect of your words on those around you. Two of the qualities required to be a good care workers are respect and sensitivity. Appropriate use of language is one of the ways in which you can display these qualities.

CASE STUDY: LANGUAGE

Glasgow City Council has published a leaflet which gives guidelines on alternative words to use for terms that are seen as sexist. They state 'Sexism continues to disadvantage women both as service users and employees. The use of sexist language, whether spoken or written, reinforces this discrimination.' Inevitably, not everyone agrees with the definitions of what constitutes sexist language, but this kind of publicity raises the point that language is an issue, because women feel disadvantaged, marginalised and ignored by terminology that is outdated. Some examples from the leaflet are:

■ Don't assume it is acceptable to address women by endearments such as **dear**, **pet** and **love** when you would not address men in such a way.

■ Some words and phrases such as **manpower** and **man the office** exclude or ignore women. Use inclusive terms like **staff** or **workers** and **staff the office**.

■ Job titles which include gender such as **Storeman** and **Clerkess** can restrict entry and encourage discrimination. **Storeperson** and **Clerical Officer** are neutral and more acceptable.

(Source: *Glasgow City Council* (1997) 'Language Matters: A guide to Good Practice)

Questions

1. Why do you think people are often hostile to suggestions that they should change some of the language they use?

2. Why is it important for some groups to 'reclaim' words that have been used against them, and change their meaning from a negative to a positive one, e.g. gay people using the term 'queer'?

LEVELS AT WHICH DISCRIMINATION TAKES PLACE

There are many levels on which the different types of discrimination can occur. Discrimination can take place at **individual**, **institutional** and **cultural** levels. In reality, these levels are not separate: our individual views are influenced by the culture in which we live, and the institutions we encounter, but it is useful initially to look at the way in which each level operates independently. It is important to analyse at what level we believe discrimination occurs, because then we will know at which level to challenge it. It is of little use treating a broken leg with a sticking plaster, and it is equally pointless trying to tackle large-scale inequalities only with small-scale solutions.

1. Individual discrimination

When one person attacks a black person because of his colour, bullies a child with learning disabilities, or sexually harasses an employee, he or she is individually discriminating against that person. Although this individual behaviour exists because he or she has been brought up in a culture that devalues certain groups, it is still individual discrimination because it is that person acting alone. It doesn't need to be literally only one person. If a small group of people harass or intimidate someone, this can still be described as an example of individual discrimination, because the essence is that they are operating independently and not as part of a wider structure. There is no official backing for their behaviour.

Individual responsibility for discrimination also occurs when we see an act of discrimination and don't seek to stop it or change it. We say 'I don't want to get involved, it's not my problem, someone else will do something about it.' Discrimination continues to exist because people don't challenge it. It is not just the perpetrators who keep groups oppressed by acting against them, it is also the people who do nothing to stop it or change it. The system of discrimination is perpetuated by individual people doing nothing to challenge it. In care settings this might mean not reporting an incident of bad practice, or failing to support someone who is experiencing harassment.

2. Institutional discrimination

Discrimination is institutional when it operates within the rules, regulations and practices of an organisation. When an individual incident of discrimination is backed up by an organisation, or when it happens so often that it is part of everyday practice, it can be seen as being institutional discrimination. It is part of the way an organisation or section of society is structured. Institutional discrimination operates through the normal, routine working of a system. This can occur in a variety of ways, so a number of different examples will be considered.

A) Rules and regulations

Discrimination occurs because it is built in to the rules and regulations of an organisation.

- A pregnant woman was sacked after her pregnancy made her too ill to work. The rules of the company were that anyone who was off for 26 consecutive weeks could be sacked. She claimed she was exempt from this rule because her illness was related to her pregnancy and was thus covered by the Sex Discrimination Act. The woman took her complaint to two Scottish Industrial Tribunals, the House of Lords and finally all the way to the European Court of Justice which judged, eight years after the sacking, that she had been a victim of sex discrimination.

- In the financial and insurance sectors, all disabled people are labelled as having the same high risk, with no distinction made between people with a stable state and average life expectancy and those who have a progressive illness.
- Gay people are not allowed to serve in the armed forces in Britain, although they are in other European countries such as Holland. They will be sacked if it is found out during their service that they are gay.
- A white woman was told on starting her job as a receptionist with a van hire company that it was not the company's policy to hire vehicles to 'coloureds or Asians'. She resigned and claimed she had been asked to carry out discriminatory instructions.

B) Everyday practices
Within an organisation

Many organisations have rules and regulations which prohibit discrimination, but nonetheless discrimination still occurs. The culture of the organisation allows certain bad practice to occur, and people don't do anything to challenge it. There has often been no formal discussion among the people involved about what is happening – it is just 'the way things are done around here' and there is a strong pressure to fit in or leave.

- A special needs lecturer at a college in the north of England was awarded £30 000 compensation because he had suffered 'vulgar abuse' and numerous racially disparaging remarks from his colleagues, on account of his Irish origin. This would have been an example of direct, individual discrimination by some lecturers if the college had followed their own procedures and backed the person's complaint. However, the college had compounded matters by ignoring its own harassment policy, and dismissing the remarks which the lecturer had complained about as 'innocent banter'. The fact that the college management chose not to support his claim meant it became institutional discrimination, because it was now the organisation as a whole that supported the discrimination, not just a few individuals within it.
- A female assistant director of finance in a London borough was awarded £234 000 damages for sex discrimination. She had been undermined by a network of male managers who had left her feeling worthless. It had been a slow, steady process which undermined her strength and confidence. She was kept in the dark about matters that should have been her responsibility, her decisions were countermanded and projects which should have been given to her were handed to colleagues. Finally, she was made redundant. There was no rule or regulation which said 'treat women managers badly', it was just part of the culture of that workplace. It was not just one event, or harassment from one person, but a number of events over a period of time, from a variety of people. This is often difficult to pinpoint, because individual events can be

apparently trivial and not obviously linked. However, there is now increasing legal back-up for people who feel they experience this type of bullying, intimidation or harassment in the workplace.

Within society

The way society operates can disadvantage certain groups. Sometimes this is enshrined in law, but often it is due to the way society has developed historically. Similar instances of discrimination can occur in so many different places, that it can be said to be part of the 'normal' functioning of that part of society. It has been institutionalised in the way that section of society operates.

- Domestic violence against women and children accounts for a quarter of all reported crime. Over 95 per cent of adult abusers of children are male. Sexual, physical and mental abuse of women and children still happens on a routine, regular basis across all sections of society because of the power that a man has as a husband and father. Despite the fact there is legislation to say this behaviour is illegal, it is still extremely difficult for a women or child to go through the process of telling the police, going to court and challenging the behaviour, because the right of men to treat their family as 'their property' is still ingrained in society.
- It is still routine for architects to design houses and public buildings without fully recognising the needs of people with disabilities, older adults, or parents with young children.
- There is an under-representation of women, ethnic minorities and disabled people in key positions in society. Some individuals in these groups have managed to break through the invisible barrier – the 'glass ceiling' – and gain positions of power. Compared to their numbers in society, however, these groups are still significantly absent from key positions. This pattern of structural disadvantage is evident in many sectors: 82 per cent of MPs after the 1997 general election were male; only 4 per cent of directors in the top 100 companies in Britain and 7 per cent of High Court judges in England and Wales are female. The fact that this discrepancy exists in a number of different areas denotes that it is not just isolated examples of discrimination but part of the systematic lack of opportunity for women.

CASE STUDY: SCOTTISH WOMEN ARE 'SECOND CLASS CITIZENS'

Scottish women are still being relegated to a 'minority interest' and continue to lag behind men in pay and promotion prospects, according to a government survey. A report being published today by the Scottish Women's Minister, Helen Liddell, shows that almost two decades after the Sex Discrimination Act, average female weekly earnings are 72 per cent of the male equivalent.

In Scotland nine out of ten single parents are women and women are also twice as likely to suffer from depression. Almost six out of ten carers in Scotland are women. Although women make up 52 per cent of secondary school teachers, only 9 per cent have been promoted to headteacher.

Mrs Liddell has promised to make concerted efforts to rectify the disparity and said: 'From now on, not only will we be working to continue to improve life for women, but we will be able to measure our progress.'

The survey showed that more than half of Scottish women in prison have been locked up for defaulting on fines, with only one per cent convicted of violent crime. It also found that, despite a rapid increase in female intake in recent years, women still only make up a third of Scotland's GPs. Women consultants have doubled in number since 1980, but they still only account for a third of those under 40.
(Source: *The Scotsman*, 'Scottish women "second class citizens" ' by Nick Thorpe, 20.11.98)

Questions
1. What examples of institutional discrimination are mentioned in the article?
2. Can you think of other ways in which women might face institutional discrimination?

3. Cultural discrimination

We learn our culture through the process of socialisation. We learn about religion, about music, about the beliefs in our society and what meaning our language has. We learn about what is considered humorous, what stereotypes there are about people and who has power in our families and communities. Our culture is the sum total of all these different kinds of influences on us – it is the shared assumptions we make about the world and how it should work.

We come to view the world through our own cultural lenses, a perspective which is based on our individual experiences and the society we live in. We often don't hear things or see things accurately because of these lenses – we don't get the full picture because we are only seeing things from our biased view. This is where our prejudices and stereotypes develop. The Commission for Racial Equality produced an exhibition called 'Roots of the Future' which looked at the history of migration to Britain. They ran workshops for schoolchildren who made the following comments: 'I didn't know that curry didn't come from here', 'I didn't think there could be 20 000 black people in London in 1787', 'I've always related Jews to the Holocaust, never back to the Norman Conquest'. Lack of knowledge about the variety of groups in society enables discrimination to continue, because our false and negative impressions of what needs people have, and what rights they should expect, limit their opportunities. Our culture – schooling, entertainment, religion and so on – helps to create and perpetuate this lack of understanding.

Activity: Effects of discrimination on deaf people

Below are excerpts from two articles on the impact of discrimination on people who are deaf. These raise a number of points about the cultural aspects of discrimination. After you have read the articles, consider the following questions:

1. What kinds of discrimination do deaf people experience at individual, institutional and cultural levels?

2. What effect does this have?

3. What variety of needs are there among different people who are deaf?

Signs of improvement

There is little knowledge in mainstream society or mainstream social work about the problems that confront deaf people. This can be quite isolating for deaf people and the social workers that deal with them.

Mainstream social workers are unlikely to be aware of many areas of specialist knowledge that social workers who work with deaf people need: things like the use of 'Deaf' as opposed to 'deaf' to express the fact that some people who use BSL would see themselves as a cultural minority and do not identify themselves as disabled at all. Things like the fact that, for a variety of reasons, the average reading age of a deaf adult is eight. This means that writing things down as a form of communication is woefully inadequate for most deaf people.

Whilst I realise this lack of information is not specific to deafness, the lack of awareness of deaf culture and language, and the assumptions made by hearing people that deaf people are 'hearing people who can't hear', make this a particularly pressing problem.
(Excerpts from: Stapleton, K. (1998) 'Signs of Improvement' in *Community Care* 30 April–6 May, pp. 26–7)

Deaf people from ethnic minorities feel isolated

Deaf people from ethnic communities feel isolated because of a lack of appropriate services, according to a report from the Joseph Rowntree Foundation. Access to information services is hampered by poor provision of community language interpreters. Statutory sector initiatives were led largely by hearing workers, while in the voluntary sector deaf people were more involved as workers. Deaf young people had limited access to family languages, customs and religion and found it hard to participate in family and community life. They also felt marginalised in the deaf community which did not respect their ethnic identity.

> Outside London there were few initiatives which focused on groups other Asian and African-Caribbean. There was also little provision for older deaf people and deaf-blind people.
>
> African-Caribbean deaf people felt particularly disadvantaged because they believed their own cultural needs were being ignored. It was felt that because they spoke the same language as white deaf people they were assumed to share the same culture by workers and so few provisions were made.
> (Excerpts from: 'Deaf people from ethnic minorities feel isolated', *Community Care* 13–19 Aug 1998, p. 15)

How do the different levels of discrimination interact?

Developing an awareness of the institutional and cultural aspects of discrimination helps to change the focus of discussion away from the personal limitations of individuals towards the barriers they face in society. At these levels, it can be seen that disadvantage is not just a random, individual problem, but is systematic and embedded in the day-to-day rules and practices of the institutions that make up society.

The cultural, institutional and individual levels interact in a different way for every individual. We share some similarities in the wider cultural influences we experience, but even at the cultural level, we develop a unique interaction with the society in which we live. This individual relationship with our surroundings continues throughout our lifetime in the experience we have within the institutions we come into contact with and the family and friends we have. Figure 2.5 shows how each individual shares certain experiences within the dominant culture and institutions but at the same time has a unique interaction with different aspects of each level. We all live with the same laws, we all have access to the media in one form or another and we all receive some kind of education. However, our experience of schooling will have been quite varied. We might have attended a Catholic school, a special school, a private school or a Steiner school. We might feel our needs were met within school or – as a girl, a Sikh, or a person with visual impairment – that our needs were not clearly recognised, or not fully met and that had an effect on the jobs we were able to apply for. In this way, our experience of discrimination and the positive or negative messages we receive as an individual – depending on our gender, racial origin, disability etc. – will be different for each person within the wider cultural and institutional framework.

EFFECTS OF DISCRIMINATION

The net result of the various levels and types of discrimination is that someone is disadvantaged, denied an opportunity or refused access to something. Whether it happens once or repeatedly, it can have an effect on that person's identity. Their sense of self-worth is diminished because of the negative treatment and their potential to achieve what they are capable of is reduced. A person with learning disabilities is frightened to walk down a street because they are being taunted and

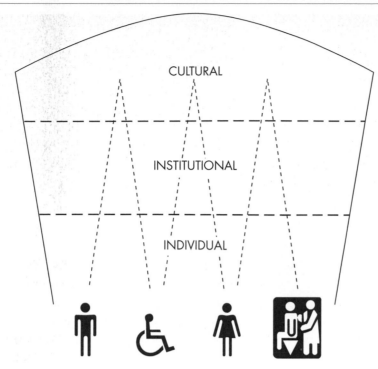

Figure 2.5 Levels of discrimination: how they interact and influence individuals in different ways

bullied, so they may miss the bus to college; a woman harassed at work takes long-term sick leave due to stress related illness; a gay person who has disclosed their sexuality to a colleague who now avoids him, is concerned that he will be isolated within his team and not gain the promoted post he has just applied for.

The result of not being accepted, not having your concerns taken seriously or not being listened to can be a feeling of alienation. Alienation is a sense that you don't belong to society and a knowledge that you are often excluded from participation in mainstream activities and events. People who are discriminated against don't have the same rights as other people, or are constrained from asserting their rights.

Another way of looking at this is the invisibility of some groups in sections of society: their needs are just not recognised or addressed. Their experience is marginalised, they feel as if they have no voice, no platform and no one to listen when they try to raise their voice. This can lead to groups feeling as if the services that are there supposedly for their benefit are seen as another way in which their experience is undervalued.

Activity: Assumptions of normality

If 1 in 10 people are gay, then in a class or workplace with 30 people, statistically there are 3 gay people. This equation can be applied to other aspects of identity which are not immediately visible – people with mental health problems, the 50 per cent of women who experience some form of sexual abuse (from flashing to rape) before their 18th birthday and nearly 40 000 people in Scotland who have epilepsy. The probability is, therefore that some of the people you live and work with will have experience of some of these situations, but because of the general 'assumption of normality' – that everyone is the same – people who are different may not feel free to talk about their experience openly. They may fear that people will misunderstand their situation because of negative stereotypes and prejudice, or that they become stigmatised and people start avoiding them or making jokes at their expense. The next time you are talking about any of these issues, bear in mind that if someone in the room was gay, had been raped, or experienced mental health problems, would you talk about things in the same way? Would you make the same 'innocent' jokes and comments? Is the way you make assumptions about the normality of people you work with one of the factors which perpetuates their silence, and therefore their continued invisibility?

All the examples of discrimination in this chapter are of real-life situations and show not only the variety of negative effects of oppression but also the desire to fight back (see Figure 2.6). A lot of people in the examples have stood up against discrimination and taken a variety of different approaches to seek redress for the negative treatment they have experienced. They have spoken out, found support and used the law in an effort to change their personal situation, and

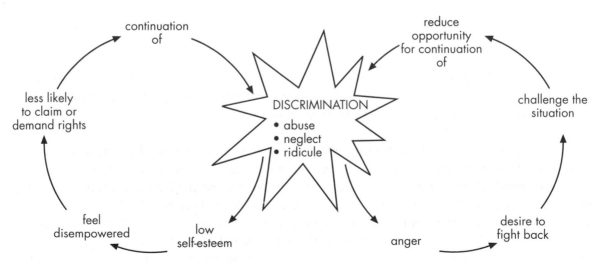

Figure 2.6 Effects of discrimination

this often has the effect that the discrimination is less likely to occur for other people in other situations. They have taken individual action or joined together in groups to campaign against the discrimination they faced.

DISCRIMINATION IN A SOCIAL CARE SETTING

In a social care setting both service users and workers can be affected by discrimination. Some of the factors which affect each group will be examined below.

1. Discrimination against service users

Care services are in an uneasy position when it comes to discrimination. They are part of the social service, benefits, housing and health systems in which people may have experienced institutionalised oppression, but part of their function is to help these same people challenge this discrimination and assert their rights.

The NHS and Community Care Act (1990) emphasised the need to promote choice and develop needs-led services, yet the experience of a lot of service users is that their choices are limited and their needs are not being recognised. One of the aims of the Act was to reduce the number of people in large institutions which clearly could not meet their individual needs. However, discrimination can still be seen to be institutionalised in community based services, because many people with disabilities or mental health problems still do not have access to resources which would enable them to live an autonomous life. There is not enough money to provide the required services, and there is no consistency of the rights and services available to people in different parts of the country. Care can be seen as a service which has increasing demands on it because of problems in society such as poverty, addiction and homelessness, whilst it has diminishing resources to deal with these problems because of changes in the funding and organisation of the welfare state.

Although the aim of caring is to improve the quality of people's lives, there are many instances in which discrimination occurs in a care setting against service users. Discrimination can occur in care settings both because certain groups are over-represented in some areas (e.g. black people defined as schizophrenic) or under-represented in other areas (e.g. lack of black people in residential homes for the elderly). Tossell and Webb (1994, p. 239) describe a number of other instances of discrimination against service users:

Many female carers have been denied support from social services because of the implicit assumption that they 'should' provide care. In similar circumstances male carers have been granted services to enable them to cope. Within the health service older people have not always had similar access to services such as psychotherapy as younger people. It may be felt that mental stress is inevitable and synonymous with growing older and therefore untreatable. Disabled people and people with special needs continue to be unfairly discriminated against when the physical environment remains inaccessible to them ... Gay service users have not always found it easy to express their sexuality in care regimes which may be hostile.

The role of care worker implies a certain amount of power and in any situation of power, abuse may occur. It is possible to behave in a way that devalues, suppresses, or dismisses the beliefs or needs of the service user. Not all examples of bad practice in care settings are necessarily also examples of discrimination, but when the misuse of power by workers is based on a denial of the rights of certain people, then it can be seen as discrimination.

Elder abuse – the systematic mistreatment of an elderly person – is increasingly recognised as a major problem for people not just in residential settings, but also those living in their own homes. It might involve physical, emotional or financial mistreatment, sexual abuse or the denial of basic rights and choices. In common with many who use care services, older adults are often frightened to speak out for fear of further abuse. If they do disclose the abuse to someone, they may not be listened to. In almost all of the enquiries into abuse in children's homes, the experience of the children was that adults just had not believed what they were saying and failed to take their claims seriously. Since abuse is often well hidden by the perpetrators, it is often difficult to prove without corroborating evidence, and this allows the abuser – often a 'respected' care worker – to maintain his or her power. The behaviour of the people who experience abuse may be challenging and disruptive because of their anger, frustration, fear and sense of powerlessness, and their allegations of abuse can sometimes be regarded as just more evidence of trouble-making from difficult service users. Care organisations should develop clear policies for dealing with allegations against staff and other service users to protect the rights of all parties if there is an allegation of abuse.

2. Discrimination against staff

Staff in care services can experience discrimination from colleagues, their organisation or service users. As a potential worker, staff can face discrimination during the recruitment and selection process, and once they have a job, they can face discrimination when applying for promotion. Workers can experience harassment and bullying from colleagues and service users. Violence against staff by service users in care settings is an increasing problem. Women workers have been sexually assaulted and black workers have been racially abused by service users. As a worker, you still have the right to be respected as an individual and expect to have your rights recognised by colleagues and service users.

CASE STUDY: DISCRIMINATION AGAINST A MEMBER OF STAFF

Mr Singh had been a social worker in a local council's children's services department since 1991. When he became a target for racist remarks by one member of staff, and complained, his manager dismissed the incidents as 'office banter' and told Mr Singh to ignore them as the offender was due to retire shortly. Because of the way the complaint was handled, Mr Singh was branded a 'trouble-maker', and staff relations broke down. The Industrial Tribunal found that the council did nothing to put matters right. Mr Singh was awarded a total of £16 615 in compensation: £5000 for the racial discrimination he had suffered and £11 615 for unfair dismissal.
(Source: Commission for Racial Equality (1995) Annual Report, p. 26.)

Questions

1. Give an example of how each level of discrimination might have contributed to this situation:
   a) individual
   b) institutional
   c) cultural.

2. How could each of the participants have acted differently to avoid the eventual confrontation?

ANTI-DISCRIMINATORY PRACTICE

We have looked at the different levels at which discrimination exists, so now we need to consider the variety of levels at which we can challenge, and prevent, discrimination in care settings. It is easy to develop a 'melting pot' theory of anti-discriminatory practice where you add all the forms of discrimination into the pot and stir, so that they are all seen as the same kind of problem. Although all forms of discrimination have some similarities irrespective of the group being discriminated against, each has a unique way in which it operates and therefore in how the problem needs to be addressed. The processes by which different discriminations occur and the forms they take, have to be included in any analysis of how to combat them. Questioning the cultural assumptions and institutional patterns of each type of discrimination will allow us to develop the best ways of combating them. Anti-discriminatory practice is not about treating everyone the same: it is about recognising the differences, negotiating with service users how best to meet their needs, assert their rights and challenge the inequalities they face.

Strategies for combating discrimination fall into four broad categories: **1. personal**, **2. group**, **3. policy/legislative** and **4. workplace strategies**.

1. Personal strategies

There are a number of things any individual can do to combat discrimination. Firstly, you can increase your self awareness to ensure that you don't discriminate; secondly, you can increase your knowledge of other groups so that you are more aware of their rights and can respond more appropriately to their needs; and thirdly you can challenge discrimination when you see it.

Increase your self awareness

The most immediate action you can take is to examine your own attitudes and behaviour. The first step to being a good care worker is the development of self awareness, because we can only change those aspects of our attitudes and behaviour that we have recognised. Workers need to become alert to the ways in which they present themselves to, and respond to, service users. Increased self awareness reduces the likelihood of unconscious discrimination. Becoming more aware of your value and belief systems is essential for competent care practice and will be dealt with more in Chapter 6.

Activity: Ways of increasing self awareness

Becoming more self aware is a lifelong process you can start working on today. We also need to make plans about what we can do in the longer term to increase our self awareness and respond to the new situations which we face. Below are suggestions for three different strategies for improving our self awareness. Think of one other thing you might be able to do within each time scale.

■ **1. Today:** Write down your thoughts and impressions of the last piece of care work that you did. What qualities did you show, what skills did you use? If you have not had any recent experience in a care setting, write about an incident in your personal life when you helped someone.

Your idea:

■ **2. Within a month:** Complete a self assessment questionnaire and ask some one who knows you to complete it about you. Compare how you assess your strengths and qualities with their assessment. You will find questionnaires in books in your workplace or local library.

Your idea:

■ **3. Within a year:** Attend a training course or workshop on a subject such as assertiveness, time management, basic counselling skills, working in groups or improving your communication skills.

Your idea:

Increase your knowledge of the rights and needs of a variety of groups

In addition to becoming more aware of how you relate to people, you need to develop an awareness of the needs and rights of a range of groups. There are many ways in which you can do this.

■ Voluntary work and placements organised as part of a college course will extend your practical experience of working with a variety of groups.

■ Choose a group you want to investigate and find out what the issues are for that group. Evaluate which needs are being met and which are not, and find out what rights the group have and others for which they are still campaigning. What legislation and organisations can they use if they have a complaint of discrimination?

■ A lot of groups have specific programmes on radio or TV outside peak viewing times which are made by, and for, people with hearing or visual impairment, ethnic groups etc. Make a point of watching some of these programmes and see if this extends your awareness of the experiences of, and issues for, other groups.

Challenge discrimination when it occurs

This requires you to be clear in your own mind about what discrimination is, and to develop interpersonal skills so you can tackle situations assertively. Challenging is not the same as confrontation. If you are prepared and informed there are non-aggressive ways of discussing your views with people. You will be more prepared to challenge discrimination if you have completed some of the tasks in the activity above, because you will be more certain of what your own values and attitudes are, and your point of view will be backed up by strong information. A lot of training courses use role plays to help people plan and prepare how they would tackle difficult situations. This gives you a chance to 'try things out' in a supportive atmosphere, so that you are more able to deal with the problem in real life.

Activity: I'm not prejudiced, but what about . . .?

When talking about prejudice and stereotypes, people often start sentences with 'I'm not prejudiced, but what about . . .' and go on to speak negatively about a group, based on prejudices they have picked up from newspapers, TV etc. An example would be 'I'm not prejudiced, but what about the girls that just get pregnant to get a house – they shouldn't go to the top of the council house list', or 'I'm not prejudiced, but I know a Pakistani grocer who sells cigarettes to under age kids and the police are too scared to get him into any trouble in case he says it's racism'.

It is important to note that when discussing prejudice with people, the point is not to score points or be more politically correct than someone else, but to become aware of the kind of assumptions that are being made and on what evidence they are based. Since prejudice is based on lack of knowledge you could ask 'What evidence do you have for what you have just said?'. Or, if it is accepted that due to our upbringing in a society where discrimination is structured into all levels of society we will all have a number of unconscious prejudices, you could say 'Everyone has some prejudices, why do you think you don't have any?'

Question

What comments might you use to counter the prejudices shown in the above statements?

The secret of success when challenging discrimination is to choose the best time and place to raise the issue. It is impossible to counter every statement or action we see that is directly or indirectly, consciously or unconsciously, individually or institutionally discriminatory. It is also too easy to think that the time is never right, because there is always the potential for hassle when you raise it as an issue. However, if we choose not to tackle a phrase or an action, we are colluding with the discrimination: we are part of it; we are part of the culture of acceptance. Things will never change if we just leave it up to other people, or to Parliament, to make a difference. If people did not allow phrases and actions to pass by unchallenged, a culture of non-acceptance would develop. There would be zero tolerance of discrimination. In this way anti-discriminatory practice would become institutionalised – it would be the accepted way of doing things; the routine, regular way of dealing with things. This has already been established in some organisations and workplaces because individuals in them had the strength of their convictions to start challenging bad practice.

2. Group strategies
Support groups

Many people find belonging to a support group gives them a chance to discuss the things that only people who share the same experience really understand. A member of a mental health support group who has manic depression said, 'Going along to these groups has been the best thing I could have done. Even if the others don't have specifically the same problem, you know they have all got a mental health problem and you can feel safe knowing they are not judging you'. Being a member of such a group means that the person can gain a wider perspective on their situation and feel empowered when they help other people in the same situation as themselves. In this way, support groups often take on a campaigning role when the members have developed the strength to challenge the prejudices and disadvantage they face.

CASE STUDY: LESBIAN MOTHERS GROUP

A workshop on parenting at a conference held by the Equality Network, a Scottish organisation which campaigns for lesbian, gay, bisexual and transgender rights, came up with the following difficulties facing gay and lesbian parents: co-parents not being recognised legally as the other parent; difficulties around maintenance when lesbian couples split after having a child together; the fears of prejudice and discrimination faced by gay parents, leaving heterosexual marriages, that they will lose their children; difficulties and fears about coming out to your children; the lack of confidence that schools are equipped to deal with bullying of children with gay parents; discrimination against children of gay parents by childminders, and/or their refusal to accept them. Lesbian mother groups help provide support for women dealing with these kinds of issues. The workshop concluded that one of the ways of addressing their concerns was to network with similar groups in order to attempt to raise the profile of gay parenting, and complain to organisations when discrimination occurs.

Advisory groups

These groups inform people of their rights in relation to the law or obtaining the right amount of benefit. They give advice on ways to bring complaints, pursue grievances and seek compensation. Trade Unions fulfil this role in relation to employment and other groups such as Welfare Rights Officers, Citizens Advice Bureaux and Ethnic Minorities Law Centres deal with a large range of queries.

Pressure and campaigning groups

These provide a focus for both one-off and long-term challenges to discrimination. People might mobilise a group overnight to highlight a particular incident of racial violence, while many organisations run campaigns for many years to highlight inadequacies in the law and campaign to change the way they are treated. Many of these groups are well funded and are very powerful. They provide statistics and information for MPs to use when issues are being discussed in Parliament. For example, the magazine *Community Care* ran a campaign in 1998 called 'A Fair Hearing', which focused on trying to improve treatment within the criminal justice system for people with learning disabilities.

CASE STUDY: ONE PLUS

Often one group can provide all these functions. One Plus, a group for single parents, provides information and advice to parents and their children and provides support groups for single mothers, single fathers and separate support groups for children. It challenges the negative stereotypes about single parents, campaigns vigorously against cuts in welfare provision to single parents and provides training to enable single parents to return to work. It has also developed a theatre group and creative writing groups. Responding to the changing role of the voluntary sector in the 1990s, it now runs a number of community business ventures in childcare and crèche provision. It takes an active role in responding to the needs not only of those in urban areas, but deals with the different needs of single parents living in rural towns and villages and the particular types of stigma and isolation they face.

---

3. Policy and legislative strategies

Personal and group strategies are crucial to raising awareness of discrimination and developing ways to counteract the effects of discrimination, but if they are to have any major effect they need to have a strong and clear backing at the institutional level. If there is not a legislative framework to provide people with rights and the freedom to make choices, then individual and group strategies are merely isolated acts which are less likely to make an impact at institutional and cultural level.

Each country decides what rights their citizens will have, and these are often enshrined in laws and charters. These rights are always subject to change, and people have often fought long and hard battles in order to achieve even some basic human rights. British legislation has to be seen in the context of International documents which preceded it and also the European legislation which now affects many aspects of domestic economic and social policy. See Figure 2.7 for a summary of relevant legislation.

Scope of legislation	Examples of legislation	Brief summary of each piece of legislation
International	Declaration of human rights 1948	All human beings are born free and equal in dignity and rights. Describes in detail what basic rights and freedoms are.
	International covenant on economic, social and cultural rights 1966	Defines the right to freedom of expression, highest standards of physical and mental health and the right to education.
	International covenant on civil and political rights 1966	Defines the right to freedom of opinion, the right to life and freedom from torture and violence.
European	Treaty of Rome 1957	Article 119: Each member state has to apply the principle of equal 'pay' between men and women at work. 'Pay' covers more than just wages.
	Directive on equal treatment 1976	Guarantees men and women the same conditions at work. Can be used to challenge sexual harassment.
	Directive on health and safety of pregnant workers 1993	Provides the right to maternity leave, to return to work afterwards and to health and safety considerations whilst pregnant.
	Recommendation on promotion of positive action for women 1984	Suggest measures from raising awareness to practical measures to achieve equality.
British	Sex Discrimination Act 1975	Direct and indirect discrimination on the basis of gender or marital status was made illegal. Certain exemptions to this were allowed, if gender was considered to be a 'genuine occupational qualification'. The Equal Opportunities Commission was set up with powers to monitor and implement the Act.
	Race Relations Act 1976	Direct and indirect discrimination on the basis of race was made illegal. Certain exemptions to this were allowed, if race was considered a 'genuine occupational qualification'. The Commission for Racial Equality was set up to implement and monitor the Act.
	Disability Discrimination Act 1995	Defines disability and encourages employers, transport providers and others to make reasonable efforts to respond to the needs of people with disabilities.
	Children (Scotland) Act 1995	Clearer definition of children's rights and parent's responsibilities.
	Data Protection Act 1998	Gives people the right to see personal information held about them.
	Education (Scotland) Act 1981	Children over 2 with 'special educational needs' are to have a record of needs established and resources to implement it. Enabled these children to attend mainstream schooling.
	Human Rights Act 1998	Brings UK legislation on human rights into line with Europe.
Local authority	Community care plans	Outline the council's plans to provide and finance care provision. Written after consultation with users and providers of the social care services. Funding for services is often dependent on having an equal opportunity policy and good practice.
	Other policies and strategies	For instance, Equal Opportunity statements on treatment of staff and in how they will provide a service to the community.

Figure 2.7 Legislation

INTERNATIONAL LEGISLATION

The United Nations (UN), set up in 1945, has developed a number of policies which have established general principles about the human rights and freedoms expected throughout the world for all groups. This is based on the premise that the denial of human rights and fundamental freedoms not only is an individual and personal tragedy, but also creates conditions of social and political unrest.

The most important of these policies is the **Declaration of Human Rights**, adopted by the UN General Assembly in 1948, which states that 'Recognition of the inherent dignity and of the equal and inalienable rights of all members of the human family is the foundation of freedom, justice and peace in the world'. A Declaration is not legally binding but it sets a standard against which all countries can be compared. Its authority is mainly moral in that it lays out the principles on which countries should base their actions.

There are 30 'Articles' in the Declaration which outline particular aspects of equality and how it should be ensured. The defining statement is found in the first paragraph: 'Article 1: All human beings are born free and equal in dignity and rights. They are endowed with reason and conscience and should act towards one another in a spirit of brotherhood.'

An example of another clause with particular relevance to a care setting is Article 25: 'Everyone has the right to a standard of living adequate to the health and well-being of himself and of his family, including food, clothing, housing, and medical care and necessary social services, and the right to security in the event of unemployment, sickness, disability, widowhood, old age or other lack of livelihood in circumstances beyond his control.' Motherhood and childhood are entitled to special care and assistance. All children whether born in or out of wedlock, shall enjoy the same social protection.

The United Nations also produce Covenants which are legally binding treaties on the states that ratify them. Two Covenants were later added to the Declaration of Human Rights and together they are seen as the International Bill of Human Rights. The two pieces of legislation were the 'International Covenant on Economic, Social and Cultural Rights' and the 'International Covenant on Civil and Political Rights'. They were both adopted in 1966 and entered into force ten years later. Basic social and cultural rights include the right to freedom of expression, the right to the highest standards of physical and mental health and the right to education. Basic civil and political rights include the right to freedom of opinion, the right to life and protection from torture and violence.

The United Nations have a number of ways of promoting these documents through conferences, decades of action which highlight particular issues, and investigations into abuse of human rights. However, it also sees the education of children in primary and secondary schools as paramount in order to provide youth with the opportunity to grow up in a spirit of respect for human dignity and equal rights. Their Internet site gives lots of exercises and activities that you can use with groups to stimulate discussion on issues of identity and rights.

EUROPEAN LEGISLATION

The principle of equality was written in to the Treaty of Rome in 1957, the document which set up the **European Economic Community** (known today as the European Community or EC). Article 119 of the Treaty of Rome states 'Each member state shall . . . ensure the application of the principle that men and women should receive equal pay for equal work'. In this instance, 'pay' is more than wages or salary: it is taken to mean all the considerations that are associated with reward in employment.

Since 1957, there have been many pieces of legislation from the EC which have extended this basic definition of equality. There are now Directives on Equal Treatment between women and men at work and the Health and Safety of Pregnant Workers. Directives require a national government to create or amend laws to tackle the discrimination they describe.

The EC also produce Recommendations, which are guidelines for good employment practice. Issues covered by Recommendations include encouraging childcare initiatives, preventing sexual harassment and adopting positive action measures in the workplace.

> ### CASE STUDY: PART-TIME RIGHTS
> Ms Wright and Ms Hannah were employed part-time as domestic assistants by the Greater Glasgow Health Board. On their redundancy, they received no redundancy payment because neither of them had worked enough hours per week to qualify for the Health Service Scheme.
>
> Ms Wright and Ms Hannah took the case up with their union, UNISON, and they argued that it was sex discrimination to treat part-timers differently from full-timers because many more women than men are employed part-time. Their employers in their view, had infringed Article 119 and the Equal Treatment Directive as they had been discriminated against for being part-time. They went to an industrial tribunal to argue their case.
>
> This case (which was eventually settled out of court) is one of several cases which have helped to establish the employment rights of part-timers.
> (Excerpts from: Bamford, C. (1995) *Equal Treatment and the Law: A Guide to European Community Law in Scotland* (European Commission Representation in Scotland)

Test cases on the interpretation of a British law will often end up at the **European Court of Justice** if all avenues of appeal in the British legal system have been used. Rulings from the European Court of Justice are final on the matter of European law, and these take precedence over national laws of the member states of the European Community. Its judges must ensure that Community law is not interpreted and applied differently in each member state. They are responsible for maintaining a balance between the power of the Community institutions and those retained by each Member state. The court has decreed, for instance, that a European worker who decides to settle in another Community country, and who may thus experience direct or indirect discrimination, now enjoys the same rights and benefits as regards conditions of work or benefits as those given to national workers.

The European Convention for the Protection of Human Rights and Fundamental Freedoms came into force in 1953 and is binding on member states, including the United Kingdom. It was the European version of the UN Universal Declaration of Human Rights. It set up a system of enforcing the provisions of the Convention, including the European Court of Human Rights which was established in 1959. Serious violations by member states can lead to them being asked to withdraw from the council, and failure to comply could lead to them being expelled.

CASE STUDY: EUROPEAN COURT OF HUMAN RIGHTS

Parents are to be banned from hitting their children following a European ruling that corporal punishment violates the rights of young people. The European Court of Human Rights ordered the Government to pay £30 000 in damages and costs to a boy who, when nine, was beaten with a cane by his stepfather. The judges decided that corporal punishment by parents violated article three of the Convention of Human Rights which Britain has signed. It states that 'no-one shall be subjected to torture or to inhuman or degrading treatment or punishment'.

Anne Houston, the director of Childline in Scotland, said her charity's telephone helpline took 2300 calls last year from children complaining about physical abuse, mostly at the hands of their parents. She said 'Children should be afforded the same rights to physical safety that adults get'.

A spokesman for Save the Children said: 'Every child has the right to a life free of violence'. The National Children's Bureau said: 'The purpose is not to prosecute more parents but to change attitudes and practice'.
(Excerpts from: 'Parents hands tied by Euro judgement' *The Scotsman*, 24.9.98)

BRITISH LEGISLATION

Since the mid-1970s there have been a number of important pieces of legislation passed by Parliament which have started to define the rights that certain groups can expect. Acts are only passed by Parliament after a series of debates about each clause, and anti-discrimination legislation attracts a lot of media coverage, thus raising the issues among the wider public.

Sex Discrimination Act 1975 and Equal Pay Act 1970

The Equal Pay Act (1970) enshrined the principle of 'equal pay for equal work' and the Sex Discrimination Act (1975) – with amendments in 1986 – gave legal definitions for the first time of what constitutes direct and indirect discrimination on the basis of gender and marital status.

- **Direct discrimination** means treating someone unfairly because of their sex; **indirect discrimination** means setting conditions that appear to apply to everyone, but in fact discriminate against one sex.
- **Victimisation**: the Act protects people from being victimised if they exercise their rights under the Acts and report discrimination. It is illegal to treat people less favourably if they report, or are a witness to, an act of discrimination.
- **Areas covered by the Acts are**: employment and training; education; advertising; the provision of goods and services (e.g. when you are buying or selling a house).
- People have the right to take a complaint of discrimination to a sheriff court or, if the discrimination is at work, to an Employment Tribunal. People who have a complaint can send a Sex Discrimination Act Questionnaire (SD 74) to the person they believe has discriminated against them. The questions answered on the form can be used as evidence in the court or tribunal, and if the person refuses to co-operate with the questionnaire, this may also be used against them.
- **The Equal Opportunities Commission (EOC)** was established with a statutory duty to promote equal opportunities and to investigate and enforce the removal of sex and marriage discrimination.

CASE STUDY: THE EQUAL OPPORTUNITIES COMMISSION IN SCOTLAND

The EOC has an office in Scotland which promotes issues of gender equality through campaigns, research and advice within the Scottish context. One of the main issues for the EOC is that of 'mainstreaming': making sure that gender issues are built right into legislation, policies and plans from the beginning, and not just added on at the end. The EOC advises local authorities and the Scottish Parliament on how to assess their policies at the initial stages to make sure they consider equal opportunities from the outset. The EOC publishes statistics and research so that people have a clear picture of what problems exist and they also encourage other people to research into gender issues. The EOC offers training and seminars to Scottish employers and trades unions, and keeps the legal profession up to date with discrimination law as it applies to Scotland.

Improving equal opportunities in the education and training sector is a vital aspect of their agenda. In partnership with voluntary organisations, the EOC is campaigning for a National Childcare Strategy which reflects the changing needs of children and their parents. A particular focus of the campaign is on parental leave from work, and pointing out the benefits to employers of family friendly work practices.

Particular attention is being paid to the needs of people in rural communities and from ethnic minorities. Over 20 years since the Equal Pay Act, the Commission is still campaigning to reduce the 20 per cent gap between the earnings of men and women, and is drawing attention to inequalities in the benefit system and the particular problem of women's poverty in old age.

In 1997, the EOC in Scotland received 154 complaints about employment, of which 44 were about pregnancy dismissal, and the other complaints included sexual harassment, maternity and family responsibility and training and promotion.
(Source: 'Making Equality Work: the Challenge for Government', 1997 Annual Report Scotland Extract, EOC)

Cases brought under the Sex Discrimination Act

How useful has the legislation been? Below are examples of some of the cases people have won using the Sex Discrimination Act to challenge the discrimination they faced.

- Two women claimed that actions and comments at a staff dinner they attended were obscene and degrading to women. They claimed at an Industrial Tribunal that the behaviour was 'environmental harassment'. This covers cases where the offence takes place where people are gathered, rather than being directed at one specific individual. After complaining about the behaviour of the chief executive, one woman claimed she was forced to resign and the other was picked for voluntary redundancy. They won an undisclosed sum and received an apology from the company.

- 400 school 'dinner ladies' won a case under the SDA and the Equal Pay Act when they challenged reductions in their pay rates, sick pay and holiday entitlements in a compulsory competitive tendering exercise.

- A manager with an insurance company complained of indirect discrimination when the company refused to allow her to job-share a management post after she returned from maternity leave. The case was settled for £20 000.

- Initially, the SDA was seen as legislation which protected the rights of women, but in recent years it has also been increasingly used by men to assert their rights. In one case, the Labour Party was successfully challenged by two male party members who said that women-only shortlists discriminated against men. In another case, a 6ft 2in male poultry worker claimed that a factory which required workers to be under a certain height was discriminating against men. The company was found guilty of indirect discrimination because fewer men could comply with the height regulations than women.

Race Relations Act 1976

This Act quickly followed the SDA in a similar format, defining direct and indirect discrimination and victimisation on the basis of racial grounds. Racial grounds are grounds of race, colour, nationality – including citizenship – or ethnic or national origins. A more precise definition of racial group, based on ethnic origins, was later developed in a House of Lords ruling. This stated that essential characteristics of a racial group were a long-shared history and a cultural tradition of its own. Other relevant characteristics are a common geographical origin or a common language. In this definition Sikhs are an ethnic group, as are Jews and Gypsies, but Muslims are not. They are seen primarily as a religious group and discrimination on the basis of religion is only illegal in Northern Ireland. It is within these definitions that recent judgements on whether the English and Scots are separate racial groups have been discussed.

The Commission for Racial Equality (CRE) was set up to monitor the enforcement of the Act, take up test cases and provide money for relevant projects. The CRE can conduct a formal investigation into suspected discrimination in an organisation and can issue a non-discrimination notice if problems are found. They have powers to monitor the situation and check whether the employer makes the suggested changes to policy and procedures.

The CRE gives grants to the seven Racial Equality Councils in Scotland to promote and monitor equality at a local level. The Commission plays an active part in raising public awareness of race issues through campaigns like 'Kick it out', which focuses on racism within football, and works with local government, private sector and trade unions to ensure that standards are improved on race issues. For instance, it worked with the Royal College of Nursing to draw up a comprehensive new policy to protect staff from racial harassment from patients.

Cases brought under the RRA are taken to an Employment Tribunal if discrimination is in the workplace and to sheriff courts for other cases. Substantial awards can be made by employment tribunals if racial discrimination in the workplace is proved, and the tribunal can also recommend action that should be taken to address the problem, with financial penalties if the organisation does not comply.

Cases brought under the Race Relations Act

A number of different cases show the scope of the Race Relations Act.

- A kitchen worker of Pakistani origin was called racist names and his work was made deliberately difficult by some colleagues. His complaints to management were ignored. Tensions mounted, there was a confrontation and the kitchen worker was dismissed. He took his case to an industrial tribunal and was awarded £7297 in compensation for his dismissal and racial discrimination.
- A woman of mixed ethnic origin applied unsuccessfully for jobs at two branches of a large supermarket chain. When she rang head office to say that she felt she had been discriminated against on racial grounds, she was told that he reason she did not get the second job was that she did not have relatives working at the store, whereas the successful candidate did. She brought a complaint of both direct and indirect discrimination against the supermarket and it was settled for £4000 before the hearing.
- An employee of a recruitment consultant was subjected to both racial and sexual harassment by the directors of the company and this caused her to leave her job. Her case was jointly supported by the CRE and the EOC. She was awarded £12 000 and the company agreed to adopt an equal opportunities policy and meet with the local Racial Equality Council to monitor its implementation.
- In four separate cases, ten young men from ethnic minorities were refused entry to a popular night club in Birmingham. The reasons given ranged from there being no space, to the applicants not being properly dressed. These same reasons did not seem to apply to the white people entering the club at the same time. The cases were settled for £20 000, with the company agreeing to introduce an equal opportunities policy and ensuring that its contracts for door security include a clause requiring compliance with the policy.

■ A Jewish woman applied several times over four years to join her local tennis club in Glasgow, without any success. Her non-Jewish friends who applied at the same time had already been accepted without difficulty. The case was settled when the club admitted discrimination and gave her and her family free membership.

■ An English man successfully argued that the Scots and English have distinct national differences because they have separate cultural traditions. Therefore, for the purposes of the Act, they can be seen as separate racial groups. His complaint that he had been discriminated against as an English person when seeking a senior position with the Police Force in Scotland was accepted by the Industrial Tribunal.

■ An Irish woman made a complaint of discrimination against a civil engineering company in Dunbartonshire and had her case settled before it came to a tribunal. However, she had to take a further claim of victimisation against an employment agency who failed to offer her jobs because she had made the original complaint. She won her case and was awarded compensation.

■ In an out-of-court settlement, a bar in Perth paid £2000 compensation to a woman they had refused to serve because she was a traveller.

Disability Discrimination Act 1995

The Disability Discrimination Act introduced measures aimed at ending the discrimination which disabled people faced in relation to employment, accessing goods and services and buying or renting land or property. It aimed to put an end to 'blatant and gratuitous' discrimination and to 'unconscious' discrimination made through ignorance. It does not use the concept of indirect discrimination.

Definition of disability

■ A person is considered disabled if they have, or have had, a disability (mental, physical or sensory) which makes it difficult to carry out normal day-to-day activities. The disability must be substantial and have a long-term effect, i.e. it must last or be expected to last for one year. Conditions which have a slight effect on day-to-day activities, but are expected to become substantial, are covered, as is severe disfigurement. The Act has been applied to people with injuries to the spine, ME and epilepsy.

Employers

■ Employers will have to take reasonable measures to make sure they are not discriminating against people with disabilities. However, an employer will not be treated as discriminating against a disabled job applicant or employee if he can show that the treatment in question is 'justified'. The onus is on the employer to prove that it was 'justified', but this is a departure from the Sex Discrimination Act and Race Relations Act where there is no justification allowed for direct discrimination. An employer has to look at what changes they could make to the workplace and to the work that is done in order to help a person with disabilities do a certain job, but they can take into account how much the changes would cost when considering what is reasonable.

■ The Act does not apply to employers with fewer than 20 employees, or staff employed by the uniformed services or to people on board ships, hovercrafts or aeroplanes.

Goods, facilities, services and property

- It is illegal to refuse to serve someone who is disabled, or offer them a service which is not as good as the service offered to other people, e.g. putting people with facial disfigurement in a corner of a café. It is illegal to provide a service to people with disabilities on terms which are different from those offered to other people, e.g. to ask a person with disabilities for a bigger deposit when booking a holiday.
- People will have to provide equipment or other items which will make it easier for people with disabilities to use their service – again only if it is reasonable to do so. Examples of this would be a handrail beside stairs, or an induction loop system in a cinema for people with hearing aids. Service providers should remove physical obstructions, e.g. narrow doors, or provide other ways of enabling disabled people to use their services.
- If a person feels that they have been wrongly excluded from the provision of goods or services, they can go to court to seek damages for any financial loss they have suffered and for injury to their feelings.
- Positive discrimination is allowed under the Act, whereas it is illegal under the Sex Discrimination Act and Race Relations Act. It is possible to give preferential treatment to people on the basis of their disability, e.g. to give people with disabilities priority on a housing waiting list.

Other measures in the Act

- **Transport**: the Act allows government to set minimum standards for new public transport vehicles (taxis, buses, trains) in order that people with disabilities can use them more easily.
- **Education**: the Act requires schools, colleges and universities to provide information for parents, pupils and students. For instance schools will have to explain their arrangements for the admission of pupils with disabilities, how they will help these pupils gain access and what they will do to ensure they are treated fairly.

Enforcing the Act

There is no provision in the DDA for creating a body with the power to give assistance to individuals who consider they may have suffered from unlawful discrimination, along the lines of the EOC or CRE. What was established was a National Disability Council. This has an advisory role, and will inform the Secretary of State about matters pertaining to the elimination of disability discrimination. It advises the Government on how well the Act is working and on whether any changes need to be made. It produces Codes of Practice about the new rights for disabled people in relation to goods and services.

Disability campaigners criticised the lack of powers held by the National Disability Council, so the Labour Government proposed in a 1998 White Paper, 'Promoting Disabled People's Rights', that a Disability Rights Commission should be set up to enforce the Act, help individuals take cases to court and encourage good practice. This agency will have much more power to ensure the Act is implemented more rigorously.

Cases brought under the Disability Discrimination Act

■ An employee had experienced severe abdominal pains, for which there was no exact diagnosis, over a long period of time. He was dismissed without warning after a period of sickness absence. He took his case to an Edinburgh industrial tribunal and was awarded £12 659 for unfair dismissal and disability discrimination.

■ A visually-impaired chemist was awarded £103 000 after he was unfairly selected by his company for redundancy.

■ An employer took expert advice on the needs of an employee with a club foot, but then sacked her for not achieving production targets. She won her case at an Industrial Tribunal which found that the company had not made reasonable adjustment. They knew a special type of chair would aid her situation but they did not buy it.

Children (Scotland) Act 1995

The UK ratified the United Nations Convention on the Rights of the Child in 1991, committing itself to ensuring that UK law, policy and practice relating to children was brought into line with its provisions. The three main rights contained in the Convention are:

■ protection from ill-treatment and harm;

■ participation in decisions affecting them;

■ provision of services to meet their needs.

The Children's (Scotland) Act 1995 reflects these basic principles. Among the rights which receive specific attention in the Act are:

■ due regard shall be given to children's views, subject to the child's age and maturity;

■ the welfare of the child should be the paramount concern in the determination of any matters affecting them;

■ no order should be made unless it is better for the child than making no order at all;

■ due regard shall be given to a child's religious persuasion, racial origin and cultural and linguistic background.

Parents have traditionally been regarded as having rights over their children, but this Act introduced the concept of parental *responsibilities* towards children for the first time in Scots law. Children have a right to sue if these responsibilities are not fulfilled.

Parents have responsibilities:

■ to safeguard and promote the child's health, development and welfare;

■ to provide direction and guidance in a manner appropriate to the stage of development of the child;

■ if the child is not living with the parent, to maintain personal relations and direct contact with the child on a regular basis;

■ to act as the child's legal representative.

The Act also introduces new provisions for children in need, the residential care of children; children with, and affected by, disability; children's hearings; adoption, and child protection. One of the new provisions in the child protection section is the introduction of an Exclusion Order which allows the exclusion of an alleged abuser from the child's home, instead of removing the child.

Data Protection Act 1998

The Data Protection Act (DPA) gives people the right to see personal information held about them. This includes computerised records held by private companies, employers and public sector organisations such as hospitals and doctors, housing departments and social work departments. People can also see housing, education, social work and health records which are kept in manual files. The first Data Protection Act became law in 1984, but this has now been replaced by the 1998 Act which brings Britain into line with European standards.

If someone wants to see their record, they should apply in writing to the relevant organisation. There are certain kinds of information which may be withheld. This includes information that could cause serious harm to the applicant or another person's physical or mental health, or which would help to prevent or detect a crime. The data user does not need to tell the applicant if information has been withheld. Applicants have the right to complain to the Data Protection Registrar, or take their case to court, if they are dissatisfied with the way a data user has dealt with their request.

The implications for care settings are obvious. Anyone who writes a report knowing that the subject of the report may seek access to the record is under a much clearer obligation to make sure that not only facts are true, but that any opinions can be justified by the evidence. As Dalrymple and Burke (1995, p. 139) note, 'One of the steps towards empowerment of users is the sharing of information. A concrete way of sharing information is through access to one's records. Sharing of records equalises the relationship between the users and the provider of a service and enhances participation ... Sharing information in an open and honest way demonstrates respect.'

Education (Scotland) Act 1981

This Act required education authorities to assess any child aged two or over who appeared to have a 'special educational need'. If the child is assessed as having pronounced, specific or complex special needs, a record of the needs would be opened for the child. The Act stated that children with special educational needs should, in principle, be educated in mainstream schools, contingent on certain conditions.

The experience of exclusion from mainstream provision for disabled people has often happened before school when playgroups and other clubs fail to respond to their particular needs. Whatever their experience in the pre-five years, a child with disabilities will generally face a challenge to stay within mainstream provision when they start formal schooling. This is often the beginning of a life-long struggle for children and their parents to have their needs recognised and their right to adequate services acknowledged. If children are not given the opportunity to participate in education on an equal footing, then it has implications for how they will manage to live independently as an adult.

Human Rights Act 1998

This Act brings British legislation into line with the rights and freedoms guaranteed under the European Convention of Human Rights. The Act is intended to protect individuals from the misuse of state power.

The rights and freedoms it enshrines include the right to respect for private and family life, freedom of thought, conscience and religion and Article 14, prohibition of discrimination. This last clause states that 'The enjoyment of the rights and freedoms set forth in this Convention shall be secured without discrimination on any ground such as sex, race, colour, language, religion, political or other opinion, national or social origin, association with a national minority, property, birth or other status'. The obvious omissions from this list are discrimination on the basis of sexuality and disability. The Act was introduced to cut the costs and time involved when British citizens take a claim to the European Court of Human Rights.

During the public debate while the Bill went through parliament there was a concern that the wording would undermine the right of separate religious schools to practice a selective employment policy. The wording has been changed in the Act and now religious schools, for Catholic, Jewish or Muslim pupils for example, will not be penalised for employing only people whose way of life and faith is compatible with the ethos of the school.

STRENGTHS AND WEAKENESSES OF LEGISLATION

The process of debate which a piece of legislation stimulates as it goes through the legislative process in the Houses of Parliament helps raise awareness in the general population about the issues at stake. The amount of TV coverage that disability rights campaigners received from TV and newspapers in 1994 and 1995 as they campaigned against the weakness of the legislation, forced politicians and public alike to consider the points they were making. This process of public debate sends a message to the general population that certain behaviours are not acceptable and should be changed.

Any piece of legislation, however, has a number of limitations. It cannot make people change their attitudes or private behaviour, even though it does tell them that certain types of behaviour are now proscribed. What many people do is comply with the letter of the law, that is they will do the minimum required not to be prosecuted, but they do not comply with the spirit of the legislation, or attempt to make improvements above the basic requirements. Sometimes, people just aren't clear about what the law expects.

Any 'watchdog' organisation set up to monitor the working of the Act cannot oversee every case that is raised. The Equal Opportunities Commission and the Commission for Racial Equality, for instance, are only able to choose test cases which extend the range of areas that an Act is able to cover, or which might set a legal precedent. Many of these test cases take many years before they exhaust the process of appeals all the way though the British and European courts.

CASE STUDY: CHILDREN (SCOTLAND) ACT 1995

Most Scottish voluntary organisations feel ill-informed about their new responsibilities under the Children (Scotland) Act 1995, according to Children in Scotland. A survey of 132 organisations working with children found that 54 per cent did not have adequate information about the legislation which came into force in 1997.

Many voluntary organisations believed the positive aspects of the Act were being undermined by an overall lack of resources. More than 40 per cent said they had not been consulted about children's services plans while others wanted to be involved in the process much earlier.

Bronwen Cohen, Director of Children in Scotland, said: 'Although the Act has been welcomed in principle, some organisations feel ill-informed and are concerned about the lack of information, training and resources to make it work.'
(Source: 'Scots unclear about Children Act legislation' *Community Care* 9–15 July 1998, p. 4.)

Dr Enderby, a speech therapist with the National Health Service, started her case for equal pay in 1986 and it was only settled in 1997 after hearings at an Industrial Tribunal, the Court of Appeal in London and the European Court of Justice. This process, inevitably, is very expensive and it is only the most persistent complainants, who tend to be backed by a Commission or trade union, who manage to see this process through to the end. The EOC helped support Dr Enderby's claim because it challenged the undervaluing of women's work across an entire profession.

There are many gaps in existing legislation. Both the EOC and CRE are campaigning to extend the remit of the legislation and clarify a number of points that have been raised in the 20 years of their existence. Also, legislation could be extended to include more positive action clauses such as compulsory ethnic monitoring, to ensure that all employers instigate good practice. If employers had to publish results annually to show whether there had been improvements of ethnic group representation in the workforce and promotion within the organisation, they would become more accountable. In wider terms, discrimination on the basis of age or sexuality is still not illegal although there are campaigns to include these in future legislation.

EQUAL OPPORTUNITIES AND THE SCOTTISH PARLIAMENT

The Scottish Parliament cannot develop its own equal opportunities legislation: that is one of the powers reserved for Westminster. The issues that are the responsibility of the Parliament – education, social work, transport, health, housing and crime prevention – do still provide an opportunity to make an impact to the inequality and disadvantage people face. The Equal Opportunities Commission campaign to encourage policy makers to 'mainstream' equality could be used by the

Scottish Parliament to ensure that equality issues are scheduled in from the beginning of each piece of legislation, and not just drafted on at the end.

The Scottish Parliament is a unique opportunity to develop a whole system which from the beginning builds in anti-discriminatory practices and is seen to represent the range of lifestyles and choices of people in Scotland. There are suggestions that the Parliament should enable access not just in the building itself but by convening some business outside Edinburgh, and using information technology to allow information to be more freely available and consider the hours it operates so that it doesn't reproduce the institutional disadvantage of the House of Commons with all-night sittings, access, way issues are presented, consultation etc. The White Paper on Scotland's Parliament states

The Government expect that the Scottish Parliament will adopt modern methods of working; that it will be accessible, open and responsive to the needs of the public; that participation by organisations and individuals in decision making will be encouraged; and that views and advice from specialists will be sought as appropriate.

(The Scottish Office (1997) *Scotland's Parliament*. HMSO: London)

Activity: The Scottish Parliament

At the time of writing the Scotland Act had just been passed and no elections had yet taken place for the Scottish Parliament, so there was no opportunity to evaluate whether the rhetoric of equality will be turned into action.

In the Act equal opportunities is defined as 'the prevention, elimination or regulation of discrimination between persons on grounds of sex or marital status, on racial grounds, or on grounds of disability, age, sexual orientation, language or social origin, or of other personal attributes including beliefs or opinions, such as religious beliefs or political opinions.'
(Scotland Act, 1998, Schedule 5)

After the Parliament is in progress, read through the Scottish Press for the last month and see if any comments have been made on how the Scottish Members of Parliament are challenging discrimination, both through the way they organise their business and in the policies they make.

LOCAL GOVERNMENT

At Local Government level, there are a number of plans and polices which promote anti-discriminatory policy. Within each council there are often staff or committees whose remit it is to ensure issues for women, black people or people with disabilities are taken into consideration when new policies are being prepared – whether the policy is to do with social work practice, environmental management or roads and transport planning. This integrated approach ensures that issues for disadvantaged groups are not drafted on at the end when the council is too far down the planning process to make fundamental changes. This process of consultation is particularly evident when a council has to formulate its new Community Care Plan. Consultation and monitoring have been built into the planning process. The council has to prepare a draft plan, hold meetings and take representations from interested parties. When they publish their plan, they have to document what consultations they undertook and explain which points they have incorporated. These activities make the process of planning much more public and inclusive, because the views of a range of people are being actively sought.

4. Workplace strategies

Employers are responsible under the law for acts of discrimination conducted by employees, whether or not they are done with the employer's knowledge or approval. Employees can be personally responsible for discriminatory acts if the employer mounts a defence to show that they took all reasonable and practical steps to prevent the discrimination. Employers are responsible if they instruct employees to act in ways which discriminate.

Within an organisation, there are many actions which can be taken to prevent discrimination and promote equal opportunities for staff and service users.

Positive action

Positive discrimination is not allowed by law, except in the case of people with disabilities. This means that an employer cannot give a job or promote someone only on the basis of their gender or race. However, *positive action* is allowed under section 47 and 48 of the Sex Discrimination Act and section 37 and 38 of the Race Relations Act. Certain groups are more likely to be unemployed or in lower grade jobs because of the discrimination they have faced, not only in a specific job but due to poor access to education in the past, lack of response to their needs etc. The main aim of positive action is to make equality of opportunity more of a realistic possibility. Even if racial discrimination, for instance, could end immediately, many people from ethnic groups would continue to experience the effects of discrimination and disadvantage from the past. They would still not be 'on a level playing field' with white people and able to compete equally with those who have not been systematically disadvantaged over a period of time.

In a work setting, positive action can take the form of encouraging people from certain groups to apply for vacant posts. Employers might put 'applications especially welcome from members of ethnic minorities' or 'people with disabilities are currently under represented in our workforce' in an advertisement. The job can only be awarded on the basis of merit of the applicants, but the message is intended to encourage under-represented groups to apply. The Equal Opportunities Commission had the following statement on a job advertisement in 1997: 'The EOC is committed to the promotion of equality in all fields. Men are currently under-represented in the EOC Scotland Office. We therefore particularly welcome applications from men as well as women'.

An employer might advertise in newspapers and magazines aimed at gay people or members of an ethnic group, or go and talk to community groups to convey the positive desire to increase the diversity and representation of a variety of groups in their workforce. They might organise training specifically aimed at groups under-represented at certain levels, e.g. 'Women in Management' courses. The purpose of such training is to equip people with skills and abilities that they have not had the opportunity to develop in the past, so that they are qualified *on merit* to be appointed or promoted. Workplace awards such as Investors in People emphasise this need for training and utilisation of existing staff as being good for morale and commitment to the organisation.

Occasionally, there will be an aspect of a job for which it is essential that the employee is of a certain gender or race. In this instance, an exemption from the discrimination laws is allowed, if it is agreed that the gender or race of an employee is a 'genuine occupational qualification'. For the purpose of authenticity, you may for instance require a male actor to play Hamlet or a female to model women's clothes. In relation to social care, there are quite a lot of jobs which due to the personal care required, it is possible to ask for same sex workers for reasons of decency and privacy. For many jobs, it is essential that the worker has knowledge of a specific language, but they would only need to seek an exemption from the Race Relations Act if the person also had to be a member of a specific race.

CASE STUDY: GENUINE OCCUPATIONAL QUALIFICATIONS

An advertisement for a Health Project in Edinburgh stated: 'The Health Action Project works with black and ethnic minority communities to enable them to access health services and raise awareness around health issues. We need a Healthworker with the ability to speak in one or more minority languages such as Urdu, Persian, Punjabi, Cantonese as well as English.' This does not break any discrimination laws, because it does not specify the racial background of the person. Theoretically a white Scottish person who had learnt Urdu or Cantonese could apply for the job. The employer would only need to seek an exemption from the Race Relations Act if they specified that they needed someone from a specific racial group to apply.

A service for young people leaving care in London advertises for a 'Black Aftercare Support Worker' because many of the young people they had to work with were from African-Caribbean and African backgrounds. The advertisement stated that Section 5 (ii)(d) of the Race Relations Act applied. A project for adults with learning disabilities advertised for a Resource Centre Worker (Man) and Support Worker (Woman) in order to meet the particular needs of their service users. Section 7 (2) of the Sex Discrimination Act applies in this case.

Equal opportunities policy

Positive action measures are just one piece of the equality jigsaw in the workplace. If the measures aren't embedded into a clear equal opportunities policy which is applied and monitored effectively, they will be little more than window dressing. A lot of organisations have a written equal opportunities policy which states behaviour that is not acceptable, outlines avenues of complaint and provides strategies for monitoring and evaluation of the policy.

It is crucial for any social care organisation to have a statement of equal opportunities to safeguard the rights of workers and service users. Most established organisations should have a policy and all new groups should develop one as a priority. Often new groups will not be able to access funding until they have a written policy. It is important, however, that they are not meaningless pieces of paper, full of fine principles that cannot be implemented or measured, which have been decided only by management.

It is important to have a process of consultation when developing or changing an equal opportunities policy in order to give all workers and service users a sense of ownership over the policy (i.e. they helped draft it and so have a sense of responsibility for implementing and monitoring it too). They will have thought about the reasons why certain things are included and how they might need to change to conform to the requirements. Management will have had to listen to all points of view and make some attempt to integrate them into a policy which is acceptable to everyone who has a stake in the process. Employees and service users who have participated in the process will not feel hostile to the policy because they feel that they are a passive recipient of something handed down from on high. There is a parallel here with good care planning, because it involves consultation with all relevant people and is not determined solely by orders from above.

Equally the process of developing action which results from the principles of the policy is important. The statement of intent is not enough: the organisation has to make plans to change practices, give training and support new developments which will bring the issue forward. The British Nursing Association, the largest nursing and homecare organisation in Britain, has amended its equal opportunities policy to remove the possibility of staff prompting or accepting race related instructions from clients, unless there was a genuine need such as language difficulties.

How will anyone know if the equal opportunities policy has made a difference? There has to be some form of measurement from year to year to see if there has been any progress. An organisation might include statistics on such questions as: Have under represented groups had more success in gaining promotion? Does the mix of service users reflect that of the target population? What training have employees had? It might also include some more subjective data on the quality of service and levels of satisfaction that staff or service users feel they receive. This could be obtained by questionnaires, interviews, group discussions, personal development meetings with staff and re-assessment of care plans with clients.

Benefits of an equal opportunities policy

There is both a moral and a business case to be put forward in support of equal opportunities in the workplace. Organisations with an effective equal opportunities policy report that it helps increase staff morale and commitment to the organisation because it is seen as a safe, pleasant place to work. Organisation costs are reduced if there is not a high staff turnover or sickness rate. No employer wants the adverse publicity, or costs involved, of challenging a case of discrimination brought to an Employment Tribunal by an employee and reported in the newspapers. For care organisations it is a visible sign that they are committed to providing a quality care service.

Activity: Elements of an Equal Opportunities Policy

Obtain a copy of an equal opportunities policy from a care organisation and arrange to talk to someone from the organisation about how it is implemented. Some of the issues you might want to discuss are:

- What groups are covered by their policy?

- What is included: recruitment, training of interviewees, childcare provision, flexi-time agreements, harassment policies, anti-violence policies aimed at protecting their staff carrying out duties?

- Is there a clear procedure for bringing complaints?

- What induction and training is carried out with staff to ensure that they know about the policy?

- How does the organisation know if the policy is working? What evidence do they use to monitor and evaluate its effectiveness?

- Is there anything else which could be included to improve the policy?

Anti-discriminatory practice

The commitment to equal opportunities in an organisation extends much further than developing and implementing a policy. A commitment to anti-discriminatory practice can be shown in many ways. It can be demonstrated with service users in everyday practice by promoting independence, maintaining dignity, supporting choices, respecting beliefs and valuing opinions. Many care agencies have a published 'Charter of Rights' which specifies the rights and choices a service user can expect. These rights include the right to confidentiality, the right to take risks and the right to make relationships.

The right to knowledge and access to information is an integral part of being an active citizen and a care worker, as an advocate, can assist service users to access information or to represent their views when necessary. The service an organisation provides should reflect a range of ways of communicating with the variety of potential service users. Technology can be used to break down certain barriers and with facilities such as voice recognition software, or a screen reader which outputs text as speech or Braille becoming more affordable, this is an option more organisations are considering for both workers and service users.

Anti-discriminatory practice is about visibility. It is about promoting positive images of people in publications and leaflets about your organisation, and it is about having a representative workforce and range of service users. Anti-discriminatory practice is also about impacting on the way services are delivered. It has to address the wider issue of re-distribution, not just of scarce resources such as funding or accommodation, but of the power imbalances which exist between workers and users, staff and management, funders and providers of services.

> ## Activity: Current examples of anti-discriminatory practice
>
> Many care organisations have in-service training for their workers on anti-discriminatory practice. Contact some organisations in your area and see what recent initiatives there have been in this field.

Managing diversity

There is a move away from anti-discriminatory practice in some organisations towards a 'managing diversity' approach. This recognises and values the differences between all employees rather than categorising certain groups as needing specific help. This approach is based on the proposition that all employees have a right to be valued and respected as individuals because it will create a more flexible, motivated workforce. There are a variety of visible and non-visible differences in any workforce, and these differences should be harnessed to utilise individual talents and meet organisational goals. The criticism of the equal opportunities approach is that some groups (men, white people) are alienated by the special attention given only to certain other groups (women, black people). The focus of the managing diversity approach is on people as individuals and not as members of disadvantaged groups, and if backed by resources and a real commitment to organisational change it could obviously make improvements in the workplace culture.

The managing diversity approach can be criticised, however, because it fails to recognise the historical and structural aspects to difference and inequality which can't be addressed within the practices and procedures of any one organisation. Blakemore and Drake (1996, p. 214) note:

Managing diversity stresses integration and the harnessing of individual differences to a common effort. However, this model, in the end, seems to stress individual rather than structural change: the emphasis is still upon changing outlook and individual behaviours, not upon a complete overhaul of the systems of power and status which underpin discrimination and patterns of blocked opportunity. This reveals a fundamental dilemma of equal opportunities policies: are they in existence to change individuals and possibly to 'compensate' for earlier disadvantages, or is their object to challenge the definitions of normality or acceptability which are so often used to exclude women, black people, people with the 'wrong' accents or with working-class backgrounds, disabled people, and so on?

Barriers to achieving equality in the workplace

There are a number of barriers to achieving equality in the workplace. There might be

- insufficient funds to implement changes or provide staff training;
- resistance or hostility from some staff or service users to changes;
- lack of information about policies and how they work for new staff and service users;
- ineffective policies with no monitoring mechanism;
- fear of 'political correctness' impinging on people's natural behaviour.

An organisation should be aware of these potential problems and try to address them when developing their anti-discriminatory policies, procedures and ways of working.

SUMMARY

Discrimination exists in a number of different forms throughout society. It is based on prejudice and stereotypes that individuals learn from being socialised in a particular culture, and is endorsed and enforced by the institutions that people live and work within. Our personal identity is formed within our culture and many of us come to learn that what we are is devalued or disliked by society. We get this message in many ways throughout our life and even when we work in and use care services, we sometimes still find ourselves disadvantaged or silenced. Sometimes the bias is direct and obvious, other times it is indirect or unconscious – but however it is expressed, it is experienced as yet another negative event in somebody's life.

There are a number of ways in which we can tackle discrimination and prevent the process forever repeating itself. We can become more aware of the part our own values and beliefs play in maintaining prejudice and we can become active in or support many of the pressure groups that challenge discrimination at local and institutional levels. We can ensure that within our sphere of influence – our family, friends, workplace or social, political and voluntary groups – we do what we can to challenge prejudice and prevent discrimination. In a care setting we can provide conditions which are responsive to individual needs and which are based on a firm notion of rights. This is developed by being aware of the legislation which exists to protect people from discrimination and the groups which exist to support and advise people who face inequality. The care organisation itself should implement good practice by having clear equal opportunities statements and a variety of measures to ensure that discrimination doesn't exist in any policies or practices. Anti-discriminatory work in care settings won't always change the historical and structural inequalities people face, but it can provide a basis for people to feel able to fight against the bias and disadvantage they experience.

SUGGESTED READING

Annual Reports of the Equal Opportunities Commission and Commission for Racial Equality
These give up to date information about cases of discrimination, how the law is working and a variety of initiatives to promote equality. These publications are free and very informative. You can find the address and number of the EOC and CRE in the phone book.

Dalrymple, J. and *Burke*, B. (1995) *Anti-Oppressive Practice – Social Care and the Law*. Buckingham: Open University Press.
Looks at the importance of knowing the legal background to issues in social care settings. The authors use a lot of case studies and activities to back up a thorough discussion of rights, discrimination and oppression in a care setting. Interesting, informative and stimulating.

'Equal Opportunities: Ten Point Plan for Employers'. Prepared by the Department for Education and Employment.
This is a pack which gives lots of clear advice on practical measures to promote equality in an organisation. It takes the reader through the steps of developing an equal opportunities policy, and looks at what kind of training staff might require. It assesses the benefits of different strategies and looks at how an organisation could start to review its policy and practice.

Moore, S. (1996) *Sociology Alive*. Cheltenham: Stanley Thornes (Publishers) Ltd.
Clear, easily accessible discussion of many of the issues discussed in this chapter including: socialisation, gender, sexuality, race and ethnicity, age and the role of the media. Other relevant issues such as poverty, class and unemployment are also considered.

Thompson, N. (1997) *Anti-Discriminatory Practice* 2nd Edition. London: MacMillan Press Ltd.
Discussion of the historical background and theoretical base of anti-discriminatory practice. A variety of areas of discrimination are discussed, with chapters specifically for gender, race, age and disability. Discussion of the debate about the differences and similarities between oppression and discrimination.

CHAPTER 3

An introduction to human development and behaviour

Janet Miller

What we perceive as development over the life span is invariably a complex blend of inner and outer change, biological and environmental influence.

(Bee and Mitchell, 1984)

INTRODUCTION

This chapter is about all of us – you, me and everyone else. One major source of information is yourself and those with whom you live and work. These are not the only sources of information however. In a multi-cultural society your analysis needs to be wide-ranging in order that you can take account of the influence of cultural and socioeconomic factors. But **you** do provide a good starting point.

> **RELATIONSHIP OF CHAPTER TO HIGHER STILL** The material covered in this chapter corresponds to the outcomes for the **Intermediate II** unit **Human Development**. In the chapter you will look at human development and behaviour and the strands which make up these processes. These are considered under the four main headings of **physical**, **intellectual/cognitive**, **emotional** and **social**. The influences upon development and behaviour are also considered, ranging from genetic to environmental and social. There is reference to the nature/nurture debate and to the importance of socialisation. Human development is examined from birth to older adulthood. There is an emphasis upon seeing life as a process, with development taking place throughout the life cycle.

The chapter is full of generalisations and outlines what people in general do or could do. Individuals, of course, are another matter. Eric Rayner (1986) emphasises this when he says: '*It is quite different to recognise what a specific person, from a specific background at a certain point in his life, actually does experience and do.*'

By the end of this chapter you should be able to answer the following questions:
- What is human development?
- What is human behaviour?
- What are the strands of human development and behaviour?
- What are the influences upon human development and behaviour?
- What is socialisation?
- What do you understand by the nature/nurture debate?
- How do people in general develop and behave at each stage of development?
- How can the understanding gained be applied to care practice?

Development

Development can be seen as a gradual unfolding, as an increase in complexity involving change and movement. Where there is change there is also transition, passing from one stage or situation to another. There is also loss and gain connected with change, with transitions being associated with both of these in varying proportions. Development can be distinguished from **growth** which is an increase in size which can be measured (e.g. height, weight).

Behaviour

Behaviour refers to how people conduct themselves, the way they do things themselves and in their relationships with others. Development and behaviour are very much interconnected and though they are not the same thing, they exert influences upon one another. Some **behaviour patterns** are typical of certain **stages in development** whilst other behaviours reflect personal traits which, although they may alter in many ways during the life cycle, are characteristic of a particular individual and are woven into the way they do things throughout life.

Activity

To make a start in the study of human development and behaviour, examine how **you** have changed since you were born and the things you do well and not so well.

Your answer may mention such things as:
- I can run really fast
- I've learned a lot
- I have developed the ability to have conversations
- I have made a lot of friends, different ones at different ages

- I have developed an interest in music
- I've learnt to swim and play basketball
- I've just got my first boyfriend/girlfriend
- I can do things for myself – as a baby I needed to be fed and now I can cook
- I'm good at languages
- I'm terrible with figures

The changes and skills noted above have formed part of your development and can be grouped into four main strands knows as physical, intellectual/cognitive, emotional and social.

These strands can conveniently be remembered as making the word **PIES**. They are not entirely separate from one another and their separation here is only because that is a convenient way to discuss them. In fact development is holistic, with all of the strands interacting with one another and inseparable from the others. **Physical development** refers to how our bodies change. **Intellectual/Cognitive development** refers to how we make sense of the world especially through the development of language and learning. **Emotional development** concerns the ways in which we gain a sense of our own identity and cope with our feelings. **Social development** is about how we interact with others, develop relationships and take on social roles.

These strands will form the basis of a discussion about development and behaviour throughout the life cycle. Another set of factors which must also be considered before tackling the life cycle stage by stage are the **influences** upon development and behaviour. Why are people different from one another? Why do some people develop different skills from others? Why do some people experience differences in physical development? Why are you different from me? These differences can largely be explained by looking at influences. There are many influences upon development and behaviour which, though they may not on their own determine how an individual develops and behaves, do in combination make for many differences among individuals.

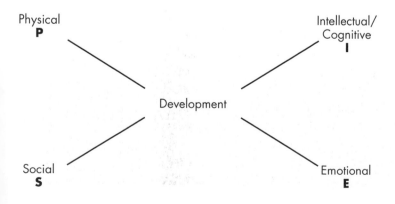

Physical
P

Intellectual/
Cognitive
I

Development

Social
S

Emotional
E

Figure 3.1 PIES

Physical
I can run fast
Learnt to swim/play basketball
First boyfriend/girlfriend
Can do things for myself

Intellectual/Cognitive
I've learned a lot
Able to have conversations
Interest in music
Learnt to swim/play basketball
Can do things for myself
Good at languages
Terrible with figures

Social
Able to have conversations
Made a lot of friends
Plays basketball
First boyfriend/girlfriend

Emotional
Made a lot of friends
Interest in music
First boyfriend/girlfriend

Figure 3.2 Aspects of development

Activity

Draw an image of yourself surrounded by four boxes. Label the four boxes: physical, cognitive/intellectual, emotional and social, and place the changes and skills which you listed in the previous activity, in the appropriate box(es). You will probably find that some things fit into several boxes as in the example below.

Activity

Read the three short descriptions below and say what you think are some of the influences upon the individuals concerned.

John is seven. He was born prematurely to his mother Jan, who was then a lone parent. He is quite small but is lively and about average for his age at school. Jan lost contact with John's father before he was born and says that she doesn't mind this since he was a drug user and very unreliable. Jan is very determined to be a 'good' mother. She is warm and loving and believes that children should be given time and attention. She gave up smoking when she was pregnant and now struggles to provide a decent environment for her son. She makes her local authority house on the outskirts of Dundee comfortable and always keeps it clean and tidy. She spends her spare money on toys and even though she works part-time she always makes time to spend with John. Jan's mother lives nearby and helps with childcare. John loves going to see his gran who gives him a lot of love and encouragement. Two years ago, when John was five, Jan married Frank (not John's father) and shortly afterwards John's half-sister, Rita, was born. John at this time started to be really upset about going to school and started bed-wetting during the night. Frank had little patience with him at first but gradually John and Frank started to enjoy a few activities together, especially football. They still have some furious arguments but gradually during the past year John's behaviour has improved and he is almost back to being the happy and loving child he was two years ago. His bed-wetting is only very occasional now.

Karen is fifteen. She has cerebral palsy and cannot walk or speak very well, though she struggles with both. Recent tests show that she has an above average intelligence. She lives with her Mum and Dad in a cottage in Portree on Skye where she attends the mainstream secondary school. Her Mum was determined that Karen would lead as normal a life as possible in spite of her disabilities and fought a long battle with the education authority to keep her at the local school. Her Mum was ill throughout a lot of Karen's early childhood but now teaches art part-time. Her Dad is a postman. They have no other children.

Nadia is 24. She is a student at a Scottish university though she grew up in Birmingham. She is black. Both of her parents emigrated from Pakistan before Nadia was born, and lived with her father's brother and his wife and two children in a terraced house in an area of predominantly immigrant families not far from the centre of Birmingham. Nadia's father is a doctor at a large hospital and is increasingly frustrated that he has never been appointed as a senior consultant. Her mother helps in her brother-in-law's shop occasionally, as Nadia did throughout her childhood. The family are very close-knit and, although they have never been wealthy, they have given priority to education. They have also encouraged their children to feel proud of their culture, which is Muslim, and of their colour. Although Nadia went through a phase of identifying with white people and wanting to be white when she was about twelve, she is now very positive about her black identity. Sometimes she jokes and says she has four disabilities in Scotland: being a woman, being black, being English and being a student. She is, however, really very cheerful and confident about her identity.

When you have read these accounts and written down what you think are some of the influences upon development and behaviour, you can check these against the list below. Each of these influences will be dealt with in more detail. The main influences are:

■ genetic/hereditary;

■ socioeconomic;

■ cultural (including the influence of socialisation);

■ gender;

■ disability;

■ unexpected/unplanned life changes.

Genetic/hereditary influences

Every individual, with the exception of identical twins, has an absolutely unique set of genes at birth. Genes are present in all human cells and are responsible for inherited characteristics. Sometimes one gene codes for one characteristic of an individual such as blue eyes, though it is much more usual for the products of several genes to combine and interact with one another and the environment to create particular individual characteristics. Genes play a part in appearance, in intelligence and in some illnesses such as cystic fibrosis and Huntington's disease. The figures below from Thomson (1995) illustrate that there is a link between genes and intelligence.

The average correlations between IQs of relations are as follows (the higher the number, the greater the link between genes and intelligence):

Between parents and their natural children	.40
Between identical twins	.86
Between fraternal twins	.60
Between siblings reared together	.47
Between siblings reared apart	.24
Between parents and their adopted children	.31

Although these figures do show a link between genes and intelligence they also indicate that other influences are at work here. If there were no other influences than the genetic, then the intelligence of siblings whether reared together or apart would be the same and there would be very little correlation between parents and their adopted children. This raises the whole issue of the nature/nurture debate in relation to human development – are people a product of their inherited, genetic characteristics or a product of their environments and the way they are brought up? This is a convenient place to examine this issue before proceeding to an examination of other influences.

Activity

Research an inherited illness such as haemophilia, cystic fibrosis or Huntington's disease and show how it is a genetic disorder.

The nature/nurture debate

Although some theorists lean more in one direction than the other, some attributing more to nature (i.e. inherited characteristics) and some more to nurture (the environment in which people develop and grow and the way in which they are looked after and socialised), it is generally agreed that the ways in which people develop depend upon a mixture of these factors in inter-action with one another. The **interaction** of factors is a very important point to grasp. Think about baking a cake. There are certain given ingredients: the flour, the sugar, the margarine, the eggs and often some additional items such as flavouring and colouring. These can be compared to inherited characteristics. Many things can affect the way the cake turns out: the vigour with which the ingredients are mixed together, the order in which they are mixed, the kind of oven used, the temperature of the oven, the care taken to line the cake tin and so on. It is the nature of the ingre-dients, the nurturing of them into a cake and the interactions between these two sets of factors which determines the eventual nature of the cake. So it is with people in the interaction of nature and nurture.

The section above, describing genetic/hereditary influences, has dealt with the 'nature' side of the nature/nurture debate. It is now appropriate to consider influences on the 'nurture' side. These include the influences of socioeconomic factors, culture (including socialisation), gender, disability and unexpected life changes.

Socioeconomic influences

Socioeconomic influences include social class (based upon occupation), income and wealth, housing situation and educational opportunity. In Chapter 1 it was shown that there is substan-tial evidence that the gap between rich and poor people in Britain is getting wider, not only in terms of income but all kinds of associated opportunity. Approximately 80 per cent of service users of Social Work Departments have incomes at or below income support levels, as a result of being unemployed, experiencing long-term illness or disability or earning a low income from unskilled labour. Carstairs and Morris (1991) in their study entitled 'Deprivation and Health in Scotland' demonstrated that people living in affluent middle class areas enjoyed considerably more favourable health than those living in deprived working class areas. In areas of affluence in general babies' birth weights were higher, fewer of them died at birth or during their first year of life and there was less illness and longer life expectancy. They found deprivation to be most severe in health boards in the west of Scotland, with Glasgow's average score more than twice that of any other health board. This has enormous implications for the development of indi-viduals in the areas of greatest socioeconomic deprivation.

Cultural influences

Cultural differences exist in society which influence development and behaviour from conception to death. Every culture views pregnancy and birth, for example, in particular ways and, even though the biological process of birth is the same the world over, the rituals and attitudes which surround it vary from culture to culture. In an article entitled 'Doing the Month', Barbara Pillsbury (in Black, 1984) describes the rituals surrounding a mother and baby in rural China. There, new mothers are forbidden to do housework, are supported by female members of the extended family, must eat a specially prepared nourishing diet and keep away from draughts. Compare this to the experience of some new mothers in Scotland who return home from hospital to relative isolation, housework, the care of older children as well as the demands of a new baby. Most fathers don't get any time off work (paternity leave) to help, though many are supportive, and extended families are often miles away. Rates for post-natal depression are much higher in Scotland than in rural China.

Cultural differences may be related to nationality, religion, social class or geographical variations. Island populations may have different practices from mainland, urban areas, Protestants have different cultural practices from Catholics and working class people have cultural differences from middle class people.

Socialisation is the process or way in which people learn the **culture** of their society. Its consideration forms a large and important section of this chapter and although it is appropriate to look at it when examining culture, its importance is emphasised by devoting a special section to it.

Socialisation and its influence upon development

Socialisation is relevant to a discussion of development from both a psychological and sociological perspective, from the viewpoint of the individual's development in society and the influence of society upon the individual. It has, therefore, a place both in this chapter and in Chapter 5. Rather than discuss it twice, the main examination takes place here with only brief reference made to it in Chapter 5. Socialisation, defined above as the process or way in which people learn the culture of their society, begins at birth and continues throughout life. It can be seen as preparation for taking adult roles, for taking a responsible and acceptable part in society. Socialisation takes place at both a formal level (e.g. in school) and at an informal level (e.g. through play). What is learned through socialisation in early life is critical to what happens later on. For care workers an understanding of socialisation is essential. John Bowlby (1965) argued that children deprived of emotional stability failed in all sorts of ways. They were often unable to form lasting, meaningful relationships later in life. Although this failure was to a very great degree one of emotional deprivation, it was often compounded by a lack of positive socialisation. Socialisation is influenced by and influences the other topics discussed in this chapter, and is itself determined by what are known as the main agents of socialisation: the family, education, work, religion and the mass media, each of which is examined in turn below.

The first agent of socialisation is the **family** and it is here that most, but not all, children learn how to behave appropriately, how to relate to other people, how to eat, drink and so on in ways which are socially and culturally acceptable. This initial socialisation is called **primary socialisation**. Its impact becomes evident through contrast with situations in which no primary socialisation has taken place. The following account was taken from a newspaper in 1998 and demonstrates what is likely to occur in the absence of socialisation:

Police who entered a house in The Hague found a scrawny girl in the attic unable to walk or talk. She had not been let outside by her mother since her birth nearly four years ago. A police spokeswoman said the girl, who was surrounded by rubbish, flies and mosquitoes, was now being treated for malnutrition.

(The *Guardian Weekly*, 2.7.98)

Activity

When you have read the above account, write down the things you would expect a four year-old brought up in a communicating family or family-like setting to have acquired through the socialisation process.

Not all children in the same culture gain the same things about that culture during primary socialisation. Rayner (1986) makes this same point as follows:

Since each child is exposed to and has to adapt to a different environment from other children, he must structure his mental life differently from the child next door or in the next continent. He is being socialised in ways particular to him.

Thus socialisation is both a general cultural concept and a particular individual concept. Your family will provide you with some aspects of culture which are common to others of your culture but it will be served up in a particular way, with some things emphasised more than others, so that your experience of socialisation is different from everyone else's. An example here is the way people are socialised into gender roles of male and female within the family.

In British society it is common for families to encourage girls to think of themselves as budding housewives and mothers, but the emphasis on this varies from family to family. Some girls are bought tea sets and encouraged to play with dolls; they are usually encouraged to think of themselves as less aggressive, less adventurous, less career-minded than boys. This kind of socialisation is called **anticipatory socialisation** because it anticipates adult roles. Other girls are encouraged to think of themselves as equal to boys in their career prospects, but even here there are likely to be cultural influences at work. Ann Oakley (1997), the sociologist who has studied housework, says that even her father, the sociologist Richard Titmus, relied upon her mother to do most of the housework and childcare whilst he wrote his books. Although she was socialised to think of herself as equal to boys, her parents presented role models of very differentiated roles, with the father's career taking precedence over that of his wife. The development of gender identity is further discussed on page 104.

As a child grows up he or she comes into contact with more aspects of society than the family, and these are responsible for **secondary socialisation. Education** provided through the school system is the second main socialising influence upon the developing child. Schools and other agents of secondary socialisation promote learning in relation to appropriate conduct in society and in behaviour towards people with different degrees of status and authority. The sociologist Emile Durkheim emphasised the importance of education in the development of the individual as a social being. The social being comprises the beliefs and behaviours which express a person's awareness of being a member of society. The culture transmitted by the education system is a subject of debate. Do schools transmit the culture of one social class in preference to another? Do schools perpetuate a patriarchal society in which women take on subordinate positions? Whose culture do they pass on to pupils? The whole subject of education is discussed in much greater detail in Chapter 5.

Activity

Think back to your attendance at school. Suggest five attitudes or behaviours which your school promoted and three ways in which you think that secondary socialisation in school took place.

In the activity above you may have suggested smart appearance, hard work, helpfulness, participation in school events or good time-keeping as attitudes and behaviours, and school rules, prizes for good work and praise as ways in which secondary socialisation took place.

Work is also an agent of secondary socialisation. People do exercise some choice about the kind of work they do but once they are in work roles they need to learn the appropriate behaviours and attitudes of these roles. In this way they are socialised into the world of work. In order to maintain their place within it they must conform, at least to some extent, to the beliefs, aims and regulations of the workplace. Many sociologists argue that work is gendered, that 'society' has views about what is woman's work and what is men's work. Ann Oakley (1982) has suggested that the sexual division of labour is socially constructed – that is, it is not based upon biological differences but upon what has become accepted and perpetuated within society.

Activity

Consider three occupations which you think are usually regarded as 'men's work' and three regarded as 'women's work'. What part has socialisation played in this view?

Religion has throughout the history of the modern world been a powerful source of socialisation. Different religions promote different cultures comprising teachings about morality, the place of men and women in society, marriage and the family. Religion can be regarded as a belief in some form of supernatural power and every known society has some form of religion. What religions can you identify in the area in which you live? You may have identified Protestants, Catholics, other Christians, Jews, Hindus, Sikhs, Muslims and perhaps others. All of these include a set of beliefs and practices into which followers are socialised. For Christians the Ten Commandments set out principles which include instructions to members to honour their parents, not to steal, not to kill, not to commit adultery. For Muslims the Qur'an sets out the rights and functions of men and women, expounding a philosophy of equal but different, with women playing a major role in family affairs and men in social affairs.

Activity

Research one religion which is different from your own, if you have one, and list the ways in which it socialises individuals.

The mass media are the final agent of socialisation to be considered here. They consist of television, radio, newspapers, books, advertisements, films, recorded music, the internet – anything which reaches a very large audience. Most people are exposed to some of these agents. They fill in where the rest of experience stops. It is impossible to experience directly more than a small portion of culture, life and the world. It is the media which form the link, mediating between the real world and what we come to think of as the real world. The media are responsible to some degree for what people share in common. Whether what is received from the media can be trusted is another matter.

The influence of gender

The different experiences of males and females in society do exert an influence upon development. These differences result from a mixture of biology and culture transmitted through socialisation. They are certainly not all necessarily biological in origin. Ann Oakley (1982) argued that although biologically it is women who give birth, there is no biological reason why women should do all, or even most of the childcare and housework.

Activity

Look at yourself and consider how gender may have affected your development. You could write a short essay about this giving consideration to some of the issues mentioned below:

- what was the influence of biological factors (male or female body)?
- what kinds of toys was I encouraged to play with?
- who did I play with?
- what subjects was I encouraged to study at school?
- what did I want to do in adult life?
- what career advice was I given?

The influence of disability

When you think about disability what image springs into your mind? You perhaps thought about someone in a wheelchair who has problems getting about. Yet the term 'disability' covers many conditions and degrees of disability. People can be born with disabilities or acquire them through accidents or sudden or progressive illness. Some people have a physical disability, others a learning or behavioural or sensory disability or a long-term mental illness. Some people have a combination of some or all of these. It is estimated that about 6 million people in Great Britain are disabled, of whom 360 000 are children (HMSO, Social Trends, 1998). The influence of disability varies from person to person but has two strands: the effects of the disability itself and the effects of social factors including attitudes and access to such things as buildings, jobs, education and leisure facilities.

Imagine John, who was born with spina bifida as a result of which he is unable to walk. This is certainly a limiting factor upon development because it is difficult for him to get from place to place. He has also spent quite a lot of time separated from his family in hospital and experiences times when he is so ill that he has to stay in bed for a few days at a time. John is now 21, he has a wheelchair which gives him a great deal of mobility and a specially adapted car, further enhancing his mobility. He is very intelligent, has completed a college course in computing and is trying to get a job. This is proving extremely difficult. Usually he doesn't even get an interview and when he does he finds that the job always goes to someone who is not disabled. What factors are at work here? John has to a very great degree overcome the physical disadvantages of his condition but other factors are involved. Many workplaces are not well-adapted to wheelchairs, many employers have an image of people in wheelchairs as less able intellectually and socially than people who are not. Social factors are at work here. These include prejudice, language and lack of social consideration for the needs of people with a disability who should have the same civil rights as anyone else.

A student at Aberdeen University wrote the following about her experience of an epileptic seizure:

My first memory on coming round afterwards is of saying . . . 'Oh no, I'm epileptic!' and bursting into tears. It was the stigma associated with epilepsy . . . that frightened me – the fear that people would think me different, or strange, or weak, or that my life would no longer be 'normal'.

(Scotland on Sunday, 7.2.99)

It can be the case that the label and stigma attached to disability can be worse or as bad as the disability itself. This can lead to a process of devaluation which has been set out in a diagram by Taylor and Field (1993) reproduced below.

The prospect for people with a disability may present difficulties but it is not all negative. These are exciting times for challenging long-held attitudes. Disabled people themselves are increasingly playing a political role and The Disability Discrimination Act (1995) begins to tackle some of the problems which people with a disability have faced. There *are* opportunities to break the cycle presented in the diagram below (from Taylor and Field, 1993), but this requires great determination by service users, care workers and politicians.

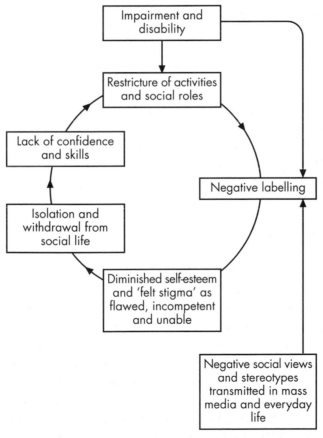

Figure 3.3 Process of devaluation (from Taylor and Field, 1993, p.128, reproduced with permission of Blackwell's Publishers, Oxford)

Activity

Look at the descriptions of Linda MacDonald and Nabeil Ahmed in the case study in Chapter 10. Give an account of the ways in which you think that their disability may influence their development.

The influence of unexpected/unplanned life changes

For most people there is a fairly steady progression through the life cycle. There will be good times and bad, sad times and happy times, gains and losses, but usually the impact of these will not profoundly affect the course of development. Some changes though are not expected or anticipated and can have profound effects. Edward Rainey's account (in Alexander, 1995) is an example:

> I had an ordinary happy childhood with my younger brother and older sister at our home in Pollok . . . I just enjoyed life as it came. After leaving school I worked in a butcher's until one day I felt there was more to life than working inside all the time. So I joined the Royal Highland Fusiliers because I wanted adventure . . . Then, when I was twenty four I went to Spain for a holiday with my friend Eddie – we were known as 'the two Eddies' – and as soon as we arrived at our hotel in Marbella we decided to have a swim in the pool. I dived into the shallow end by mistake and struck my head on the bottom.

Eddie's spinal chord was severed and he faces the rest of his life in a wheelchair. He has experienced some of the influences of disability discussed above, but there have been other adjustments to be made because this event was so sudden and unexpected. He goes on to say:

> I was so depressed that I cried an ocean at the beginning. I kept asking 'Why me?'

Eddie's response was characteristic of what many people experience when something as major and as catastrophic happens to them: he experienced depression, then anger, and then gradual adjustment to completely changed circumstances. In the next chapter there is a more detailed account of adjustment to loss. Eddie went through all of the stages of grief, explained in Chapter 4, before coming to terms with what had happened. The outcome for Eddie was influenced by many factors: a lot of support from family and friends, his strong religious convictions, his previously high level of physical fitness, his previous optimism and positive outlook, and chance. The chance was a calendar which an aunt gave to him from the Mouth and Foot Painting Artist's Association. Eddie, who had never painted in his life before, decided to give art a try and is now the only Scottish student to be sponsored at art school by the Association. He now says:

> At times I enjoy a wonderful sense of peace and I am happier than I was before the accident – it has made me a better person spiritually.

Of course the outcome could have been completely different, and is for many people who experience dramatic change. Eddie, if he had not been supported and encouraged, may have remained depressed. If he had not been sponsored he would have remained relatively poor. If he had not been strong before the accident he may have experienced more physical complications and would probably have died. The influence of unexpected events can be positive or negative or a mixture of the two, but they often do alter the course of development.

Activity

Unplanned pregnancy is an example of an unexpected change. How may this influence development? List four possible negative influences and four possible positive ones. What factors are likely to affect the outcome?

DEVELOPMENT AT DIFFERENT AGES AND STAGES

It is interesting to look at the process of development as it occurs at different times in the life span. You will quickly realise if you look around you that people differ enormously in what they do at different ages and stages, and that any account here can only be about what can generally be expected. Joe at twelve months is already saying a few words and can walk. Ryan at twelve months is still crawling everywhere and makes a few incomprehensible sounds. By five Ryan might have overtaken Joe and be able to catch a ball and give a good account of his day to his Mum, whereas Joe may not yet have mastered these skills. Linda at 50 may be very tired, overweight, unfit and depressed. Pat is 50 too but she is active, optimistic and thinking about taking a college course and changing her job. We are all different and affected to different degrees by all of the influences considered in the previous section. Below is an account then of what generally happens from **infancy to older adulthood** which is considered in the separate sections 0–2; 2–5; childhood; adolescence; adulthood and older adulthood. Physical, cognitive/intellectual, emotional and social development will be examined at each stage.

BIRTH TO TWO YEARS

At birth a baby undertakes a phenomenal journey from being totally connected to the mother to being outside her body. Although the baby is still completely dependent upon others for the fulfilment of needs, this transition has enormous implications. One day 'ventilation, nutrition and excretion take place through the placenta and umbilical cord' (Rayner, 1986). The next day the baby breathes independently, feeding by sucking starts in the next couple of days and so does excretion. Other people have to reorganise their lives around this new, dependent person.

Physical development

Here are some of the physical developments you may have noticed in a child from birth to two years. There is increasing control over the body beginning with control of head and upper body. This progresses to the ability to sit independently, then to crawl, then to pull up onto two feet and stand, then to walk with help, perhaps in a walker or pushing a toy trolley. Then that remarkable day arrives, usually between ten and eighteen months, when the child takes those first independent steps. Hand movements become finer with the ability to grasp things and then to finely hold objects in a pincer grip at around nine months old.

Rachel

As a short example of one child's physical development, here's Rachel. At seven months she has learned to turn over from front to back. She can sit momentarily without support but soon flops forwards or backwards; she can hold a cloth book but can't yet turn the pages. By fourteen months Rachel is walking and can sit in a small chair at a small table holding crayons or small objects and transferring them from one container to another. She can turn the pages of a book, usually several pages at a time. By eighteen months she is running, though not very confidently and with rather a lot of falls. She can walk upstairs one at a time holding someone's hand but comes down on hands and knees backwards. She pushes a small trolley full of toy bricks everywhere. By two years she runs confidently and has learned to turn door handles to open and close doors. Climbing is one of her new discoveries and she can 'escape' from her cot. She has a little tricycle and moves it by walking her feet along the ground. She now turns book pages one at a time. It has become evident that she is left-handed. She likes to build a tower with bricks, picking them up very carefully with her thumb and first finger; and she loves to knock the whole thing down again – with great hilarity.

Cognitive/intellectual development

Cognitive/intellectual development includes the child's thinking, language development, some aspects of play and the whole process of learning and understanding about the world. The five senses of sight, smell, touch, taste and hearing are used to learn about and explore surroundings. **Memory** is used to store up information which can be adapted, initially to the same situations and subsequently to different ones. At first there is memory of the same face(s) meaning the same things: usually food and love. **Recognition** of one meaningful person, usually but not necessarily the child's mother, is among the first cognitive steps the child takes. For example, at a few weeks old a baby will stop crying at the sight of his or her mother's face, or the face of whoever happens to be the most significant person to that baby.

One way in which babies seem to learn is through imitation of those in their surrounding world. Even though adults and older children may not realise it they are having an effect upon a baby. What they do is very important from the earliest days of the child's life, not only in terms of the child's emotional security but also in terms of intellectual growth. There is evidence that babies imitate their mothers mouth movements from the age of about a month, even though they can't speak; similarly, body movements are imitated and learned.

Exploration develops to the stage where by eighteen months a child remembers where objects belong, explores new environments with great interest and can manipulate building blocks so that they become towers. The development of **language** is perhaps one of the most fascinating aspects of cognitive development. From crying and cooing at three months of age the child develops to babbling a whole mixture of sounds by six months. By nine or ten months the language of a child's culture can be recognised and by twelve months the first words are usually spoken. By two there is usually a vocabulary of a hundred words or so. Andrew was saying Da, Ma, do (dog), ca (cat) and something which resembled 'hello' by his first birthday, whereas his friend Sam called everything 'ducker'. As the second year progressed both boys grasped the meaning of 'me' and 'mine' and parts of the body: nose, face, feet. By two they could also recognise most colours. They pretended to 'phone' one another on their toy telephones and had 'conversations'.

Emotional development

A child's early experiences are crucial to emotional development. The presence of at least one consistent, caring and loving individual has been shown to be invaluable to the child's ability to thrive and to develop emotional stability, an integrated sense of self and relationships with others. Babies deprived of a close relationship may lose vitality, become apathetic and show many symptoms of depression. Sometimes they die. This is why there is so much emphasis upon preventing the separation of young children from their families. When such separation cannot be prevented or is not in the child's best interests, as in abusive situations, it is important to provide a situation which is as close as possible to a loving, warm parent/child relationship. Fortunately the days of routinely separating children with disabilities from their parents have passed. Whenever possible the emphasis is upon support within, rather than outside, the family. Parents are now encouraged to stay with their children in hospital, nurture their babies as soon as possible after birth and to respond to a baby's need for warmth, love and physical closeness.

At first a baby is not able to distinguish between him/herself and other people, to distinguish the breast or bottle as something separate. At this stage begins what Rayner calls the synchrony between a close parent or parent substitute and a baby. They fit themselves around each other, are in tune and a baby establishes communication with at least one close significant other within the first few weeks of life. Both parents and babies vary in the nature of the synchrony which is established but without it a baby is likely to be distressed. This synchrony is the basis for bonding and attachment between parent and child upon which depends the baby's later ability to gain a separate sense of self. It is also the basis of love, trust and a feeling of security.

Slowly but surely the baby begins to gain a sense of him or herself as separate from other people and things, so that somewhere between six months and a year a separate identity begins to emerge. Crying changes in nature and becomes a call for someone else. Smiling, which has probably been present as a sign of pleasure from the first month of life, becomes increasingly a response to other people. Crying and smiling are the baby's main ways of communicating pain and pleasure and need a response in order that the child can begin to gain a knowledge of communication as an exchange. At this stage too the child begins to test the world, to throw things away which are then put back, to get anxious if the closest person to her goes out, and to be reassured when she or he returns. As long as the person does come back the child learns to **trust** other people, to see that they can be relied upon, and to form a close **bond** with at least one significant other person. Initial synchrony helps in this bonding process, though bonding at this stage is entirely possible for children who have had early health difficulties and/or have been separated from their parents. Continued separation though, increases the difficulties of bonding once a child reaches the stage of seeing him/herself as separate.

Although children thrive and survive all kinds of different parenting and can and do recover from short periods of separation, children deprived of love and closeness and the opportunity to bond and form a consequent **attachment** to an adult are unlikely to trust others or to develop a satisfactory self-concept. This can lead to difficulties in their relationships with others. Such **emotional deprivation** has also been shown to be associated with slow intellectual development and poor physical health. Spitz (1965), for example, observed children in large institutions where they were well-fed and clean but had little personal attention or stimulation. These children had extreme difficulties with learning, emotionally responding to others and were prone to infections. Their illness and death rates were much higher than those for children in less clean but more warm and friendly places.

Social development

Most people who have been with small babies a lot will be convinced that they are sociable from a very early age. Whether or not they have any sense of a separate identity, a small baby's smiles and cries elicit responses from others to play, to comfort or just smile back. From these beginnings the child between two and eight months usually bonds with and shows attachment to one or more adults who are close to the child. This early sociability is thus very much linked with the emotional development discussed above. There is little interest in other children in the first six months of life, though familiar children, such as brothers and sisters, are recognised and often elicit a response such as a smile of pleasure. From about eight months onwards the young child begins to spread his or her sociability to other people, though will often seek the reassurance and closeness of the most meaningful person if threatened or unsure (or hungry or uncomfortable or tired).

PHYSICAL	INTELLECTUAL/ COGNITIVE	EMOTIONAL	SOCIAL
How the body changes	How sense is made of the world	Beginning to gain a sense of identity	Interacting/getting on with others
• increasing control over body	• recognition of meaningful people	• need for warmth, love and closeness	• bonding and attachment
• sitting, crawling, walking, running	• development of memory	• developing trust or mistrust	• importance of early close relationship
• co-ordination, finer hand movements	• developing concept of objects	• secure or insecure base	• increasing interest in other children
• focusing on objects	• communication and language	• distinguishing self from others	• parallel play
• beginning to manipulate toys and other things	• beginnings of number skills	• emotional responses to others; smiling, crying	• communication with others
	• exploration		

Figure 3.4 Summary of general pattern of development: Birth to two years

Life becomes a series of going forth into new situations and retreating back for comfort. There is increasing interest in other children. Most children of one will happily be with other children but actions are not yet an exchange between them. For example, at one Rachel went to playgroup where she would happily play alongside other children for up to an hour, but then she would retreat to her mother for comfort. By two she was becoming much more independent and sociable but still her play was what is known as parallel play, it did not yet rest upon ideas of sharing and exchange. That has to wait for the next stage of development.

TWO TO FIVE YEARS

Physical development

Parents will often have been preoccupied with 'toilet training' for several months preceding the second birthday. Some time from eighteen months to three years magical things seem to happen: the child becomes increasingly able to control both bladder and bowel and can now communicate so well that he or she can begin to predict the need to use a pot and say what is required. This new-found control is very important, for it further frees the child from dependence on adults for physical care. By two most children are fully weaned and can eat and drink independently. Development is very much tied up with growth at this stage. As the body grows bigger and stronger it also gains in co-ordindation and strength. Walking, running, climbing and balancing are increasingly skilled.

Matty

Matty is two and a half. He loves to visit the swings and slides. Tentatively he'll climb the ladder and slide down the slide. After ten minutes he's running from the end of the slide to the ladder, up one step at a time and whizzing down with great glee . . . time after time after time. He loves to go to the swimming baths and flap around with arm bands on, but needs to know that there's someone close by to help him. By five he may be going up the really big slide, co-ordinating climbing steps with alternate legs and confident enough to go head first as well as feet first. Also by five a lot of children are learning to swim without the support of arm bands.

This period from two to five is one of consolidating skills, of increasing co-ordination of lots of movements, of running around and climbing. Gradually a child can learn to throw a ball and then to catch it, to pedal a tricycle and then to begin to balance on a bicycle. There is increasing skill gained in holding and manipulating toys so that children by five can usually thread beads, build buildings with lego or other building toys and draw by holding crayons quite skilfully and with increasing control.

Cognitive/intellectual development

Language is one of the main avenues through which cognitive/intellectual development can be gauged at this age. Not only is vocabulary increasing but children are very creative with their language. They do not completely mimic adults but often, once they have learned a few rules of language, come up with entirely original constructions. Here are some sentences of children in this age range:

I was tired. My eyes did lie down a little while.
I not naughty. I just a little terror.
I knowed Andrew at nursery school. I done some drawing.

Here is a conversation between a three year-old and a six year-old quoted in Bee and Mitchell (1984) about the relative dangers of forgetting to feed the goldfish versus overfeeding them:

Six year-old: It's worse to forget to feed them.
Three year-old: No, it's badder to feed them too much.
Six year-old: You don't say badder, you say worser.
Three year-old: But it's baddest to give them too much food.
Six year-old: No, it's not. It's worsest to forget to feed them.

These examples show really creative use of language which, although perhaps not grammatically correct, is inventive and wasn't learned from copying adults. One of the delights of this age is this remarkable grasp of some basic rules of grammar combined with experimenting with them in original ways. By three children are constructing quite long, complex sentences. They have often replaced their own names with 'I' in their conversations as they gain confidence in themselves and their self-concept becomes more fully developed.

Children of this age are also learning about colours and shapes, numbers and time, what things in their environment are like and what they do. They will play shapes games, putting different shapes through appropriately shaped holes in boxes, they will investigate things to see what they do and feel like, and they will be trying to work out things like distances. One favourite word is often 'why'. Why is sometimes asked out of sheer habit but can also indicate a real desire to know why something is the way it is. 'How far' is also a favourite one, especially on a long journey. 'How far is it? Are we nearly there?' comes from a small voice ten minutes into a three-hour journey, and at five minute intervals thereafter, unless there's distraction and/or fun going on. It's certainly not far to five now, but there's still a lot of life's journey to pursue.

Emotional development

Emotional development usually, though not always, goes hand in hand with intellectual development. As a child learns communication skills these facilitate interaction with others and the development of relationships. During the period two to five years children become considerably less dependent upon their parents and strive towards greater autonomy. They can usually be separated from parents for short periods without becoming too distressed. They begin to enjoy the company of others, especially brothers and sisters (siblings), spending as much time with them as with their parents. Siblings often begin to form strong bonds with one another at this stage, talking, playing, imitating, arguing, experiencing difficulties and attempting to sort them out. Sibling relationships are certainly not all plain sailing and some siblings never gain fulfilling, integrated relationships with one another for reasons of both nature and nurture. But there is the potential in sibling relationships for strong bonds to develop which are different from and additional to those with parents and friends. Parents still play a prominent part at this stage, an emotional retreat when the child needs love, stability and reassurance.

It is at this stage that **gender identity** emerges and girls and boys become more fully aware of the differences between them. Even before the age of two there are signs that boys and girls are aware that they are different from one another. Physical differences have emotional implications since these differences become part of identity, and children begin to pay attention to the different **roles** of boys and girls, men and women. The gaining of gender identity can be seen as progressing in four stages:

■ **Awareness:** the child begins to notice gender differences (12–14 months);
■ **Labelling:** the child correctly identifies gender in self and others (2–3 years);
■ **Stability:** the child understands that gender remains over time, that a boy becomes a man and a girl becomes a woman (3–5 years);
■ **Constancy:** the child understands that gender doesn't change when outward appearance changes (5+).

Social development

Not only is the child moving outwards emotionally but also socially: from parents to siblings to other children and other adults. The child's social world is usually expanding and spreading beyond the family to nursery, playgroup, public places (shopping, swimming, holidays) and is a mixture of child and adult relationships.

Play is an area which combines all facets of development – physical, intellectual/cognitive, emotional and social. It is useful to examine here, not only how play is part of social development at this stage, but also how it acts to integrate the various facets of development in the process of the growth of a well-balanced person.

At two a child generally participates in parallel play. Children play alongside each other rather than with each other. If you watch children at this age, they can be very absorbed by a toy car, or by the toy car with which another child is playing which they will then proceed to try to obtain. This is more important than any kind of relationship with the other child. Play here is a learning process, it serves to develop physical and cognitive skills and is preparing to be a much more social and emotional experience – but it isn't quite there, yet. This process continues slowly until by five children begin to co-operate, to divide roles and to share, though play is by no means always an harmonious experience.

Activity

Watch a group of three to five year-old children playing. Note what they are doing and make a list of which aspects of play fall into each of the categories of physical, intellectual/cognitive, emotional and social behaviour and development.

PHYSICAL	INTELLECTUAL/COGNITIVE	EMOTIONAL	SOCIAL
How the body changes	How sense is made of the world	Developing sense of identity	Building upon relationships
• control of bladder and bowel	• creative use of language	• less dependence on parents	• moving outwards; expanding social world
• eating and drinking independently	• talking and using words and symbols	• greater autonomy if emotionally stable	• playing with other children
• increasing physical independence	• learning about everything: colours, shapes, numbers	• emergence of gender identity	• taking on roles in play, including gender roles
• increasing skill in co-ordination	• curiosity: often asks 'why'	• begins to verbalise emotional responses	• relationships with siblings

Figure 3.5 Summary of general pattern of development: Two to five

CHILDHOOD

Childhood has a different time span for different children and for different cultures. In the UK it generally spans the ages of five until about twelve or thirteen when puberty and adolescence occur. It is the time of starting school, making friends and moving further out from the confines of the family and home to the wider society.

Physical development

Of course, children get bigger and bigger, though at different rates. How else do they change and develop before they reach that notorious adolescence? Skills and sex are the two clues to physical development from five to twelve or thirteen. **Skills** involve more meticulous dexterity in manipulating their hands and bodies. At six children can usually tie laces and cut meat at the table. At seven, lo and behold, a small person balancing on a plank, leaping down several stairs at a time, dressing ... and its reverse, undressing. By eight here we are roller-skating or roller-blading on Saturday evening at the Sports Centre, skipping in the playground and riding a bike at full speed down the local hill. **Sexually** children are inexorably moving towards puberty, girls usually at a faster rate than boys. Girls begin to develop pubic hair and breasts and some begin menstruation before they are twelve, though in Britain the average age for the onset of menstruation is thirteen. Boys do not usually reach puberty at this stage or undergo any major growth spurts. Both sexes make steady progress in their ability to perform complex physical tasks with the effects of puberty dominating not this stage of development but the next.

Cognitive/intellectual development

Play continues to have a vital role in cognitive/intellectual development, though formal learning at school plays an increasing part at this time. **Thinking** changes in a number of ways. The child usually develops numerical/mathematical ability. For example, at five a child can count sweets if they are placed in a straight line (though not in a circle). By eight most children can count sweets placed in a circle. By twelve concepts of addition, subtraction, multiplication and division are being grasped. Measuring and recording can be practised in both formal and informal situations through seeing how long and wide things are, now much items weigh when baking a cake and so on.

Time becomes increasingly meaningful and by eleven most children can tell the time, understand the calendar in some detail (weeks, months, years), know the date and grasp that it is the same date and time everywhere in the UK. **Writing** ability is often more developed than speech. The use of increasingly complex sentences indicates growing language competence.

Emotional development

Most children become more self-assured between the ages of five and twelve, developing a self-concept which is more confident about their abilities and showing more insight into their own identity. Children from five to twelve start to question family relationships and emotions and quite frequently push their parents to the limit of their patience. They like to see how far they can go, though if limits are imposed they are usually adhered to ... eventually.

At five a child can count sweets placed in a straight line

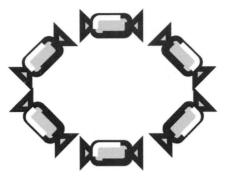

At eight most children can count sweets placed in a circle

113 + 47 = 160   **3000 ÷ 12 = 250**
1,620 - 742 = 878   **524 x 13 = 6,812**

By twelve concepts of addition, subtraction, multiplication and division have usually been grasped

Figure 3.6 Development of numerical cognition

Seonaid wrote the following description of herself at age eleven:

My name is Seonaid. I live in Dundee. My home is a flat. I was born in Fort William and when I was six weeks old I moved to Glasgow and stayed there for seven years. My school in Glasgow was . . . and my best friend was called Joanne. I have brown hair cut short and I wear earrings. My best friend in Dundee is Ellie. I have a younger sister in primary 2 and an older sister in third year. My Mum works in a shop and my Dad is a taxi driver. I go dancing after school every Wednesday. I go swimming quite often too. I collect pictures of cats in a scrap book and I also collect stamps. I have a one year-old cat called Snowy. My ambition is to look after lots of animals that have been abandoned. I am average size. My home has three bedrooms, a living room, a kitchen and a bathroom. I like skateboards and bikes.

Activity

What was important to Seonaid? From this account identify which parts refer to emotional, intellectual/cognitive, physical or social development.

Social development

'Friends' would be an apt title for a TV series about childhood. The peer group, children of the same or similar age, gains in importance as children move increasingly away from social dependence upon adults. Competitive and co-operative play develop alongside one another. Children compete in sports activities, in classroom situations and in their attempts to gain the attention of adults and other children. They also learn co-operation, enhanced in play situations where they act out such co-operative and competing roles as mothers, fathers, doctors, nurses, older brothers and sisters, shop assistants, school teachers and pupils.

Play enables children to learn roles and to emphasise with those who perform other roles in their lives. The self-concept, seen as part of emotional development, is developed to some extent through the social situations which the child experiences and through the increasing ability of the child to put him or herself in other roles, to stand outside and to look in. Ideas about self-concept are further developed in Chapter 4.

Group participation, whether through the family, school group, interest group or friendship group, provides avenues not only for co-operation with others, but also for the expression of opinions and the development of relationships. Children of this age have an enormous need for acceptance which leads to what many adults see as an annoying conformity; children have to dress in similar ways to their peers, develop language patterns which are similar, hair must be just so and things not 'in' are viewed as very 'uncool'. Conformity sometimes looks cripplingly stifling of creativity and achievement, but for many children acceptance by the peer group is of much greater importance. The peer group itself, though, can be a source of creativity, interaction and the opportunity for co-operation and leadership. By eight or nine boys and girls are beginning to drift apart into same sex groups, only to come together again in adolescence.

Adult relationships continue to retain a great deal of relevance, the family is still an important social focal point but other adult attachments often develop. Hero worship of teachers, sports coaches, instructors, guide and scout leaders, youth club leaders, even social workers, can develop. These are usually healthy attachments if the role models are positive and the power which could be associated with these roles is not abused.

For most children this is a happy time socially, with some friendships formed at this stage lasting well into adult life. There are fallings in and out, but gradually as the child develops confidence in him/herself, so confidence develops in relationships. Social development rests firmly in its emotional partner.

ADOLESCENCE

Indeed, all the terms that we use for the age group have an awkward feel. There is no neutral way of describing it: 'youth' has an air of causing trouble and needing clubs, 'juveniles' are obviously delinquent, 'adolescents' are most likely to have problems and 'teenagers' to have spots.

(Open University U205 Course Team, 'Birth to Old Age', 1985)

PHYSICAL	INTELLECTUAL/ COGNITIVE	EMOTIONAL	SOCIAL
How the body changes	How sense is made of the world	Developing sense of identity	Moving outwards from the family
• developing skills and coordination	• play: make believe and dramatic	• developing self-image, self-esteem	• importance of peer group
• beginnings of sexual development	• numerical and language ability	• questioning about emotions	• competitive and cooperative play
• progress in doing complex tasks	• grasp of the concept of time	• increasing independence	• learning roles and social competence
	• learning by doing	• play and its role in identity	• group participation
	• distinguishing fact from fiction		• family still a focal point

Figure 3.7 Summary of general pattern of development: Childhood

Think about being a teenager. You may still be one, you may have just passed that stage or you may be well past it, not that adolescence is ever entirely left behind. What do you think are its most significant aspects? Is it a time of calm, natural transition from childhood to adulthood or a rather stormy passage or a mixture of the two? A lot has been written about this period, which in Western society is often associated with problems, storm and stress; but is adolescence necessarily problematical? Is turbulence in adolescence a biological necessity or are social and cultural factors of paramount importance? Writers and theorists vary enormously in their views. The sections below, combined with your experience and thinking, should enable you to come to a few of your own conclusions.

Physical development

Adolescence is a time of rapid physical growth and development, more so than any other period except infancy. Babies, though, are not aware (as far as we know) of the changes in their bodies, while adolescents most certainly are.

(Bee and Mitchell, 1984)

The physical changes which an adolescent undergoes are not just ones of growth but of transformation associated with the eventual ability to reproduce and to work as an adult. They have many emotional implications. This period of adolescence usually begins with puberty which occurs at different ages for different individuals and is generally earlier for girls than for boys. The physical development of adolescents can be viewed as falling into three types:

1. **General changes in body shape**, including changes in the way fat and muscle are distributed. In girls fat is laid down around the hips and breasts whilst boys generally lose fat and develop greater muscle mass than girls. The strength and stamina of both sexes greatly increases and they become more greatly differentiated as adolescence progresses.

2. A **growth spurt** occurs in adolescence between the ages of eleven and sixteen. There is usually a rapid increase in height.

3. There is continuing **development of the reproductive system**, with changes in the level of sex **hormones** in the bloodstream giving rise to internal and external changes. For boys these changes include a deepening of the voice, enlargement of the penis and the growth of pubic and body hair. For girls the changes include enlargement of the breasts, growth of pubic hair and the onset of menstruation (called the menarche). Menstruation can begin at any age from about ten to sixteen but is usually at around thirteen in the UK. This period of sexual development is known as puberty.

Cognitive/intellectual development

As adolescence progresses each individual is usually moving towards more abstract thought. Thought is not confined to things which can be seen and recognised, but can be applied to unseen things. Ideas and reasoning about one problem can be transferred to similar problems, experiments in thinking can be performed not only with concrete objects but with ideas. The individual is capable of envisaging many possible consequences and not just one or two.

Linda

Sixteen year-old Linda decides to get a part-time job. She thinks around this problem and initially says something like 'I'd like to work in Asda'; phone call to Asda; told you have to get an application form from the job centre; told by job centre no application forms available since Asda doesn't have any vacancies at present. Linda doesn't stop there but now starts to think more widely around the problem. She realises that she has to use a lot of different strategies and has to keep persisting until she gets a job. She has to telephone, visit, answer advertisements, ask her friends and, if she still wants to work in Asda eventually, has to keep contacting the job centre until they have application forms. This strategy worked. She heard through a friend that people were needed to serve in a café. That's what she did until she did eventually gain employment at Asda. A pre-adolescent child would have been capable of thinking it would be good to get a job at Asda but it is unlikely that he or she would have had the ability to see alternative avenues, conduct the experiments needed to find out about how to arrive at an alternative solution or have the intellectual persistence to get to Asda in the end.

Some other aspects of cognitive development in adolescence are the ability to understand the impact of the past on the present and of the present on the future, to begin questioning the views of adults which have previously been accepted (arguments with parents, 'debates' with teachers), to look behind the obvious in books and paintings to appreciate that there is often more than is explicitly stated about life or the world. Adolescents do not confine themselves to progression in logical thought but also progress in creative thought. Some adolescents develop immense creative ability through making imaginative leaps. One famous example is Einstein who, at sixteen, imagined himself as a particle of light travelling away from a planet. This sparked off his thoughts towards what eventually became known as the theory of relativity. Many young people begin to see the world with new eyes at this age and to make creative and imaginative leaps in the production of masterpieces. If you go round a school to look at work produced for Standard Grade and Higher Art the combination of analytical thought and creative leaps of imagination is often quite staggering.

Not all adolescents progress at the same rate or in the same way in their cognitive development. Some have reached a stage of analytical thought well before adolescence, some never really reach it, some don't reach it until well into adult life, and some are slow starters but suddenly have an intellectual growth spurt somewhere between fifteen and twenty-two. This is one of the reasons why some people who do only moderately well in Standard Grades end up gaining first class honours degrees at university.

Emotional development

A lot of people would say that the word 'emotional' is quite an apt one to apply to adolescence but would question the relevance of the word 'development'. Is all that storm and tempest really development? Well, yes, it is all part of life's rich, wondrous and varied passage. For many people it is not a period of great trauma and upheaval, although it is certainly a period of change and transition. Children enter in and adults come out (though usually continuing to be adolescent in some aspects of their lives) and a lot of emotional development goes on in between. What is the nature of this development?

The continuing development of a sense of self is one of the main issues of this stage. The adolescent is quite intensely focused upon this self and behaviour is often rather egocentric. The main question is 'who am I?', a question which people often continue to ask themselves throughout their lives. If you look at Seonaid's description of herself, aged eleven, on page 00, she's not really asking questions about who she is but is content to describe herself in terms of where she lives, her interests, her parents, her average size. By sixteen she's writing some quite powerful poetry:

I feel rejection
And search for my world
In a mild way which does not make
It obvious to them
Who I really am.
Maybe one day
I will be happy
Not in the way that they believe they are
But in a way purer than the water I drink
Where I'm doing what I want
And don't care what they think
Because then I'll be at ease with me
And maybe then they'll see
That it's not important to be smart and rich
Because satisfaction is what matters to me
I could be in the gutter
And have people mutter
'What a waste of a life'
As they wander by
But I'd smile to myself
And think secret thoughts
At least I am happy and true to my heart
I don't pretend to be something I'm not.

Activity

What aspects of adolescent emotional development are evident in the above poem?

You may have mentioned the focus upon feelings (in this case feelings of rejection), searching for something, a separation from 'them', who are presumably adults, a focus upon 'I' (where I'm doing what I want), a rejection of what she considers to be adult ways and an attitude of 'I don't care what they think'. There's an emphasis upon being honest to yourself and upon not pretending to be something you're not. Not every adolescent has all of these feelings or feels them so intensely but most adolescents have some of them. There is a lot of questioning which is working towards resolution of what many theorists see as the identity crisis of adolescence.

Connected with the developing sense of self are issues related to **sexuality**. Part of the 'who am I' questioning is also about being heterosexual, homosexual or of other sexual orientation. Some people find themselves intensely dissatisfied with the conventional options open to them. Many adolescents and young adults experiment with aspects of sexuality until they resolve the conflicts within them. Some adult problems are associated with a lack of resolution of the question of sexuality because it comes into conflict with other aspects of themselves or with the society in which they live.

Separation, both physical and emotional, is one of the aspects of growth and also one of anxiety for many adolescents. They desperately want to be independent people but many, especially if they continue into further or higher education, are financially dependent upon parents. The nuclear family is less and less important as partnerships, friendships and sexual relationships increase in importance, yet the family is still a source of financial support, and emotional support in times of crisis. The back and forth away from and towards the family, away from and sometimes back to and sometimes away from again long-established relationships, the contradictions and a move towards their resolution are all part of adolescence.

There are particular issues in relation to emotional development in adolescence for those who belong to various ethnic and/or cultural groups, for children who are 'looked after' in children's homes or by foster parents, and for children who are adopted. Can you think of others for whom adolescence may present particular problems?

You may have thought of adolescents with a disability, those who are or have parents who are gay, lesbian or transvestite, those who come from abusive or unstable environments. Although a whole book could be devoted to the issues surrounding all of these groups there just isn't the time or the space here to do the subject justice. Instead two short case studies are presented below for you to consider and discuss.

CASE STUDY

Cathy is fifteen. She is looked after in a small, homely children's home. She has had a very difficult emotional life. Her mother was a lone parent and a drug addict who died when she was four years old. Even at the age of four Cathy was showing signs of disruptive behaviour and an inability to make friends. At the age of six she was adopted by a loving couple who had one daughter of their own, five years older than Cathy. The adoption was a disaster, with Cathy and her adoptive mother in constant conflict. Cathy had temper tantrums for no apparent reason, used abusive language and didn't seem able to respond to any kind of love or affection shown to her. The adoption completely broke down a year ago and Cathy came to the children's home at that time.

CASE STUDY

Tanveer Ahmed appears in the case study in Chapter 10. He is fifteen, his parents were born in Pakistan though he was born in Edinburgh. He is part of an extended Muslim family. He is expected to attend the mosque with his father and uncle and to speak Urdu with his grandmother. His family hopes that when he marries he will marry within his own faith and community. Tanveer attends the local secondary school where he is one of only three other Asian pupils. He is doing well there, wants to feel part of the social life of the school but is expected to come home straight from school to help and to do homework.

Activity

Discuss the above case studies in the light of adolescent emotional development. Make two lists for each study, the first stating the main factors which affect most adolescents and the second, factors which may be additional or different for these adolescents. When you have read the next section, the exercise can be repeated in terms of social development.

Social development

Social development is greatly influenced by all other aspects of development in adolescence and bears many resemblances to emotional development. Sexual maturity leads the individual towards sexual relationships. In Western society the search for self and emotional independence from parents establishes a new and different kind of relationship with them and with the peer group. The end of formal school education leads to a transition into the worlds of work or further or higher education or other experiences such as gap years of travel. For some there is the frustrating world of unemployment, uncertainty and lack of money. Whatever avenue is taken by the adolescent, new and often meaningful and long-lasting relationships develop, usually with members of both the same and the 'opposite' sex.

Parents, including step-parents, are a source of support, annoyance and aggravation at this age. One observer (Montemayor, 1983) noted that adolescents and their parents are in conflict in all families some of the time and in some families all of the time. Sometimes serious conflicts can lead to serious problems, which can include running away, drug abuse, under-age pregnancy, attempted and actual suicide and illness, including eating disorders such as anorexia nervosa (Open University, 1985). Not all conflicts have serious repercussions and not all serious problems are caused by conflict with parents or others. Rayner (1986) also points out that a *child's adolescence brings the opportunity for his parents to be rejuvenated in mind if not in body.*

The peer group or friendship group is of prime importance in adolescence. 'Do I look OK?' doesn't mean 'do I look beautiful?' but 'do I conform to the norms of the peer group?' 'is my

PHYSICAL	INTELLECTUAL/ COGNITIVE	EMOTIONAL	SOCIAL
How the body changes	How sense is made of the world	Developing sense of self	Moving further away from the family
• rapid development/growth spurt	• More abstract and creative thought	• change and transition	• influences of emotional factors
• development of reproductive system/puberty	• understand impact of past on present/present on future	• focus upon self/identity/feelings/ who am I?	• sexual attraction
• changes in body shape	• presenting arguments	• issues related to difference e.g. ethnicity, sexuality	• changing relationship with parents
	• questioning views of adults	• separation	• importance of peer group
			• changing roles

Figure 3.8 Summary of general pattern of development: Adolescence

skirt short enough, are the heels high enough, is the hair spiky enough, is the nose-ring in the right place, do the eight ear-rings in one ear conform to the peer group norms but still mark me out as 'different'?' Many sets of relationships are being balanced at this stage; those with parents (including step-parents), those with teachers and/or employers, those with peers and those with whom the individual has a sexual or potentially sexual relationship. A fifth relationship, the relationship with oneself, is also vying for attention. The ways in which these relationships develop depend upon all of the influences and other aspects of development considered earlier. The person who emerges, the young adult, is the subject of subsequent sections of this chapter.

ADULTHOOD

If you look at the case studies of the MacDonald and Ahmed families in Chapter 10, several adults make an appearance: Linda and Joe MacDonald, Hassan Ahmed and Aisha Bibi among others. Below are another two short case studies.

CASE STUDY

Fiona and Alistair are in their early thirties. They are married. Alistair works as an engineer and at the moment Fiona, who was a teacher and hopes to be a teacher again, is at home looking after their new baby son, Christopher, and three year-old Sam.

CASE STUDY

Alex is a journalist in his mid-forties. He lives alone and has never married but plays an active role as uncle to his four nieces and nephews. His career is very, very important to him and he loves his work, the unpredictability of it and the fact that he is frequently sent on assignments abroad. He is writing a book about motorbikes in his spare time. He has a boyfriend who is a doctor with whom he has a long-standing sexual relationship. They have considered living together but decided to maintain independent households, especially as they lead such different lives. They do, however, spend holidays together every year.

All of these people are **adults** but their differing experiences reflect the enormous range of factors to be considered in this section. The period of adulthood examined here is from about 21 to 65, though some people much younger than 21 are functioning as adults, some people of 26 still appear to be experiencing adolescence and some people over 65 are not really older adults but are performing as adults in their middle years. Rayner (1986) emphasises that features of adolescence recur throughout adulthood stating:

However, if 'adolescing', with its regression, romance and madness, is not kept alive throughout our lives then we neither have the means to change ourselves nor can we provide the environment for others to change. We become either very dull, shrunken people unable to face crisis, or arthritic martinets, self-satisfied with power and unable to be either humble or flexible.

Physical development

Until adulthood physical development has been a prime force influencing social and cognitive development. In adults cognitive, emotional and social forces influence physical change, development and health to a much greater degree than in earlier life. There are some physical changes, however, which are characteristic of adult life, some associated with younger adult life and others associated with middle adult life. By adulthood physical development, including sexual development, is virtually complete, though sexual identity in terms of heterosexuality, homosexuality or other sexual orientation may not be. Young adulthood is usually the healthiest period of life, when people are at peak fitness. Footballers, for example, usually play at their best in their twenties; athletes are then also at their peak. Serious illness in young adulthood is quite unusual, with the greatest threat to health being accidents, especially road traffic accidents among men in their late teens and early twenties. Of these accidents 80 per cent are car accidents and 5 per cent are motorcycle accidents, usually to young men who take risks for the kind of 'reward' expressed in the following quotes:

You can forget drugs – at speed on a bike, you're the closest to flying you're ever likely to get.

There are times when it might have been wiser to slow down, yeah ... but you just think, what the hell – go for it.

(Open University, 1985)
(Statistics taken from HMSO 1998, the Scottish Abstract of Statistics)

Activity

Find out the ages of ten key players in the Scottish premier football league. Calculate the average age by adding all the ages together and dividing by ten. This should give you some indication of the age of peak fitness.

Pregnancy and childbirth are among the major physical events for young women. These have enormous implications for their emotional and social lives and the subjects receive much more attention in subsequent sections. The age at which women have their first child is on average much later than it was 20 years ago, though the number of teenage pregnancies has also risen. There are now possibilities for women who would previously have been unable to have children to receive fertility treatment. Pregnancy and childbirth are still risky events in terms of health, though both maternal and infant mortality are at their lowest levels ever. In 1997 only 4 deaths were recorded in Scotland as a result of complications of pregnancy and childbirth. There were 140 child deaths in the peri-natal period, down from 230 in 1987 (HMSO, 1998).

As adulthood progresses the individual's way of life determines to some extent the physical changes which take place. Many people from the thirties, forties or fifties onwards gain weight and lose physical fitness, but these gains and losses are neither universal nor inevitable. Lifestyle is a major influence and a combination of diet, exercise and low stress levels can combine to promote good physical health throughout the adult years. Low alcohol consumption and no smoking also contribute to the maintenance of good health. There is some inevitable loss of speed of reaction and of muscularity as adulthood proceeds. This is why winners of the Tour de France, for example, do not usually exceed 30 years of age. On the other hand, stamina often increases with age and compensates for some of the physical losses. Mountaineers such as Chris Bonnington continued to conquer high peaks well into their fifties and Beryl Burton, the woman cyclist, continued to compete in 100-mile races into her forties. Bortz in Bee and Mitchell (1984) gives a lovely summary of the benefits of exercise:

It is wrong to suggest that exercise might halt the fall of the grains of sand in the hourglass. It is proposed, however, that the dimension of the aperture may be responsive to the toning influences of physical activity, and consequently the sand may drain more slowly. A physically active life may allow us to approach our true biogenetic potential for longevity.

One major physical life event affecting women in middle adulthood is the menopause. This is caused by a decrease in levels of the hormone oestrogen, which leads to a cessation of menstruation and the ability to produce children. It does not lead to a cessation of sexual activity, though levels do usually decrease considerably for both men and women as young adulthood gives way to middle age.

Cognitive/intellectual development

In adulthood cognitive/intellectual development is associated with knowledge and skills gained through further and higher education, work, hobbies and interests. The application and development of knowledge in relation to everyday life especially though parenthood, and the passing on of knowledge and skills to other people are also of importance. Individuals make choices about cognitive development and also differ in the opportunities open to them. Some people see leaving school as the end of their need to think or develop intellectually, though many feel the frustration and stagnation of this in later years and return to some form of education and/or training. Others lack the opportunities to develop to their maximum potential. The virtual abolition of student grants has meant that many people who do not have parental or other support find it extremely difficult to survive in further or higher education, especially if they have family commitments. High rates of unemployment, especially among school leavers with no qualifications, can mean that the alternative intellectual stimulation of work is not available. Cognitive development is, as a consequence, impaired or delayed. For some adults the intellectual demands of partnership and/or parenthood provide an additional or alternative route to cognitive development and they direct their thinking and learning towards making a success of family life.

Assuming that one or more of the above avenues of cognitive development is available, most adults show a fairly steady or improving level of ability throughout their young and middle adult years. For example, in a long-term study by Schaie and Labouvie-Vief (1974), mathematical ability and verbal comprehension only began to decline after the age of 67. Many adults show improving ability on tests of vocabulary, comprehension and general knowledge, especially if their everyday lives present opportunities for learning or they purposefully pursue intellectually stimulating interests, read a lot and/or travel.

If you look back at the case studies at the beginning of this section you will see that the people discussed there have developed cognitively in many different ways in adulthood. For example Fiona and Alistair have undergone training for their respective careers. They have also embarked upon parenthood through which they can pass on their own learning and develop the skills of child care.

Activity

Choose two of the adults mentioned at the beginning of this section. State how you think they may have developed cognitively during their adult lives and consider the factors which have contributed to this.

Emotional development

The self continues to emerge throughout the adult years and is presented with many life experiences and events which contribute to this process. Work, partnership (marriage and other sexual relationships), friendships, parenthood, transitions, crises, achievements and interests all play a part. The emerging self is constantly faced with choices and questions which influence the course of this development and the resulting adult identity. Women in their thirties, for example, may be asking themselves 'should I have a baby?' or 'another baby?' or 'should I go back to work, change my career, change my partner, am I happy with him or her?' Some periods of adulthood can be very emotionally stressful. Even quite positive events such as marriage and holidays can create tension. A sufficient number of tense or stressful events or one extremely stressful one can lead to a **crisis**. Usually in a crisis the individual's normal coping mechanisms do not work too well and support from others may be of vital importance. It is quite interesting for you to look at your own level of stress. One indicator of this is the scale devised by Holmes and Rahe (1967), outlined on page 160 of Chapter 4. Do not become too concerned if you score very highly (i.e. in excess of 300). You may just thrive on change and/or be very well supported. You are not necessarily in crisis at all.

Most of the events on this scale are either **transitions** or **losses** and you are referred to pages 158–170 for a much fuller discussion of these; only brief consideration is given to them here. Two factors which are important in coping with transition and loss are the degree of support which is available to the individual and the individual's coping mechanisms. Part of emotional development is to find **positive** ways to deal with the many transitions and losses which adult life presents. If this is not achieved, either because the individual has not found ways to cope or because of lack of support or because the level of stress or crisis is just too great, or a combination of all these things, the consequences for psychological and physical health can be severe. Below is a comparison of two possible routes to adjustment in adulthood.

POSITIVE ADJUSTMENT	NEGATIVE ADJUSTMENT
Excited about life	Anxious
Keen to seize opportunities	Dissatisfied
At home with self	Feelings of inadequacy
Happy about the future	Feelings of guilt
Well supported by friends and family	Doesn't feel well supported
Able to take transition in stride	Very stressed by transition
Works through loss by facing it and grieving	Experiences prolonged depression as a result of loss

Activity

The emotional adjustment of the adult depends upon many factors. From the above account and your own thinking, list as many of these as you can.

You may have thought of: past history; heredity; level of support; personality and attitude; state of physical health; stage of life. Perhaps you had a completely different list. Think about these factors in terms of your own adjustment to life.

Support has been mentioned several times as important in adult emotional development. Where does this support come from? One important source is through **relationships of intimacy** with partners, spouses, friends and relatives. These relationships of intimacy are, at their best, reciprocal, satisfying and a source of stability from which the individual can face the outside world and its challenges. They also contribute to the individual's identity. The roles of partner, husband, wife, friend, daughter, son, etc. all become ways in which the individual identifies him/herself in the outside world. Identity is also enhanced through the creative roles which the individual plays through parenthood, work and/or creative pursuits.

Parenthood is one major life transition which brings change in relationships, lifestyle, roles and responsibilities. Ideally for most people this experience is shared with someone they love and to whom they have made a meaningful, lasting and intimate commitment. This is not always the case, however, though statistics indicating that over a third of all children are born to people who are not married does not mean that their parents are not living together or providing support. Nevertheless in the West of Scotland approximately 20 per cent of children do grow up in single parent households where no other adults are present (Strathclyde Social Trends, 1992).

Social development

The major factors involved in emotional development are also those which influence social development. Forming and maintaining intimate relationships, including friendships, the changing roles brought about by parenthood, work and partnership, and the social networks which individuals form as a result of these roles and relationships, are all part of the pattern of social as well as emotional development. Rather than repeat most of the above section in social terms, the subject of **work** is discussed as a link among all aspects of development.

Work

It is a great matter for a man to find his own line, and keep to it. You get along faster on your own rail . . .

(Janet Aitken in the Glasgow School of Art's magazine, 1893 – 'man' here is really an all-encompassing term for 'person'. Quoted in Jones, A., 1990)

The case study below demonstrates some of the links among various aspects of development.

CASE STUDY

Stuart and Eileen are both senior care workers in a residence for people with sensory and learning disability. They both enjoy their work and in their desire to further their knowledge and career prospects they signed up for an evening class in social sciences. They didn't know that they had both signed up for the same course until they met at the first class. They got into the habit of going for a drink after the class and often discussed homework if they were on the same shift. Before long they were seeing each other for social events at the weekend and eventually decided that they would like to spend their lives together.

In this passage you can see how **work** can link cognitive, social, emotional and physical development. The work is care work which is both a practical and a cognitive process; through mutual interests, empathetic relationships developed which were physical, cognitive, social and emotional in nature. Try to find similar examples in your own experience which demonstrate the links among the different strands of development.

Work is one of the many sources of self-esteem in the individual and one way in which individuals identify themselves. If someone is asked to describe him/herself, the kind of work done is usually one of the ways in which the individual wishes to be known and seen. In the short case studies at the beginning of this chapter and the longer ones at the end of the book you will see that Alex's role as a journalist is very important to him, Alistair is an engineer, Fiona was a teacher, Senga is a care assistant, Hassan is an accountant and Aisha works for a voluntary organisation. All of these work roles are bound up with other aspects of the individual's emotional life to promote self-esteem and form identity. Self-esteem and identity are part of emotional development. Work, though, is also a social role and can be a source of friendship and partnership. In this sense it is also part of social development.

Work is usually a term used to refer to paid employment, but many people do work for which they receive neither pay nor recognition. Anne Redpath, a Scottish artist born in

Galashiels, makes the point that for many years she devoted herself to her family and her home, rather than to painting, and that this was just as relevant as any other kind of work. She says:

> I put everything I had into house and furniture and dresses and good food and people. All that's the same as painting really, and the experience went back into art when I began painting again.

(Long, 1996)

This passage shows that here can be links between paid work and the work of being at home, and that the one has great relevance for the other. The experience of running a household and bringing up children does go back into and enrich later work experience, yet it is so often undervalued by employers.

Activity

Re-read the sections on physical, cognitive and emotional development and select those factors which are also part of social development. Write a sentence for each one which illustrates the social aspects.

You may, for example, have mentioned parenthood. This provides the social roles of mother and father, it creates social as well as emotional bonds between parents and their children. Parenthood also provides networks with other parents through meeting at such places as playgroups, health centres and schools. It is often a source of change in social relationships and roles. You can now analyse other examples in the same way.

THE OLDER ADULT

Age is opportunity no less
Than youth itself, though in another dress.

(Longfellow, Morituri Salutamus, quoted in Slater, R. 1995)

In this section a conscious effort is made to get away from the 'all doom and gloom' view of old age. Many older people, even those with illnesses and disabilities, do lead rich and fruitful lives. A class of care students was asked whom they thought were good examples of famous older adults. Here are their suggestions: Sean Connery, the Queen Mother, Jimmy Savile, Dot Cotton, Nelson Mandela, Omar Sharif, Richard Wilson and Clint Eastwood. Their teachers added Paul Newman, the Pope, Shirley Bassey, Michael Parkinson, Henry Kissinger and Thora Hird, who is still acting at the age of 87. You can probably think of other examples of older people who are active and content in old age. More opportunities are available than ever for older people to learn, to participate in exercise, to live in better health. Relative poverty is, unfortunately, still a problem for many and efforts need to be made to maximise benefit uptake, for example, and to

PHYSICAL	INTELLECTUAL/ COGNITIVE	EMOTIONAL	SOCIAL
How the body changes	How sense is made of the world	Developing sense of identity	Relationships
• importance of cognitive, emotional and social factors	• different choices and opportunities	• influences of work, partnership, friends, parenthood	• intimate relationships/partnerships
• peak fitness in young adulthood	• often improving level of ability in young and mid years	• transitions, crises and achievements	• roles and changes in role
• pregnancy, childbirth and menopause	• applying knowledge to work, parenthood, and other life situations	• positive or negative adjustment	• social networks
• relationship between lifestyle and health		• importance of support	• effects of poverty and discrimination
• often loss of speed/increase in bulk		• roles and identity	
• increase in stamina		• relationships of intimacy	

Figure 3.9 Summary of general pattern of development: Adulthood

ensure that those who are young adults now, make adequate financial provision for when they are old.

Physical development

Anthony Quinn's lust for life results in 11th child at age of 78.

(Sharrock, 1993)

When you first look at old age the evidence does seem somewhat negative: hearing, vision and balance do tend to deteriorate, speed of movement decreases, skin loses elasticity and is more likely to wrinkle, there is usually some hair loss and hair pigment loss so that most 'old people' have grey or white hair. The major organs of the body do deteriorate, but much more slowly than you probably think. This is all balanced to some extent by fewer physical demands. The physical effects of aging can be affected by exercise, attitude and nutrition as well as inherited genetic characteristics and other environmental influences. When you actually look at older adults the variation is enormous. One person of 80 may be confined to a wheelchair or able only to walk very short distances with a zimmer; she may have a multitude of minor ailments; another will be cycling to play cards with her friends and ploughing up and down the lanes at the swimming pool three times a week. He or she may have several minor ailments but when asked about his or her health will say I'm fine . . . and mean it. There are those still having a reasonably active sex life into their seventies and eighties. The example of Anthony Quinn above is a prime example. Others are more content to enjoy one another's company and are quite relieved that sexual pressure is diminished in their relationships.

On the positive side, then, gains in health, nutrition and hygiene in recent years mean that fewer people are dying prematurely and that those who do survive into their eighties are generally healthier than they would have been ten years ago. People are living longer, in general, with 50 per cent more people over 85 in 1991 than in 1981. In 1997 20 per cent of the residents of Scotland were over 60 (HMSO, 1998). A large majority of these people are able to live rich, full lives with health which is at least moderately good. The negative view of old age results not from the effects of **primary** aging, which is slow and gradual, but from the results of **secondary** aging resulting from disease, lack of exercise and such pursuits as excessive drinking and smoking. People who continue to be fit and active can usually expect to reap the benefits in a healthier old age.

Cognitive/intellectual development

Slowing down is generally regarded as one of the features of the cognitive state of older adults. This is different from deterioration for which there is scant evidence except in people experiencing specific illnesses such as Alzheimer's disease.

Here's an example quoted by Slater (1995):

I am a 73 year-old 'wrinkly' who, determined not to become a cabbage after retirement, took up the piano at the age of 70. So far I have obtained Grades 1 and 2 . . . Three days a week I work for an international trading company. My shorthand is still 120 plus and touch typing is second nature to me. I would like to take up other things but time is too demanding at present . . .

Longitudinal studies (which study the same people over a period of time) show little, if any, drop in mental ability with age (Schaie, 1988). Although there is some slowing down in the rate at which people **process** information and some decline in tasks which need speed, 'there is no sizable decline in **memory, knowledge or the ability to learn**'. It is interesting that on a test of 'obscure knowledge' older adults actually did better than younger ones. Do you know what 'deliticulate' means or for what the Greek writer Antigorus was noted. Older people (over 65) scored higher on such items than younger persons (Slater, 1995).

Evidence from studies of older adults on adult learning courses (e.g. those run by the Open University or that wonderful institution, the University of the Third Age which now has 38 000 students in the UK) illustrate that although older people may be slower, they have more time to grasp things, persevere more than younger learners and bring wisdom and experience of life which compensates for a lack of speed (Slater, 1995). Birren and Fisher (1992) indicated a link between physical health, exercise and cognitive ability concluding that exercise may help to ameliorate some of the slowing down in responses related to age. 'Mastermind', that long-lived test of knowledge on the TV was the subject of a study by Maylor (1994) who found that aging didn't seem to affect performance at all on the 'specialised subject' round and that older masterminds did *better* on general knowledge.

While there are many adults who do show a decline in cognitive functioning in later life, as with physical aging there are enormous variations often related to such **secondary** causes as disease, lack of exercise and high alcohol consumption. In general, although there is a decline in the **speed** at which intellectual tasks can be performed there is stability in solving the problems of everyday life and in knowledge and verbal comprehension.

Emotional development

There is an emotional roller coaster in older age: down for bereavement and loss, up for becoming a grandparent; down for retirement for some, up for retirement for others; down with more bereavement and loss, up for a sense of contentment; down when ill health occurs, up if health is maintained; down when friends are lost, up when new friends and activities are gained; down for dependence, up for independence. Some of the losses of old age can have profound effects of either a short- or long-term nature. Loss and bereavement are fully considered in Chapter 4 and are not therefore mentioned here. One major transition of old age which has both emotional and social consequences is that of retirement. For many people a part of self-image and identity is their paid or unpaid work. Paid work usually ceases at around 60 to 65 and this, for some people, results in a loss of both status and self esteem. This is to some extent a reflection of negative attitudes of society to retired people, but there can be compensations. Some people see this not as a loss but as an opportunity.

> **CASE STUDY**
> Alistair has been employed all of his working life in a brewery but what he had always really wanted to do was to have a beautiful garden. He had always kept his

fairly large garden neat and tidy but had never been able to devote much time to it. When he retired he was able to pursue his lifelong passion for plants. He bought a greenhouse, grew some unusual varieties of plant from seed and entered horticultural competitions. He was so successful that within a year of retirement he exhibited some begonia plants in a competition, gaining first prize.

A less positive reaction to retirement is quoted in Rayner (1986).

Mrs F went on working in a pub until she was over 70, when she slipped and bruised herself one day. She lost her job through being off sick. She recovered quite quickly but never went back to work . . . she slowly became quiet and apathetic . . . She usually shuffled about the house in boots and several layers of clothing.

Activity

Research reactions to retirement among four older people whom you know or are able to talk to. Write a short account of their response in terms of positive and negative consequences for their emotional lives, including self esteem and self-concept.

In **care settings** it is most important that the way in which care is provided maintains or enhances self esteem as far as possible. This means promoting empowerment and independence and minimising possible effects of institutionalisation which can lead to what Goffman (1968) called 'mortification of self' (see page 213) and a state of learned helplessness. Learned helplessness is a **decline** in the desire and ability to do things beyond what may be expected in relation to a person's state of health. It usually occurs among people who 'give up' because other people won't let them do things or exercise any control over their own lives.

The emotional situation of older people from ethnic minorities deserve some special attention. Most people of Asian and Caribbean ancestry place a very high value upon the care of their older people. If they have few or no supports, however (Fenton, 1987, illustrated this in relation to research in Bristol) this can result in shame, loss and depression. Emotional problems may be compounded by isolation, poverty, racism and discrimination. Building positive self esteem among this population can be a vital part of the care task.

To end on positive notes, for many older adults, grandchildren can be a source of great joy and emotional satisfaction. Grandchildren come without many of the financial and emotional stresses of parenthood. Grandparents can enjoy their company and care in time-limited amounts, though they still need to work to create positive and fulfilling relationships. Slater (1995) writes about Mrs Patel who loves the noise and laughter her grandchildren bring. Old age presents a sense of freedom for some older adults. Marjorie Dickens appears to have a great deal of emotional satisfaction in her present state:

I like it that I can do as I please, go where I want, and if I can afford it, buy what I want to, and eat what I want.

(Slater, 1995)

Ford and Sinclair (1987) researched what women were seeking from old age and they used phrases such as 'having some pleasure, peace, meeting people, enjoyment, pleasing myself, not having to fight.'

Social development

The fifties are probably the low point for social activity but by the sixties off we go again: for some this is a time of rejuvenation, increased social contacts, more friends and **time** to pursue social activities. Friendship plays a major part in the lives of many older adults. Ishii-Kuntz (1990) found that

... 'older people's satisfaction with life has little relationship with the quantity or quality of their contact with the younger members of their own family, but shows a strong correlation to the quantity and quality of their interaction with friends.

The functions of friendship in later life can be summed up through the three As: aid, affect and affirmation. Friends give and receive help, provide love and affirm people's self concepts. This demonstrates a link between emotional and social well-being.

The initial average increase in social contacts tends to diminish in older adulthood as contact with friends can be lost through death and ill-health. Unless an older adult or others such as care workers and family members make a conscious effort to maintain outside links, isolation can result, which for many is a very depressing experience. Some isolation is aggravated by the restrictions placed upon elderly people by low income, though facilitating claims for appropriate benefit entitlements can go some way towards alleviating this. Empowerment can sometimes only be gained through access to cash.

Here is an example from Slater (1995) which relates to the social lives of some older adults:

Police had to be called to Highwood Court old people's social club ... after neighbours complained about the noise coming from a Karaoke session.

Mrs Harman now prefers the company of people her own age who can talk about the same things ...

Other older adults may enjoy attendance at the community centre, going line dancing, step and tone classes, working in an allotment or going to the library. Heim's (1990) research indicated that though physical confidence decreases with age **social** confidence increases.

Bee and Mitchell (1984) sum up social development as follows. From ages 65 to 75:

PHYSICAL	INTELLECTUAL/ COGNITIVE	EMOTIONAL	SOCIAL
How the body changes	How sense is made of the world	Developing sense of self	Relationships
• usually gradual loss of abilities	• wisdom and experience	• identity issues often related to changing roles	• friends, family and social networks or isolation
• importance of exercise/diet	• may be slower to grasp new things	• transition and loss e.g. bereavement	• changing roles e.g. due to retirement
• enormous variation	• linked with health	• influence of isolation, discrimination, poverty	• social confidence
	• may be short-term memory loss		

Figure 3.10 Summary of general pattern of development: Older adulthood

Usually a maintenance of social contacts, particularly with family. Friends are important here especially for maintaining life satisfaction. Little evidence of any withdrawal or disengagement. Retirement, which occurs during this time for most adults, appears to cause relatively little trauma for most.

From age 75 on:

There appears to be some social disengagement, at least for some older adults, during this period, although most elderly adults continue to see their children and other family members with some regularity and spend time with friends.

SUMMARY

This chapter has encouraged you to look at development as a process which continues throughout life. You should by now understand the meaning of behaviour and development of the physical, intellectual/cognitive, emotional and social strands of which they are constituted. The influences upon development and behaviour have been considered and throughout this chapter you have been encouraged to apply your learning to case study situations. The following areas have been covered in this chapter:

- the meaning of development and behaviour;
- the strands of development and behaviour (physical, intellectual/cognitive, emotional and social);
- influences, including socialisation;
- the nature/nurture debate;
- development at different stages and ages from 0–2 to older adult;
- case studies which encourage you to apply your thinking.

The following activities, in common with all activities in this chapter, are at Intermediate II level.

Activity

Read the accounts below and then answer the questions which follow them. The people referred to are described in the case study in Chapter 10 (the MacDonalds and the Ahmeds).

- Linda MacDonald, aged thirteen, is having a week of respite care at 'M' unit near to her home. She is about to go on an outing with the other young people in the unit. She gets very upset when you try to put her red coat on her and insists that she wants her blue one. The blue one is very thin and it is quite a cold day.

- Nabeil Ahmed, aged eleven, is attending a day care centre during the summer. He loves the company of the other children and always gets very upset when it is time to go home.

- Alistair, aged fourteen, Maureen's son, is in a children's unit and has tried to run away on several occasions.

- Hassan and Afzal's mother, aged 74, has recently been very confused and is in a nursing home for a temporary period to give the family a rest from her care.

Choose two of the above situations and answer the following questions in relation to each one:

1. State three physical factors which you would expect to be part of normal development for a person of this age.

2. State two physical factors which may affect development for **these** people.

3. How may the physical factors identified in question 2 affect: i) emotional development – give two effects; ii) social development – give two effects.

4. State three cognitive factors which you would take into account if you were working with these service users.

5. Give two ways in which cognitive factors would affect the way you work.

6. Draw two columns for each service user and in each column make the headings physical, intellectual/cognitive, emotional and social. In the left-hand column give two features of 'normal' development for a person of this age, for each strand, and in the right-hand column give features of development for each service user (they may be the same, or different from, the norm).

7. Identify four influences upon the development and behaviour of each service user and state how you think each of these influences may affect two strands of development.

SELECTED BIBLIOGRAPHY

Bee, H.L. and Mitchell, S.K. (1984). *The Developing Person: A Life-Span Approach*. 2nd edn. New York: Harper and Row.
An interesting and entertaining guidebook to human development which has relevance both to this chapter and Chapter 4.

Rayner, E. (1986). *Human Development*. 3rd edn. London: Unwin Hyman.
Provides a very readable introduction to human development written by a psychoanalyst.

Sheridan, M.D. (1997) *From Birth to Five Years*. London: Routledge.
Designed as a source of information and reference for all who wish to increase their knowledge of the developmental progress of infants and young children.

Slater, R. (1995). *The Psychology of Growing Old*. Buckingham: Open University Press.
A very positive book about the challenge of later life.

CHAPTER 4

The contribution of developmental psychology and its applications

Doris Graham

Life can only be understood backwards; but it must be lived forwards.

(Kirkegaard, in Peter, 1982)

INTRODUCTION

This chapter will look at explanations of how people develop and change over time. You already have some understanding of the many factors which influence human development and behaviour from the previous chapter. It will now be useful to look at a range of explanations which belong to a branch of psychology known as developmental psychology. By so doing you will come to understand more fully the process of human development and behaviour. This understanding will allow you to offer a more effective approach to caring for others.

The chapter covers human development and behaviour at Higher level, Outcome 1. It also has relevance to Outcome 3.

By the end of this chapter you should be able to answer the following questions:

- What is developmental psychology?
- How does it help us to understand service users?
- What needs do people have?
- When does development occur?
- How do we learn to behave?
- How do people form attachment to others?
- Why is self-awareness important?
- How do changes and losses affect individuals?

Psychology is the scientific study of individuals. It is concerned with their behaviour and how their minds work. Human beings are very complex and psychologists have tended to study them from a range of angles to try to make a complete picture of them. This has created different branches of psychology which have different areas of interest. Although these branches are separate areas of study, they do overlap and together they seek to provide a comprehensive explanation of the individual.

Figure 4.1 below sets out the main branches of psychology and briefly explains the area of

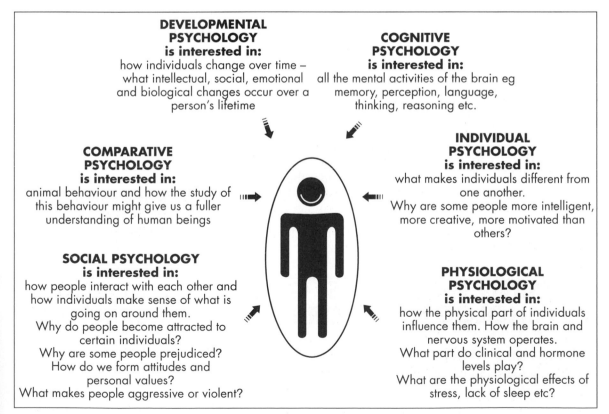

DEVELOPMENTAL PSYCHOLOGY is interested in:
how individuals change over time – what intellectual, social, emotional and biological changes occur over a person's lifetime

COGNITIVE PSYCHOLOGY is interested in:
all the mental activities of the brain eg memory, perception, language, thinking, reasoning etc.

COMPARATIVE PSYCHOLOGY is interested in:
animal behaviour and how the study of this behaviour might give us a fuller understanding of human beings

INDIVIDUAL PSYCHOLOGY is interested in:
what makes individuals different from one another.
Why are some people more intelligent, more creative, more motivated than others?

SOCIAL PSYCHOLOGY is interested in:
how people interact with each other and how individuals make sense of what is going on around them.
Why do people become attracted to certain individuals?
Why are some people prejudiced?
How do we form attitudes and personal values?
What makes people aggressive or violent?

PHYSIOLOGICAL PSYCHOLOGY is interested in:
how the physical part of individuals influence them. How the brain and nervous system operates.
What part do clinical and hormone levels play?
What are the physiological effects of stress, lack of sleep etc?

Figure 4.1 The main branches of psychology

study in which it is interested. As you can see, psychologists are interested in a wide variety of areas of study.

Developmental psychology is concerned with the study of how individuals develop biologically, intellectually, socially and emotionally over the period of their life. As you have learned in the previous chapter, people develop as a result of an *interaction* of factors – the genes they inherit and the environment in which they are brought up. This is known as the nature/nurture debate. Developmental psychology is concerned with the examination of this interaction of factors and how it affects the development and behaviour of individuals.

Activity

Can you think of someone you have known for a number of years? Under four headings – biological, intellectual, social and emotional – can you record how that person has changed over a period of time. You can choose a person from any age group – child, teenager, adult or older adult or you could even choose yourself!

You are no doubt aware that a variety of changes do take place in all individuals. All individuals experience a process of change as they progress through life. Developmental psychology seeks to understand this process and explain why people develop and behave in the way they do. By learning different explanations of this process, you will be able to apply this knowledge to help you understand more fully the people for whom you care. It will help you in the assessment process to understand more fully why service users have developed in the way they have and help to explain their behaviour. This approach to assessment should encourage more effective care planning, helping processes and evaluation.

How can you use developmental psychology to help explain human development and behaviour? It may be perhaps useful to consider the ways of explaining human development and behaviour as 'tools' in a tool box. You will not use *all* the tools every time we want to understand or assess a client. Rather, you will choose one or perhaps several of the tools to help you understand your service users – their past experiences, changes in their lives or their behaviour now or in the past.

USING THE 'TOOLS' OF DEVELOPMENTAL PSYCHOLOGY – THEORIES AND PERSPECTIVES

Developmental psychology has two main types of 'tools' which should help you to understand people – theories and perspectives.

Theories are ways of explaining how people develop and why they behave in certain ways. No one theory offers the complete answer to explaining human development. This is because they do not concentrate on exactly the same issues. Sometimes you can use two or more theories together to gain a better understanding. These theories are based on research. The research can take many forms: observation, surveys, questionnaires, interviewing, experiments, case studies and secondary sources such as journals, newspapers and Government reports. (This will be covered in more detail in Chapter 9.)

Theories can be challenged or disproved because of their research methods, lack of evidence or because new data or information comes to light. Theories may therefore fall from grace and new ones become accepted.

Not so with perspectives! Perspectives are *not* based on evidence, they cannot be disproved by new findings. Perspectives are ways of seeing people, ways of understanding why they behave in certain ways, ways of understanding why they develop in the way they do. They are areas of thought based on assumptions about human beings.

Unlike theories, perspectives cannot be used in conjunction with each other. They are separate views of human behaviour and development. They are in themselves another group of tools which you can utilise.

Carers must learn from each of these perspectives and guard against a selective approach to service users. It is important to realise that there are different assumptions about the explanation of human development and behaviour.

An understanding of different perspectives combined with an understanding of different theories should help you to understand more fully service users. There are several perspectives prevalent in psychology. Detailed below are four, each of which have a different view of human development.

Psychodynamic perspective
This perspective was originated by Sigmund Freud (1856–1939). Put simply, psychodynamic means energy or forces of the mind. The underlying assumption of this perspective suggests that the way a person thinks and behaves is determined by experiences they had in their early years. Emotional disturbance is caused by unresolved conflicts stemming from childhood. During these childhood experiences, energy or drives are created which motivate people to behave in certain ways throughout their lives. Behaviour, therefore, is largely seen as being determined by past experiences.

Humanistic perspective
This perspective is based on a positive view of human development and is associated with the work of Carl Rogers (1902–1987) and Abraham Maslow (1908–1970). It regards both past and present as having equal importance. It assumes that all human beings are unique, rational and self-determining, and that they continuously strive to grow and develop. It sees human beings as having an inherent need to develop their potential to the full. Emotional disturbance happens because individuals are not allowed to 'be themselves'. In an attempt to be accepted by others,

individuals suppress their own true nature and make choices not to please themselves but to please others.

Lifespan perspective

As its name suggests this perspective sees development as a life-long process. It starts from the time the baby is developing within the womb and finishes at the point of death. Biological, intellectual, social and emotional changes continue to occur throughout a person's life and are not confined to childhood or adolescence. One of the first theorists to construct a theory from this perspective was Erik Erikson (1902–1994) who described the 'Eight Ages of Man' in which each stage of life offers a new development task to be achieved.

Behavioural perspective

The behavioural perspective explains human development in terms of what a person has learned. Whilst it recognises that human social experiences are complex, this perspective sees development as a process of learning from a wide range of experiences – interaction with family, friends, partners, work colleagues, making decisions and choices, holding values and attitudes and thoughts about yourself. These are all formed through a process of learning. Two exponents of this view are the theorists B.F. Skinner (1902–1990) and A. Bandura (1925–).

These perspectives offer different views of human development. Used in conjunction with some psychological theories, they will provide a body of knowledge which will help you with your work.

Some theories which try to explain how people develop are now examined. It is important to remember that individual theories do not explain everything about human development and behaviour. Each theory tries to explain a particular aspect of its subject. It does not cover everything and its explanations will have strengths and weaknesses.

MASLOW'S HIERARCHY OF NEEDS

One of the main ways in which developmental psychology can help you in your work with service users is in the process of care planning (see Chapter 7). The assessment of needs with the service

Activity

Make a list of human needs. Try not to focus on material possessions such as TVs, videos, computer games, cars etc. Try to consider needs which are common to humans throughout the world.

How many items did you have on your list? 5, 10, 50? Did you list your items in order of priority?

user represents one of the major components in the care planning and helping process. All human beings have needs. All service users have needs. But how do you know what these needs are?

As early as 1954, Abraham Maslow put forward the idea that human beings have a number of complex needs. Coming from a humanistic perspective, Maslow believed that all of us constantly strive towards fulfilling these needs. Maslow formulated the idea that needs are not always equally important. Rather that some are more important than others at a given time.

He believed that human beings are motivated by two systems of needs – deficiency needs and growth needs. The basic needs are termed deficiency, because when they are not satisfied individuals engage in behaviours designed to remedy this lack of satisfaction. For example, hunger represents a deficiency that can be satisfied by eating. The growth needs are termed growth needs because activities that relate to them do not fulfil a lack but lead towards growth.

According to Maslow needs are organised as a hierarchy – that is, they can only be satisfied if the one below has already been achieved.

As you can see from Maslow's Hierarchy of Needs in Figure 4.2 on page 138, the needs at the base are the needs which are necessary to sustain life itself – food, water, rest, shelter and security. It is towards these needs that a person's energy or motivation will be directed as a means of survival and security. Only when these basic needs are satisfied will a person become focused on the next level of needs – social/emotional. As these needs are met, the person moves up the pyramid towards the highest point of self-actualisation. This is quite a difficult concept (or idea) to grasp. It refers to the potential within all individuals for personal growth – to be the person you want to be, to make full use of your talents and capabilities. Maslow believed that all human beings are born with an innate tendency to strive towards self-actualisation – that is, they are motivated towards reaching their full potential.

The satisfaction associated with self-actualisation comes from within the person rather than without. In contrast, satisfaction of lower order needs, such as self esteem is associated with external sources of reinforcement (approval and recognition).

Maslow himself only found one person he considered to be actualised, in a study he carried out among 3000 college students. It is probably more useful therefore to consider self-actualisation as a process that guides a person towards growth rather than a state that can be attained.

Those who fail to move towards self-actualisation do so because of circumstances in which they find themselves, e.g. people living in an area of famine or war. Other circumstances may cause an individual not to reach self-actualisation such as being in the middle of a divorce, losing your job, having relationship problems with your family or living in a poor area and being unable to afford to buy things or take part in leisure or recreational facilities. These circumstances and many others will act against the individual being able to move towards the top of the pyramid, towards self-actualisation.

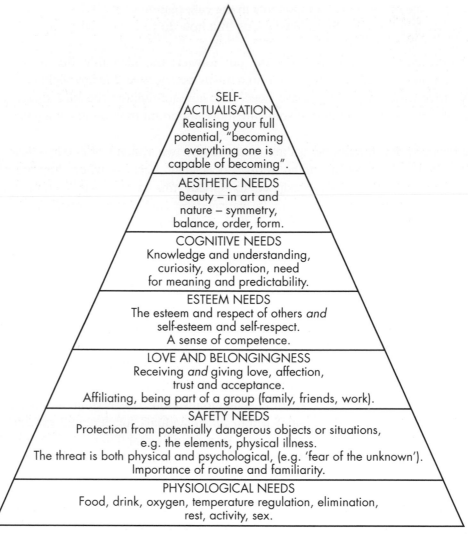

Figure 4.2 Maslow's Hierarchy of Needs (based on Mastow, 1954)

CASE STUDY

Ampin is an 84 year-old woman who has been in residential care since her husband died a year ago. Her health is relatively good and she eats and sleeps well. She has her own room which has many items from her previous house – chair, photographs, clothes, ornaments and a TV.

Ampin's only daughter moved away six months ago when her husband's job was relocated to Canada. She writes to her mother once a month and plans to visit her at Christmas time.

> The staff in the home are very caring towards Ampin. They are concerned however that Ampin has not made any friends in the home and tends to sit in her room or on her own in the lounge.
>
> How does Maslow's theory help you to understand Ampin's needs?

Using Maslow's Hierarchy of Needs as a guide, it would appear that Ampin's physiological needs are being met – she has food, warmth, shelter and rest. It would also appear that her safety needs are being met – she feels safe, secure and out of danger. Her room contains mementoes and familiar objects from her own home. There are things she knows, things which evoke fond memories and which in themselves make her feel secure.

However it seems evident that Ampin's needs of love and belongingness are not being met. She is obviously missing her daughter and has not made any friends in the home. Since these needs are lacking, Ampin cannot progress towards self-actualisation.

It is towards the love and belongingness part of Maslow's Hierarchy of Needs that Ampin, with the help of the staff, may now want to focus. If Ampin wishes this will become part of her assessment and the helping process should work towards meeting these needs and help her progress towards the peak of the pyramid – self-actualisation.

Maslow's Hierarchy of Needs is a useful 'tool' to help us understand the needs of service users. It can safely be used as a rough guide to what *most* people do in *most* situations, but it does not offer a complete explanation of all human motivation. Can you identify any weaknesses in Maslow's theory?

Probably the major flaw in the theory is the idea that lower needs have to be satisfied first before higher needs become important. Some people, for example workaholics, will often neglect their personal needs such as food and sleep in their pursuit to complete a work project. Others will live without work and in poverty rather than leave their partner and children to go to look for work in another part of the country.

Nevertheless, it remains a model which sees individuals in a positive light. The humanistic perspective from which it derives encourages a view of service users which demands that they are seen as individuals who are all striving to meet their basic and growth needs. Effective assessment and care planning should be designed to help them to achieve this.

LIFE SPAN THEORY

For much of this century developmental psychology focused on the changes which occurred during childhood and the effect this had on a person's later life. Freud in particular was interested in conflicts which happened in the first five years of life.

However, as the century progressed, influences from the humanistic school of thought which emphasised the continual and positive growth and development of individuals, encouraged psychologists to consider the importance of what is known as life span psychology. This is based on the idea that people develop throughout their lives, from the moment of birth (and even before as they grow in the womb) to the moment they die.

One of the foremost theorists to consider life-long development was Erik Erikson. He was influenced by the work of Sigmund Freud and like him agreed that individuals face a number of conflicts which must be resolved if they are to develop a healthy personality. Erikson differed from Freud in that he believed development took place throughout a person's entire life and the conflicts which they encounter are concerned with the individual's relationships with others in society. His theory is known as a psychosocial theory of development.

Underlying the whole notion of life span theory is the assumption that an individual's development needs to be seen within the social context in which they live – family, partners, friends, school, college, work. Within the social context, the individual relates to many people in many different ways and in so doing develops socially, emotionally and intellectually. Life span theorists are also aware that the socio-cultural context will affect how people develop. This may involve factors such as the person's social class, the political regime in which they live as well as the cultural expectations of their society. Erikson thought that an individual would develop a healthy personality if they were able to resolve basic psychological conflicts which they met at different stages of their lives. He identified what he called the 'Eight Ages of Man' (1968): 4 in childhood; 1 in adolescence; 3 in adulthood.

Each stage is given a name which represents two opposing outcomes – one positive and one negative. Resolution of each stage does not result in one or the other being achieved. Rather, Erikson saw the individual as having a mixture of, for example Trust or Mistrust. However he saw healthy developments as having more Trust than Mistrust, a demonstration that this conflict had been successfully resolved. He also believed that it was possible to make up for unsatisfactory experiences at a later stage (although it was harder to do so). Conversely positive early experiences of, for example, trust could be shattered at a later stage.

Figure 4.3 outlines the main stages and the conflict which has to be resolved.

Erikson's theory is not without limitations. His 'Eight Ages of Man' were meant to be universal, that is, they were meant to apply equally to men and women and to different cultures. Clearly it is very difficult to achieve a theory which is able to do this. However, the significant

EARLY INFANCY	
Trust versus Mistrust	To gain a balance between trusting people and risking being let down or being suspicious and mistrustful and therefore being unable to relate to others fully.

LATER INFANCY	
Antonomy versus Shame and Doubt	To develop a sense of personal agency and control over behaviour and actions, or to mistrust one's personal abilities and anticipate failures.

EARLY CHILDHOOD	
Initiative versus Guilt	To develop an increasing sense of personal responsibility and initiative, or to develop increased feelings of guilt and doubt.

MIDDLE CHILDHOOD	
Industry versus Inferiority	To learn to overcome challenges through systematic effort or, to accept failure and avoid challenges, leading to an increasing sense of inferiority.

PUBERTY AND ADOLESCENCE	
Identity versus role confusion	To develop a consistent sense of personal identity faced with the changes in social role and expectations of adolescence, or simply to become overwhelmed by choices and expectations and to fail to develop a sense of consistent inner self.

YOUNG ADULTHOOD	
Intimacy versus isolation	To develop intimate and trusting relationships with others, or to avoid relationships as threatening and painful.

MATURE ADULTHOOD	
Generativity versus stagnation	To develop a productive and positive life incorporating recognition of personal achievements, or to stagnate and fail to grow psychologically.

LATE ADULTHOOD	
Integrity versus despair	To become able to look back on one's life in a positive fashion and to evaluate one's achievement, or to feel that life has been meaningless and futile.

Adapted from Erikson (1968), in Hayes (1994)

Figure 4.3 Main stages and conflicts

feature of his theory is the assumption that all individuals continue to develop throughout their lives.

Can you think how Erikson's theory could help you work more effectively with a service user?

Perhaps you might be able to understand why service users are very under-confident and will not take any responsibility for their actions. Perhaps you can see why they will not take part in any new activities, meet new people or establish relationships. Perhaps you can understand more fully why they may look back on their lives and feel that it has all been meaningless. Erikson's theory goes some way to offer an explanation and it also helps you to understand that the service users for whom you care are people who have been through a process of development and are continuing to develop.

BEHAVIOURAL THEORY

Behaviourism (a perspective) explains human behaviour as a process of learning. One of the foremost theories was developed by B.F. Skinner who invented the term 'operant conditioning'. His systematic research led him to believe that behaviour which produces the desired results for the individual will be repeated. These behaviours which 'work' are called operants (or reinforcers) and it is these operants which cause the individual to repeat the behaviour. Skinner believed that the individual does not actually decide to behave in a particular way, they do not plan or make individual choices about their behaviour. They are controlled by the *outcomes* of their behaviour. If the outcome of behaviour in the past has been effective (if it has been reinforced) then this behaviour will be repeated. Reinforcement actually encourages the behaviour to be continued or repeated.

> **CASE STUDY**
>
> Josh is a 34 year-old man with learning disabilities who attends a day centre near his home in Motherwell. At 10.30 a.m. the tea bar is opened for the morning break. The centre is a very busy place and the queue is very long. Every morning as he stands in the queue Josh becomes very agitated. He begins to shout and swear and becomes abusive to anyone who is standing beside him. His carers are concerned that he will hurt someone so they take him to the front of the queue. Having chosen his cake and drink Josh sits quietly at his table with his friends until it is time to return to the activity room. His carers have tried to stand beside Josh in the queue but have decided that he does not like queues and it is easier to get him served first.

Activity

Can you describe what is happening here. Why does Josh continue to behave in this way? Perhaps you have said that Josh's agitated behaviour gets him what he wants. He has learned that his behaviour is 'reinforced'.

If you now have some understanding of why Josh is behaving in this way, the obvious question is to ask what his carers should do? Should they ignore Josh's behaviour? Skinner's extensive experimental research into operant conditioning suggests that ignoring his behaviour may only lead to Josh displaying even more challenging behaviour.

What about restraining or punishing Josh? The carers could make him stay in the activity room until all the people in the queue had been served. Or they could tell him that if he 'misbehaves' again he will not be allowed to go on the group outing to the bowling alley. Do you think this will help?

Skinner was very clear about this and stated that while unpleasant experiences *might* stop a particular behaviour at the time, it does not mean that future behaviour will be affected. Josh might experiment with different behaviour – screaming, kicking, lying down on the floor – the list is endless! So what is the answer? The answer, according to Skinner, lies in understanding how reinforcement is working in the present situation, to examine that reinforcement and look for alternative ones.

Perhaps Josh's carers could start by placing him near the very front of the queue, spend time with him, talk to him and use effective communication skills to keep him calm. Gradually they could encourage him to stand further back in the queue. They could tell him how good his behaviour is, praise him for his patience while standing in the queue and make him feel good about achieving this new behaviour. According to Skinner, Josh will have learned a new piece of behaviour which has been reinforced and this behaviour will be repeated in the future.

Behaviourism helps you to understand behaviour. By analysing behaviour you may be able to understand the causes and outcomes of certain situations. Looking for patterns in the behaviour is one way of trying to understand it. Three questions may shed light on this.

1. What happens before the behaviour?   ANTECEDENTS   (A)
2. What is the behaviour like?   BEHAVIOUR   (B)
3. What happens after the behaviour?   CONSEQUENCES   (C)

This is called the ABC approach.

Let's look at Joshs' behaviour and see if the ABC approach helps you to understand it.

A   Josh stands in the queue;

B Josh swears and shouts;

C Josh gets taken to the front of the queue to choose his cake and drink.

The reinforcement for such behaviour is that he gets his drink and cake quickly. It is important to analyse this a little further by looking more closely at the antecedent. Why does Josh behave this way in the queue at the morning tea break? Is it really because he does not like queues? Or is there another reason?

One of the care workers has a chat with Josh's mum who explains that Josh gets up very early, normally at 6 am. He hates to eat early in the morning and goes out to the centre every morning with an empty stomach. By 10.30 am. he is really hungry and is desperate to get something to eat. He has learned that his 'challenging behaviour' gets him access to food very quickly – it works every time. According to Skinner, Josh does not set out to behave in this way, he does not plan it. It happens because the operants or reinforcers have encouraged a particular pattern of behaviour.

It would seem that an analysis of Josh's behaviour, using a behaviourist approach, might help the carers to work more effectively with him. Perhaps a cup of tea and toast when he arrives at the centre in the morning combined with reinforcement to encourage a new behaviour in the queue might help Josh to learn new operants.

Behaviourism and its theories suggest that the individual's behaviour is the result of conditioning – people do things because they have been conditioned to do them. They have not planned the behaviour, there is no reason or thought process attached to the behaviour. It happens because they have learned to behave in this way because past reinforcement has encouraged them to it.

For *some* of their behaviour this may in fact be the case. *Some* of their behaviour is carried out without deep intellectual or emotional reasoning. It just seems to be the 'best way' to behave at the time.

While this approach does offer a 'tool' of understanding behaviour, in practice it has a more limited application. There are two reasons for this. Firstly, it fails to acknowledge that behaviour can be guided and directed by reason, emotion and planning and secondly it does not take account of the value base of care which promotes the rights and choices of service users. There is a danger that carers may exercise power over service users to make them behave in ways which are acceptable to the carer or to the establishment. This may result in the service user being denied the right to make choices.

SOCIAL LEARNING THEORY

It is therefore useful to examine an additional theory which might act as an extra 'tool' to help understand behaviour. This is known as 'social learning theory' (sometimes referred to as social behaviourism). One of the foremost theorists in this field is A. Bandura.

Bandura agreed with Skinner to some degree with the role of reinforcement in determining behaviour, but his research indicated that the process of learning was much more complex than Skinner had detailed. He did not believe that development and behaviour could be explained in terms of conditioning processes alone. He believed that thought processes allow the individual to interpret the consequences of their behaviour. The interpretation of these consequences exerts its influence forward to future behaviour by giving the individual information about what effects can be expected if they behave that way in a similar situation.

In particular, Bandura and other social learning theorists believe that a person's development and behaviour is the result of social interaction with others. Social interaction starts a few minutes after a baby is born and continues throughout a person's life. It involves the process of socialisation, which is discussed in Chapter 3. It is the process whereby a person learns to conform to the norms of society and to act in ways that are considered acceptable. It is therefore a helpful tool in understanding the different social expectations and practices of different cultures and the effects these can have on the development and behaviour of individuals.

Social learning theory in general highlights three main ways in which socialisation is encouraged:
1. imitation and identification;
2. punishments and rewards;
3. social expectations.

Imitation and identification

From children's earliest stages they will observe the behaviour of others and copy or imitate it. This allows the child to learn a range of physical skills very quickly and efficiently and they will often incorporate this learning into their play activities. Small children love to 'play' at being a grown up. They will play at being mummies and daddies, doctors and teachers, soldiers and fire-fighters.

Imitation can be a powerful influence on behaviour as shown by some studies carried out by Bandura et al (1963) with 96 children between the ages of three and six years of age. The children were split into four groups. The first group saw an adult behave aggressively towards a large rubber, bottom-weighted, 'bobo' doll. The adult shouted at the doll, punched it and hit it with a hammer. The second group saw exactly the same scene but only on film. The third group saw the same scene but this time portrayed as a cartoon and the last group were shown no violence at all.

The children were then put into a room with a one-way mirror. The children were given toys to play with including a 'bobo' doll. The children's favourite toys were deliberately taken away from them to annoy them and then their behaviour was observed for 20 minutes and each aggressive action was recorded.

The average number of aggressive acts from the groups were as follows:

Group 1: 99
Group 2: 92
Group 3: 83
Group 4: 54

Bandura noted that the children who had not witnessed aggressive actions displayed less violent behaviour than those who had seen aggressive actions. He also noted that the children who had observed the real-life adult reproduced more of the specific aggressive actions than those children who had seen the film or the cartoon characters.

He also found that children did not imitate all models (adults) equally – they were much more likely to imitate models who were similar to themselves, such as those of the same sex.

In a later study (1965) Bandura set up a similar 'Bobo' doll experiment. This time one group saw the adult behaving aggressively towards the 'Bobo' doll because the doll was being disobedient. A second group also saw this scene, but this time a second adult entered the room and chastised the first adult for striking the doll. When the second group was observed, they did not display as many aggressive actions as the first group.

Bandura then offered rewards to the second group to imitate what they had seen the adult doing to the doll. He then recorded that there were no differences between the two groups. Although the second group had not displayed the aggressive behaviour immediately after seeing it they had learned it and were able to replicate it at a later time. Bandura's findings seemed to show that there can be a difference in what children learn and what immediately shows in their behaviour.

Identification is the second part of the process. Not only do the children imitate behaviour, but as time goes by, they begin to model themselves on another person, the learning becomes internalised and they come to identify with that person or that role. Role models act as a blueprint of behaviour, attitudes and values which the child may adopt in later adult life. It is believed that identification is responsible for individuals learning social roles such as gender roles.

CASE STUDY

Chloe and Jack have two children, William (4) and Katlin (3). Jack goes out to work while Chloe has temporarily given up her job to look after her children. Jack is the more dominant in the partnership and makes all the major decisions regarding the running of the household and bringing up the children. He never involves himself in any household tasks as he regards this as Chloe's work. The toys which are bought for the children are always gender specific. William is given cars, lorries, guns and swords, construction kits and boys' books. Katlin is given dolls, dolls houses, doll's prams, dressing up clothes, toy kitchens, and girls' books. He has recently bought a season ticket for William for the local football team. Katlin goes to her dancing class with her mother on a Saturday afternoon.

What do you think William and Katlin will learn about gender roles from their parents?

Punishments and rewards

Another important way in which a child learns to behave is through direct reaction from adults. Behaviour may be rewarded or punished and through these means the child learns to act in ways which are appropriate and acceptable.

There have been several studies carried out to investigate the effects of punishment and rewards. Rewards teach the child the types of behaviour which are likely to bring about a pleasant outcome. Punishment only teaches the child what they should *not* do, not what they should or may do. Rewards will vary from culture to culture. They may take the form of paying attention to the child, playing with them or giving them sweets, treats or hugs and praise. These rewards do act as reinforcers of appropriate behaviour, however studies have shown that they are only effective if there is a strong affectionate bond between the child and the adult.

Punishment can take many forms – smacking, hitting, beating, withdrawing privileges, stopping pocket money or grounding (not letting the child go out of the house). Many social learning theorists believe that punishment often produces hostility and resentment as well as fear and avoidance of the punisher. The child also quickly learns to suppress the punishable behaviour in the presence of the punisher but tends to be more likely to carry out this behaviour out of sight of the adult who has punished them. It may also teach children that behaviour can be controlled by another person by virtue of their age, gender, strength or status. The child may learn to follow this model and could in later years use punishing strategies to control the behaviour of others (their own children, their partner, their friends, their work colleagues or members of the opposite sex).

Social expectations

Social expectations (the type of behaviour which is regarded as appropriate in particular situations) can vary dramatically from one culture an another.

Activity

Can you make a list of different types of behaviour which are regarded as appropriate between children and their parents in your own culture? You have probably noted such behaviour as:

- doing what adults tell them;

- sharing toys/sweets with others;

- being respectful of adults;

- helping others;

- going to bed when they are told;

- not being selfish.

The list is endless. You probably have many more examples on your list.

The way in which a society's culture is constructed can play a large part in determining the kinds of expected behaviour. In the west for example there is an expectation that in the adolescent period teenagers will be 'difficult', moody, move further from their parents' influence and move closer towards their peer group.

An interesting study by Bronfenbrenner (1974) looked at the behaviour of teenagers in the USA and what was then the USSR. He identified a specific youth culture in the USA which highlighted the gulf between adult and youth activities. Because of cultural restraints, teenagers were not supposed to participate in activities such as sexual relationships, drinking alcohol and drug taking. He noted that the differences between adult and teenage activities caused a segregation and this in turn contributed to the anti-social attitudes held by some American teenagers. Teenage delinquency was seen as 'daring' by the peer group, especially among boys.

In contrast, in the USSR, Bronfenbrenner found that Russian teenagers tended to be much more pro-social and did not respect anti-social behaviours from their peers. This, he believes, was because Russian culture was very inclusive of teenagers and encouraged them to be involved in numerous aspects of adult activities. The expectation was that teenagers behaved to a large extent like adults and the result of this was that they did. The culture in the former USSR has since changed dramatically. Each of the Soviet states are now independent in their own right and capitalism has replaced communism. Russia itself has now opened itself up to influences from the west.

Activity

Do you think that social expectations have changed? Do you think that the behaviour of the Russian teenagers will have changed? Can you give reasons for your answers?

Social learning theory therefore gives you an important insight into how people develop and behave and how the culture in which they live affects this process.

ATTACHMENT AND SEPARATION

Macoby (1980) has defined attachment as 'a relatively enduring emotional tie to a specific other person'. While attachments can occur at any point in a person's life, psychologists are particularly interested in the first relationships which are formed as they are regarded as crucial for healthy development. This is because these first relationships act as a model or example for all an individual's later relationships. Psychologists are concerned with how these relationships are formed and what happens if these relationships are disrupted or disturbed. One of the most well-known theorists to first examine this area was John Bowlby. He was asked by the World Health Organisation to investigate the effects on children's development of being brought up in orphanages. In his report, published in 1951, Bowlby argued that babies form a special attachment with one particular person – their mother ('monotrophy'). They do so by displaying certain behaviours which help to keep them close to their mother, such as crying, smiling, crawling. He also found in his research that there was a *critical* or *sensitive* period in which attachment has to take place. For most children, Bowlby thought that this has to take place within the first six months of life.

In 1953, his study of 44 delinquent children who had a history of stealing showed that 17 of them had been separated from their mother before the age of five. He concluded that *maternal deprivation* (being separated from one's mother) before the age of five had a serious effect on the children's social development, making them unable to form meaningful relationships with others. This, Bowlby noted, would affect the child as they developed into adult life. Bowlby thought that in many cases the child could develop a syndrome which he called *'affectionless psychopathy'*. This meant the child was unable to develop a sense of social responsibility and would most probably become delinquent.

Activity

What are your thoughts about this theory? Can you write down any parts of the theory which you feel are weak?

You probably think that it does not offer a complete explanation about attachment and the consequences children face if they do not have a mother to look after them. Other psychologists thought the same and carried out more research looking at the same subject.

Shafter and Emerson (1964) published the result of a longitudinal study which found that infants, rather than establishing a relationship solely with the mother, were in fact able to develop *multiple attachments*, that is equally important relationships with more than one person. Most importantly the infants formed relationships with people who interacted with them in the most sensitive way. This study found that infants formed attachments with people based on the *quality* of the relationship.

The role of fathers was also examined in this and other studies. The studies found that infants may seek mothers and fathers for different reasons – the mother as a source of comfort when distressed, the father for particular types of stimulating and fun play. However the father is *not* seen as a poor substitute for a mother, rather he offers a unique contribution to the development of the infant. The child is able to form equal attachments with its mother and father as more than one type of satisfaction can be derived from an attachment figure. Lone parents whether male or female can offer a range of behaviour, some like a mother and some like a father. The main factor which determines attachment is based on the quality of the relationship rather than specific behaviour (e.g. rough and tumble play, singing songs, cuddling and comforting are all equally important).

One of the most serious criticisms of Bowlby's theory was his belief that failure to form strong attachments during infancy is related to later adjustment problems and to difficulties in establishing loving relationships in adulthood. Studies published in 1979 and 1981 by M. Rutter questioned Bowlby's notion that maternal deprivation was the cause of children's failure to establish relationships in later years and become delinquent. Rutter found that other factors were much more likely to have caused these problems. In particular he found that the effects of physical and emotional neglect, stress within the family home and the lack of any positive relationships were factors which were more influential than maternal deprivation in affecting children's ability to form relationships. He was also interested in the effects on children who had spent time in institutional care, as he considered the impact of this could have a detrimental effect on the ability of children to form positive relationships.

Other psychologists also thought that Bowlby had failed to address the question of whether early deprivation was reversible. That is, would children who had experienced early deprivation be able to form positive relationships at a later date? Studies were carried out by Tizard and Hodges (1978) on children who had experienced early deprivation and had been looked after in children's homes. By the age of eight, it was found that some of the children who had returned home and the majority of those who were adopted had formed close attachments with their parents. More of the children returned to their natural parents did however display more difficult behaviour, in particular attention seeking.

By the age of sixteen the relationships of most of the adopted children seemed satisfactory both from the young person's and the parents' point of view. It appeared that early institutional care had not necessarily resulted in a later inability to form positive relationships.

In contrast, the children who had been returned to their own parents still experienced many more relationship difficulties within the family than within the adoptive families. This was attributed to problems within the family caused by financial, emotional, psychological and social problems. Interestingly, both groups of children experienced difficulties developing positive relationships with their peers or with adults *outside* the home.

The study came to the conclusion that children who are deprived of positive attachments within their first years of life *are* able to make firm attachments later in their life, but this is not automatic. Positive attachments depend not solely on the child being placed within a family but on how parents work at nurturing these relationships.

These later studies seemed to produce evidence that although early experience can certainly cause damage, there is little evidence to suggest that maternal deprivation alone is the major cause of the failure of children to form attachments. More important are factors such as neglect, abuse and stress within the family.

Activity

Can you comment on the types of attachments highlighted in the two case studies below? Compare the following situations.

CASE STUDY

Ryan is one and lives with his mother Emma and his sister (aged three) and his brother (four) in a deprived area of Aberdeen. Emma works full-time and sees the children for a short time in the morning before going out to work. The full-time carer for the children is Emma's mother, who is 62. Granny is a lively and energetic woman who spends a great deal of time talking and playing with the children. They do not have a lot of toys but Granny devises games with things from around the house – sheets, pillows, pots etc.

Emma returns home about 6 pm and is usually very tired from her work in the factory. The children go to bed at 7.30 pm, so Emma only has a short time to be with the children. During this time she sits down to tea with them, baths them and gets them into their pyjamas ready for bed. Emma talks a lot to her children and makes tea time and bath time as much of a fun time as she can before reading them a story in bed.

CASE STUDY

Katie, who is eighteen months also lives in a deprived area of Aberdeen. She lives with her mum and dad, Vicky and Stuart. Neither of her parents work and Vicky is with her all day. Stuart goes out every day to meet his friends and does not spend much time at home. Vicky spends a lot of time with Katie in the house, but often becomes tired and stressed and cannot be bothered to play with her. Katie loves her Teletubbies video and most days sits in front of the TV for hours while her mother lies on the couch. Vicky loves Katie and always keeps her neat and clean and tidy.

Bowlby's theory of maternal deprivation might seem to suggest that Ryan is deprived while Katie is living in the better situation since she has the company of her mother all day. However, as you examine their situation it becomes obvious that the quality of care might be as least as important as the quantity of care. Ryan has another adult with whom he can build attachments – his granny.

SEPARATION

It is apparent that maternal deprivation in itself may not be the sole cause of emotional disturbance in later years. It ignores the possibility that the *reasons* for separation may be more influential in creating emotional problems than the actual separation itself. It is therefore important to look at a range of reasons why children are separated from their parents and what, if any, effects it may have on an individual's emotional stability.

Activity

Draw up a list of reasons why children might be separated from their parent/s. Your list might include short-term separation and more permanent separation.

Short-term separation
Parents who work

In the 1950s Bowlby's research, which stressed the importance of the infant's relationship with his or her mother, had a major effect on attitudes towards working mothers, who had become a politically sensitive issue at this time. Large numbers of servicemen were returning home after the war and it was argued that the jobs which had been undertaken by women during the war should be given up for the men. Bowlby's explanation of maternal deprivation was used as an effective political tool to support the view that women should be at home looking after their children. Subsequently, in the 1950s and even into the 1960s, it was regarded as the norm for women to give up work (either voluntarily or in some occupations such as teaching, compulsory) when they became pregnant.

Attitudes to working mothers have changed and today just over half the working population is composed of women. It is interesting however that there still exists an element of debate about the benefits of mothers staying at home.

There are various ways in which young babies, infants and children experience separation from parent/s. The main types of care provided for children when parent/s are at work are:

Outside the child's home:
- day nurseries;
- childminder (in the childminder's home);
- relatives;
- before and after school care.

In the child's home
- relatives;
- childminder;
- nanny;
- au pair.

Self-care ('latch key')
- children being alone in the house before and after school.

It is clear that not all separations lead to long- or even short-term distress and that different children who experience similar separation respond differently. Overall there is a general consensus that children who have the benefit of a secure home life with strong attachments and who receive a good quality of care when not with their parent/s will not suffer from any emotional disturbance as a result of being separated on a daily basis while their parent/s are at work. Indeed some psychologists believe that children may benefit from the stimulation of nurseries and playgroups where they learn new intellectual, social and physical skills, while 'latchkey' children may become more independent. Mothers and fathers may benefit from time away from their children and feel more able to spend more 'quality' time with them when they are not working.

Children may also be able to form what are known as *transitional attachments*, attachments to objects (teddies), friends or substitute figures. These can act as bonds to their main attachment figures, thus causing less emotional distress.

Other experiences of childhood separation
Hospitalisation

An early study in 1946 (Spitz and Wolf) carried out on children who had experienced a period in hospital, found that apparently 'normal' children reacted to the separation by becoming quiet, apathetic and sad when in hospital but quickly recovered when restored to their mother if the separation had lasted less than three months. In 1975 Douglas found that longer separations however did not result in complete recovery and the evidence suggested that there was an increased risk of behaviour disturbance and poor reading in adolescence.

It is fair to say that the experience today of most children who have to stay in hospital is much changed even from the 1970s. Then, parents were not allowed to stay with their children and were only allowed to see them at visiting times. Children were not told what was going to happen to them and treatments were often uncomfortable and sometimes painful. Even favourite teddies and dolls were considered to carry infection and had to be left at home.

There is evidence to suggest that children in hospital do experience a considerable amount of stress. This is helped greatly in today's modern hospitals where facilities are made available for parents to stay. Yorkhill Hospital for Sick Children in Glasgow has a block of apartments with all kinds of modern facilities next door to the hospital and are available to parents free of charge. This allows parents to be near to their child at all times. Parents can also sleep and eat beside their child and children are encouraged to be involved in play therapy which helps them to understand the procedures/operations which they will have to undergo.

Separation anxiety can therefore be greatly diminished for most children today. However for a small group of children who have to be in hospital for long periods, or have frequent periods of hospitalisation and where their parents because of work or family commitments cannot be with them all the time, there may well be some effect on the child's emotional well-being.

Long-term separation
Divorce and the breakdown of relationships

Increasingly in Britain today, children find themselves living apart from their parents. In 1996 in Scotland, 41 per cent of marriages ended in divorce. (*Scotland on Sunday* 31 January 1999). This figure does not take into account couples with children who live together and split up.

Much debate has centred around the effect of divorce or separation on children. Generally the evidence would seem to suggest that children who have experienced the divorce or separation of their parents do have lower levels of academic achievement, a higher level of behavioural problems both at home and in school, health problems and lower self esteem.

Amato (1993) has shown that these effects should not be seen *exclusively* as a result of divorce or separation. He has drawn from a number of studies to identify five main reasons why children experience a range of difficulties when their parents separate.

■ absence of the one of their parents;
■ inability of the remaining parent to adjust to the separation which may result in poor parenting;
■ economic hardship;
■ stressful life changes (changing home, school, losing friends);
■ parents in continual conflict.

The effect of the separation can be made worse by the way in which the divorce or separation is managed by the parents. If the child receives no explanation about why their parents have separated, they might feel that the separation is their fault. The parents' own difficulties may force the child to take sides, and the child's emotional vulnerability may be severely increased as a result. The child may lose contact with one of the parents and grandparents because of the acrimonious relationship between the parents. These other aspects of separation may well in themselves be as central to the negative effects of divorce as the other social and economic factors discussed above.

Parental death

The death of a parent is a special kind of separation which thankfully happens only to a small group of children. Studies have shown that there is a high rate of depression, particularly in adult women whose mother died when they were a child. However, as with the experience of divorce, other factors are important in fully understanding the effect of parental death. In particular the quality of care which is subsequently provided, the way in which the child is encouraged to grieve (this will be examined later in the chapter) and the effect the death has on the rest of the family (especially the remaining parent). If no other parent remains then the care from grandparents or other relatives is a crucial factor in allowing the child to manage this difficult experience.

DEVELOPMENT OF SELF CONCEPT

What is self concept?

One of the major differences between human beings and animals is the ability of human beings to be aware of themselves. This is called *self-consciousness* or *self-awareness*. Animals may have *consciousness* and feel hunger or pain, but only humans have *self-consciousness*. It does not mean that people feel shy or embarrassed. When you think about yourself you are the person doing the thinking but you are also the person being thought about. Cooley (1902) described this as the 'looking glass self'. What he meant by this was that human beings are aware of what kind of person they are, what they think about themselves and what kind of personality the have. They are able to do this because the have *self-consciousness*. Individuals are able to do this because we have an awareness about what others think about you and it is how you develop an impression of what you are like. Robert Burns, the national poet of Scotland, obviously understood this idea. In his poem 'To a Louse' he notes:

O wad some Power the giftie gie us
To see oursels as ithers see us!

This notion of self-awareness is known as self concept, which does not have a universal definition. It may vary from culture to culture. Indeed in some cultures the notion of 'self' does not exist. African culture has two principles which affect an individual's self concept – 'survival of the tribe' and 'oneness with nature'. African philosophical tradition has a sense of the collective self 'we' rather than 'I'. This is also true of many of the Asian cultures.

African people ... realise that one's self is not contained only in one's physical being and finite time ... [it] transcends through the historical consciousness of one's people, the finiteness of both physical body, finite space and absolute time.

(Flanagan, 1996)

In contrast, in the West, there is a strong cultural notion of individuality, uniqueness, competition, independence and separateness. Western psychology therefore tends to see an individual's self concept as being made up of three major parts:
- self image;
- ideal self;
- self esteem.

Self image

Self image is how individuals describe themselves.

Figure 4.4 Animals do not have self-consciousness

Activity

Try this activity either on your own or with a group of friends or family. Ask each person to write down a list of words or phrases which describe themselves. Ask them to list about 20 things. Remember they can write down some negative aspects about themselves!

Their list will probably include three main categories. It is these categories which make up a person's self image. They have probably described themselves in terms of their **social role** – student, sister, father, friend, son. These roles can be verified by others.

They might also have described themselves in terms of **personality traits**. These traits or characteristics will be formed from their own opinion about themselves – friendly, under-confident, generous, nervous, bad-tempered. These may be traits they consider themselves to have but others may not hold the same view.

The last group on their list might be descriptions of how they look, their **body image**. They might have included descriptions such as tall, fat, thin, blue eyes, attractive, unattractive etc. One of the important features of body image is biological identity – whether someone is male, female or what is known as third or intermediate gender (neither purely male nor female). The other important feature of body image is that as individuals grow and develop, so too do their bodies and appearance. It may be something simple like getting a haircut or having their nose pierced or it may be more significant such as the change in the bodies during puberty or their skin becoming wrinkled and their hair turning white when they get older.

Ideal self

Your ideal self is the kind of person you would like to be. Perhaps you would just like to be a little thinner, younger, a bit more intelligent, or better at sports or perhaps you would like to be a better friend, be a more caring person or a better mother. At a more extreme level, you may even want to be someone else!

Self esteem

Self esteem is what an individual thinks about themselves, how they value themselves as a person, how much they like themselves. To a large extent this might depend on the relationship between their *self image* and their *ideal self*. If they are very unhappy with their self image and want to be like someone else (ideal self) then most likely their *self esteem* will be low. However if they are happy with the person they are, then their *self esteem* will be high. The wider the gap between *self image* and *ideal self*, the lower a person's *self esteem* will be.

The type of culture in which people live has a large influence on how individuals view themselves. British culture today holds certain physical attributes in high regard. Women are deemed to be attractive if they are young, tall, slim, have beautiful faces, good skin and long shapely legs. Men are seen as attractive if they are young, tall and slim with a 'six pack', have good skin and look as if they 'work out'. In contrast other cultures, in particular third world cultures, regard overweight people as attractive.

Other aspects of culture, status and orientation will also affect how people see themselves – race, gender, age, social background, education, marital status or sexual orientation.

Activity

Can you list which characteristics would be most valued in a society like Britain?

One list would probably look like this:

- white;

- male;
- young (20–40);
- affluent background;
- university degree;
- married;
- heterosexual.

CASE STUDY

Emma is 23 years old and is of mixed race. She is a lone parent with two children under five and lives in a high-rise block of flats in one of the large housing schemes in Glasgow. She left school at sixteen with no qualifications. She has been using drugs for several years and her children were in foster care for quite a long time. With help from the local drug rehabilitation team and her social worker Emma has stopped using drugs and her children have been returned to live with her.

Emma's self esteem is very low and when her social worker suggested that she attended a college course for adult returners, Emma felt that she was not 'good enough' to go to college with 'a lot of brainy people' from the 'posh area'. After a year off drugs however Emma did attend a basic computer course at her local community centre and showed a real aptitude for this subject. The out-reach tutor from the college who taught the course eventually persuaded her to attend a full-time computer course at the college the following year. Emma is now studying for an HNC in computer studies and sees herself as 'as good as anybody else'. Her self esteem continues to grow.

TRANSITION AND LOSS

As individuals go through life they experience many changes. These changes affect an individual's development and behaviour and are known as transitions. Adams, Hayes and Hopson (1977) have described a transition as 'a discontinuity in a person's life space'. For a transition to occur, two conditions must be met. Firstly, the person must be aware that a transition is occurring and secondly, the person is expected to behave differently.

Transitions can be categorised into two main groups.
- personal development;
- major life events.

Personal development

We grow from children to adolescents to adults and finally to older adults. As we age we move from the home environment to school, perhaps to work and a life of retirement. In so doing, individuals change in appearance, develop social and emotional and intellectual skills, develop and change their behaviour and extend or diminish relationships with other people. Many transitions take place in childhood – going to playgroup, to nursery, to school, joining clubs, growing bigger, becoming an adolescent, reaching puberty.

Gould (1978) has identified the stages of personal development for men and women which take place in adult years (see Figure 4.5). Each stage of development is linked to a series of tasks which indicate that all of life is about change. The ages which Gould uses are of course approximations and should be used as useful generalisations. His study was carried out in California in the 1970s and is therefore more representative of personal development in the West. His model may not be so applicable in countries where life expectancy is between 30 and 40, where marriage takes place at a younger age and the notion of career is absent.

Stages	Task
1. Pulling up roots (ages 16–22)	Autonomy. Self-sufficiency.
2. Provisional adulthood (ages 22–29)	Select a career. Establish personal relationships. Achieve a place in society.
3. Age 30 transition (ages 29–32)	Search for personal identity. Re-assess future objectives. Search for meaning of life.
4. Rooting (ages 33–39)	Establish long term goals. Receive recognition in career or career success.
5. Mid life transition	Confrontation of gap between aspirations and achievements. Re-examination of career. Re-examination of personal relationships.
6. Restabilisation and flowering (ages 43–50)	Acceptance of time as infinite.
7. Mellowing (ages 50–60+)	Confrontation of mortality. Autonomy. Acceptance of what I have. Fewer personal relationships.

Gould (1978)

Figure 4.5 Stages in personal development

Major life events

The other main group is concerned with transitions which occur because of things which happen in our lives, which are called life events. Holmes and Rahe (1967) compiled a list of life events and gave each a scoring value (see Figure 4.6). Their research showed that people who scored between 200 and 300 points in a given year were statistically very likely to develop major health problems during the course of the following year. People who scored over 100 points were statistically likely to suffer a moderately serious period of illness.

Death of a spouse (partner)	100
Divorce	73
Marital separation	65
Prison sentence	63
Death of parent or close family member	63
Personal injury or illness	53
Marriage/moving in with partner	50
Being sacked from work	47
Reconciliation with spouse/partner	45
Retirement	45
Change in health of family member	44
Pregnancy	40
Sexual difficulties	39
Gain of a new family member	39
Business readjustment	39
Change in financial state (more or less)	38
Death of a close friend	37
Change to a different kind of work	36
Foreclosure of mortgage	30
Change in work responsibilities	29
Son or daughter leaving home	29
Trouble with in-laws	29
Outstanding personal achievements	28
Spouse/partner begins or stops work	26
Begin or end school/college	26
Change in living conditions	25

Change in personal habits	24
Trouble with boss at work	23
Moving house	20
Change of recreation	19
Change of social activities	18
Change in sleeping habits	16
Change in eating habits	15
Holiday	13
Christmas	12
Minor breaches in the law	11

(Adapted from Holmes and Rahe, 1967)

Figure 4.6 Life events

Psychologists today would perhaps challenge the rather simplistic relationship between life events and illness which Holmes and Rahe claim. However the link between transitions, stress and illness is now well established and their scale is still widely used as a useful tool. It is interesting that even desired events such as marriage, a lottery win or a new baby may be stressful to individuals and if combined with other transitions may lead to ill health

Unwelcome transitions such as divorce, unemployment or bereavement may cause great emotional and social difficulty for individuals, but the experience of these events will be fundamental in understanding the changes in their development and behaviour. For some individuals unwelcome events may even offer the chance to find new avenues for growth and development. The Chinese have two words for crisis. One means 'danger' and the other means 'opportunity'.

Adams, Hayes and Hopson (1977) created a general model which tries to explain transitions (see Figure 4.7). The seven-stage model tries to show how the experience of transition affects an individual's self esteem. An understanding of the model can help to understand that individual's experience a range of feelings when they go through a transitional experience. The feelings are 'normal' and in time they will pass. There is also the idea that the person can have some control over what happens to them.

The phases represent a cycle of experiencing a change. At first the individual may feel in a state of shock, they may 'play down' what has happened, they may feel depressed. As they move through the transition, they may begin to acknowledge the reality of the change, test out new ideas or behaviour, understand themselves and use the experience of the change to change their behaviour. The level of the person's self esteem varies across the phases and follows a predictable

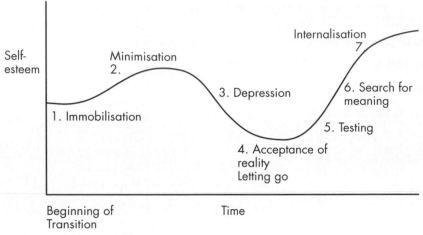

Figure 4.7 Self esteem changes during transitions (Hopson and Adams, 1977)

path. For a transition to be effectively managed, all seven stages would have to be worked through.

Individuals seldom move smoothly through all seven phases. Some may never move beyond the earlier phases, others may become 'stuck' in a state of depression. As life unfolds, an individual who has successfully reached the end of the phases may experience a major problem and be catapulted back to the beginning of the cycle.

CASE STUDY

Ifrah is 35 years old and has multiple sclerosis. Two years ago she was a senior partner in a large firm of architects in Glasgow. The changes in Ifrah's life have had a profound effect on her and she became quite depressed. She no longer went out as she was embarrassed to be seen in her wheelchair and her mother had to move into her house as Ifrah had lost interest in looking after her husband and children.

After three years the doctors told Ifrah that her condition seemed to be in remission and that they were confident that her condition rather than deteriorating any further would be stable at least for a number of years. This news had a profound effect on Ifrah and she seemed to come to terms with her condition. She began to go out again and even did some work for her old firm from the house. Her mother moved back to her own house and with some assistance from a firm of private cleaners, Ifrah was able to manage the upkeep of her house. She began to take an interest in her husband and children again and she felt that her life was beginning again. Five years after her condition was first diagnosed, Ifrah's husband left her, unable to cope with a wife who was disabled. Her transitional cycle was beginning all over again.

One of the changes which happens in everybody's life is the experience of loss. It is part of everyday life. Some losses are trifling, such as the loss of a book on the bus. Other losses can be more significant, for example if your house is burgled and you lose a ring which your mother has given to you or you lose all your family photographs in a house fire.

Activity

Can you think of any other losses which may occur in people's lives which may have an even more significant effect on them?

Here are some that may be on your list.

- loss of friends when you move house;
- loss of a job;
- loss of freedom (prison);
- loss of a pet;
- loss of a limb;
- loss of hearing;
- loss of sight;
- loss of mobility;
- loss of health;
- loss of a loved one.

fearful	vulnerable	anxious
sad	hurt	afraid
numb	helpless	unloved
insecure	worthless	powerless
apprehensive	vengeful	burdened
dazed	distressed	alienated
misunderstood	grief	unhappy
bewildered	restless	self-pity
pain	angry	disbelief
shocked	panic	denial
guilty	tired	unwanted
lonely	disoriented	fearful

Loss can have a devastating effect on those who directly experience the loss and it also has a powerful effect on friends, family and carers. The most difficult and painful emotions are when someone close to you dies or when someone is facing their own death. Ward and Houghton (1987) compiled an extensive list of the feelings which may be associated with the death of a loved one.

It is important to try to understand more fully the emotions experienced by someone who is dying and also by partners, family and friends who are left after the person has died.

Today it is also recognised that the loss of a baby due to stillbirth, miscarriage or termination (at any stage in the pregnancy) is also an experience of death and should be regarded as such.

It is important to examine how death is viewed in society today because this will largely determine attitudes and behaviour at the time of death and in the weeks, months and years which follow.

In the past, death was part of everyday life. Caring for the sick and dying was seen as the responsibility of relatives. Babies were born at home and people died at home surrounded by family and friends. Large families stayed in one household and death was an occurrence which was witnessed by all who lived there, including the children. Once the person had died they remained in the house and family members would clean and prepare the body for burial. The body would remain in the house until it was taken for burial. The normal running of the house continued – cooking, cleaning, going to work, as well as welcoming friends and family who came to pay their last respects.

Today dying has become a more professional affair. Field and James (1993) have shown that only one quarter of people die at home (see Figure 4.8). The medical profession have taken on the responsibility for the care of the dying and now most people die in hospitals. Funeral directors remove the body to a chapel of rest, prepare the body for burial or cremation and organise most details of the funeral arrangements.

It would appear that the process of dying is being removed from everyday experience. Katz and Siddell (1994) describe this process as the 'unfamiliarity of death' and go on to say that Britain is a 'death denying society'.

The whole issue of death and dying has been removed from the family into the hands of the medical profession. The ever-increasing progress of public health and medical science has meant that people now live longer than they have ever done in the past. No longer do epidemics kill thousands of people, children do not die of childhood diseases such as diphtheria and small-pox, and mothers and babies are seldom lost in the process of birth. While this progress has no doubt had a positive effect on the health and welfare of the population, it has had a profound effect on how death is viewed. Nowadays death is often seen as a failure of the medical profession to keep someone alive. It is not seen as an integral part of everyday life. Even the language that is used offers some insight into how death is viewed.

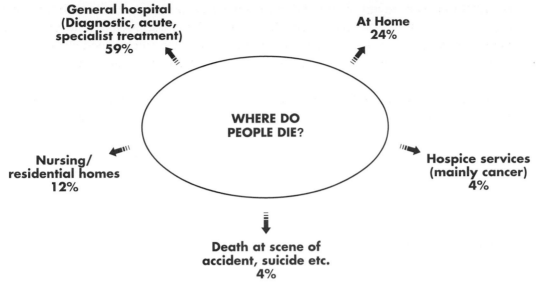

Figure 4.8 Where do people die?

Activity

Can you make a list of some of the words and phrases you have heard which either try to be humorous about death or which try to 'soften' the idea of death (euphemism).

Here are some you could include:

■ gone;

■ left us;

■ is pushing up the daisies;

■ kicked the bucket;

■ snuffed it;

■ had the big 'C' (cancer);

■ turned up his toes;

■ popped his clogs;

■ caught the train;

■ gone to the last resting place.

Can you think of any others?

The death of a loved one represents a profound change in people's lives. If there is some agreement that society today has more and more come to ignore the reality and inevitability of death and to a large extent sanitises the whole subject, what implications does this have for individuals who face their own death or experience the death of others.

Much work has been carried out to research the process of death and dying and it is widely acknowledged that mourning or grieving for someone who was close is an essential part of coming to terms with the loss.

*Grief:	the emotional *feelings* people have about death, the *feelings* of sadness or loss you have going on inside you.
*Mourning:	the way in which grief is *expressed*. How emotions are *shown*. How feelings are *demonstrated*.

When a loss occurs it is inevitable that transitions or changes will occur in people's lives. Transition can be very challenging because people gain a feeling of security from the present pattern of their life. Colin Murray Parkes (1975) describes this as a person's 'assumptive world', or ideas of their world which are based on how it has always been. It is assumed that this is how it will always be. To think otherwise would cause feelings of insecurity.

When loss happens ideas have to be changed about what is normally taken for granted in order to cope with the world which has changed. The individual has to understand the feelings they are experiencing and face the practical aspects of life after loss.

Worden (1983) has carried out work which involved counselling people who had been bereaved. This work allowed the bereaved person to talk through their feelings and work through their grief. This work led Worden to identify 'four tasks of mourning'.

Task 1
When death occurs, the first reaction is shock and disbelief. This does not only apply in the case of sudden death. The person may have been very ill for some time and the family may have known that they were dying but it may still be difficult to accept that the loved one is actually dead. The first task is to accept the reality of the loss.

Task 2
At this point those who are grieving experience the pain of grief. They should express all the feelings whether they be anger, sorrow, guilt or sadness. They need to realise that all these feelings actually help them to come to terms with the loss.

Task 3
Now they need to adjust to the environment (home, relationship, family, friends, pastimes) from which the dead person is missing. Bereaved people must restore their self-confidence if they are to overcome their grief.

Task 4

In this last task they should take 'emotional energy' from the relationship with the dead person and reinvest it into different aspects of their lives, such as relationship(s), work, hobbies, activities etc.

Managing to achieve these four tasks, in Worden's view, ensures that the person will be able to mourn or grieve for the person they have lost in a way that allows them to move on from the pain of the loss towards a positive readjustment of their own lives.

Worden's tasks do offer some help in understanding the grieving process, but care must be taken in applying this model to everyone. All experience of death are individual and not everyone will 'achieve' Worden's four tasks. There is no time limit to mourning or the feelings of grief. Each person will determine this process for themselves.

CASE STUDY

Ken is 35 years old with a successful career in the computer industry near Edinburgh. Two years ago his wife Angela died of breast cancer. Ken was devastated by his wife's death. Everyone was very supportive of Ken and offered both emotional and practical help for quite a long time after Angela's death.

After two years this support began to scale down as both friends and family felt his period of mourning had 'elapsed' and he should now 'get on with his life'. His married friends began to invite him to parties and barbecues. Ken was initially quite happy to go as it got him out of the house, but he soon realised that there always seemed to be 'an available woman' at these events and it was expected that they would get together. Similarly, his male friends wanted him to 'get back on the scene' again and come out to pubs and clubs. When Ken refused, his friends accused him (behind his back) of wallowing in his grief. Their attitude was that he had no children to look after, he was still young and had enough money to enjoy himself. So he should put Angela's death behind him and start to enjoy life again.

But grief and mourning do not adhere to rigid time scales and Ken was not yet ready to adjust to life without his wife. It may be that Ken needs some help to come to terms with his wife's death in order that he can come through the grieving process.

> **CASE STUDY**
>
> Jin-ming was a 78 year-old woman who lived in Glasgow on her own in the house she had lived in for over 50 years. Nine years ago when she was 69 her husband Han-chen died suddenly of a stroke. Jin-ming was completely broken-hearted. They had recently celebrated their golden wedding anniversary (50 years) and had a good and happy marriage.
>
> As the breadwinner of the house Han-chen had always been the one to deal with all the money matters in the home. He had paid the mortgage, council tax and all the household bills. He had dealt with all the details of his pension and insurance policies. Han-chen had also taken responsibility for all the DIY tasks in the home. Jin-ming, meanwhile, did all the cooking, cleaning and shopping. Theirs was a traditional type of relationship.
>
> When Han-chen died Jin-ming found she could not cope with either the emotional or practical aspects of life without him. She stopped going to her church groups and instead never ventured out of the house. She became quite depressed and her family became worried about her. She refused to go and live with any of them and would not accept a place in a sheltered housing complex in the street next to her eldest daughter. Her GP prescribed anti-depressant tablets which helped a little but in the nine years she lived after her husband's death, Jin-ming never came to terms with this death and when she died she was still in the process of grieving.

Mourning is the way you express your feelings of grief, and it is how you behave when someone dies. In all cultures mourning has two main parts;
- how you show the feelings associated with grief;
- the behaviour which is expected or accepted within your particular culture or society.

Showing feelings can take on a variety of forms. In Britain showing feelings such as crying in public has not always been regarded as 'the right thing to do'. The expected behaviour of men at funerals was to 'keep a stiff upper lip' while women were described as being 'very brave' if they did not cry. Society has recently been showing a move away from this. The death of Diana, Princess of Wales, saw mass crowds openly weeping in the streets, politicians have been filmed crying at their own or other's distress and even male football players have been seen crying on the pitch or at news conferences.

Each culture has its own mourning rituals which for the most part are associated with particular religions. Today in Britain large numbers of people seek the help and guidance of the Christian religion at the time of a death. However not everyone practises a religion and individual approaches to mourning must be accepted. This is becoming more apparent in a secular society (having no particular affinities with religion) such as Britain. More people are now seeking alternatives to a religious funeral, for example a Humanist funeral which places emphasis on the relationships and achievements of the person during their lifetime rather than on the notion of an afterlife.

Other religions have their own particular rituals. Muslims bury their dead within 24 hours and the body is buried in a deep grave facing Mecca. Some Muslims like to embalm the body and take it back to the country their family originally came from. Mourning goes on for three days in which the grieving family is supported by family and friends. The official end of mourning is at the end of 40 days when a special meal is prepared and readings are heard from the Qur'an (Holy Book).

Hindus and Sikhs believe that the body has to be cremated. Hindus place food in the coffin of the dead person to help them on their journey in the afterlife. Sikh male bodies are dressed in the sacred symbols, the 5 K's – uncut hair, a wooden comb holding the hair, a metal bracelet on the right wrist, a symbolic sword in a sheath, and short trousers (or underwear). A Sikh man's hair should always be covered even when he is dead.

The Jewish religion prefers to bury their dead in a Jewish cemetery. The close family remain at home for a week and pray three times a day. Mourning ends after 30 days, except for children of the deceased who mourn for a year.

So far you have examined the impact of the death of a loved one on those who are left. However it is also important to consider the feelings associated with the prospect of a person's own death. Doctors can now largely tell when an illness, such as cancer, is terminal (the person will not survive). They may even be able to estimate how long the person will remain alive.

Elizabeth Kubler-Ross (1970) studied terminally ill patients and came to the conclusion that they also went through a transition or stages of grief. Her model of grief is outlined below.

Denial	There has been some mistake. This is not happening to me.
Anger	Why me? I don't deserve this. This has been someone's fault. I will blame someone and rage at them.
Bargaining	What deal can I do to prevent this happening? Maybe I can put it off until after my birthday, wedding anniversary etc.
Depression	The full impact of death becomes a reality, perhaps due to failing physical health. Fear of death, helplessness takes over.
Acceptance	In this final stage the acceptance of death becomes a reality. The person no longer 'fights' the inevitable. This brings relief to the person, although it may not necessarily be a happy stage.

This model is still widely used in the care of terminally ill people. It is often viewed as the 'best way' to die. While you can use this as a helpful general 'tool' to help you understand the process of dying, you must also be aware of its limitations.

Not everyone will go through all the stages and perhaps not even in the particular order shown. Not everyone will experience denial, anger or bargaining. In the final stages not everyone will accept their death. Some may even pretend in order to ease the pain of relatives. Other factors such as age or cultural traditions may have a deep impact on the final stage. Someone who is 87 may well be prepared to die, to consider that they have had their life. Another 87 year-old may think they still have much to do, much to experience and will not be ready to accept their death.

Lou Grade, a famous British television impresario, died in 1998 at the age of 92. He knew he was dying and shortly before his death wrote his own epitaph for his gravestone. It read 'I didn't want to go'.

So while models do help you to understand the experience of death, you must always remember that everyone is an individual and does not always neatly fit into the restrictions of a particular model.

SUMMARY

This chapter which is at Higher level, has attempted to look at ways in which developmental psychology can help care workers to understand more fully the way in which their services users develop and behave.

A variety of 'tools' have been used in the form of perspectives, theories and models which help to explain aspects of the people in your care. These 'tools' offer general guidelines and explanations. They cannot be used as precise answers or explanations because all service users are individuals with individual life experiences, but they do go some way at least to give you a body of knowledge which can help you to provide a more effective service of care.

This chapter has examined the following areas which together provide a useful way to develop your work with service users:

- the needs of individuals;
- explanations of behaviour;
- the stages of human development;
- the importance of attachment;
- the relevance of self-consciousness;
- the effect of loss and transition.

Activity at Higher Level

1. Using Erikson's 'Eight Stages of Development', outline the stages of development of the members of the MacDonald and Ahmed families (see Chapter 10).

2. Choose one person from each of the families in the case study and using a psychological theory of need, describe how far their needs are being met.

3. Using psychological theory, describe the transitions and losses experienced by the adults in the MacDonald and Ahmed families and the effects they have on their development and behaviour.

4. What is self concept? Describe the self esteem of the teenagers in the MacDonald and Ahmed family.

FURTHER READING

Hayes, N. and Orrell, S. (1993). *Psychology an Introduction*. London: Longman Group Ltd.
This book provides a good basic textbook for this level of study. It has a helpful range of exercises and self-assessment questions. It also attempts to show examples of how psychology can be applied to every day contexts, or in social or political life.

Moonie, N. et al (1995). *Human Behaviour in the Caring Context*. London: Stanley Thornes (Publishers) Ltd.
This book provides a good source of reference for students who are interested in working in the care sector. One half of the book is devoted to the understanding of psychology and its application to work with service users. The other half looks at aspects of work within care organisation.

Flanagan, C. (1996). *Applying Psychology to Early Child Development*. London: Hodder and Stoughton.
This is a well written and easily read book. It looks at child development from both a psychological and sociological view.

More challenging reading

Hayes, N. (1994). *Foundations of Psychology: An Introductory Text*. New York: Routledge.
This book is more challenging than those above and its examination of the subject is more wide ranging.

Gross, R. (1996). *Psychology the Science of Mind and Behaviour* 3rd Edition. London: Hodder and Stoughton.

CHAPTER 5

The sociological contribution and its applications

Janet Miller

Sociology may make us see in a new light the very world in which we have lived all our lives.

(Meighan, 1981)

INTRODUCTION

This chapter aims to provide a clear and interesting introduction to sociology. The meaning of sociology is examined together with a consideration of four different sociological perspectives: functionalist, conflict, interactionist and feminist. Several aspects of society are studied from each of these perspectives. The aspects considered are the family, education, deviance and institutionalisation. The chapter is relevant to the Higher unit 'Human Development and Behaviour' and covers material for outcomes 2, all pcs, and 3, pc b.

By the end of the chapter you should be able to:

■ give an account of the various ways in which 'sociology' can be interpreted;
■ distinguish and explain four different sociological perspectives;
■ examine the aspects of family, education, deviance and institutionalisation from various sociological perspectives;
■ apply your knowledge to the care context.

SOCIOLOGY

Sociology is exciting. It provides useful and sometimes unexpected insights into the way society and its parts work. It enables us to look through different eyes. In common with psychology, it is an alternative to 'common sense' and often turns 'common sense' on its head. There is no one single definition of sociology and the more you study it the more you will realise that definition depends to some extent upon the viewpoint or perspective which you are taking. Before reading further imagine that you have said to a friend that you're going to study sociology and your friend says 'what's sociology?' What ideas do you have in your mind about sociology and what it is that you will be studying?

To get you started in your thinking about sociology some brief statements are given below, but do not take these as the whole story. At the end of the chapter you will be asked again to try to define sociology and you might conclude that this is a very difficult thing to do.

Some statements about sociology:

*Sociology can be seen as a modern attempt to explain the workings of the **social world**.*

(Lawson, T., 1991)

Sociology: the science of the development and nature and laws of human (esp. civilised) society; study of social problems.

(Oxford Dictionary)

One difficulty about attempting to answer the question 'what is sociology?' lies in the fact that there is disagreement amongst sociologists on the kind of approach to take ...

(Heraud, B., 1970)

Sociology is left-wing rubbish.

(Edwina Currie, formerly Conservative Minister of Health, in Dominelli, 1997)

Sociology is a vast discipline characterised by a variety of theoretical approaches and perspectives.

(Dominelli, L., 1997)

And finally ...

(Sociology is) the study of society. (It) ... includes the social structure of society, its social institutions and how people live ... (And) culture ... (which) deals with the ways in which ... individual behaviour, values and attitudes are culturally conditioned; and how different people handle the great life experiences of courtship, marriage, birth, growing up, work, old age, death.

(Younghusband, E., 1964)

Sociology and care practice

Some people have seen sociology as potentially damaging to care workers – too much insight or too much analysis may make workers unduly critical of the structures and ways in which they work, of the bureaucracies in which they are enmeshed, of the institutions which provide social care to thousands of vulnerable people. Others see sociology as potentially empowering, as providing some insights into society, culture and institutions which can enable care workers to contribute to improvements in the quality of life of those with whom they work. It is this latter view which is promoted in this chapter. A single chapter devoted to sociology cannot hope to give you more than an introduction to a fascinating subject. You are encouraged to read some of the recommended texts if you wish to take your thinking further.

SOME SOCIOLOGICAL BACKGROUND AND CONCEPTS

Comte, or, to give him his full name, Auguste Francois Marie Xavier Comte (1789–1857) was the first person to use the term 'sociology' in the late 1830s. Comte saw sociology as the scientific study of society. He stated his belief in these words: 'Savoir pour prevoir et prevoir pour pouvoir'. This may be translated as: 'To know in order to predict and to predict in order to empower'. For Comte sociology could be seen as the scientific study of society seeking to provide understanding of it. Although the scientific status of sociology continues to be an area of debate and dispute, Comte's aim to understand society and through this understanding to be able to promote change, continues to be relevant to this day.

There are in sociology some very fundamental **concepts** or ideas which it is as well to consider at the very beginning of your study in order that in later discussion they can be used without further explanation. From the many sociological concepts some brief consideration will be given here to **society, culture, institution, role, status and social class. Socialisation** is also a sociological concept of prime importance but, since it was examined in Chapter 3, it is only briefly touched upon in this one. These concepts form what O'Donnell (1997) has called the sub-culture of sociology. They are not the only concepts which are relevant to your study and many others, e.g. deviance and the family, will receive consideration at appropriate points in the text.

Society

Activity

Sociology leads to the careful and close examination of society and the way it works. But what is meant by 'society'? Before going further a useful activity (adapted from Brown, 1979) is to draw a very simplistic picture which represents 'society' for you. Don't use words, only shapes and pictures, and spend no more than five minutes doing this. What did you draw? Why did you draw what you drew? What does this say about your view of society? The diagram or picture which you drew may say something about your viewpoint or perspective of society, about where you see people fitting into it, about hidden assumptions you make about the world around you.

Now examine Figure 5.1 below adapted from Brown (1979) and answer the questions.

Questions

1. What do you think each of these illustrations suggests about society?

2. What is the main difference between the diagrams in Row 1 and Row 2?

3. What do you think the boxes in (c) stand for? Fill in the boxes.

4. Explain your own diagram and what it says about your own interpretation of society.

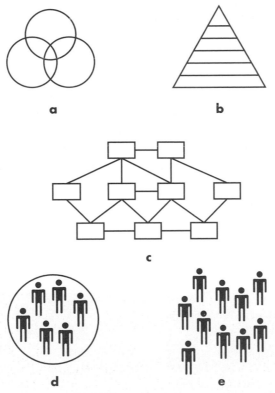

Figure 5.1 Examples of diagrams which illustrate 'society'

Although some theorists argue that we are moving towards a global society, 'society' is usually regarded as the country or nation-state in which you live. For example, Scotland is increasingly seen as a society which is distinct from other parts of Britain in many ways, though having a great deal in common in others. Language often defines a society; laws, education, religion and other aspects of culture distinguish one 'society' from another. Although Scotland shares a language with the rest of Britain there are distinct Scottish meanings and dialects, Gaelic is still spoken in the Highlands and Islands and increasingly is being taught in other parts of Scotland. Scotland has its own legal system, education system and religious denominations. Scotland is also a multi-cultural society and is still part of Great Britain in many social, economic, political and cultural ways, even though it has many differences from the rest of Britain and has its own parliament.

Activity

Make two lists which show a) similarities between Scottish society and that of the rest of Great Britain and b) differences between Scottish society and that of the rest of Great Britain.

Often 'society' is referred to as something distinct and independent, as a thing in itself rather than just the sum total of the members who are part of it. 'Society' is often blamed for things like inability to progress or for the problems which people face. Avril Taylor (1993), for example, in her study of women drug users in Glasgow talks of 'the inability of society either to recognise or to cater for such women's needs'.

Culture

Human beings, unlike animals, learn most of their behaviour. They do not just behave instinctively but use their intelligence and learning. They learn how to behave and share much of this behaviour with other members of the society to which they belong. This learned, shared behaviour is known as culture. Culture is the way of life of society's members. It includes values, beliefs, customs, rules and regulations which human beings learn as members of a society. Without culture human society would not exist.

Activity

Write down ten things which you think are part of your culture.

Read the passages below from George Mackay Brown and J.R. Allan and pick out the things which you think are part of 'culture'.

Three nights later, on Christmas Eve, I saw the old fiddler beside his barn lifting the upper quernstone from the lower stone, and slowly and solemnly, taking it inside.

> *Then, crofter by crofter, the same piece of ritual was enacted: the stone that turned and ground the bread lifted and removed to a safe place.*
>
> *'For why?' said Betsy. 'For this is the night that the trows come and turn the quern wheel against the sun. And if that happens, the stones will be barren, ther'll be no meal and bread next harvest, the countryside'll starve. And your father won't get a penny in rent . . .*
> (from 'Winter Tales, George Mackay Brown, 1995)
>
> *The etiquette of the bothy and stable was equalled in rigidity only by that of the court of Louis XIV. Each man had his place and was taught to keep it. For the second horseman to have gone in to supper before the first horseman would have created as much indignation as an infringement of precedence at Versailles. The foreman was always the first to wash his face in the bothy at night; it was he who wound the alarm clock and set it for the morning, and so on, and so on. The order of seniority was as strictly observed between the second horseman and the third, while the halflin always got the tarry end of the stick . . . But the foreman had pride of place in everything. He slept at the front end of the first bed – that is, nearest the fire: he sat at the top of the table in the kitchen; he worked the best pair of horses; and he had the right to make the first pass at the kitchen maid.*
> (From 'Farmer's Boy' by J.R. Allen, 1935)

Culture need not be something which is fixed, though it often is. It is something which can and does change. Sometimes it changes because attitudes change, because things which have previously been accepted as 'right' or inevitable come to be seen as unnecessary or oppressive or disempowering. Can you think of five cultural changes which have taken place in the twentieth century which would illustrate this point? What other factors do you think might lead to cultural change?

Institution

In sociology the word 'institution' is used in two main ways. The first use, which also incorporates the second, refers to the component parts of society, thus society is made up of institutions. Mike O'Donnell (1993) has defined a social institution as: *a group of people organised for a specific purpose (or purposes)*. The family can be seen as one institution of society. The second interpretation, closely linked to the first but somewhat more specific, refers to buildings and their functions, in which people live or do things or are looked after or controlled or just lead their lives or two or more of these things. In this sense a hospital is an institution, so is a factory, a prison, a school and a residential home. Erving Goffman (1968), who will be referred to in greater detail when institutionalisation is examined, was very interested in looking at institutions, especially what he called 'total institutions'. He defined a total institution as:

. . . a place of residence and work where a large number of like-minded individuals, cut off from the wider society for an appreciable period of time, together lead an enclosed, formally adminis-tered round of life.

(Goffman, E., 1968)

These different interpretations of institution are not entirely separate in that institutions in the second more specific sense are also institutions in the first sense since they are 'groups of people organised for a specific purpose'. It is useful to look at institutions under four separate headings:

- economic (for example, factories and offices);
- political (for example, political parties);
- kinship (for example, families);
- cultural and community organisations (for example, schools, churches and other religious bodies).

Activity

Make a list of the social institutions of which you are a member and think about their meaning in terms of how they affect your life.

Role and status

All the world's a stage,
And all the men and women merely players:
They have their exits and their entrances;
And one man in his time plays many parts, . . .

(William Shakespeare, *As You Like It*, 1599)

In a sense, society provides individuals with scripts which enable them, like actors in a theatre, to play their roles.

(Heraud, B., 1970)

The above quotations are referring to people's social roles. Role and status are two further fundamental sociological concepts. A fairly straightforward definition of role is that it is the part which an individual appears to play in a group and the behaviour which is expected from a person in that position. It has the three constituents of part, behaviour and social expectation. A role can be **ascribed** or given, for example son, daughter, or **achieved** and chosen, for example teacher. Most people have multiple roles. For example, the roles of wife, mother, teacher, daughter can all be held by the same person at the same time, sometimes in harmony, sometimes in conflict with one another. The roles which a person has will, to a large extent, determine the **status** which that person has in society. Status refers to position in society and the degree of respect which this position commands. As with role, some statuses are achieved and some are ascribed. One status which is largely ascribed is that of social class, though change in social class can be achieved (either up or down) through social mobility. Thus a bank manager has a fairly high status and can be defined as being a member of the middle class. But if he or she loses his or her job, takes to alcohol, can't pay the mortgage, ends up homeless living under a bridge, what has happened to that individual's roles and status?

Socialisation

In Chapter 3 socialisation was defined as the process or way in which people learn the culture of their society. At this point you are advised to go back to Chapter 3 to read the account of socialisation again, bearing in mind that it has aspects of both psychology and sociology, human, personal development and growth and social development.

Social class

Sociologists have been concerned to look at social class as one of the ways of describing and explaining the different **life chances** of individuals in society. Social differences can be of many different kinds and as well as class **gender and ethnicity** are important. These receive consideration elsewhere in the text (see Chapter 2 and later sections of this chapter). Social class in Scotland was the subject of a book by McLaren (1985) who was concerned to assess its importance in determining attitudes, beliefs and relationships within the total society. He drew attention to the relationship between **class and culture**, illustrated in his quotation from J.R. Allen on page 177. But what is social class? As with every other question in sociology this is not as straightforward as it seems. Class is a way of stratifying society into different levels. There are different points of view about the criteria which are appropriate to distinguish these different levels. Karl Marx, for example, saw class in a strictly economic sense with capitalist society divided into two main classes: those who owned property and controlled the means of production and those who were workers and propertyless – the **capitalist** class and the **proletariat**.

Max Weber divided society into four main classes and differed from Marx in seeing that other factors than the ownership or non-ownership of the means of production and property were important in distinguishing class groups from one another. As well as capital he also emphasised the importance of skill, education and status. Weber's four classes were: the propertied class; the intellectual, administrative and managerial class; the traditional petty bourgeois class of small businessmen and shopkeepers, and the working class. For the purposes of this chapter the Registrar General's division of society into classes by occupation is used for practical purposes whilst still recognising the analysis of both Marx and Weber as important in any consideration of class. It should also be emphasised that official statistics about social class based upon occupation often take the occupation of the person identified as the head of the household. This tends to diminish the importance of the occupational status of women. It also excludes people who are unemployed.

The five classes identified by the Registrar General are as follows:

I	Professional occupations
II	Managerial and technical occupations
III N	Skilled non-manual occupations
III M	Skilled manual occupations
IV	Partly-skilled occupations
V	Unskilled occupations

In everyday language society is usually divided into three classes: upper, middle and working class with a fourth class of people who are socially excluded because they have neither work nor enough money to provide for an adequate standard of living. This division is also used in the text where it seems appropriate and is particularly useful when looking at the relationship between class and culture. Some people argue that class is not relevant in Scotland today and that we are now a classless society.

Activity

Answer the following questions:

1. What do *you* think are the ways, if any, in which people are divided into classes?

2. Do you think that Scotland has become a classless society? Give three reasons for your answer.

3. Give some comments upon the Registrar General's classification of social class based upon occupation.

SOCIOLGOICAL PERSPECTIVES

So far you have been introduced to a number of **concepts** which will be woven through this chapter and the rest of this book. The present fundamental ideas and building blocks upon which thinking about society and the behaviour of people in society can be built (see Figure 5.2). In order to gain a fuller understanding of sociology and the way in which it sets out to explain the

Society	country or nation state; often distinguished from other societies by language, laws, education, religion etc.
Culture	learned, shared behaviour; the way of life of society's members.
Institution	a group of people organised for a specific purpose (or purposes) e.g. the family, school etc.
Role	the part which an individual plays in a group and the behaviour which is expected of a person in that position.
Status	position in society and the degree of respect which this position commands.
Socialisation	the way in which people learn the culture of their society.
Social class	the division of society usually according to occupation, status and/or power.

Figure 5.2 Conceptual building blocks

social world it is also necessary to look at the different viewpoints or perspectives which sociologists take. Just as you can have a point of view about many things which differs from that of other people (the way you view education, for example, might differ from that of a friend you meet on holiday) so sociologists differ among themselves about the way they look at people and society. These different viewpoints are called **perspectives** and four different perspectives are discussed. They are:

1. a **functionalist** perspective;
2. a **conflict** perspective;
3. an **interactionist** perspective;
4. a **feminist** perspective.

Try not to be put off by long words here, for what these perspectives set out to do is to clarify ways of looking at society. The ideas presented in these perspectives are usually quite straightforward once you have grasped the main ideas. These are not the only sociological perspectives but provide an introductory spectrum which can be enlarged through further study.

A functionalist perspective

Functionalism is one of the earliest sociological perspectives and has fluctuated from being in and out of favour. This perspective still remains useful in its emphasis upon function and in looking at society as something more than the sum total of individuals who go to make it up. Its early emphasis on scientific method or positivism also retains some relevance in sociological thought, as long as this is balanced with other approaches.

Emile Durkheim (1858–1917), a professor at the University of Bordeaux and then the Sorbonne in Paris, a great thinker and writer, developed ideas about society using the term functionalism for the first time. In its earlier stages the essential ideas were that social groups and institutions perform **functions** which are useful to society as a whole. Society is seen as being made up of inter-related parts which form a system, the social system. Understanding of each part can only be gained by looking at the functions which it plays in relation to the whole. A comparison with the human body was made, seeing the body as a system and society as a comparable system. In a human being the heart has specific functions in relation to pumping blood around the body, but its function can only be understood in relation to the whole body. Similarly, a functionalist perspective emphasises the importance of looking at parts of society, such as the family, in terms of their function in and maintenance of the social system as a whole. Two quotations here from Durkheim and Radcliffe-Brown sum up this early thinking:

Consequently, to explain a social fact it is not enough to show the cause on which it depends; we must also, at least in most cases, show its function in the establishment of social order.

(Durkheim, E., 1938)

The function of any recurrent activity, such as the punishment of a crime, or a funeral ceremony, is the part it plays in the social life as a whole and therefore the contribution it makes to the maintenance of the structural continuity.

(Radcliffe-Brown, 1935)

Talcot Parsons, an American sociologist, writing over a period of 50 years from the 1930s to the 1970s, further refined functionalist thinking. He was the son of a Congregationalist minister and spent his whole adult life in teaching and research positions in the USA, with a short period of training in Europe. Parsons saw societies as having certain needs which must be met if they are to survive and that social institutions function to meet these needs. Although Parsons is seen as developing previous functionalist theories, the emphasis of the functionalist perspective remained, and continues to remain, centred upon four assumptions:

- society is seen as greater than the sum of its parts;
- the various parts of the social 'system' perform functions in relation to the whole;
- the parts of society are integrated and inter-dependent;
- 'society' is seen in terms of a consensus or agreement about the values and norms which guide social life.

Criticisms of functionalism

One of the main criticisms levelled against functionalists is that they fail to take adequate account of conflict in society. Functionalists do not ignore conflict but often attempt to explain it in terms of the contribution which conflict can make to social order or as being dysfunctional and something which society should try to correct. Functionalists do not see conflict as fundamental or inherent in society.

A further criticism is that functionalists, in concentrating upon social facts, social functions and the social system failed to take account sufficiently of the individual in society.

Feminists have seen much of functionalist theory as being gender blind and conservative, promoting traditional views of such institutions as the family and in so doing perpetuating patriarchy, the roles of women as housewives and mothers and contributing to continuing inequality and disempowerment.

Finally, through seeing society in terms of functions and harmony functionalists have failed to emphasise change and the need for progress.

Advantages of functionalism

In spite of the above criticisms, functionalism continues to be useful in encouraging a focus upon the functions of the parts of society and their contribution to the whole. This continued usefulness, if balanced against the views of other perspectives, is demonstrated in the sections which examine aspects of society: the family, education, deviance and institutionalisation.

A conflict perspective

Society is like a more or less confused battle ground. If we watch from on high, we can see a variety of groups fighting each other, constantly forming and reforming, making and breaking alliances.

(Ian Craib, 1984)

Unlike the functionalist perspective which emphasises equilibrium, balance, shared values and norms and a concentration upon the function of various aspects of society in contributing to the maintenance of the whole, conflict perspectives rest upon the view that conflict is fundamental between various groups in society which have differing interests from one another. The interests of some groups are better served by the way in which society is organised than the interests of others, i.e. some groups of people in society get a better deal from 'society' than other groups. This is not because some people work harder or deserve more but results from the way in which society is structured. In this section two major theorists who have put forward conflict perspectives will be considered. These are Karl Marx and Ralph Dahrendorf.

Karl Marx (1818–1883) was born in Germany, lived for a time in Paris where he met Friedrich Engels with whom he formed a life-long friendship, moved to Brussels and finally settled in London in 1949. He is best known for his views about economic life, especially capitalism expressed in *Das Capital* and for promoting Communism in *The Manifesto of the Communist Party* (see Bottomore, T. and Ruben, M., 1963). He put forward a conflict view of society believing that in capitalist society there is a conflict of interest between two groups: the ruling class which owns and controls the means of production, e.g. factories, and the subject class or proletariat which produces labour but which is exploited and oppressed by the ruling class. In Marx's view only when the means of production are communally owned (i.e. equally owned and shared by everyone) will classes and conflict disappear. For Marx economic class and ownership of the means of production were the most fundamental divisions in society and the source of conflicts of interest.

The second conflict theorist to be considered is **Ralph Dahrendorf** (born 1929). By coincidence he too was born in Germany and subsequently moved to London. In London he became Professor of Sociology at the London School of Economics. Dahrendorf took Marx's theories as a staring point but argued that in the twentieth century changes have taken place in society which necessitate a re-evaluation of Marx.

In *Out of Utopia* (in Coser and Rosenberg, 1966), Dahrendorf sees functionalist perspectives as being utopian or idealistic in their analysis of society and proposes that at least one other way of looking at society is required. For Dahrendorf this is the conflict perspective. This perspective emphasises change as continuous and normal in society and that 'the great creative force that carries along change . . . is social conflict'. He goes on to state that 'wherever there is social life there's conflict, and the surprising thing in society would not be the presence of conflict but the absence of conflict.' He is not here just talking about conflicts like wars and revolutions but what happens in Mrs MacDonald's house or the local pub. Thus so far two main concepts in the conflict model are **change** and **conflict**. For Dahrendorf a third important concept is **constraint**.

Unlike the functionalists who hold that agreement holds societies and organisations together Dahrendorf argues that they are held together 'not by consensus but by constraint, not by universal agreement but by coercion of some by others'. Thus for Dahrendorf some groups in society coerce and others are coerced, some groups constrain, others are constrained. This has some similarities to Marx who argued that the owners of the means of production constrain and coerce workers. Dahrendorf differs from Marx in seeing the situation as much more complicated than this, in seeing other sources of conflict than economic ones and the possibility that in some situations a person may be the source of constraint and in other situations may be constrained. For example, a teacher might constrain students in the classroom but might herself be constrained in what she can teach by the education authority. The essential point to grasp is that conflict, change and constraint, and not consensus, are points of departure in any analysis of social situations.

Dahrendorf again differs from functionalists in stating that the conflict perspective is not the only way of looking at society, in a way building in his own criticism of the perspective. Functionalists usually claim that theirs is a comprehensive model and can be used to explain all social phenomena. But Dahrendorf states:

As far as I can see, we need . . . both the equilibrium and the conflict models of society; and it may well be that . . . society has two faces of equal reality: one of stability, harmony and consensus and one of change, conflict and constraint.

An interactionist perspective

In contrast to the large or macro perspectives presented by functionalism and conflict theories an interactionist perspective focuses attention upon the meanings which **individuals** give to social actions. Here interactions among individuals are seen as the starting point rather than society. The importance of society is not denied but social structures are seen as changeable through individual actions and as open to varying interpretations.

There are many variations upon the interactionist theme. They go under such names as symbolic interactionism, social action theory and labelling theory. Just a note here about the word

theory. A theory can be seen as an organising principle, a statement about what are held to be general laws about a subject. A **perspective** is the view about society based upon a theory or group of theories. You may if you read other sociology books see the word theory used where in this book perspective is used. This is because here the emphasis is upon enabling you to see society in different ways, from different viewpoints. These viewpoints are often the result of combining several theories and are very broad rather than narrowly focused around a few ideas. This distinction between theory and perspective has already been considered in Chapter 4 (page 00).

To return to an interactionist perspective, this section takes ideas from three thinkers: George Herbert Mead who developed ideas about symbolic interactionism, Max Weber who developed what has come to be known as social action theory and Howard Becker (1966) who developed labelling theory. The main emphasis here is upon Mead's symbolic interactionism which is explained in some detail. Becker's labelling theory is developed in the section on deviance and Weber is written about briefly, though a thorough consideration of his work is beyond the scope of this book.

In symbolic interactionism symbols are seen as the foundation upon which interactions are built. A symbol can be defined as:

Any gesture, artifact, sign or concept which stands for or expresses something else . . .

(Abercrombie et al, 1994)

A word can be a symbol. For example, the word 'table' has a symbolic meaning – it stands for a particular set of ideas about a thing called a table which is immediately understood by those using the symbol and includes some meanings and excludes others. What does the symbol 'table' mean to you? Does it mean somewhere to eat? Does it mean a potentially useful weapon? A gesture such as a handshake is also a symbol, which signifies a particular meaning, and in many societies is used as a welcome. This meaning is, however, culturally determined. The handshake on its own, without its symbolic meaning, would be meaningless to people in interaction situations.

Symbolic Interactionism originated in the USA. Among the founders was George Herbert Mead. Mead (1863–1931) was an American philosopher whose ideas had a great influence upon sociology. One of Mead's central ideas was that individuals develop their interactions and their ideas through their ability to put themselves in the position of others. The individual imagines the effect of symbolic communication (verbal and non-verbal communication, words, gestures etc.) on others and so can anticipate their response. This is done through internal 'conversations' which individuals have with themselves and the responses imagined become internalised in the individual as what Mead called 'the generalised other'. According to Mead, without symbols there would be no human interaction and no human society. It is the use of symbols which distinguishes human interaction from the interactions of other species. It is only through symbols that the responses of others can be imagined. The process of imagining responses is called by Mead 'role-taking'. If I see you crying, for example, my response will be largely determined by me imagining myself in your position. It is likely that my response will be appropriate because I have internalised how to respond to crying and can, in my imagination, take the role of someone crying and respond to it. This process of role-taking is also central to the development of a concept of **self**.

Mead, in developing his thoughts about self distinguishes between the 'me' and the 'I'. To quote Mead (in Coser and Rosenberg, 1976):

The 'I' is the response of the organism to the attitudes of the others; the 'me' is the organised set of attitudes of others which one himself assumes. The attitude of the others constitute the organ-ised 'me', and then one reacts towards that as an 'I'.

The distinction between 'me' and 'I' is an important, though rather, difficult, one to grasp. 'I' is the self concept, 'me' is the definition of yourself in specific roles. 'I' has been built up from your reactions to others, their reactions to you and the way in which those reactions have been interpreted. This combination of social reaction and individual interpretation gives rise to people making choices about which roles they take on board and how those roles are performed.

This rather brief introduction to symbolic interactionism hardly does a rather complex per-spective justice but it does emphasise the main ingredients:

- an emphasis on the individual in society rather than society determining the indi-vidual;
- symbols as the basis for human interaction and therefore of human society;
- role-taking, i.e. imagining yourself in the role of the other;
- the development of a self concept.

Criticisms of symbolic interactionism

Among the criticisms which have been levelled against this perspective are the following:

- the importance of the historical aspects of society and the influences of institutions, power and class are given insufficient consideration;
- symbolic interactionism does not look at the how or the why of social behaviour which takes place in terms of social norms;
- symbolic interactionists fail to explain the source or origin of the symbols upon which communication and interaction depend.

But, as William Skidmore (1975) has pointed out:

. . . on the positive side, it is clearly true that some of the most fascinating sociology is in the symbolic interactionist tradition.

Max Weber and social action theory

Max Weber is often regarded as the founder of modern sociology. He was born in Erfurt in Germany and studied at the universities of Heidelberg, Gottingen and Berlin. His ideas do not really fall into any particular category and he is often placed by himself between Marxists and interactionists. He developed ideas about society which fall both within the conflict and interactionist perspectives. One of his contributions was the development of **social action theory**. Weber thought that sociology should aim to understand the meaning of social actions, to step into the shoes of the society being studied and understand it from the perspective of its people. He also thought that a good way to build theories about society was to develop what he called 'ideal types' which were exaggerations of social characteristics, rather like caricatures, with which particular aspects of society could be compared. For example, he developed an 'ideal type' bureaucracy with which actual organisations could be compared. Max Weber was such a wide-ranging and complex thinker that it is impossible to do him justice here and the reader is directed to other sources, such as Paul Stevens et al (1998), for a more detailed examination of his work.

A feminist perspective

Feminism as a perspective, though covering a multitude of theories and ideas, sets out to explain the position of women in society and to focus attention upon how women have been subordinated and oppressed. The perspective is closely linked to feminism as a social movement, which advocates equality of opportunity for women and men and the eradication of inequalities which exist between them.

As a sociological perspective feminism has only relatively recently made its way into general sociological literature. For example, a book entitled 'Sociological Perspectives' (Thompson et al) published in 1971 had no mention of feminism and out of 44 readings not a single one was written by a woman or addressed issues specifically in relation to women. By 1991 Haralambos, in *Sociology – Themes and Perspectives*, was giving considerable attention to feminist thought.

In spite of the relatively recent emergence of feminist perspectives in sociology, feminist ideas have been around for a lot longer. Mary Wollstonecraft expressed an equal rights doctrine as early as 1792 in her 'Vindication of the Rights of Women'; the Suffragettes fought for votes for women at the beginning of the twentieth century; feminist writers such as Simone de Beauvoir in France and Germaine Greer in Britain gained prominence in the 1950s to 1970s. More recently feminist thinkers have emphasised the diversity of feminist thought and several branches of feminism can be identified such as liberal feminism, radical feminism, Marxist feminism and black feminism, all of which will receive some attention later in the text.

All of the above developments can be referred to as the three waves of feminism:
- **Wave 1** – the beginnings of feminism, fighting for women's civil rights, especially equal rights to vote and to property;
- **Wave 2** – a more radical focus seeking reform of society in order to promote an equality of power in society and to eradicate male domination of women from all spheres of life;
- **Wave 3** – postmodern feminism, emphasising the diverse needs of different groups of women, e.g. black women, working class women, though retaining the main focus of eradicating all inequalities.

In order to understand more fully the ideas behind a feminist perspective, ideas associated with gender and patriarchy are further explored. Many men have argued that differences in biology between men and women justify the domination of women by men and that they should occupy different roles in society. For example, one argument runs: because women can become pregnant and bear children they should stay at home to look after the children they produce, this is their 'natural' role. Since it is their 'natural' role to bear and look after children and be at home with them, it is also 'natural' that they should do the housework whilst they are there. Women, it is argued, make unreliable workers anyway, always taking time off to have children or to look after them when they are ill.

A feminist perspective seeks to give insight into why there is absolutely nothing 'natural', there is nothing in female biology, which determines that women should perform childcare or housework or should be any less reliable than men, given the same opportunities and rights. Ann Oakley (1974) is a sociologist who has researched and discussed the role of women in Britain. She gave research status, for the first time, to the subject of housework. She argues that although male and female are biological terms, gender roles in society are **culturally** and not biologically determined. Most feminist thinkers support this view and feel that confusion between sex (male and female) and gender (masculine and feminine) has been used as an excuse to promote the subordination of women, through placing them in roles which are given inferior status in society. Both the roles and their inferior status are culturally and not biologically determined and are the basis of patriarchy or male dominance in society.

Culture, as transmitted through the socialisation process and through the use of language, has reinforced patriarchy by determining, or at least influencing, the ways in which men and women think of themselves and of one another psychologically. Cultural ideas about gender have led to differences in **power** in the broadest sense (power to make decisions and choices) between men and women with men retaining the balance of power and being dominant in society. Feminism in all of its forms has consistently argued against any biological, social, cultural or rational basis for men to have dominance over women. The different perspectives of different groups of feminists are now briefly explained in order to demonstrate the various emphases which feminists place upon issues.

Liberal feminism works within the democratic structures of society to promote gradual change in the political, economic and social systems. Equality of opportunity, especially in education and in work, is the main aim of liberal feminism. It is a continuation of the first wave of feminism and has built upon early efforts to gain property, rights and the vote, to support such pieces of legislation as the Sex Discrimination Act and the Equal Pay Act and their implementation and to eradicate stereotypes of women and men presented by, for example, TV and children's books.

Radical feminism emphasises patriarchy or the rule by men as the fundamental cause of the oppression of women. Politically this movement promotes revolutionary change to liberate women and has promoted women's rights to control their reproduction and their bodies, as well as changes in social structures to promote sexual equality.

Marxist feminism does not see men as the only cause of women's exploitation, but attributes the main cause to capitalism and places stress on the exploitation of women in both paid employment (in the workplace) and unpaid work (in the home) resulting in their lack of power. The aim is the overthrow of capitalism and the emergence of communism which would, it is hypothesised, give women and men equality.

Black feminism presents many diverse views belonging to all of the above perspectives but also emphasises the particular issues surrounding black women in both Western and Third World countries. It attributes the oppression of women to racism, whether intended or not, and to class oppression, as well as to male domination. Black feminists have developed the special concerns of black women, for example for refugees and for the promotion of reproduction rights.

Criticisms of feminist perspectives

There are criticisms of feminist perspectives both from within the ranks of feminism and outside them. From within feminism radical feminists feel that liberal feminists don't go far enough in the reforms which they are promoting and supporting. Black feminists feel that liberal and radical feminists are often blind to the particular concerns of black women and the racism they experience. Critiques of feminism often rest upon a misconception about the aims of feminist thought or come from groups who feel threatened by the prospect of equality of power and opportunity between men and women. Sociological research and reasoned philosophical thought provide no sound basis for such a misconception and the uphill struggle for feminist thinkers to promote equal rights for women and equality of opportunity rests upon a sociological perspective which has sought to explain women's oppression through analysis of culture, including socialisation, the use of language, development of psychological thought patterns and ideas about the distribution of power.

In summary, the following points can be made about feminist perspectives:
- there is an emphasis upon gender as a starting point in sociological analysis;
- they direct attention to the unequal distribution of power of men and women in society;
- they direct attention to the study of culture, roles, socialisation and patriarchy;
- they act as an academic base for the feminist movement which advocates equality of opportunity for women and men and eradication of inequalities.

Activity

Draw up a table which illustrates the main sociological perspectives, summarising the most important points of each one, the advantages, disadvantages and main theorists. You will then have this to refer to as you read the following sections.

ASPECTS OF SOCIETY

So far this chapter has tried to give you different ways of looking at society, different viewpoints from which to look at what is familiar to you. In doing this you are developing what the American sociologist, C. Wright Mills called 'the sociological imagination'. With these viewpoints or perspectives and the resulting sociological imagination, which constantly looks at the relationship between the individual and the social structure of the social structure and the individual, depending upon your starting point, some aspects of society are now considered which are of particular relevance to care practice. These aspects of society are the family, education, deviance and institutionalisation.

THE FAMILY

We used to be able to talk about the family; now we've got to talk about families because there are lots of different forms of the family.

(Neil Frude, 1997)

The family – that dear Octopus from whose tentacles we never quite escape.

(Dodie Smith, 1938)

The family as an institution is not a static entity, stereotyped in its forms, or unchanging in its functions. It is a dynamic system, susceptible to change; it's influenced in the short term by the personality, development and relationships of its members, and in the longer term by the pressures of economic events and historical processes.

(Martin Herbert, 1986)

The first thing to recognise when talking about 'the family' is that there is no one family type but many differing manifestations of the family in terms of such variables as size, composition, gender and values of family members. In addition, families are part of the social structure and as such are affected by and affect the culture in which they exist. This culture is in turn influenced by many social, economic and historical forces such as social class, ethnicity and regional differences. Scotland in the late twentieth century is characterised by a great variation in family patterns and this has repercussions on how 'normal' families are defined. What do you see as a 'normal' family? What percentage of the 20 people you know best in your age group live in what you have defined as a 'normal' family? An article in *Scotland on Sunday* (Gill, A., 1999) begins:

Jane and Trevor Bechtel are a rapidly vanishing breed: a married couple with two young children where the wife chooses to stay at home while the husband goes out to work.

Morag Henderson is becoming much more common: an unemployed single mother living with her two children in an inner-city flat.

Activity

Figure 5.3 below entitled 'Nuclear fallout' provides statistics which relate to the family in Scotland. Using this table indicate at least four changes which have taken place in the family between 1977 and 1997.

A definition of the family, such as George Peter Murdock's of 1949 quoted on page 192, can no longer be seen as universally relevant. Murdock took a sample of 250 societies ranging

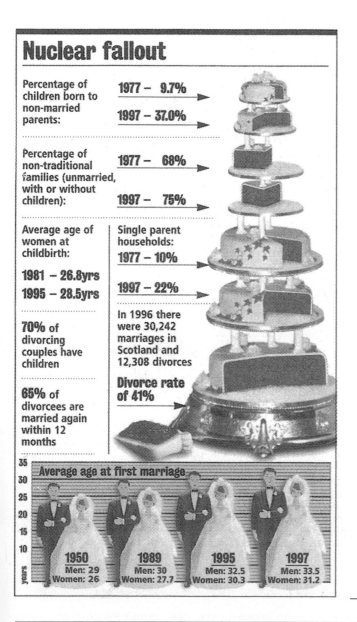

Nuclear fallout

Percentage of children born to non-married parents:
1977 – 9.7%
1997 – 37.0%

Percentage of non-traditional families (unmarried, with or without children):
1977 – 68%
1997 – 75%

Average age of women at childbirth:
1981 – 26.8yrs
1995 – 28.5yrs

70% of divorcing couples have children

65% of divorcees are married again within 12 months

Single parent households:
1977 – 10%
1997 – 22%

In 1996 there were 30,242 marriages in Scotland and 12,308 divorces

Divorce rate of 41%

Average age at first marriage
1950 Men: 29 Women: 26
1989 Men: 30 Women: 27.7
1995 Men: 32.5 Women: 30.3
1997 Men: 33.5 Women: 31.2

Figure 5.3 Nuclear Fallout
(*Scotland on Sunday*, 31 January 1999)

from small hunting and gathering bands to large-scale industrial societies and developed the following definition:

A family is a social group characterised by common residence, economic co-operation and reproduction. It includes adults of both sexes, at least two of whom maintain a socially approved sexual relationship and one or more children, own or adopted, of the sexually co-habiting adults.

Although this might have been acceptable in 1949, even then it hardly encompassed all possible family types. Married or co-habiting couples in the absence of children, for example, can be regarded as a family in the support which they provide for one another. A definition more applicable to the realities of twentieth century Britain is taken from *Social Trends*. This is a definition of a nuclear family, explained below.

A family is defined as a married or co-habiting couple, with or without their never married children who have no children of their own, or a lone parent with such children. People living alone are not considered to form a family.

(*Social Trends*, 28, 1998)

Sociological concepts which relate to the family

Before going on to discuss the family in terms of different sociological perspectives there are some family concepts which contribute to an understanding of the family and changes which are taking place within it. The first distinction to be made is that between the nuclear and the extended family. The **nuclear family** accords with the definition from *Social Trends* above and usually takes one of three forms: a couple in a socially recognised union and child or children; a single parent and child or children; or a couple without children, all sharing the same household. 'Socially recognised union' includes married and co-habiting couples, step-families, adoptive and foster families, but as yet there is little social recognition of lesbian or homosexual relationships incorporated into family structures, though this is slowly changing. An **extended family** consists of all family members beyond the nuclear family and this has both vertical and horizontal dimensions.

Rosser and Harris (1965) defined the extended family as:

. . . any persistent kinship-grouping of persons related by descent, marriage or adoption, which is wider than the nuclear family, in that it characteristically spans three generations from grandparents to grandchildren.

Activity

Look at your own family and draw a diagram which illustrates this. Label each family member and draw a line round the nuclear family to which you belong, to distinguish it from the extended family.

In order to clarify further the present nature of the family in Britain an excellent article by Peter Willmott, reproduced in O'Donnell (1993), is summarised below. In 1957 Peter Willmott and Michael Young published a now famous study of family life in Bethnal Green, London. At that time this was a fairly stable working class community where most residents had lived for a long time and over 90 per cent of residents had some relatives living in the district. Kinship was a very important element in people's lives and kinship contact from and to the extended family, in the form of face to face support, was a common part of life, with a high proportion of married women with children seeing their own mothers on a daily, or at least weekly, basis. Willmott makes the point that by the 1980s, although enormous changes had taken place in what were old established areas and in the way society functions, the role of kinship and the role of the extended family were (and still are) very important in the lives of a high proportion of the population. In a study of a London suburb (Willmott, 1986) the proportion of couples seeing relatives at least weekly was precisely two thirds. Two important changes have served to influence contact with relatives: greater mobility, especially by car, and the telephone. To quote Willmott:

Greater mobility has helped give kinship a new face: proximity no longer matters as much as it did . . . Today the wider family could equally well be called the 'telephone family'.

Willmott goes on to suggest that there are now three broad kinship arrangements in Britain:

- the **local extended family** with relatives living near each other providing mutual aid on a continuing basis. This kind of arrangement applies to approximately one in eight of the adult population of Britain and is more common in Scotland, the Midlands and the North of England than in Southern England;
- the **dispersed extended family** where members of the extended family still maintain contact and, although they are not all living in one locality, support is still provided both in an emergency and on a regular basis. Research evidence from many sources suggests that this operates for about half the adult population.
- the **attenuated extended family** is a term used to describe people who still have an extended family but only maintain limited contact with it either from choice or because distance or finance prevents this or for a mixture of reasons. For example many students break away for a time from their family of origin (though they often return in the vacations) and for them friends matter more and family less than at other stages in their lives.

So the evidence points to the continuation of the family as an important institution in its continuing relevance to people's lives. But what about the family and sociological perspectives? How can different perspectives enhance our understanding of this major aspect of society? The four perspectives outlined earlier in the chapter are now returned to and assessed in terms of their contribution to the understanding of the family in Britain today.

Functionalism and the family

Functionalist sociologists concentrate on looking at the family and society in terms of its functions both for society and for the individuals in that society. Some functionalists have made the leap from trying to demonstrate that the family is universal to saying that if the family is universal then it must also be necessary. For example George Peter Murdock (1949) after studying a sample of 250 societies, suggested that the family is found in every society and has four main functions which he called sexual, reproductive, economic and educational.

Activity

Read the case studies of the McDonald and Khan families in Chapter 10 and say how you think these families achieve the four main family functions suggested by Murdock.

In a similar way to Murdock, Talcott Parsons argued that there are two 'basic and irreducible' functions of the family: primary socialisation (i.e. early childhood socialisation which serves to internalise culture and develop personality) and the stabilisation of adult personalities through emotional security and the performance of appropriate social roles.

Both Murdock and Parsons have been criticised for presenting a rather idealised picture of family life, especially since their theories implied families which are harmonious and integrated. There was little consideration of the problems which beset many families, e.g. divorce and single parenthood, or of diverse family patterns and cultures in a multi-cultural society, or of the ways different families allocate and perform social roles.

Some of these criticisms have been partly met by later functionalist sociologists who appreciate the problems which families may experience and the changes which have taken place in family structures, but maintain that families in some form or another still perform useful functions in the late twentieth century. Sociologists such as Ronald Fletcher (1988) and Young and Willmott maintain that family functions may have changed but they have not diminished. Young and Willmott, using their research in London claim that the family:

...*can provide some sense of wholeness and permanence to set against the more restricted and transitory roles imposed by the specialised institutions which have flourished outside the home.*

(Willmott and Young, in O'Donnell, 1993)

Activity

1. What do you think? Set up a small research project among your friends to look at what their families do.

2. Look again at the case studies of the McDonalds and Khans in Chapter 10 and analyse them in terms of the functions which the families perform for the individuals and for the wider society.

Fletcher maintains that the functions of the family have increased in detail and importance. The family's role in socialisation is as important as ever, the family has a responsibility for the health and welfare of its members, the family is a major consumer of goods and services.

THE FAMILY FROM A CONFLICT PERSPECTIVE

By contrast with the functionalist view which emphasises the family as a positive force, conflict theorists present a perspective which views the family as serving the needs of some sections of society more than, and often at the expense of, others. For example, from a Marxist viewpoint the family favours the interests of the owners of the means of production. Marx's friend and colleague, Friedrich Engels, was a major proponent of this view. He saw the monogamous nuclear family developing alongside and supporting capitalism. A nuclear family structure for Engels provides the owners of the means of production with a way of passing wealth from one generation to another through the male line. At the same time workers are stabilised within families and inadvertently perpetuate the system by being dependent upon their waged labour to support themselves and their families. Later Marxists have emphasised that in modern society the family consumes the products of the capitalist system and that people must continue in waged service and manufacturing jobs in order to maintain their families. They depend upon the products produced through their labour and perpetuate the need for them which gives the owners of the means of production (capitalists) the power to continue to make a profit.

The somewhat different emphasis of Dahrendorf's conflict theory provides a more complex and complicated analysis of the family in conflict terms. If you look back at the account of Dahrendorf's perspective you will be reminded that the three central concepts were change, conflict and constraint. **Change** in Dahrendorf's view is a natural social phenomenon. Society and its parts are in a perpetual state of change, a phenomenon which is not adequately accounted for if society is viewed from a functionalist perspective. Change in the family is illustrated in many ways. Increases in divorce rates, increases in the number of step families, the presence of single parent families as an accepted part of the social structure, the emergence of gay and lesbian families, multi-cultural families; all of these illustrate changes in the family which are neither good nor bad, functional nor dysfunctional, but part of the inevitable move and shift which is always taking place in society.

Constraint upon the family by external factors is illustrated through the promotion of norms and values and through the law and social policy. The present Labour government, for example, through promoting 'family values' is encouraging people to behave in particular ways, interpreted by conflict theorists as constraint. Parents have legal responsibilities to their children (emphasised in the Children (Scotland) Act of 1995), social norms can still be critical of divorce, The Christian Church and most other religions continue to promote marriage and the procreation of children within marriage as the most acceptable way of leading family life. These laws, norms and values constrain individuals, and, according to many conflict theorists, prevent individual creativity and achievement. These theorists do not present the alternative view that the family can provide the emotional stability from which individual creativity and achievement can emerge. Do you think that different families achieve different results in different ways?. Does conflict theory apply to some families and not to others?

Conflict (and also constraint) is illustrated through the occurrence of domestic violence and child abuse. Many critics of the family were expressing a conflict view of it, usually alongside an interactionist perspective. When Edmund Leach (1971) made the following statement he was expressing a conflict perspective of the family:

Far from being the basis of the good society, the family, with its narrow privacy and tawdry (grubby) secrets, is the source of all our discontents.

He goes on to say that within the family 'parents fight, the children rebel' and his solution was not that dissimilar to that of Engels when he says that

... children need to grow up in larger, more relaxed domestic groups centred on the community rather than on mother's kitchen ...

Dobash and Dobash (1980), in a Scottish study of domestic violence, said:

For most people, and especially for women and children, the family is the most violent group to which they are likely to belong. Despite fears to the contrary, it is not a stranger but a so-called loved one who is most likely to assault, rape or murder us.

They gave the extremely alarming statistic that the women they studied, drawn from refuges for battered women, had suffered 32 000 domestic assaults. Only 517 of these were reported to the police, i.e. fewer than 2 per cent.

Criticisms of the conflict perspective in relation to the family in twentieth century Scotland

(Before you read these criticisms, list five of your own views of conflict perspectives; these views may agree or disagree with the perspectives presented above).

1. The views of Marxists, such as Engels, do not take into account the changes which have taken place in society, which now has a large middle class, lots of people, who though not owners of the means of production do own property and/or shares, and who do not see themselves as oppressed and alienated.
2. Like functionalists, many conflict theorists do not account for or take into account the enormous variations in families.
3. The Conflict perspective puts too much emphasis upon conflict and does not account for the fact that many people continue to live harmoniously within nuclear families and see their families as a major source of comfort and emotional support. Only a small proportion of the population doesn't have any contact with at least one other family member.

These are only a few of the criticisms of a conflict perspective. As illustrated above, even among sociologists who hold a conflict perspective of society there is disagreement. Dahrendorf, for example, has attempted to address some of the criticisms levelled at Marx but in doing so has made the whole process of looking at society much more complicated and difficult to understand; but then society is complicated and difficult to understand and Dahrendorf does at least provide some conceptual tools which help in this process.

The family from an interactionist perspective

One of the most relevant features of an interactionist perspective in relation to the family is its part in the development of a self concept. If you look back at the account of this perspective (page 184) you will see that the starting point is the individual interacting with society. The **individual's** experience of family is one of the structures upon which the self is constructed. For most people the family contributes to the framework of the self, it is part of what Mead called the 'generalised other'. Individuals learn the symbolic meaning of family and family roles initially through play. They gradually acquire knowledge of the expectations and attitudes of others about family roles, and experience of roles, including family roles, enables people to be members of 'a community' or of society. There are, however, still choices which the individual 'I' can make about which roles are taken on board and how these roles are performed. The interactionist view, in seeing individuals as both shaped by and influenced by their social environment, and in turn actively creating and influencing this environment gives rise to the diverse ways in which family roles are performed or even chosen at all. The symbolic interactionist view of the family differs fundamentally from the functionalist view of the family in emphasising the part the individual plays in creating his or her own social world, whilst at the same time recognising that this world is also being influenced through the performance of social roles.

Activity

Now look at the case studies of the McDonald and Khan families in Chapter 10 from this perspective and look especially at Andy and Tanveer.

How have Andy and Tanveer acquired knowledge of family roles? What other facts, as well as their families, do you think have influenced Andy and Tanveer in the creation of their self-concepts?

A feminist perspective of the family

Feminist theorists have had a field day with the family, backed up by some very substantial evidence that even in the late twentieth century women still perform most of the housework, most of the childcare, still experience violence in the home and are far from equal in their status as family members or as members of the workforce. Paternalism and oppression are alive and well and a feminist perspective of the family focuses upon the relationship between women, the family and society. It is closely related to the more political stance of pursuing equality and empowerment within the family and elsewhere.

In this section the main features of the various feminist perspectives identified on page 000 will be examined in terms of 'the family', remembering that there is not a single but many kinds of family manifestation in Britain and also several feminist perspectives, not just one.

Gender is the starting point for examining what happens in the family from a feminist perspective. Here the research of Ann Oakley (1985) into participation in housework and childcare is especially relevant. Although her research was fairly small-scale (a study of 40 families) she attempted to make her sample as representative as possible. She found that few marriages could be defined as egalitarian and although there was greater equality among middle class than working class families, in only 15 per cent of the families she studied did men have a high level of participation in housework and in only 25 per cent in childcare. Figure 5.4 below illustrates this point.

Lena Dominelli (1998) also discussed housework in terms of black women and states:

Black women have, therefore, carried the burden of doing the housework for the world. This included working as domestic servants for white middle class women ... Consequently black women's oppression is not the same as white women's even if they share the same gender and class.

	High	Medium	Low
Husband's participation in housework			
Working class	10%	5%	85%
Middle class	20%	45%	35%
Husband's participation in childcare			
Working class	10%	40%	50%
Middle class	40%	20%	40%

Figure 5.4 Husband's participation in domestic tasks

Adapted from Ann Oakley, *The Sociology of Housework*. Basil Blackwell, Oxford.

The second area of family study from a feminist perspective is the distribution of **power**. Power may be exercised through decision-making, agenda setting and choosing what issues are raised and discussed. Edgell (1980), in a study of middle class couples, looked at family decision-making. He examined decisions which were perceived by the couples as important or unimportant and found that in most of the families in his sample the male decided the overall allocation of money and made most of the decisions which were regarded as important, whereas women were relegated to making decisions which were considered minor, e.g. interior decoration, children's clothes and domestic spending.

Both the areas of gender and power are linked to the other areas of study from a feminist perspective, the study of **culture**, **roles**, **socialisation and patriarchy**. All of these areas are illustrated by the above studies. Thus when Oakley showed that women still do most of the housework and the childcare she also demonstrated that these tasks are associated with culture. Women are **socialised** to perform these **roles** and it continues to be in the interests of men to keep women in these roles. The role of mother/wife, even in an age of enlightenment, is still passed from one generation to the next and as Graham Allen (1985) said

. . . the female is chronically disadvantaged from the start by the socially constructed framework of values and norms which constrain her options.

Paternalism in terms of the domination of the female by the male is part of the socialisation process and is perpetuated through the roles which women continue to perform and through the decisions which they are permitted to make. It is also perpetuated through the response of some officials towards women. Dobash and Dobash (1980), for example, found in their Scottish study of violence against women, that police officers were 'very unlikely to make an arrest when the offender had used violence against his wife', though practice in relation to this is slowly changing.

EDUCATION – THE SECOND ASPECT OF SOCIETY

We may see education as enhancing every child's (and every person's) development, and at the same time as transmitting values that maintain cohesion and order in society. But education can also be seen as an agency for the selective and unequal distribution of opportunities – or life chances . . .

(J. English and F. Martin, 1983)

The sociological study of education has traditionally focused upon several issues, among which are the part played by schools in the socialisation process, the functions of education, including an examination of the contribution of education to life chances in society, a Marxist/conflict analysis focusing upon social class differences in educational achievements; also since the 1970s there has been an increasing emphasis upon looking at the social systems of schools and pupil/teacher interactions in terms of educational attainment, as well as the ways in which education, gender and ethnicity are associated with one another.

Education may be defined as 'a form of socialisation that involves the deliberate, directed and systematic imparting of knowledge'. (P. Stephens et al, 1998). Most studies of education focus upon schools and other establishments formally established to educate people, though it is acknowledged that some families choose to educate their children themselves. Some of these families have formed an organisation called 'education otherwise'. Some form of compulsory education has existed in Scotland since the Education (Scotland) Act of 1872 when responsibility for formal education was transferred from the church to the state.

Much of the very interesting research which has been conducted in relation to education is illustrated through the various sociological perspectives. It is therefore useful at this stage to return to the four perspectives focused upon in this chapter, beginning with a functionalist analysis.

Education from a functionalist perspective

A functionalist perspective looks at two main issues in relation to education: firstly the function of education in society, including its function in relation to the economy and the world of work; secondly, the social functions which education performs for the individual in society. These two sets of functions are related and similar to one another and can be seen to fall into four main categories. These are economic, political, cultural and selective. 'Economic' refers to the relationship between education and employment; 'political' refers to the relationship between education and political ideology and dogma; 'cultural' refers to the part which education plays as an agent of secondary socialisation; and 'selective' refers to the function of education in providing advantages for some groups through the educational process.

Activity

In terms of your own education write down what functions you think education performs for you. Answering some of the following questions might help.

1. Do you think education helps people to get a job?

2. Do people know more about the culture of their society through going to school?

3. Do school and college students have to abide by certain rules? What influence do you think this will have upon their future behaviour?

4. Can pupils choose some of their school subjects?

5. Do pupils socialise with one another, have friends in school, talk to the teachers?

6. Are there streams or sets in schools, with some students in the top stream, others in the middle and some at the bottom?

7. In your area are there different kinds of school e.g. private, local authority, etc.?

8. Do schools have assemblies? Do they have houses which compete with one another?

9. Is there a hierarchy in schools i.e. some people who are ranked above others

   a)   among the teaching staff?

   b)   among the students?

When you have answered these questions think about each one in terms of **function**. You may initially see something as performing a function in a school but try to think more widely than this. For example, every school has some rules and a start time and a finish time. This may enable the school to function reasonably effectively but do these rules also play a part in the wider society? By learning to get up for school do people also then know how to get up for work? By choosing subjects do students begin to find where they will fit in to the world of work? By abiding by rules are individuals able to transfer their appreciation for the need for (some of) them to a work situation? Do discussions in school lead to an understanding of some of the things going on in society? Do students learn some things about the culture of their society, its history, art, science, politics and religion?

Functionalists, such as Durkheim and Parsons have seen education as one of the main links between the individual and society, one of the ways in which individuals develop a commitment to the norms and values of their society. They see schools as models of the 'social system' as a whole, a place where individuals learn social rules about interaction with other people and rules about social behaviour in any setting. They also develop skills which prepare them for the world of work. All of these things contribute to social unity and stability.

It was announced in *The Guardian* newspaper (August 1998) that schools in California which have previously held lessons in Spanish will now only conduct lessons in the English language. Why do you think this is? There is now a Scottish curriculum which all Scottish schools must follow. Why do you think this has been established? What could some of the unstated consequences of these measure be?

One of the main criticisms of a functionalist perspective is that it assumes that the value system transmitted through education is the value system of 'society' as a whole. In reality this value system may be only that of some members of society and not of others. The needs of some sections of society may be totally ignored by such a blanket view of the functions of education and some whole sections of society may see the education presented to them as irrelevant and unimportant. They feel socially excluded from education and often are physically excluded from school for disruptive behaviour. Is this the fault of the students? of the schools? of that vague thing we call 'society'? Think about this, and discuss it with others if you can, in relation to what has been said about a functionalist perspective.

There is also an underlying assumption within the functionalist perspective that the functions of education are promoted fairly and equitably in society. This view is contested by those who view society from differing perspectives, especially the conflict perspective which is considered next. On the other hand education does perform undoubted functions in relation to the economic and social structure of society. Whether the way in which this is done is fair, is based upon merit and real equality of opportunity is one which a conflict perspective seeks to examine.

Education from a conflict perspective

If you look back at the account of conflict perspectives you will be reminded that conflict, and especially Marxist, theorists view society in terms of conflict and the oppression, exploitation and/or constraint of some members of society by others. A conflict perspective emphasises that social class plays a major part in educational attainment, regardless of individual ability. Although not usually anti-education, most conflict theorists feel that only through radical reform of society as a whole can a fair and equitable education system emerge. A conflict perspective draws attention to what is called 'the hidden curriculum' of education which is to promote uncritical conformity to the values of the capitalist system.

One piece of research and theoretical writing which exemplifies a conflict perspective of education is that of Samuel Bowles and Herbert Gintis (1976). The authors outlined what they called 'The Correspondence Principle', arguing that the hierarchical social relationships of the educational system replicate the equally hierarchical social relations of the economy. Young people are socialised through education to take their place uncritically in the capitalist system. Bowles and Gintis studied 237 students in the final year of a New York high school and found that the highest achievers were students who were punctual, dependable, hard-working, accepting of authority and the direction of teachers. Students who were inventive and creative tended to get low marks and their originality was not encouraged by teachers. Conformity to the norms of the capitalist system was being replicated in the school.

Other studies, though not necessarily Marxist, have demonstrated that class and not ability is the most important determinant not only of educational achievement but also of post-education highly paid employment. One famous study by Douglas the results of which are contained in 'The Home and The School' (1964) followed the progress of 5000 British children from birth until they reached sixteen. Douglas found that education begins at home, that middle class parents provide greater individual attention and set higher standards for their children from birth and follow this through in their school lives through higher attendance at parents meetings, help with homework and encouragement to stay on at school for as long as possible. The greater achievement of middle class children is hardly surprising given these class advantages. Class differences are perpetuated within the school system through teacher attitudes, as demonstrated by Bowles and Gintis among others. Thus Douglas found that 77 per cent of upper middle class, 60 per cent of lower middle class, 53 per cent of upper working class and 37 per cent of lower working class students gained good certificates at GCE 'O' level.

In a Scottish study of children in upper secondary school, Andy Biggart and Andy Furlong (1996) identified three groups with differing attitudes towards education. They called these three groups the 'High-flyers', the 'Plodders' and the 'Drifters'. They found that the high-flyers 'are predominantly middle class and had typically been regarded as having a strong academic potential at an early stage in their careers. Here are some quotes from high-flyers:

Since I was wee, it has always been said that when you leave school you go to university. So I have just taken that as the accepted thing.

All the time I was growing up it was sort of expected of me, from my Mum especially, to go to university and I suppose I always did, I always wanted to like have a degree. It's always sort of appealed to me.

I got on with (the teachers) really well, especially the last couple of years. I found it was more a sort of informal relationship, sort of more your friend than teacher.

The informal and friendly relationships between high-flyers and their teachers was important in their integration in the school and their adoption of the values which the school promoted.

Plodders had a mixture of backgrounds but were predominantly from lower middle class and upper working class families. Before the 1990s many of them would probably have left school at sixteen but a lack of employment opportunities for sixteen year-olds now means that they stay at school, sometimes reluctantly and begrudgingly and sometimes willingly. One begrudging attitude was reflected by the student who said:

You feel there's no relaxation, it's just work, sleep and school; work, sleep and school.

Other plodders gained some of the benefits of high flyers. One student said:

The teachers relate to you a lot easier and they treat you more as adults . . .

A lot of plodders, though, felt pressured by their lower attaining friends or friends who had left school to show a lack of commitment to school. They often did less well than they felt they could have done because of the pressure on them to conform.

The drifters were more likely to come from working class backgrounds, though this wasn't always the case. They would almost certainly have left school if there had been any prospect of a job. Boys seemed to have more difficulty than girls in adapting to staying on at school, with girls more often involved in mixed ability friendships. Some quotes from this group are as follows:

The only reason I stayed on was till I found something to leave for.

To me school is for my mates and having a laugh . . . I don't take things that seriously.

Although this study showed that many more students of all social classes now stay on at school it also demonstrated that especially among the high flyers and the drifters, social class differences determined to a large extent not only attitudes towards education but also attainment levels in exams.

From such evidence conflict theorists would argue that education replicates and perpetuates an unequal class system. Far from remedying inequalities which exist, the education system both intentionally and unintentionally perpetuates the inequitable class system of capitalist society.

Education from an interactionist perspective

The above study by Biggart and Furlong illustrates not only a conflict perspective but also an interactionist one. Individual perceptions of school and interactions between teachers and pupils form part of the evidence. Another theorist who crossed the boundaries from a conflict to an interactionist perspective was Paul Willis (1977) who studied a Midlands school. In true interactionist tradition he began with individual perceptions of school using techniques of observation, informal interviews and diaries. He focused his study upon twelve working class boys whom Willis refers to as 'the lads'. Findings differ from a conflict perspective in stating that these 'lads' only found their place in the economic structure through the unintended consequences of the education system. They avoided work, gave a bad-tempered tut-tutting to the simplest request, regarded themselves as definitely superior to teachers and hard-working, conformist pupils whom they called 'ear 'oles'. These 'lads' were not in any way persuaded to behave as they did by the school, the opposite being the case, but they did at the end of their school lives seek manual labour. The unintended consequence is therefore the perpetuation of the class system. In many ways this study also supports a Marxist perspective using an interactionist approach, with the individual as the starting point.

Education from a feminist perspective

Feminists focus upon many issues in relation to girls and women in the education system. On the political front early feminists promoted the rights of women to equality of opportunity in education, their rights to enter university and to have equality with boys/men to study the subjects of their choice. A sociological, feminist perspective has drawn attention to such issues as perceptions and expectations of girls by their teachers and the different ways in which teachers communicate with girls from boys. Dale Spender (1983) in her book *Invisible Women: Schooling Scandal* argues that girls get less attention than boys in the classroom. She even studied her own class contact as a teacher, where she consciously tried to give equal attention to girls and boys.

When she listened to tape-recordings of her classes she found that boys received 62 per cent of her attention and girls 38 per cent. She also argued that in discussions female contributions are usually treated dismissively by the males present.

In spite of receiving less attention than boys during their school careers, the achievements of girls, in terms of exam results, surpass those of boys. In 1997, for the first time ever the percentage of boys and girls entering university was roughly the same in Scotland. Does this represent equality of opportunity?

DEVIANCE – THE THIRD ASPECT OF SOCIETY

Deviance is a crowd puller. It generates curiosity and interest. Perhaps this has something to do with the fact that deviance, as Durkheim reminds us, is exciting and innovative.

(Stephens, P. et al 1998)

There's something fascinating about deviance. Perhaps most people are sometimes attracted by, as well as sometimes repulsed by, things which go considerably beyond the bounds of what is considered to be 'normal' behaviour. As with most other sociological concepts, there is a great deal of controversy about what deviance is and how it should be defined and no one single definition can be completely satisfactory. Definition to a large extent depends upon the perspective being taken. At this point some definitions are presented which you can alter and refine as you read through the chapter.

Deviance is action that offends the norms of a particular society or of a particular group.

(Stephens, P. et al 1998)

Deviance refers to those acts which do not conform to the norms and values of a particular society.

(Haralambos, M., 1996)

The deviant is one to whom that label has successfully been applied; deviant behaviour is behaviour that people so label.

(Becker, H.S., 1963)

(This definition illustrates an interactionist/labelling perspective further developed on page 209.)

Deviance has generated much discussion within all branches of sociology and to look at it from only one to two perspectives is almost as limiting as it is illuminating. A combination of perspectives is needed, and although perspectives are examined separately, a grasp of several is necessary in examining all of the ways in which deviance occurs and in seeking explanations for it. Explanations cannot be complete without also taking into account psychological factors which may contribute to deviant behaviour. These were examined in the previous chapter.

Crime is one of the main ways in which people deviate from the norms of society. Although a lot of research into deviance has been research into criminal behaviour sociologists, unlike criminologists, consider a much broader range of issues including sexual deviance, drug and alcohol abuse and football hooliganism. Two small points are emphasised at this point, which may seem obvious but which need to be made:

- all crime is deviance but not all deviance is criminal;
- deviance is not only negative; it can be positive and lead to social change.

Sociological studies of deviance, however, usually focus upon those forms of deviance which are regarded negatively, especially since positive deviance in the form of non-criminal innovation is really only partial deviance since it is often carried out within the framework of socially approved norms and values.

Activity

From your understanding of deviance so far, write down ten things which you consider to be deviant. Why do you consider them to be deviant?

As you read though the chapter, try to relate the reasons you have given, to the different perspectives of deviance given below.

A functionalist perspective of deviance

Our old friend Durkheim was among the first sociologists to study deviance, and his theories still receive serious consideration in sociological literature. He saw the potential for deviance to be functional in society, as long as its levels were not too high or too low, arguing that a lot of social change begins with some form of deviance.

Activity

Here are some positive social changes which began with deviance:

- Nelson Mandela became the president of South Africa. He spent more than 25 year of his life in prison for committing terrorist acts in his fight against apartheid.

- Former gangland killer, Jimmy Boyle, who served 15 years for murder, became, in 1998, a member of a Scottish task force to tackle social exclusion. He is also an author and sculptor.

- Oscar Wilde, the author of many famous plays including *The Importance of Being Earnest*, who was arrested for being a homosexual in 1895, has come to be seen as a pioneer in the fight for equal rights for homosexuals. A statue of him was unveiled in London in November 1998. The Culture Secretary,

Chris Smith, said of him: *'It's due to Oscar Wilde in many ways that we today can celebrate a society that generally appreciates diversity and the richness of diversity in our community.'*

Can you think of two other examples of deviance which have led to positive social change?

Durkheim developed the concept of **Anomie** in relation to deviance. He saw this as a condition which occurs when people want, even need, things but don't have the means to get them. For example, if people want to live in a comfortable house, own a car and have a job, observe other people in society with these things but can't have them and really want them, this results in anomie. It is an incompatibility between ends and means, an inability caused not by individual characteristics but by the structure of society, where some people are prevented by social structural factors from achieving what are the 'accepted' values and norms of society.

Durkheim studied suicide, a form of deviance, in one of the first great sociological studies to use statistical evidence, and concluded that increases in suicide rates occurred when anomie increased. R.K. Merton (1968) developed Durkheim's theory of anomie in his studies of North American society in the 1930s to the 1970s and saw the USA as a particularly anomic society. The goals of success through the attainment of wealth and material possessions are stressed without providing the means to attain them for large sections of the population. Jeremy Seabrook's account of property crime in the UK in the 1990s echoes what Durkheim and Merton said about anomie:

The upsurge in crime is the only logical response by certain sections of the poor to the exacerbation of their condition ... They are not only relatively poorer, but they also see the good life, which requires ever more money, receding from them at an accelerating pace.

(Seabrook, 1990)

Other studies of deviance have examined deviant sub-cultures which provide a 'solution' to the 'failure' of members within conventional society. These sub-cultural theories often combine several perspectives including functionalist, conflict and interactionist.

A conflict perspective of deviance

One of the main criticisms of a functionalist perspective is that it fails to take sufficient account of the power structure of society. This has been addressed by Marxists and other conflict theorists who have examined deviance, particularly criminal deviance, not only in terms of who commits crime but in terms of who makes laws, which crimes are acted upon by police and the different treatment received by 'criminals' of different social classes. Marx saw the law as one means by which one class (the rulers/owners of the means of production) kept everyone else in check and maintained their position of power in society. Other Marxists have supported this view.

Criminal legislation has historically given prominence to the protection of property, a factor emphasised by Hermann Mannheim (1960).

Big corporations are among the dominant forces in modern society and the law is often very slow to deal with big-time, big-business crime or to curb the activities of large corporations even when they are known to be causing harm to large numbers of the population. William Chambliss (1978) in a study of crime in Seattle, Washington from 1962 to 1972 concluded that power, in the form of money and influence, is the key factor which determines who gets arrested and who does not. His study showed that 70 per cent of arrests in Seattle were for drunkenness and that it was crime committed by poor people which preoccupied the police rather than the much more expensive crimes of fraud and corruption. The courts and the prisons were and are full of the poor and the powerless. Top executives found guilty in the Guiness share-support trial which involved billions of pounds were given only short sentences. One of those found guilty of the fraud, Ernest Saunders, had his five-year sentence commuted on the grounds of ill health.

Many non-functionalist sociologists have thought that Marxism is an inadequate perspective for looking at deviance, feeling that it goes too far in its emphasis upon relative power and in diminishing the importance of working class crime. A group of sociologists, known as **left realists**, have developed a perspective which seeks to redress the balance by taking all kinds of crime seriously, including domestic violence, sexual harassment, blue collar and white collar crime. Left realists, such as Matthews and Young (1992) have carried out a number of victimisation studies (studies of the victims of crime rather than criminals) demonstrating that crime is often unreported and is a very real problem to ordinary members of the population. Rather than the straightforward power/non-power explanations of Marxists they put forward an explanation for crime based upon **relative deprivation, subculture and marginalisation.**

These explanations, although often referred to as neo-Marxist, do not fall neatly into any one perspective but combine aspects of conflict and interactionist perspectives of deviance and of Durkheim's theory of anomie. Relative deprivation occurs when people see themselves as deprived relative to others in the population. Forming a sub-culture is one possible response to feelings of deprivation whereby members have their own values and norms which are distinct from, though related to, the dominant culture. Marginal groups are those which lack legitimate social organisations to represent their interests; for example they do not work or study. Terms like social exclusion are used to describe marginalised people in society. Tackling deviance, especially criminal deviance, involves tackling all three of these areas, through reducing poverty, increasing prospects of employment and through community involvement.

Activity

Read the account below and analyse why you think that an area like Easterhouse is so susceptible to crime. What can be done about it?

Nine o'clock on a Sunday morning. A trembling woman comes to our flat to phone the police. She had been woken by smoke and discovered a room ablaze from a burning missile thrown through the window. The previous evening a gang had attacked her partner outside the chippie, leaving him with 44 stitches ... Another neighbour, a member of the committee of the agency which employs me, obtained a job as a security guard at £1.90 an hour. She was alone in a disused building when five raiders burst in. While two held knives at her throat, the others made off with the gas cooker.

A mother, having just left her child at the creche run by the local community association, was knocked to the ground by two men who made off with her purse. The next day, the Salvation Army captain tells me that yet again his old van has been stolen. He grins: 'They didn't get far this time. It broke down'.

These crimes occurred within a few days in one district of Easterhouse, a peripheral Glasgow estate where unemployment is high and where 64 per cent of schoolchildren receive clothing grants – that is, they come from families with very low incomes.

(from Bob Holman in O'Donnell, M., 1993)

An interactionist perspective of deviance

Interactionist perspectives of deviance differ from functionalist, Marxist and left realist perspectives in focusing not upon the breaking of society's rules but upon the interaction between the individual 'deviant' and those who define him or her as deviant. Howard Becker is one of the first and major exponents of this perspective emphasising that it is only once someone has been **labelled** as deviant that the consequences of 'being a deviant' come into operation. Becker (1963) states that

... social groups create deviance by making the rules whose infraction constitutes deviance, and by applying those rules to particular people and labelling them as outsiders. From this point of view, deviance is not a quality of the act the person commits, but rather a consequence of the application by others of rules and sanctions to an 'offender'. The deviant is one to whom that label has been applied; deviant behaviour is behaviour that people so label.

The above passage gives the essence of the interactionist approach which emphasises the deviant label and its consequences. In saying that deviant behaviour is behaviour that people so label, Becker is implying that there are behaviours which could be labelled as deviant but they aren't. He gives the example of a brawl involving young people. In a low-income area it may be defined by the police as delinquency – a deviant label; in a wealthy area it may be defined as youthful high spirits – no deviant label is given or gained. Becker also makes the point that there are behaviours which aren't necessarily criminal or offensive but which by being labelled as deviant become deviant.

Becker went on to describe a **deviant career** which often follows once a deviant label has been applied. Firstly the label, e.g. delinquent, nutter, pervert etc. is applied to the individual. This leads to a public reaction and quite often rejection by family, friends and neighbours. This may encourage further deviance because other avenues of behaviour are blocked. The 'deviant' may also join a deviant group which develops a sub-culture with its own deviant norms and values and the deviant career is now well and truly established. The deviant identity becomes incorporated into the individual's self concept. Tim, in 'A Glasgow Gang Observed', (Patrick, J., 1973) illustrates this point very well. His identity and status became increasingly linked to his gang membership and the delinquent activities of the group. He felt that school had rejected him and he in turn had rejected school. Gang membership gave him some sense of belonging. He committed crimes of theft and violence as a member of the gang, was labelled as delinquent by the police, sent to what was then an approved school and gained status in the gang from this. Once this pattern of behaviour was established his deviant career was well and truly launched.

Criticisms of the interactionist perspective of deviance have focused upon the view that there are some behaviours which are not just deviant because they are labelled as deviant by a social audience, they are deviant because they break important social rules. For example, in Western societies a premeditated murder for personal gain is deviant and the person who commits the offence is a murderer whether or not society applies the deviant label. Another criticism of the interactionist perspective is that it does not give any explanation about **why** individuals behave in ways which lead to them being labelled as deviant. In defence of the perspective is the argument that whether or not an act is regarded as deviant and the way in which a deviant act is treated are still important. The consequences of labelling are very real to those so labelled and the consequences of deviant acts differ for individuals of different social groups/classes. Interactionism emphasises the fact that defining deviance is by no means straightforward and directs attention to social reaction as well as to the deviant act itself.

A FEMINIST PERSPECTIVE OF DEVIANCE

A feminist looking at studies of deviance before 1970 is immediately struck by the almost total absence of reference to or studies of women in the context of deviance. Does this mean that there weren't any women who were deviant? Does it mean that the deviance of women was unimportant sociologically? What do you think it means? These are the kinds of question which a feminist asks. Other perspectives are able to ignore women as independently significant or not see that a separate consideration of women in relation to deviance is important. Feminist sociologists and criminologists see the study of deviance before the 1970s as having been written by men about men with a male readership in mind. Fortunately there has been some redressing of the balance since then. Apart from gender blindness two statistical reasons perhaps account for fewer studies of female deviance, especially female crime. Firstly statistically there appear to be fewer women than men who commit crimes. Secondly, there appears to be more leniency in charging women who have committed crimes. Although there is a lot of controversy about the interpretation of statistical information the official figures do show that in 1991 in the UK the rate of females aged 21 and over in prison was 5 per 100 000 whereas the rate for men was 163 per 100 000, i.e. a man was 33 times more likely to be in prison than a woman. Even taking into account the theory that more leniency is shown towards women than men in making convictions, men do seem to commit more crimes than women. It does not, however, mean that female deviance and especially crime should not be studied just because there is less of it. In fact, one legitimate area of study is to look at why there is less female reported crime.

Another area of study is to look at why women commit crimes. Feminist sociologists also direct attention to women as victims of crimes.

Frances Heidensohn (1985) tried to explain why women commit fewer serious crimes and argued that male patriarchy with its elements of power and control make it more difficult for women to deviate from 'society's' norms, with control operating at home (women are expected to look after children and to do more housework than men), in public (women are often afraid to go out in public at night, for example) and at work (through predominantly male hierarchies).

Pat Carlen (1988) conducted a study of 39 women aged 15–46 who had been convicted of one or more crimes. She found that the most common reasons women gave for their criminality were drug (including alcohol) addiction, the search for excitement, being brought up in care and poverty. Only two of her sample had had good jobs before being convicted of their crimes. She presented a theory which had both elements of Durkheim's theory of anomie and of the left-realists, seeing women who committed crimes as being predominantly those who did not have the means to achieve the dominant norms of the society in which they lived.

Women as the victims of crime. The British Crime survey, 1987, suggested that victims reported about 1 in 3 criminal incidents. There was an enormous variation however in reporting rates for different kinds of crime, ranging from nearly 100 per cent for thefts of motor vehicles to less than 10 per cent for sexual assaults, most of which were committed against women or children. Dobash and Dobash (1980) estimated that 25 per cent of violent crime reported to the police involved violence against women by their partners. In 1990/91 1890 women were admitted to refuges in Scotland – 3900 were turned away because there wasn't room for them.

Activity

1. What do you see as the importance of a feminist perspective of deviance? Suggest the subject of two studies which could increase knowledge about the relationship between women and crime.

2. Make three comments about the statistics in the section on 'women as the victims of crime'. Try to say something about report rates and paternalism.

INSTITUTIONALISATION

Below is a description (fictionalised but based upon a true account by an SVQ internal verifier) of a 'home' for older people which has, since 1996, thankfully begun to improve its practice. It should be read as a background to what follows about institutionalisation.

Lilybank

When I walked into the place I couldn't believe this was 1996. All that literature about promoting fulfilment, providing choice, maintaining independence and respecting privacy had evidently passed this establishment by. Where was the evidence of forward-looking community care legislation and practice guidance. There were all 'the residents' ranged round the four sides of the room in their armchairs waiting. Waiting for what, for heavens sake. Waiting for lunch. And after lunch, back they came and waited for tea. And after that back they came and waited for bed-time. There were, admittedly, some pleasant members of staff who jollied people along a bit, tried to raise a few spirits with a smile and a bit of encouragement, but they were fighting a culture. Did those other experienced, established members of staff who emphasised getting the job done, keeping the place clean, treating this, that or other physical symptom, realise that for all their good intentions they were colluding in a culture of institutionalisation?

'Come on John, Fred and Andy, it's time for the toilet.' She said it nicely, she was gently persuasive, but whose time was it for the toilet? Not theirs. What a coincidence it would be if all three of them wanted to go at exactly the same time every day.

'Are we all well today?' asks the unit manager. No-one would dream of saying 'no'. She's worshipped, this paragon in a blue uniform.

'Agnes, time to get up.' For goodness sake, Agnes lives here, this is her home and she's 92. And this morning she'd like to lie in until 10.00 a.m. Unfortunately Agnes shares a room with three other people and this room gets a thorough clean every Wednesday morning. This is Wednesday morning.

As I leave, with the faint whiff of urine filling my nostrils a woman struggles forward on her zimmer frame. She comes up to me and says 'Take me with you. I want to go home.'

Institutionalisation – the fourth aspect of society

The fourth aspect of society to be considered is that of institutionalisation. In sociology this concept has been variously defined and a distinction can be made between institutionalisation as a possible characteristic of being 'in' an institution, usually residing within it, and the institutionalisation of conflict, usually referring to conflict within the field of employer/employee relationships. For the care worker the first meaning is the one which is most relevant and the one which is given most emphasis here. Erving Goffman, in his book *Asylums* (1961) has been particularly influential in promoting analysis of the process of institutionalisation. He took an interactionist perspective and concentrated upon looking at how an institution, through the interactions which take place within it and the meanings attached to those interactions, affects the 'self' concept of those residing in or attending the institution. Since this is the major sociological perspective from which institutionalisation is viewed, the interactionist perspective is considered first, followed by much briefer examinations of institutionalisation from functionalist, conflict and feminist perspectives.

An interactionist perspective of institutionalisation

Interactionism provided a perspective from which labelling theory has been developed. Erving Goffman was one of the main theorists to develop this perspective in relation to institutionalisation. He was especially interested in what he called 'total institutions', establishments cut off, in one way or another, from the outside world and from the rest of society. Although his work is somewhat dated in its terminology it is still of great relevance. He placed total institutions into five broad groupings (the terminology is Goffman's):

- places which care for people such as the old, the blind and orphans;
- places for people seen as a threat to society e.g. mentally ill people, people suffering from TB etc;
- places which protect people from perceived dangers e.g. prisons, prisoner of war camps and concentration camps;
- places which allow limited access and have a functional use e.g. barracks, ships and boarding schools;
- places designed as 'retreats' from the world e.g. monasteries and convents.

These institutions, although they have somewhat different individuals within them affect those individuals in very similar ways. Their self concepts are 'taken over' by the institution and the resulting breaking down of self is referred to by Goffman as the 'mortification of self'. Some things which may contribute to this are as follows:

- role loss;
- undressing and wearing regimented clothing;
- hair cutting;
- fingerprinting;
- expected co-operation and/or obedience;
- deprivation of clothing, name and/or possessions;
- expected verbal responses;
- humiliation and/or ill treatment;
- keeping of personal details on record open to others;
- regimentation which means deprivation of personal decisions and daily routine;
- work organisation often disguised as 'rehabilitation'.

A condition called institutional neurosis is a likely result of a combination of some or all of the above, and you may recognise some of these in 'the residents' of Lilybank and in the description of an institution given in Chapter 1:

- apathy;
- lack of initiative;
- loss of interest;
- submissiveness;
- lack of interest in the future;
- inability to make practical plans;
- deterioration in personal habits;
- acceptance that things will go on as they are;
- occasional aggressive outbursts;
- characteristic posture.

Activity

Read the account of Lilybank and of the hospital ward on page 212 again and identify:
- factors which may contribute to institutionalisation;
- characteristics of institutionalisation in the resident population;
- ways in which the accounts can be interpreted from an interactionist perspective.

A functionalist perspective of institutionalisation

At first glance you might say to yourself that institutionalisation, as interpreted by Goffman, isn't very functional at all. In terms of a care practice value base it isn't. It doesn't respect the worth and dignity of all individuals or promote social justice. But it can perform functions in terms of organisational goals. Institutionalisation is, in some ways, functional for staff members and functional in terms of efficient, smooth running of an organisation. If the particular needs of individuals are ignored and the focus is upon the needs of the organisation for efficiency, time management and physical cleanliness and hygiene then institutionalisation could be seen to be highly efficient.

Activity

Look at the accounts of Lilybank and the ward and describe how institutionalisation could be seen to be functional for the organisation.

Is the organisation functional in terms of a care practice value base? Explain your answer.

From a functionalist perspective it is the alternative view of institutionalisation which is of most relevance, the view which focuses upon institutionalised conflict. From this perspective any conflict which exists between workers and employers is neutralised through an agreed set of rules and procedures, resulting in increased stability in industrial society. Revolution does not occur because, even though there are disagreements between employers and employees, there are **institutionalised** procedures for dealing with these disagreements. Similarly in care (and control) settings there are agreed, institutionalised procedures which preclude any kind of revolutionary action on the part of service users. For example, complaints and inspection procedures established under the 1990 NHS and Community Care Act institutionalise conflict and ensure that, as long as procedures are followed, conflict does not get out of hand. Institutionalisation, in this sense, can be seen to be functional to the provision of a service.

Activity

View critically the functionalist perspective of institutionalisation and list at least three short-comings of this viewpoint.

You may have suggested that functionalism does not take into account sufficiently for whom the institution is functional; it does not take into account conflicts of interest with the organisation; an explanation of institutionalisation from a functional perspective would see the way the institution was functioning and in harmony as a reason for its continued existence. What do you think?

A conflict perspective of institutionalisation

A conflict perspective focuses upon differences in power. Marx focused especially upon worker/owner relationships whereas when examining institutionalisation it is useful to look at the power differential between service user and staff. Institutionalisation, through the process whereby a person's individuality is diminished (what Goffman called the 'mortification of self'), disempowers the service user and empowers staff. In the most extreme form of institutionalisation staff exercise what they consider to be their right to give orders, to humiliate and to regiment service users. They emphasise their power by exercising it upon every possible occasion. There develops a conflict of interest within the organisation and a conflict perspective clarifies the way in which the organisation, set up theoretically to fulfil the needs of the service user, has the potential through the institutionalisation process to divert the aims of the organisation towards enhancing the power of some staff members. There is in any care organisation a potential for the staff as well as the service users to become institutionalised. An analysis of the power structure of some privately run 'homes', for example, would indicate that the power of the owners is maintained through an emphasis upon routine and the performance of tasks of physical care at the expense of the development of meaningful and helpful relationships between staff and service users. An understanding of institutionalisation from a conflict perspective enables the care worker to identify elements of institutionalisation in the work place and to counter them through work which firmly practises the value base and aims to empower rather than disempower the service user.

In the second way in which institutionalisation is interpreted in sociology, the institutionalisation of conflict within the work situation, a conflict perspective is useful in focusing attention upon the ways in which institutionalised conflict i.e. conflict which is channelled through procedures and norms, usually works to the advantage of the employer more than to the employee and continues to promote an unequal rather than equal society. For Marx, in a society in which everyone shared the ownership and running of the means of production, there would be no conflict of interest and therefore no necessity to institutionalise conflict. The same could be said of a care organisation in which the staff were working to empower service users. In this situation the aims of the staff would correspond with the interests of the service user and a conflict of interest would thus not exist. Institutionalising conflict between service users and staff would not therefore be an issue.

A feminist perspective of institutionalisation

With its emphasis upon gender as a starting point in the analysis of any situation a feminist perspective of institutionalisation focuses upon the particular effects of institutionalisation upon women and whether women's experience of institutionalisation is different from that of men. Some writers in the field of deviance have given indicators of the effects of a process of institutionalisation within family situations. Frances Heidensohn and Pat Carlen, for example, use a theory called 'control theory' to argue that male-dominated patriarchal societies control women more effectively than they do men. Most of the ways in which this occurs parallels many features of institutionalisation. Heidensohn describes the domesticity which many women experience as a 'form of detention'. For example, endless hours of childcare and housework, accompanied by ill-treatment and humiliation from a violent partner can lead to low self esteem and 'mortification of self' which Goffman described as a feature of people who live in long-stay institutions. There is very little research into the particular effects of institutional life on women. As with much other sociological investigation, research has been gender blind and it is impossible to tell from such studies as Goffman's study of asylums whether there are any distinct differences between men and women in their experiences of and the effects of institutionalisation. Feminism raises such issues and directs research in new gender-aware directions.

Beware of perspectives

The family, education, deviance and institutionalisation have all been examined from various sociological perspectives. This is useful in directing attention to different ways of looking at social phenomena but such approaches also come with a warning. Beware of the limitations of these perspectives and beware of taking only one perspective. Although theorists may have favoured one perspective over another they have often also recognised the limitations of only one approach. Dahrendorf, for example, felt that both functionalist and conflict perspectives were relevant in studying society. Max Weber drew upon both conflict and interactionist perspectives but didn't fully belong to either 'camp'. Feminist sociologists combine or use separately all of the other sociological perspectives.

At the end of the chapter it is useful to return to the question posed at the beginning: what **is** sociology? It is also useful to examine the ways in which you think that sociology can help you as a care worker. The concluding activities should further your thinking about these questions.

SUMMARY

At the beginning of the chapter attention was given to the difficulty of providing a definitive **definition of sociology**. Definition depends to some extent upon the perspective being taken. Four sociological perspectives have been considered: functionalist, conflict, interactionist and feminist. A **functionalist perspective** emphasises a view of society as a system made up of interrelated parts which perform functions in relation to the whole. 'Society', according to this perspective is seen in terms of consensus and agreement rather than conflict and change. A **conflict perspective**, on the other hand, rests upon the view that conflict is fundamental and inevitable between various groups in society which have differing interests from one another. Both the functionalist and conflict perspectives can be regarded as macro or large-scale perspectives which take 'society' as their starting point. An **interactionist perspective** focuses attention upon the meanings which **individuals** give to social actions. One of the main proponents of an interactionist perspective was George Herbert Mead who developed **symbolic interactionism. Feminist perspectives** set out to explain the position of women and to focus attention upon such issues as the subordination and oppression of women in society. Feminist sociology may include any of the above perspectives in combination with a prime concern with the position of women.

All of these perspectives were used to examine several aspects of society. These aspects were: the family; education; deviance; institutionalisation. Throughout the chapter opportunities were provided for you to apply your thinking to social, including care, situations. Some further activities encourage you to take your thinking further in relation to the Higher Unit 'Human Development and Behaviour'.

Activity

1. Assess the relevance of any one sociological perspective in understanding either the MacDonald or the Khan family, described in Chapter 10. (If you are working in a group situation, you could divide into four groups, with each group considering a different perspective.)

2. Compare the ways in which two different perspectives can be used to examine either your own educational situation or that of the Khans or MacDonalds in Chapter 10.

3. Becker said that 'the deviant is one to whom that label has been applied, deviant behaviour is behaviour that people so label'. What sociological perspective does this represent? List arguments for and against using this perspective to explain deviance.

4. Take one of the four care situations described in the Chapter 10 case study (Ivy Unit; 16 Fir Street; Heron Day Centre; Queen's View). What would be some of the characteristics of this unit if service users were institutionalised. Assess the relevance of one sociological perspective in a consideration of such institutionalisation. (As in Question 1, if you are working in a group situation you could divide into four groups with each group considering a different perspective.)

SELECTED BIBLIOGRAPHY

Gubbay, J., Middleton, C. and Ballard, C. (eds.) (1997). *A Student's Companion to Sociology*. Oxford: Blackwell.
A stimulating and interesting book of international readings for the student who wishes to take thinking further.

Haralambos, M. (ed.) (1996). *Sociology: a new approach*. 3rd edn. Ormskirk: Causeway Press.
A clearly written introduction to sociology using an activity-based approach.

O'Donnell, M. (1997). *Introduction to Sociology*. 4th edn. London: Nelson.
A well-written and interesting introduction to sociology.

CHAPTER 6
Interpersonal skills

Ellen Lancaster

*Though people can learn about these skills by reading, writing and talking about them, if they are to become competent practitioners, sooner or later they have to learn by **doing**.*

(Richard Nelson-Jones, 1994)

INTRODUCTION

This chapter is divided into four sections:

1 the value base;
2 effective communication;
3 personal qualities and attributes required by the care worker;
4 the many roles of the care worker.

The chapter covers material for all outcomes of the Intermediate II Unit 'Understanding Care Skills', although issues relating to anti-discriminatory practice have been discussed in Chapter 2. It also covers Outcome 1 and presents relevant material for all performance criteria of Outcome 2 of the Higher Unit 'Interpersonal Skills for Care', and relevant material for the Intermediate II Unit 'Health Promotion'.

By the end of the chapter you should:
- understand and be able to apply the value base for care;
- understand the skills required for effective communication, and some of the difficulties associated with communication;
- identify personal qualities required by the care worker and understand your own personal qualities;
- describe and apply attributes of effective helpers;
- understand the many roles of the care worker.

Interpersonal is defined as 'of or relating to relationships or communication between people' (Oxford English Dictionary). **Skill** is defined as 'the ability to do something well; expertise; difficult work' (Oxford English Dictionary). Interpersonal skills are the 'heart and soul' of good care practice. The skills rest upon essential qualities, attributes, abilities and knowledge which it is important for care workers to understand and practise if they are to assist in improving the quality of people's lives. It is the intention in this chapter to look at the constituent parts of interpersonal skills through considering the objectives and content of a value base for care, looking at communication, its importance and the necessary components of 'good' communication, examining the qualities and attributes of effective helpers, and providing an overview of some of the many roles of care workers.

THE VALUE BASE

In all areas of care practice a commitment to **values** and **principles** of care is essential.

A **value** is defined as 'that which is worthy of esteem for its own sake, that which has intrinsic worth' (Oxford English Dictionary). **Principle** is defined as 'a rule of conduct, especially good conduct' (Oxford English Dictionary).

One key value, which is considered at great length later in the text, is the value of respect for the worth and dignity of **every** individual.

Activity

In the light of this value read and consider with thought the quotes below:

- Oh, that is the boy Brown – a 'no-gooder'. Of course his whole family is the same. He will never be any good.

- What is the point of taking that disabled person to the disco, he will not be able to dance!

- Just give old Mrs Smith the steak pie, she 'disnae' know what she's eating anyway.

- Why should we tell drug addicts what benefits are available to them – it only puts up our taxes and they would only buy more drugs.

- Oh what is the point of trying to help the Asian family, they are not like us and anyway they do not want to be like us.

How often have you heard such statements or similar statements made? What have you thought of them or have you just accepted them?

On reflection you may conclude that the people making these statements think that those people talked about have no value, do not deserve a chance in life, a choice in life or acceptance as fellow human beings worthy of dignity or respect.

Unfortunately in many walks of life these attitudes are apparent and reflect a lack of the understanding and acceptance to which every human being should be entitled. For these reasons excuses could be made for the general public, but in care work there should be no such attitudes. In today's society, which is multi-cultural and multi-racial, those who need the help of care services **are** entitled to **good** care practice enriched with values and principles. If care practice is anything less, then people are being let down by the workers who are there to support them. The differences between good and poor practice can be seen below.

Person receiving care Good practice	Poor practice
Happy	Unhappy
Optimistic	No hope
High self esteem	Very low self esteem
Choice	No choice (given orders)
Privacy	Exposure of their lives
Important	Lonely
Comfortable with oneself and others	Awkward and no confidence
Non-threatened	Intimidated and bullied
Safe	Scared, in danger

It is obvious from the diagram that the person receiving good care will have a far better quality of life than the person receiving poor care. Good care rests upon a solid value base and it is for this very reason that it is imperative that care values and principles are adhered to and practised devotedly at all times.

The necessity for a value base with a set of guiding principles has been outlined many times in the last decade. The Wagner Report (1988), the British Association of Social Workers (BASW) Declaration of the Twelve Principles of Social Work Practice (1988), the Social Care Association's Code of Practice (1994), the National Health Service and Community Care Act (1990) all emphasised the importance of values and principles. As far back as 1946 The Universal Declaration of Human Rights, published after the Second World War, gave prominence to 'fundamental human rights, the dignity and worth of the "human person" and equal rights for men and women'. Since this Charter there have been many Acts. Charters and policies which aim to improve on the delivery of good care, placing a duty upon care workers to constantly reassess their own practice.

Values and principles
In care practice there are **two** core values:
- the value of respect for the worth and dignity of **every** individual;
- the value of according social justice and promoting the social welfare of **every** individual.

The value of respect for the worth and dignity of every individual
The right to be regarded as having worth involves **individualisation** and respect for that particular person, whoever he or she may be. It also involves empathy, acceptance and encouragement from the care worker to heighten the self esteem of the person. (The qualities a care worker needs to do this will be discussed later in the chapter – see page 241.)

Individualisation is the recognition and understanding of each person's own qualities, distinctive character and personality. Individualisation is based upon the right of human beings to be individuals and to be treated not just as **a** human being but as **this** human being with his or her personal differences.

EXAMPLE

Consider the statement written earlier in the chapter 'Oh, that is the boy Brown – a "no-gooder". Of course his family are all the same. He will never be any good.' Imagine, for instance, that this young man is being looked after in a children's home. The care worker with genuine values would look upon and accept this young person as an individual, who needs support and guidance. The worker will not or should not prejudice or judge him in any way whatever his family background, where he comes from or the level of support he needs. It is crucial that this young person is given dignity and respect, and shown that he is valued. Only then can he begin to realise that he has positive attributes and talents which he has never been given the opportunity to explore. The care workers should, when appropriate, praise, encourage and support this young person, promoting his right to receive a service which befits his individuality.

EXAMPLE

Another statement is considered from earlier in the chapter 'Just give old Mrs Smith the steak pie, she "disnae" know what she's eating anyway.' – This, for example, could refer to an elderly lady living in a nursing home. The care workers have, it would seem, decided that Mrs Smith, because she is older than they are, does not know what she is eating.

What right does any care worker have to make this decision? Where is the dignity and respect for this lady? Would they deny this choice to their own grandmother, their mother or someone they dearly love? Irrespective of whether the lady is confused or not the workers should respect her by taking the time to explain what choice of food there is and should ask her what she would like to eat. If there is a difficulty in communication then the workers should use imaginative ways to find what she likes and enjoys, by 'reading' her non-verbal communication or by asking relatives or friends what Mrs Smith likes and enjoys.

The care workers are not giving her choice or treating her as an individual person with likes and dislikes, hence they are showing no respect for her dignity as a fellow human being.

According social justice and promoting the social welfare of every individual

Social justice means that everyone has the right to fair and correct treatment in society. Welfare should ensure that those who are in need of care should have the opportunity to improve their personal situation through the promotion of their right to services and benefits. Commitment to these should be shown by care workers in their practice through knowledge and familiarity with sources of information, benefits and services available. (See Chapter 2 for relevant legislation.) In the words of a care student:

If commitment is less than a hundred per cent, this can have a large effect on the individual's life in relation to how full a life the individual can lead. Workers should continuously be aware of any changes in legislation and government benefits if they are to promote the service user's right to the fullest extent.

The following example was experienced by the same student when he was on a placement.

EXAMPLE
A gentleman who had lived in a 'long-term' hospital for the largest part of his life had been discharged from hospital to live in the community. He has now lived in his own house with the support of paid support workers for almost a year. This man enjoys travelling into the city to shop. However, because of the expense of bus travel, he is limited to how often he can do this. When the student support worker realised this gentleman's plight, he made inquiries about why the same man did not have a concessionary travel card. Alas, this possibility had been overlooked by the support workers. Their negligence had caused this man to be deprived of his leisure pursuits and had been limited in his number of trips into the city. His right to receive the concessionary travel pass should have been available to him when he originally moved into his own home. The support workers involved in this situation were failing to ensure that this service user's support needs were being fully met and he was being deprived of living his life to the full.

From the **two core values** is derived a set of principles. The values can only be established and practised when these most essential principles are promoted. The main principles are:

■ promoting acceptance;
■ maintaining privacy;
■ maintaining confidentiality;
■ promoting the rights to protection from abuse, exploitation, violence and/or neglect;
■ promoting choice, empowerment and risk-taking;
■ promoting fulfilment and potential;
■ promoting anti-discriminatory practice.

Each principle will be discussed in turn. It should be appreciated that in some literature these values and principles may be called by different names and even overlap sometimes, but what most authors talk about is the same value base.

Promoting acceptance

Acceptance is a principle of action wherein the care worker perceives and works with a person for who they really are. This includes knowing their strengths and weaknesses, their agreeable or disagreeable dispositions, their positive or negative feelings, their constructive or destructive attitudes and behaviour, and always maintaining a sense of their innate dignity and personal worth.

The care worker should not condemn or feel hostile towards a person because of who he is or her behaviour no matter how greatly it may differ from behaviour of which he or she personally would approve. In order to help those in need of care the worker must feel genuine warmth, be non-judgemental and have a certain 'outgoingness' to form a bridge across which help and support may be given. He or she must really wholeheartedly feel concern, genuinely care and have dedication towards helping to improve the service user's life.

Acceptance does not necessarily mean approval of all service user behaviour and attitudes. What it does mean is that the care worker's role is not to 'judge' or condone the behaviour but to accept the person and understand why he or she needs this in working towards fulfilment.

EXAMPLE
Recall the statement 'Why should we tell drug addicts what benefits are available to them – it only puts up our taxes and they would only buy more drugs.' If a care worker was to accept this belief then the unfortunate person addicted to drugs would, no doubt continue to take drugs because he or she would not have been given the opportunity to change his or her life. The care worker who possibly does not agree with taking drugs or even abhors drugs, should look beyond the addiction and accept the person. This acceptance is pertinent to the helping process.

Maintaining privacy

Everyone has the right to privacy, to have his or her own 'space'. It is not difficult to imagine how it would feel if someone accompanied you to the bathroom and insisted on staying, or barged in without permission when you were in your own bedroom, or listened into your telephone conversations, or discussed your financial affairs with you in front of others. If you consider the humiliation and embarrassment this would cause you, then you will appreciate the needs for care workers to give service users the privacy that is their human right.

> **EXAMPLE**
> A student on a placement in a nursing home had to assist a care worker one morning in waking up residents and then helping them to wash and dress. The student was horrified when the care worker boldly walked into each resident's bedroom without knocking, switched on the lights and proceeded to help them out of bed. The student did not follow suit. She knocked on the doors first and then, when told to enter, went up to the resident and kindly spoke to her before switching on the light, allowing time for the resident to decide when she wanted to get out of bed. The student was given a 'ticking off' for her actions by the care worker and told that they did not have time for this. Realising that this was common practice in the home, the student discussed her concerns with her supervisor. The supervisor, without hesitation, discussed with all staff this practice and it was agreed that in future this type of practice was not acceptable. It is only by not accepting bad practice and by good example that long-standing 'well that is the way that we do it' bad practice will change.

Maintaining confidentiality

Confidentiality is maintaining the right to privacy of information and is an extension of the privacy principle. It is not only an ethical obligation of the care worker but is also necessary in order that the service user will trust and confide in the worker. The principle of confidentiality appears deceptively simple. You may think that it can be equated with secrecy but this is not the case. It is about the **appropriateness** of sharing, transmitting or storing information about a service user where a number of competing factors may influence decisions about the information usage.

It may appear to present a dilemma for the care worker when a service user offers to tell him or her something of a confidential nature. In this instance the worker should explain to the service user that what is told to them may have to be shared with their line manager. Confidence needs to be instilled in the service user that this would solely be in his or her interest.

Suggested methods of maintaining confidentiality are by keeping all records in a secure place when not in use, by gaining permission from the service user if information has to be shared with other professionals, by restricting access to records, by keeping confidences unless there are limitations imposed by law and agency policy, by not talking about service users or their carers behind their backs or to others who are not members of the care team.

It is wise not to talk about any area of work in caring to anybody other than those involved, whether it is about service users, their carers, their family or any incident. Prevention is better than cure. Even to repeat something despite changing names is not recommended, as it is not difficult for some people to recognise who or what is being talked about. There could be times when you are in a place or talking to people whom you would never associate with your workplace or service user when in fact they do have connections. How many times have you started to talk about someone when you have been away somewhere only to find out that they know someone you know or are even related? Remember the familiar saying ' it is a small world'.

Promoting the right to protection from abuse, exploitation, violence, neglect or any kind of harm

It is the **duty** and **moral obligation** of the care worker to protect the service user and the **right** of the service user to be protected from any form of abuse. Abuse includes behaviour which is intended to exploit, dominate and/or damage another person. There are several forms of abuse. **Physical** abuse occurs where the one person may hit, punch, push, pull or cause pain to another. **Emotional** abuse including verbal abuse, occurs when a person is humiliated, intimidated, shouted at, belittled and/or bullied. **Financial** abuse occurs when one person is exploited by another or others for financial gain. **Sexual** abuse is exploiting another for sexual pleasure against their wishes. Lastly there is neglect, sometimes called **passive** abuse. Neglect can be intentional or unintentional and occurs when a child or other vulnerable person is deprived of the appropriate or continuous care needed, thus resulting in the deterioration of their physical or emotional well-being.

In many situations the service user's reasons for being in need of care has occurred because of one or more of these forms of abuse. Rightfully, then, they should not be exposed to the same painful treatment by those who are supposed and legally bound to ensure a feeling of safety and security. Care workers who are guilty of abusing those in their care misuse the power of 'being in charge'.

Unfortunately abuse in many forms still rears its ugly head as is apparent in examples taken from 1994 to 1998 in issues of community care magazines, such as: 'social worker sexually abuses adolescent in care', or 'private nursing home closed down because of a catalogue of neglect' or 'a resident of a home suffered horrendous bedsores and subsequently died' or 'residents found to be in a state of coma due to being drugged' or 'home care worker embezzles thousands of pounds from elderly lady in her care' or 'care officer imprisoned for grievous physical assault on children in his care'.

These acts of abuse should never happen and it is imperative that care workers should never practise in this way. They should also be aware of, prevent and report any care worker whose behaviour is considered to be abusive.

Promoting choice, empowerment and risk-taking

Choice, empowerment and risk-taking are three principles which are inter-related. Practising these three principles promotes and encourages **independence**. Independence may be defined as 'opportunities to think and act without reference to another person, including willingness to incur a degree of calculated risk'.

Many service users were previously accustomed to and capable of making decisions and choices for themselves. Others, for example people who were severely institutionalised as a result of spending many years in hospital, never had the opportunity of being independent. Irrespective of the service user's circumstances it is the care worker's duty to ensure that those in his or her care are enabled and empowered to maximise choice and independence.

Choice and empowerment can in many situations result in an element of risk. This is embodied in the following quote from the principles of practice of one home for the elderly:

Responsible risk taking is regarded as normal. Excessive paternalism and concern with safety may lead to infringements of personal rights. Those who are competent to judge the risk to themselves are free to make their own decisions so long as they do not threaten the safety of others.

(Crookfur Cottage Homes, Glasgow)

Empowerment is aimed at making service users who might be seen as powerless and vulnerable in some aspects of their lives as independent as possible. It therefore relates to service user's choice because giving service users choices, a form of control over their own lives, does **empower** them. It also involves making sure service users are given sufficient information to enable them to make informed choices, that is choices which are based on a sound understanding of their situation and any options which may be available.

Encouraging **independence** is encouraging people to take control of their own lives, having the power to make decisions and choices, no matter how small or how big. It follows then that the service user has to be given a full range of choices and not just those which are compatible with the care worker or the agency that is providing care. Too often the service user is not given the power of choice because of inconvenience, apathy or over-protection. This type of practice is in complete contrast to the key factors stated in Government reports and legislation such as The National Health Service and Community Care Act (1990), The Wagner Report (1988) and The Citizens Charter (1991), which all state that service users have the **right of choice** and should be given encouragement enabling them to be **independent**.

Examples of these principles in practice are:
- a resident in a residential home choosing to go to bed when it suited her and not the 'night shift' workers;
- a young person who is being looked after in a children's home, travelling to school on pubic transport and not in the Local Authority named bus;
- a person with learning difficulties cooking his own meal;
- a person who is blind travelling independently to and from wherever they wish to go.

Think about the choices you have and the decisions that you make for yourself.

Finally, a quote from a care worker makes points about choice and the way in which this is empowering:

People should be encouraged as far as possible to make choices. This helps to teach independence and encourages acceptable risk taking. Being able to make choices about one's life can be a sign of maturity. One service user has recently chosen to become involved in a project to help her move out of the unit, eventually to a home of her own. Making that choice has made her feel good about herself. She'll be supported in her choice, and would have been whatever she decided.

(KM, care worker, in Miller, J., 1996)

Promoting fulfilment and potential

When the principles of promoting choice, empowerment, acceptance, individuality and risk-taking are practised in entirety by the care worker then a service user has a feasible chance of achieving a good quality of life. Quality of life can be defined as satisfaction with life, contentment, happiness, enjoyment, achieving goals, pleasure or even employment. Care workers should be committed to providing more than just basic care and should enable service users to lead rich, fulfilling lives in which they are encouraged to achieve their ambitions and goals and reach their maximum potential.

The following guidelines aim to assist care workers in this task. They should:
- make themselves knowledgeable of the service user's previous lifestyle by consulting with them or someone, such as a relative, who knows them well. In this way the worker becomes aware of the expectations and wishes regarding the service user's independence;
- help and encourage the service user to think and act as independently as possible;
- encourage, enable and participate, if required, with the permission of the service user;
- provide a suitable physical environment which is safe for the service user to do as much as possible for him/herself;
- continually monitor the service user's achievements and ensure a practical and safe progression;
- praise achievements or kindly explain the justified limitations;
- offer and make the service user aware of services outside their own residence or local environment;
- offer information on training, educational provision such as Further Education Colleges, choice of outings, holidays, choice of creative and leisure activities.

With the required principles in practice, these guidelines in place and the additional attributes of dedication, vocation and positive thinking the service user will not only succeed in experiencing a fuller life but he or she will improve his or her confidence and build up self esteem.

Promoting anti-discriminatory practice

So far in this chapter the great necessity for and the essentials of **values and principles** in care work have been discussed. All of these values and principles underpin anti-discriminatory practice, which is fully discussed in Chapter 2.

The duty and responsibility of **every** carer is to:
- demonstrate an awareness of both individual and institutional discrimination;
- be sensitive to all people's needs regardless of differences;
- challenge discrimination in words and deeds.

Activity

On the list below tick the things that **you** value.

Living in your own home

Living in a rented flat with other people

Living in a hospital ward

Having to repeatedly apply for state benefit

Going on holiday abroad

Going to a seaside boarding house for a week once a year

Going to college

Going to the hairdresser

Being neat and well dressed

Having your teacher, hairdresser and doctor come to see you only at your place of work

Having your needs discussed by other people at a meeting

Going out for a drink with your friends

Being free to come and go as you please

Having to ask permission to leave your home

Having worthwhile employment

Choosing your own clothes

Sharing underwear and clothes with someone else

Spending the day doing 'arts and crafts' work for which you do not get paid

Having a speech impediment and not being able to communicate clearly

Winning an athletic event

Passing your driving test

Having the right to marry if you wish

Not being able to drink without help

Being told the truth about a medical condition you have

Consider the statements you have not ticked and think why you do not value them. It may be because they do not give you choice, because they do not give you privacy and/or because they take away your dignity.

EFFECTIVE COMMUNICATION

Communication is defined as '. . . the imparting, conveying or exchange of ideas, knowledge etc. (whether by speech, writing or signs); interchange of speech' (Oxford English Dictionary) and **effective** is defined as 'producing a desired result; impressive; operative'. From these two definitions it is apparent that communication is more complex than just speaking to a person. The ways in which care workers communicate convey to the service user how they **value** that person.

Think of someone in your life whom you admire and find it easy to speak to, perhaps a friend or a relative. It is likely that your reasons are that you know that person well, and they know you well, they accept you, they are warm and understanding, they listen to you and they do not criticise or judge you.

Effective communication involves many skills which include:
■ caring, valuable relationship;
■ listening skills;
■ non-verbal communication;
■ using appropriate language;
■ using the right pace and tone.

Caring, valuable relationship

To form and sustain a caring, valuable relationship is the main essence of effective communication between a service user and a care worker. Without a good relationship there will be no mutual respect. This is likely to result in failure to meet the needs of the service user. The ingredients necessary to form relationships are the practice of all the values and principles, a knowledge of human behaviour, a knowledge of the person and also that bit extra – **the oomph factor** (see Figure 6.1).

An explanation of the ingredients which bind together the oomph factor are as follows:

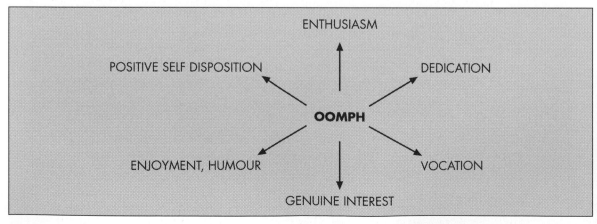

Figure 6.1 The oomph factor

- **Enthusiasm** is ardent interest, eagerness and includes encouraging and having a great faith in others. Care workers need to be energetic and possess inspiration in what they are practising.
- **Dedication** is consistent support and commitment to the well-being of the service user.
- **Vocation** emphasises the professionalism of care work and that it is 'not just a job'.
- **Genuine interest** includes being interested in **all** people, knowing people's likes and dislikes, frustrations, expectations and also being truthful.
- **Enjoyment and humour** involves the worker showing and feeling genuine pleasure in what they are doing and sharing successes or even failures however great or small.
- **Positive self disposition** emphasises that the care worker should be confident and happy with him or herself in what he or she is doing, and striving to share this confidence and happiness with the service user. If the care worker does not feel this way then the service user will sense it.

In addition to these attributes, it is necessary to involve further qualities such as **warmth, understanding and sincerity**. Without these the service user will not feel **valued**.

Carl Rogers (1902–1987) identified these qualities which will ensure a rich, safe and valuable relationship.

Conveying warmth

The care worker who conveys warmth will be seen as a warm and accepting person. This acceptance will ensure that the service user feels valued as an individual. A service user may be feeling helpless, threatened, embarrassed or a nuisance, therefore the care worker may reflect warmth by:

Non-verbal communication

- a warm smile (facial expression);
- open, welcoming gestures;
- friendly tone of voice;
- confident manner – this reassures the service user that they can be helped;
- offering physical help – for example a guiding arm to an elderly or distraught person;
- general appearance of the care worker;
- calm gestures and movements.

Verbal communication

- use of friendly words that show respect;
- expression of a wish to help;
- clear explanation of what the care worker is trying to do;
- reassurance about confidentiality;
- clear understanding of what has been achieved and what can be achieved.

In developing the skill of showing warmth it is important to be oneself, to be natural and genuine. If the care worker **pretends** to be interested, warm or understanding then the service user will sense this and it will jeopardise the whole relationship.

Conveying understanding

Understanding has to be shown through **empathy, acceptance and being non-judgemental**. It means learning about the individual identity, beliefs and needs of each person. Carl Rogers (1991) saw the idea of understanding or empathy as 'the ability to experience another person's world as if it was your own world'. Service users may have completely different experiences from the care worker so it is important to try genuinely to understand service user's thoughts and feelings. Many service users who are given the opportunity of talking freely often experience great relief at being able to tell their innermost feelings without getting a negative reaction from the care worker. This process is sometimes referred to as 'ventilation'. It can lower anxiety and can, if the care worker provides warmth and acceptance, be sufficient in itself to let the service user find their own solution to their problem.

Also, when service users feel comfortable with the care worker they will be more likely to talk about themselves, which will enable the care worker to learn more about that person and understand their views. Understanding can grow from a conversation which conveys **value** for the service user. Understanding is also conveyed when the care worker is competent in showing knowledge of a particular physical, intellectual, emotional or social need of a service user.

Barriers which impede communication

Care workers need to be aware of personal and physical obstacles which impede communication and deter a service user from expressing their feelings. Failure to understand and detect these obstacles will affect communication and make it impossible for the care worker to understand and respond to the needs of a service user. Below is a list of possible barriers:

Personal: a person
- who is very nervous;
- who is distressed;
- who feels uncomfortable with any care worker;
- who feels their problems are too personal to discuss with the care worker;
- who feels embarrassed;
- who is angry;
- who fears being ridiculed;
- who fears being abused;
- who fears being misunderstood;
- who fears being neglected;
- who has no self esteem;
- who is wary of confidentiality;
- who has a different mother tongue;
- who feels inferior and prejudiced;
- who is unable to express their feelings;
- who is uncomfortable with age difference.

Physical: a person
- who has a hearing impairment;
- who has a speech impairment;

- who has a visual impairment;
- who suffers from a mental illness;
- who suffers from dementia;
- who is very depressed;
- who has a physical disfigurement.

It is advised to consider the **environment** where communication is taking place. For instance:

- the meeting place is the choice of the service user;
- it is safe and comfortable;
- it is private and quiet;
- it is free of any interruptions;
- it is appropriate, with suitable lighting (for those with visual impairments);
- the seating arrangements are positioned in a friendly way;
- the care worker is sitting in full view (for those with hearing impairment).

The care worker who is sensitive to these aspects will be competent in achieving effective communication with those for whom they are caring.

Conveying sincerity

Being sincere is paramount. It means that care workers have to be honest, open, be themselves and giving to others. There is no room for acting or using language that confuses the service user. This only gives the impression that the care worker is superior to others. When a person talks to a friend or relative there are no barriers because each is relaxed, natural and genuinely interested. When a care worker talks to a service user it should be just the same. It is essential that a care worker conveys a little of what kind of person they are and shares information which may help the service user feel relaxed and comfortable. In some situations this could encourage the service user to be more forthcoming with information about themselves.

Like any other skills, forming a supportive relationship with a service user improves with practice and care workers should continually evaluate themselves. It is necessary for care workers to accept feedback from colleagues, supervisors and most importantly the service users. It is possible to tell if communication is effective by the response of service users. They will show trust, be honest with the care worker and show that they enjoy the care worker's company. Without these kind, humane ingredients the relationship will be doomed and very difficult to redeem.

Activity

You are unable to speak, write and walk following a stroke. You are able to understand what people say to you.

You will need a partner for this activity.

1. Tell your partner that you are hungry.

2. Tell your partner you need to go to the toilet.

3. Tell your partner you want to go out.

4. Explain to your partner that you are uncomfortable and want to be moved.

What were your feelings during this exercise?

What did your partner do that was most helpful?

What could she have done that she did not do?

How did your partner feel?

Can you suggest a method of communication that would be useful in this situation?

Activity

You are unable to speak or write following a stroke. You are able to understand what people are saying to you. You cannot use your hands.

You will need a partner for this activity.

1. Tell your partner that you are thirsty.

2. Tell your partner you would like the TV on.

3. Tell your partner you want a friend to come and visit you.

4. Explain to your partner you are concerned about how hard they are working to look after you.

5. Tell your partner that you are worried about the future.

What were your feelings during this exercise?

What did your partner do that was most helpful?

What could she have done that she did not do?

How did your partner feel?

Listening skills

Listening involves not only receiving sounds but, as much as possible, accurately understanding their meaning.

(Richard Nelson-Jones, 1983)

Listening is as important as verbally communicating. Listening should not be 'passive' but **active**, and this involves more than just hearing but also concentrating on what the person is saying, responding to what has been said and then acting on it. To be a good listener involves practising all the values, principles and attributes in caring as well as:

Being attentive – This means actively listening and concentrating on what is being said, being aware of what is **not** being said by sensing that the service user is perhaps shy, feeling awkward, embarrassed or unable to express how they feel. They may show signs of these feelings by silence, eye movements, nervous movements like wringing their hands or turning a ring on their finger. Facial expressions, posture and other forms of body language all give clues to a person's feelings. The care worker should try to understand these signs and allow the service user time to relax and feel confident to talk.

Using prompts – Service users who may be shy, nervous or are hesitant about talking for various reasons may need encouragement from the care worker. This can be done, for example, by nodding at appropriate times which shows acceptance and understanding, by eye contact which shows attention is being given, and by using words and sounds like 'oh', 'really', 'mmm' as they show that they know what they are saying and are happy to listen further.

Using appropriate questions – Questions may be asked to clarify what the service user has said and to establish more information. To encourage service users to talk, it is better to use 'open' questions which invite answers that are longer and more involved and usually start with words like 'How', 'Why', 'What', 'When', 'Where'. For example, rather than asking a young person 'Do you like your new school?' which would likely be answered with a 'Yes' or 'No', it would be better to ask 'What do you think of your new school?' The care worker is then more likely to learn more information about how the young person feels about the school.

Non-verbal communication

Non-verbal communication comprises appearance, gestures and movements. There are four main ways in which non verbal communication is used:

Eye contact – eye contact is very useful to show that the care worker is paying attention to the service user when they are speaking and also conveys sincerity and genuineness. However, it would not be appropriate to stare continually at someone: it is best to be natural.

Posture – When two people are talking they generally feel more comfortable if they are at the same level. If a care worker were to tower over a service user, they may feel intimidated, or that they cannot move away. The care worker should be sufficiently relaxed to be friendly and calm. Positioning of seating is important and it is better to be facing the service user and leaning forward slightly, showing willingness to listen. Such mannerisms as hands in pockets, playing with hands or running hands through hair should be avoided as these would be distracting to the service user.

Facial expressions – The expression on a person's face can often convey how that person is feeling and can be used effectively to communicate feelings. Therefore it is essential that the care worker shows warmth and friendliness. It is difficult to communicate with someone who shows no emotion in their face and it can be very unsettling. Of course, the expressions that the care worker show should be appropriate and not signs of laughing, sneering or superiority.

Physical contact – When a service user is distressed or frightened then a care worker might show understanding and empathy by giving a child a cuddle or perhaps an older person a reassuring arm around their shoulder. However, the care worker has to be careful that their familiarity is not misinterpreted. Knowing when physical contact is not appropriate can be difficult. Generally, when a good relationship has been formed with a service user, the care worker will know whether physical contact is appropriate or not. It should be remembered that this is a controversial subject and it helps to discuss appropriate physical contact at team meetings and to come to some agreements within the **team** on this subject.

Using appropriate language

Each service user is an individual with their own social background, culture, character and abilities. For these reasons it is necessary for care workers to adapt and tailor their language to suit each individual service user. The choice of words, the length of what is said and the content is all important. Too often care workers, without thought, use 'jargon' such as 'goal setting', 'empowerment' or 'interaction', which will only confuse the service user.

The **age** of a service user has to be considered. When speaking to an older person for example, they should never be spoken to as if they are a child by using childish words. This is patronising and shows no respect to the person. Would you like to be spoken to in this manner? Similarly, when speaking to a child, language should be kept simple in order that the child can understand. It is useful to check, in an appropriate way, that what is being said is understood.

When working with service users who have a **hearing** impairment it is best for the care workers to be familiar with sign language and know the different meanings which service users attach to signs, or an interpreter could be present. Also, when working with those who have a **visual** impairment it is advisable to describe objects and situations. It would be ineffective and insensitive for the care worker to show them something and ask 'Do you want this just now?'

Care workers may work with service users who speak in a **different language**. This should not cause a barrier in communication nor should the service user be made to feel inferior because they do not speak English. In this situation an interpreter would be required. Ideally the care worker could make an effort to learn the service user's language, or at least a few words of it.

EXAMPLE

A student, on her first day in a day centre for young adults with hearing impairments, was asked to assist a young man, called Jake who is deaf and has very little speech. The inexperienced student found she had great difficulties communicating with Jake. At the end of the day she felt despondent and unsure that she would be able to continue in her placement. However, she decided that she would try harder the next day and she would find ways of communicating with Jake. Initially she observed Jake's care worker. She learned that the care worker, through using signing, touch, giving encouragement and time, had built up a trusting relationship with Jake. She realised that it would take time and perseverance. She was given the opportunity of training in signing which she readily accepted. She learned that Jake could lip read so she made sure when she was talking to him that he could see her face and she spoke slowly, making sure that she formed words with her lips. She showed signs of expression on her face to suit what she was saying and also used her hands to express herself. At first, Jake was amused by her efforts but it helped to 'break the ice'. Jake responded well. Within a few weeks she was a good friend to Jake and was able to communicate with him. She had gained confidence and Jake felt comfortable with her. The student has now formed a trusting and valuable relationship with Jake.

EXAMPLE

A student who recently took up part-time employment as a care worker in a Local Authority home for elderly people, noticed that an Indian woman who was in the home for a period of assessment and respite, seemed very unhappy and isolated. When she asked another care worker about the woman she was told that English was her second language. It had been assumed by the staff that there was no point speaking to her as she would not understand. It was the opinion of the staff that she was in the home for a short time and that they did not have the time to communicate with her. They had attended to her physical needs, washing, dressing, giving her meals but they had not attempted to communicate with her. When they did have to speak to her they had used inappropriate language such as 'You sit up', 'Me feed you'.

The student approached the Indian woman with a smile and introduced herself. She found that the Indian woman understood what she was saying and continued to tell her her name and a little about herself. The student realised that the other staff had assumed that because English was the woman's second language she would not understand what they were saying. By not speaking quickly or shouting and by being patient and repeating some words, the student had been able to communicate with this woman. If there were words that were not understood then the student had used facial expression and hand gestures. Some of the other staff noticed the attempt made by the student and they too made more effort to speak to this Indian woman. The student found that after a few days she seemed happier and had made friends with other service users.

Service users who have a learning disability need the care worker to be patient and capable of using words that they will understand. The length of what is being said should take into account the service user's ability to understand. It is advisable to repeat what has been said so that the service user understands. Adults should not be spoken to as if they are children and time should be given for the service user to express themselves. To aid communication, facial expressions, gestures and appropriate touch is useful.

Using the right pace and tone

The pace of the communication used by a care worker should, like the language used take into account the age, the ability/disability and culture of the service user. It would be of no avail to talk on and on very quickly when in fact the service user is still trying to understand what was first said. The tone of voice that is used by the care worker should again be appropriate to who is being spoken to. They should not 'talk down' to service users and there is no room for abruptness. The tone should be friendly and warm, irrespective of who is on the receiving end. 'Civility costs nothing and goes a long way'. For example **'What do you want?'** with the emphasis on **what**, could be as easily said as 'What would you like?', said in a warm and friendly tone. The first tone and question would make the service user feel that it was a bother for the care worker, whereas the other reflects that the care worker is genuinely interested in those they are talking to. There are times when the tone of voice has to be different, for instance when the service user has received disturbing news and then the tone should be comforting. Care workers have to be sensitive about what they say and how they say it and this should stem from a good understanding and interest in the person they are caring for.

Finally, to be successful as an effective communicator, care workers need to be aware of their own ability to communicate with others and use the necessary skills to form good relationships with service users. Where effective communication is practised the service user will feel accepted, understood and know that their needs have been recognised. Effective communication is an important way of helping to promote independence, ensuring equal opportunities and achieving self empowerment.

Activity

Read the following case studies and write down how you could maximise communication with each service user, for example which methods could you use; which you should avoid and what else might help. Think about what or who might also be of assistance to you.

Case Study 1: Mrs Boyd
Mrs Boyd is suffering from dementia. Because of her confusion and occasional loss of memory it is difficult to communicate with her. Mrs Boyd lives in Sheltered Housing.

Case Study 2: Mr Meechan
Mr Meechan has a hearing impairment. He has a hearing aid but does not always use it. He attends a social club run by his church.

Case Study 3: Miss Moodie
Miss Moodie has suffered a stroke which has affected her speech. She feels embarrassed and frustrated when she is slow in communicating. She is staying in a nursing home for a short period.

Case Study 4: Mr Sloan
Mr Sloan has lost his sight in one eye and is partially sighted in the other eye after a car accident. Before his accident he was a lorry driver and this has changed his life completely. He attends a Resource Centre twice a week.

Case Study 5: Mr Wilson
Mr Wilson has learning difficulties. He has been discharged recently from a long-stay hospital where he had spent twenty years and is now living in the community.

Case Study 6: Mrs Malik
Mrs Malik has been in this country ten years but has little command of English. She is elderly, lives at home and requires home care assistance.

Improving communication in:
Case Study 1:
- use short, simple sentences; speak slowly;
- talk about one thing at a time;
- find similar ways of saying things, or repeat if necessary;
- use facial expressions and gestures;
- objects and pictures can help the service user who is confused;
- consult relatives or friends;
- do not shout or contradict the service user;
- be patient and understanding.

Case Study 2:
- try not to surprise the service user, be sure you can be seen approaching;
- make sure you have the service user's attention;
- sit close to the service user's attention;
- sit close to the service user;

- sit where the light is on your face, so the service user can see your facial expressions;
- do not cover your mouth and speak normally in sentences;
- have patience, do not rush and use different words if necessary;
- make sure the hearing aid is working properly;
- use a writing pad or sign language if necessary;
- use gestures, facial expressions.

Case Study 3:
- do not shout and speak slowly and clearly;
- do not say too much at once, then give the service user time to respond;
- do not speak to the service user in childish language;
- use a writing pad and pen;
- use facial expression, and gestures;
- be patient and calm.

Case Study 4:
- tell the service user who you are;
- do not surprise the service user, approach gently;
- you could use touch to let the service user know that you are there;
- do not shout, speak clearly;
- let the service user speak;
- describe objects and events;
- explain when you are leaving or someone else is approaching;
- make sure that lighting is not too bright.

Case Study 5:
- support the service user in expressing himself;
- let the service user take his time, do not rush;
- support your verbal communication with gestures and touch;
- work at showing the service user that he is valued;
- do not hurry to do things, give the service user the opportunity to say what he wants;
- do not speak in a childish way.

Case Study 6:
- speak slowly;
- speak clearly without raising your voice;
- if you have not been understood, repeat what you have said using the same words;
- keep sentences simple;
- do not use expressions only used in English such as 'its raining cats and dogs';
- do not use broken English such as 'you happy';
- make sure the service user understands what you have said before moving on to something else;
- try using pictures or objects;
- make an effort to learn a few words of the service user's language.

PERSONAL QUALITIES REQUIRED BY THE CARE WORKER

There are no 'golden rules' to learn in order to become an effective carer – we each do the job differently according to our own personalities.

(David Tossell and Richard Webb, 1994)

This quote is true to an extent, however there are areas and guidelines where a care worker can improve and develop. Throughout this chapter many of the required attributes and skills have been discussed, such as the ingredients of the 'oomph factor', acceptance, understanding, warmth, empathy, listening skills and communications skills. Established within these skills are the essential personal qualities. No one care worker will possess all of the personal qualities, but each individual should be aware of the qualities they already possess and build on these to develop other qualities and skills. As a comparison, a person who knows he or she is a good singer may decide to sing as a career. In order to succeed he or she has to pursue studies in music and spend hours practising to become skilful and even famous.

What qualities can potential carers possess? There are many qualities, some overlap and some with 'fine tuning' can develop into skills. Personal qualities include:

- patience and tolerance;
- respect, acceptance and empathy;
- sensitivity and discretion;
- reliability, dependability and flexibility;
- positive attitude, cheerfulness and willingness;
- politeness and kindness;
- honesty and humility;
- autonomy and teamwork;
- self awareness;
- readiness to learn;
- readiness to do a share of unpleasant tasks.

Patience: A care worker should never lose their patience or show annoyance. This could upset a service user and make her feel a nuisance.

Tolerance is patience, understanding and accepting others.

Respect is considering, accepting the views of others even if they differ from your views.

Acceptance is taking people as they are without judging them; an absence of rejection.

Empathy is putting yourself in another person's shoes and seeing the situation from their point of view.

Sensitivity is being aware of others' embarrassment, fears, discomfort.

Discretion means not making a show or a fuss; it comes with respect and maintaining privacy and confidentiality.

Reliability is always doing what you said you will, on time and in a meaningful manner.

Dependability means being reliable and giving others confidence in your actions.

Flexibility means adaptability; open-mindedness and a willingness to learn from the skills of others.

Positive attitude is being able to see the best in a situation. This is aptly explained in the phrase 'the glass if half full' and not 'the glass is half empty' or a more common phrase like 'this is not a problem'.

Cheerfulness is being a 'happy' person who enjoys their work, which makes others feel happy.

Willingness is accepting readily what you have been told to do and also performing tasks without being told.

Politeness is being mannerly, respectful and giving others recognition.

Kindness means showing compassion, interest and natural friendship.

Honesty is being truthful, trustworthy, genuine and keeping your word.

Humility is being humble, admitting that you do not know how to do something or accepting constructive criticism. This is not failure, it is evaluating your practice and being able to enhance it accordingly.

Autonomy is being able to work on your own initiative.

Teamwork is being able to work with other care workers, being tolerant of their ideas and methods of working, accepting help, guidance and support.

Self-awareness is being aware of yourself, your strengths and areas which need development.

Readiness to learn is willingness to think about what you do, to ask questions and to be ready to learn throughout your career.

Readiness to do a share of unpleasant tasks: Chapter 1 warned you that not all tasks are lovely but use empathy and respect and be willing to play your part in the team.

EXAMPLE

Jenny, a care worker in a home for elderly people, always arrives at work on time; she usually smiles at everyone and says a cheerful 'good morning'; asks people how they are feeling and she waits to hear their replies. She gets upset when a service user dies or becomes ill. She admits that there are parts of her job she does not like such as cleaning up vomit. This makes her feel sick but she says that it is not the person's fault that they are sick and that they must feel embarrassed that someone else has to clean it up.

Here the care worker shows qualities of **sensitivity, cheerfulness, politeness, positive attitude, respect, empathy, reliability, dependability, respect, kindness, and humility.** Jenny has shown that she is a cheerful, pleasant person who enjoys her work. She starts her day in a positive way and shows service users that she is happy to be with them. She is aware of her strengths and weaknesses and is able to build on the strengths. She admits that she does not like cleaning up vomit but builds on her empathy and sensitivity by understanding how the service user is feeling.

Autonomy, Teamwork and Honesty are explained in the example below:

EXAMPLE

Helen, a day release student who is employed in a small Residential Unit for people who suffer from Cerebral Palsy, works mainly on night shift. More often than not she works on her own. There is a senior member of staff available if Helen needs assistance. There are occasions when service users are not well or cannot sleep. In these situations Helen has to work on her own initiative. She has become very attached to the service users. They depend solely on her during the night and early morning. Once a week, the Unit has a team meeting and Helen has to be present at this meeting. There are times when she finds it difficult to share information about service users, and accept new methods of working from other team members. She does appreciate, however, that she is not the 'sole' carer and that any change is in the interest of the service user. At these meetings Helen has had to be truthful and not conceal any information that may jeopardise the service user.

Activity

In the above examples, can you identify the qualities that Jenny and Helen practise in their work?

A care worker may have many of these qualities but it is also important that personal qualities are well balanced. They should be practised in close relation to each other (see Figure 6.2).

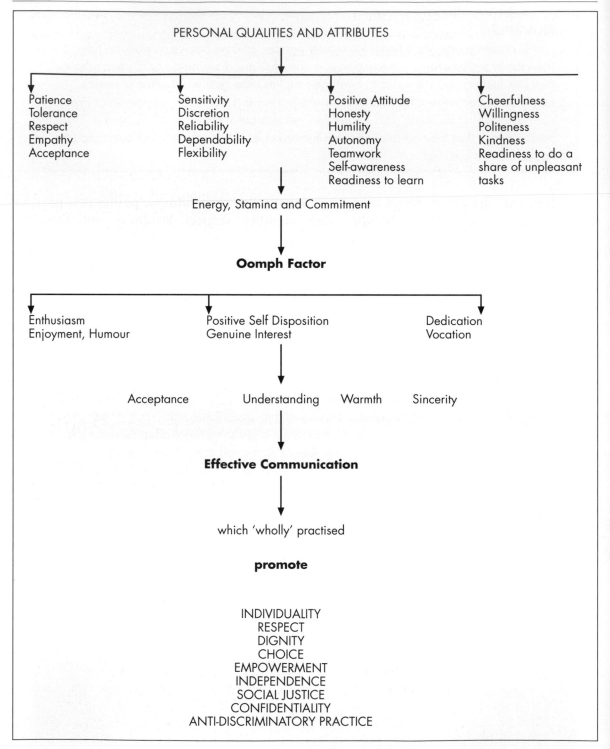

Figure 6.2 Personal qualities and attributes

Care workers should be aware of what qualities they possess, build on these and recognise what they still have to learn. To be an effective care worker requires all the above and more. It is not enough 'just to like people', because effective care work involves energy, stamina and a strong desire actively to help others.

QUALITIES AND ATTRIBUTES: A NOTE ON THE HIGHER SYLLABUS

At Intermediate II level you need to gain an understanding of the personal qualities required of a care worker and at Higher you need to gain an understanding of the attributes of effective helpers. Attributes include empathy, acceptance, reliability, flexibility, respect for others and patience. There is so much overlap between what are qualities and attributes that they have been discussed together. Although you may not possess every single personal quality you must work towards developing all of the above attributes.

A quality may be defined as a characteristic; something special about a person or a thing. An attribute may be defined as a quality that is characteristic of a person or thing. As you can see, there is not much difference in definition between the two terms.

THE MANY ROLES OF THE CARE WORKER- THE INTERPLAY OF PRACTICAL, EMOTIONAL AND MANAGEMENT ROLES AND SKILLS

The role of the care worker varies with the setting in which care takes place, the needs of service users and the position occupied by the worker in the organisation. If you look back at Chapter 1 you will see that the aim of the care worker is to improve the quality of people's lives. The three short examples which follow give outlines of the work of three different carers and these provide a good starting point for a discussion of **role**. These workers have already been introduced in Chapter 1. 'Role' was defined in Chapter 5 as the part which an individual plays in a group and the behaviour which is expected from a person in that position.

> **EXAMPLE**
> **Harry's** role is to work directly with John in helping him to build a meaningful life. This role involves communication, assisting with some physical tasks such as shaving and washing and coping with John's challenging behaviour. Harry is also a part of a community care team in the 'not for profit' organisation for which he works. He attends team meetings and communicates with other professionals involved in John's care. He prepares a review report every six months and keeps brief records on John's progress and achievements. Harry is also John's Keyworker, a role discussed in greater detail below, and is supervising a student on placement who is taking a course at the local Further Education College.

EXAMPLE

Janet's role as a home support services organiser is involved in the assessment of need with service users, ensuring that appropriate support is provided in order that they are enabled to remain in their own homes for as long as they wish to do so. Her role involves assessment, organisational and communication skills. She also has a management role in leading a team of home support workers. She provides these workers with supportive supervision, she arranges induction training for them and runs the team meetings, every two months. She also liaises with other professionals such as social workers, GPs, district nurses and occupational therapists.

EXAMPLE

Gina provides support for two children with autistic spectrum disorders who attend a mainstream school. This support involves assisting them with educational tasks, supervising them at break times and assisting with their lunch and physical needs. She also communicates with their teachers about the educational programme and with their parents about their school day, their progress and their needs. Her role includes direct care, education and liaison.

Below is an account of the role of **Laura**. She has written this description herself and describes her role as a facilitator in person-centred planning.

The role of the facilitator working with person-centred planning includes:
- talking **and** listening to the individual;
- helping the individual communicate their expectations to others;
- supporting the individual through a process of change;
- helping to deal with and work through conflicts that can arise;
- allowing everyone the opportunity to speak, so that no one person can dominate the meeting.

When an individual takes on the role of the facilitator he or she must bring with them the underpinning values and the personal knowledge of the tools of person centred-planning.

Before starting work on a person-centred process, each facilitator must have had one carried out on themselves first. This allows the facilitator to experience the emotions that can arise during these processes.

All of the work done with the individual should be shown with graphics as this is often the best way of communicating with the person and allowing him or her to be in control of the situation.

A good facilitator will check everything with the individual first to ensure it is recorded accurately as part of this process.

The role of **keyworker** is included as part of the tasks of many care workers. Ian Mallinson (1995), in *Keyworking in Social Care* has written extensively about this role and much of what follows relies upon his excellent book.

Keyworking

Many workplaces have workers who are called **keyworkers** or **linkworkers**. Their tasks vary from place to place, though they generally involve special responsibility for assisting one or more service users, forming a special relationship with them and coordinating work in relation to them. Essentially the role should be seen as a partnership which empowers service users to maximise potential and improve their quality of life. Keyworker tasks may include:

- developing a dependable relationship;
- coordinating care and coordinating the care plan;
- advocacy and empowerment;
- being there as a reliable, approachable, dependable person, an ally in good and difficult times;
- maintaining, exploring, encouraging and expanding the service user's network of links with family, friends and other agencies;
- liaising with social workers and other professionals;
- attending reviews and case conferences with the service user, ensuring that their views are heard and that decisions made are understood;
- ensuring that records are up to date and accurate;
- monitoring care to ensure that it is as good as it can be.

Keyworking is not always as straightforward as it seems. Sometimes the relationship between keyworker and service user is less than ideal: at times representing the needs of the service user conflicts with a worker's other roles, and sometimes the task is misinterpreted as favouritism. These occasional disadvantages do not detract from an otherwise valuable role. They alert the worker to the possible pitfalls and should encourage development of the role in the best interests of the service user.

Activity

If you are on placement or working in a care agency check whether there are keyworkers. What are the tasks of these keyworkers? What do you think are the good points about keyworking? What are its weaknesses? How could the system of keyworking be improved?

It is evident in the many roles of care workers that at the core of all care roles is the **respect for the worth and dignity of all individuals and the promotion of social justice**.

CASE STUDY

Rosemount View is a Day Centre for older adults. The staff have to collect the service users in the morning and escort them home in the afternoon. Many service users live alone and staff have to go into their houses to help them with coats, shoes, handbags, etc.

All the service users have a keyworker who has a special interest in their care. One day Mrs K tells Billy (her keyworker) that she is low in mood because she does not get on with her husband and has never had a happy marriage. Billy tells Mrs K that he would like to share this with other team members, and she agrees but specifically asks that her family, and particularly her husband, should never find out. At the next meeting of keyworkers Billy tells the other team members about Mrs K and they agree on ways in which they can help her.

On the way home one of the keyworkers, Harry, meets a colleague from another day centre. They start to discuss their work and Harry recounts the story of Mrs K to his friend. Harry is on duty next day and receives a phone call from Mrs K's daughter. She says she is very worried about Mrs K as she seems depressed. Harry suggests that it might be something to do with Mrs K's marriage. The daughter is very shocked and visits her mother to find out if there is any truth in the story. At her next attendance at the day centre Mrs K is very withdrawn and angry. When asked about it she says she feels 'let down' and will never 'trust the staff again'.

Activity

Answer these questions after reading the Case Study above.

1. In paragraph 1, which qualities would staff need if they have access to service users homes?

2. Which quality did Billy have which made Mrs K able to tell him about her troubles?

3. Was it appropriate that Billy told the other team members about Mrs K and why?

4. Which particular context did Billy choose to tell staff members about Mrs K?

5. What 'rule' did Harry break when he told his friend about Mrs K?

6. Did Harry break this rule when he told Mrs K's daughter about her mother?

7. Do you think there was a difference in what Billy did and what Harry did?

8. What was the result of Harry's actions?

CASE STUDY

Routenburn is a Unit for high dependency service users. The work is very hard and tiring but the staff are enthusiastic. There is also a keyworker system in place where each member of staff is allocated to a group of service users and is responsible for their total care for the duration of the shift. This makes the work more interesting and rewarding but requires staff to be reliable in all aspects of their work.

Jan lives 15 miles away from the Unit but is always on time for work and has never been off sick. Sandra is also very punctual but has had two weeks off because she had to go into hospital for a minor operation. Christine is a very good worker, has an excellent rapport with the service users, and comes forward with exciting ideas for improving service user's care. However, she also has frequent absences from work and is late at least once or twice a week. This sometimes causes friction between herself and other staff members, and also disrupts the planning of service user care as other members of the team do not know if she is going to be late or if she is off sick.

Another very good member of the team is Helen. She is extremely reliable, caring and intelligent. She is polite and professional at all times in her manner. However, Helen tends to be a bit sloppy about her personal appearance and often has an unpleasant body odour. Her colleagues feel too embarrassed to say anything and although they like and respect her they feel uncomfortable when they have to work alongside her. The service users also prefer when she does not attend them even though she is kind and caring, and visitors have been overheard to say unkind things about her.

Activity

Answer the following questions based on the Case Study above.

1. Christine appears to have many good qualities. Which two aspects of her behaviour are letting her down?

2. Which two consequences result from this?

3. Which two aspects could Helen improve on?

4. She is neglecting these at the moment. What effect does this have on staff, service users and visitors?

Activity

FEELINGS ABOUT YOURSELF

Finish the following incomplete sentences. Do not spend a great deal of time thinking about the most appropriate way to finish them – be as spontaneous as possible.

1. I get angry at myself when . . .
2. I like myself best when. . .
3. I feel ashamed when. . .
4. I trust myself when. . .
5. When I fail, I. . .
6. I feel encouraged when. . .
7. I puzzle myself when. . .
8. I'm pleased with myself when. . .
9. I get down on myself when. . .
10. I feel confident when. . .
11. When I violate my own principles, I. . .
12. When I succeed, I. . .
13. It troubles me when I. . .
14. I'm most at peace with myself when. . .
15. I feel good about myself when. . .
16. When I do not understand myself, I. . .
17. I get depressed when. . .
18. I am buoyed up when. . .
19. I get annoyed with myself when. . .
20. When I take a good look at myself, I. . .
21. When I think of what others have told me about myself, I. . .

Review the ways you have completed the sentences and see if you can identify characteristic ways you feel about yourself. How do you feel about the way you feel about yourself? How do your feelings about yourself facilitate or interfere with your involvement with others?

Activity

Check what qualities you possess by filling in the answers as you read through the questions.

QUESTIONS	MY ANSWERS
1. Anything I do regularly which helps others?	
2. Any skills I have?	
3. Any time I was generous?	
4. Anything I achieved which took a good deal of effort?	
5. Any feature of my personality?	
6. Any special relationship?	
7. Any spare time activity?	
8. Any work I do in my spare time?	
9. Any strengths/qualities I have?	
10. Any award/recognition I have received?	
11. Any membership of any group?	
12. Any way in which I have changed?	
13. Any way in which I have stayed the same?	
14. Anything I have done for myself?	
15. Anything I have won?	
16. Anything I do to: help society; protect the environment; give support to the less fortunate?	
17. Any fears I have overcome?	
18. Any time I have been positive rather than negative?	
19. Anything I do to maintain/improve my health?	
20. Anything else not covered by this list?	

SUMMARY

This chapter has introduced you to the value base for care upon which practice is based. It has explored essential components of interpersonal skills associated with communication, including relationship skills, 'oomph', listening skills and non-verbal communication. Barriers to effective communication have been examined. Personal qualities required by care workers and the attributes of effective helpers were described and opportunities have been provided to examine your own qualities. The roles of care workers, with some examples, have given you the opportunity to see how qualities and attributes, values and principles, knowledge and skills are practised in care settings.

Activity (at Higher)
Refer to the MacDonald/Ahmed case study in Chapter 10.

1. Linda MacDonald and Aishi Bibi both work as care workers. What attributes do you think they need in their work? Take four of these attributes and give an example of how each one can be put into practice.

2. Imagine that you are a worker in one of the following units described in Chapter 10:

   - Ivy Unit
   - 16 Fir Street
   - Heron Day Centre
   - Queen's View

Discuss in small groups or write down

   - the interpersonal skills which a care worker needs to develop in this setting;
   - the barriers which there may be to communication with this group of service users;
   - ways of overcoming at least two barriers.

SELECTED BIBLIOGRAPHY

Rogers J. (1990). *Caring for People, Help at the Frontline.* Milton Keynes: Open University
A warmly written, practical and relatively short introduction to caring.

Thomson, H. et al (1995). *Health and Social Care for Advanced GNVQ,* 2nd edn. London: Hodder & Stoughton.
A comprehensive guide with a lot of useful explanation and examples relating to interpersonal skills.

CHAPTER 7

Care planning and the helping process

Janet Miller

All people should be able to decide how they will live their lives. People with disabilities face the same decisions as anyone: the definition of self; the meaning of life; relationships with family, friends and others who cross their path, daily routines and experiences; and opportunities that are seized, created, postponed, rejected or simply let go.

(Pamela Walker and Julie Ann Racino in Sanderson et al, 1997)

INTRODUCTION

This chapter aims to enable you to participate in the care planning and helping process. It begins by introducing you to a model of care practice based upon assessment, planning, implementation and evaluation. The concept of need is examined in some detail, since it is upon an assessment of need which care planning is based. Two models of care planning are examined: the exchange model and person-centred planning. The helping process seeks to find the most appropriate ways of implementing care plans, that is putting them into practice. Included in this section is an explanation of two theoretical models of helping, those of Carl Rogers and Gerard Egan. At the end of the chapter boundary issues and evaluation are discussed. The relationship between the care planning and helping process and health promotion is briefly explored at relevant points, for those who are also working for the Higher Unit, 'Health Promotion'. The chapter is relevant to Outcomes 2 and 3 of the Higher Unit 'Interpersonal Skills for Care' and to Outcome 2 of the Higher Unit 'Health Promotion'. It goes beyond these syllabuses, however, to widen understanding of approaches to care work, and is useful for those going on to higher level qualifications such as HNC.

By the end of this chapter you should:
- understand the helping process;
- be able to participate in the process of assessment, planning, implementation and evaluation;
- have looked at different ways of assessing need;
- have started to develop a repertoire of helping skills;
- understand the theoretical models of helping of Rogers and Egan;
- understand the importance of boundary issues and evaluation;
- be able to relate some of the ideas in the chapter to Health Promotion.

Introduction to care planning

The foundations for helping have been laid in the previous chapter, through the development of a sound value base and the ability to build helpful, supportive relationships with people. These are really the most important things, since without them care practice is just a chore without the interests of people at its centre. They are not enough, however, to promote the best possible practice. Good practice needs to give service users as much power in their lives as anyone else, as much choice and as much say about how they wish to lead their lives. This imposes a duty on care workers to share the process of helping with service users in order to provide a quality of life which is as good as it can be, and to come to some agreed ways by which this can be achieved. The **agreement** reached between service users and those involved in their care is the **care plan**. Some writers prefer the term 'agreement' to 'plan' since it stresses that the service user is very much part of the decision-making process. This has not always been so and, unfortunately, it is still the case that some people in care situations feel that things are done to them rather than with them. Here are some quotes from service users which reflect this:

Everyone got together, staff, family and did your meeting and got my future sorted out without me.

They said you can't speak for yourself so we are doing it for you.

When I got my plan typed up the four things I wanted had been left out, but some things staff wanted were there.

(Sanderson et al, 1997)

Would you like it if other people decided how you should live your life? Glynn Vernon, who appears on a film *Stand up the Real Glynn Vernon*, has cerebral palsy, is unable to walk and uses a wheelchair, has speech which is difficult to understand when you first hear it, and experienced a lot of other people trying to make decisions on his behalf in his early adult life. He wanted to go to university, to get married and to live independently in his own accommodation. His first experience of a university interview was an apologetic rejection because the interviewer couldn't see (didn't have the imagination to see) how he would manage. Glynn gained a degree with the Open University. Glynn visited his minister of religion when he wanted to get married.

This well-meaning character tried to put him off because he didn't think that he could consummate the marriage. Glynn knew that he could and was married for seven years before the marriage broke down (40 per cent of marriages break down; there is nothing unusual here). A social worker tried to encourage him to go into residential care, saying she had his interests at heart, when it was apparent that she didn't want to take the risk of enabling Glynn to live independently. He did and does live independently in his own flat. Glynn had to fight many battles, but some people (his GP, his parents, some of his care workers) **listened** to him in pursuing his **needs and dreams**, and assisted him in helping to plan for his own future.

The care planning process

Care planning is part of a process which begins with an exploration of needs. The term **need** is used here to incorporate many kinds of need, including the top of Maslow's hierarchy (see page 000), self-actualisation. In this sense it also includes **wishes** and **dreams**. The initial exploration of need is usually termed **assessment** as a result of which a **plan** is made about how needs are going to be met. A plan will have certain aims and objectives in relation to meeting need. It may aim to improve the quality of life for a particular individual. Objectives will state the particular aspects of life which are to be worked on and changed. It is no good just having a plan, however. This plan has to be **implemented**, i.e. put into action, and it should be constantly **evaluated** through processes of **monitoring and review**. The mode and time scale of evaluation should be built into the plan. If evaluation indicates that the plan is not meeting need then it should be changed. **Flexibility** is essential in this process and frequent opportunities should be presented to the service user to discuss and evaluate the plan of care. Figure 7.1 on page 256 illustrates this process in the form of a tree. The roots of the tree represent values and principles, communication and other skills, and knowledge, some of which are explained in other parts of this book. The trunk of the tree represents the relationships which are made with service users and other relevant people, emphasising especially the qualities put forward by Carl Rogers (1991) of empathy, congruence or genuineness and unconditional positive regard. The crown of the tree is the care planning process, a process which begins with assessment and care planning and progresses to implementing and reviewing, but which goes round and round because care planning should never be regarded as complete.

The planning process in health promotion

The above model can be translated and used in the basic planning and evaluation process for health promotion. Health promotion involves enabling people to increase control over, and to improve their health. Work ranges from individual one-to-one help to group work and work with whole 'communities'. The beginning of this process is to **identify needs and priorities**, which corresponds with the assessment process. Once needs and priorities have been identified, aims and objectives are set and decisions are made about how to achieve these. Resources are identified (ones which exist and ones which may be needed), decisions are made about how work is to be evaluated and all of this results in an **action plan**, which corresponds with the care plan. The plan is then **implemented** in ways discussed in Chapters 8 and 9, and **evaluated** through looking at what has been achieved in terms of the original aims and objectives. The process is a circular one, in that once evaluation has taken place changes can be made to the plan and its

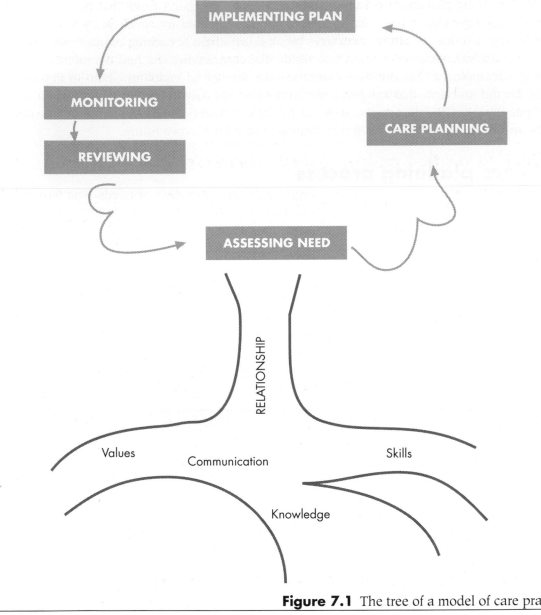

Figure 7.1 The tree of a model of care practice

implementation. Most of what follows about the care planning process can be applied with a little translation to health promotion.

Assessment

Assessment is the first step in the care planning process. It involves examining needs (including gifts, dreams and nightmares) and opportunities as a basis for a care plan which aims to ensure that the service user reaches a quality of life which is as good as it possibly can be. Right at the centre of this process, as far as possible guiding its course and making decisions, is the service user. A good assessment will also take into account the needs of other people in the service user's life, especially carers and family members, but the focus of **this** assessment should be **this** service user. Under Community Care, Disability, Carers and Children's legislation other people in the service user's life may be entitled to assessments and plans in their own right. Before proceeding to a more detailed examination of the elements of assessment ten essential points about assessment and care planning are emphasised, most of these contributed by care students.

Ten essential points about assessment and care planning

Assessment and care planning should:

1 – rest upon a firm value base with respect for the dignity of every individual and promotion of choice, rights, empowerment and, in some cases, protection, at the forefront;

2 – have good communication at the heart of the process;

3 – be **with** and not **of** the service user and be available to him or her. The aim is to empower the service user in negotiating an agreed care plan;

4 – be part of an on-going process which should never be regarded as complete;

5 – be needs led and not service led; 'needs led' means focusing upon a full examination of needs; 'service led' means the way in which, in the past, people were assessed for a particular service for which they had been referred – service came first, needs second;

6 – be based upon accurate, up to date information. It is important to distinguish clearly what is fact, what is opinion, intuition or something else;

7 – guard against labelling, stigmatising or making a scapegoat of a person. For example, if Joe is described as 'difficult' in an assessment this is a label which can lead to stigma (a negative sign) which can lead to scapegoating (being unjustly blamed for everything which goes wrong);

8 – be specific about who is responsible for what and outline the responsibilities, as well as the rights, which the individual has in the process;

9 –have a built-in evaluation procedure;

10 –emphasise that there is no one right care plan, there are no absolutes and assessment and care planning should be tailored to individual needs.

There follows a more detailed examination of needs and opportunities, which form the basis of assessment and the resulting care plan.

Needs

This section reminds you of some of the things which it is important to consider when examining need. In Chapter 3 development was examined in terms of PIES: physical, intellectual/cognitive, emotional and social development. These aspects of development can be translated into needs, though they are expanded in this section to the word PROCCCESS (with apologies for the misspelling) referring to: **p**hysical needs, **r**elationship needs (in terms of relationships with carers and other professionals), **o**rganisational and operational needs (in terms of what needs to be done to put the care plan in place), **c**ommunication needs, **c**ultural needs, **c**ognitive/intellectual needs, **e**motional needs, **s**ocial (including other relationship) needs and **s**piritual needs.

The other model of needs which it is useful to refer back to here is Maslow's hierarchy of needs, set out in Chapter 4. The aim of any care plan should be to enable and empower a person to reach as far up this hierarchy as possible through providing access, assistance and opportunities. Before further examining PROCCCESS needs, one additional way of analysing need is explained. This is known as Bradshaw's taxonomy of need (Bradshaw, 1972), which looks at needs as being of four different kinds:

- **normative needs**, defined in terms of some agreed standard, usually by professional 'experts', whose views may not necessarily coincide with those of service users;
- **felt needs**, seen as what individuals identify as needs, in other words, what they want;
- **expressed needs**, which are felt needs turned into requests or demands. Not all felt needs become expressed needs;
- **comparative needs** refer to the imputed needs of a group not in receipt of a service but similar in relevant characteristics to a group receiving a service.

It is important to bear all of these areas of need in mind when assessing need, ensuring that even when it is impossible to meet all needs, at least consideration has been given to different aspects of need. An assessment of need is relevant not only to the care planning process but also in the development of an action plan in health promotion. PROCCCESS needs are now examined in more detail.

Physical needs

Everyone has physical needs, needs associated with keeping the body in good working order and as healthy as possible. For people who need some help it is essential to identify those needs which the individual is unable to meet and to provide enough help to meet these, whilst at the same time maximising independence, maintaining dignity and promoting empowerment. An example of providing adequate housing as a way of then enabling people, including informal carers, to meet needs, especially physical needs, is illustrated in the passage below about children with physical disabilities:

The home was often these children's most restrictive environment. Often they simply could not use their equipment such as walking or standing frames around their homes because of the cramped and confined conditions.

Parents were worried that their children were not getting the exercise or therapy they believed they need because of space constraints and the two mothers of visually impaired children complained that their children spent a lot of time colliding into furniture and doors.

Compare this with the experience of Debbie after moving to a new, specially built home:

Within 24 hours of being in this house it was like – Wow! She was a different child. Her confidence increased overnight. I can't describe to you the difference in Debbie.

(*Community Care Magazine*, 1.10.98)

Relationships with carers and other professionals

One part of the care planning process which is often neglected is the need for service users and care workers to build up relationships with the providers and organisers of care. **Informal carers**, such as parents, partners and friends, **professionals** such as doctors, social workers, community psychiatric nurses, home care supervisors, health visitors, educational psychologist, **other people** with whom the service user interacts such as neighbours and befrienders, are all potentially important components of the planning process. In one school of care planning, person-centred planning, which is explained in greater detail later in the chapter, the service user chooses who is to be part of the planning process. In other situations, especially where statutory requirements must be met in relation to children or people with mental health problems, there are some people who must be part of the planning process and others who can be chosen by the service user.

Organisational and operational needs

A knowledge of organisations which have the potential to provide for need, and of the operations necessary to access their services, is a vital part of the care worker's repertoire. The more a care worker knows about what resources can be utilised or may be available, the greater the choice which can be given to the service user. Sometimes all that is needed is **information** about how to access various forms of help, for example what DSS (Department of Social Security) benefits are available, where there is a day centre, which college runs appropriate courses in computing. Armed with this information the service user may then be able to pursue avenues of interest or care independently. Agencies which are able to provide a great deal of useful information are the Citizen's Advice Bureaux in many locations around Scotland and the rest of the UK, Social Work Departments and Health Centres.

Activity

Choose one client group and find out which agencies can provide relevant help and information in your area.

Communication needs

Although communication needs could be included in the section on cognitive/intellectual needs they are considered separately here, mainly at the suggestion of service users who feel that this is an often neglected area. Many people experience some form of communication difficulty or disability such as deafness or speech difficulty or have a first language which is different from that of the care worker. It is important that their communication needs are met, for example by providing signers for someone who is deaf and communicates by signing, and/or by learning some signing yourself. Joan, a social work assistant on a disability team, wanted to gain a qualification. She is deaf and communicates by signing. She visited her local college where she was offered a place on a course. Her employer was prepared to finance a signer, Joan successfully completed her care course and is now anxious to further her education by taking an Open University degree. By meeting Joan's communication needs, cognitive needs were also achieved and Joan was enabled to reach towards self-actualisation.

Cultural needs

Cultural needs are often seen as part of social needs but are in danger of being neglected if not considered separately. Culture includes values, language and customs. The care worker should try to familiarise him/herself with the different cultural practices of those with whom he or she works and should take these into account in shared planning. Different cultural groups have different practices in relation to diet, physical care and coping with death. For Muslims, for example, Islam governs the way of life and forbids eating pigs in all forms, and other animals which have not been slaughtered ritually. Women should be covered from their heads to their feet, leaving only the face and the hands uncovered. Muslim women are often very modest and will usually prefer female to male carers. During the month of Ramadan a Muslim fasts from sunrise to sunset, although those who are sick are not expected to fast. A Muslim who is dying may wish to sit or lie with his or her face towards Mecca and after death there should be no skin contact with non-Muslims.

Activity

Find out about the practices of one cultural group which is different from your own in terms of diet, care requirements and coping with death.

Cognitive/intellectual needs

If you look at Chapter 3 you will see that there are different cognitive needs at differing stages of development. The young child needs school and stimulation at home, especially through play and communication, the adult needs opportunities to continue to develop cognitively and these should be explored as part of the planning process. Whenever possible, people should be enabled to access resources which are available to everyone. Glynn Vernon wanted a university education but discrimination and poor access prevented him from entering the first university of his choice. Many colleges at present provide special courses for people with a learning disability. It is often assumed that these students would be unable to access mainstream courses when in fact additional support rather than special courses may fulfil their needs. Care workers can be advocates for people to access resources in the community which contribute to the fulfilment of cognitive/intellectual needs. The process of promoting access to mainstream community resources is part of **normalisation**.

Activity

Investigate two services/opportunities in your local community which may be useful in promoting the cognitive development of one group of service users. Are these accessible? What measures should be taken to enable service users to attend?

Emotional needs

Emotional development depends upon the fulfilment of emotional needs. These include the need for love, belongingness, self esteem and opportunities to develop a positive self concept. Exploration of emotional needs rests very much upon spending time getting to know the service user, listening actively to verbal and non-verbal communication and, from this, gaining a picture of the individual's emotional life and the extent to which emotional needs are fulfilled. The time and patience required to explore the significance of relationships and how the individual sees and feels about him/herself can have spin-offs in many areas of life. An account provided by a care student, about a man who attended a day resource centre, provides a good example here. The service user had no speech and couldn't say how he felt. Other care staff had said this was not a great concern!

I thought about making up a chart of faces with different expressions so that the service user could show me how he feels and we could start working together and getting to know each other. By doing this it would promote effective care practice for the service user as he is getting to know how he feels and he can deal with it ... Within 2 weeks I was getting results and he was showing me and telling me how he was feeling.

Activity

Devise an exercise similar to the one above which could be used with a service user with communication difficulties to 'tell' you how he or she feels about one aspect of his or her life.

Social needs

Social needs include the need for relationships and opportunities to build these in a variety of contexts.

When you look at the opportunities which service users have to develop social relationships how far do these meet social needs and is there any support needed to develop these? Have community links been thoroughly explored in order that service users have opportunities which are as far as possible equal to the opportunities open to all citizens? The answers to these questions provide indicators for planning and implementation. Here is an example contributed by a student with the permission of the service user.

Mary has a physical disability which restricts her movement, and is a wheelchair user. She also has a mild learning disability. She loves the cinema, going to pubs and enjoys going to chapel on Sundays. She has a good friend Jean who lives in the same hostel and with whom she enjoys going out. Jean also has a learning disability but is able to walk and is physically quite fit. Because of Mary's mobility problems and her inability to travel independently she has few opportunities to go out socially with her friend. I asked if I could be of any help in enabling Mary and Jean to do something they would enjoy together. They discussed this and said that they would love to go to see the film 'Braveheart' ... I discussed this with the care team and it was agreed that I could arrange this outing with maximum help from Mary and Jean, and that I would accompany them to assist with Mary's wheelchair, but would only sit with them if they wanted me to ... the outing was a huge success and enhanced their relationship with one another, fulfilling both social and emotional needs.

Activity

Examine and write about your own social needs. Do you want to spend time talking to people you choose to spend time with, sharing activities with them, going on holiday with others whom you like and whose interests you share? Do you appreciate the opportunity to spend time with your family, friends, colleagues in pleasant surroundings? Where do you gain your social contacts? Do you meet people at work, through organisations to which you belong, through your family?

Spiritual needs

Spiritual needs could perhaps have been encompassed in the discussions of emotional and social needs, but there is a danger that they are given insufficient emphasis. Spiritual needs include the need for contemplation, for the pursuit of religious belief and/or the sharing of ideas about the meaning of life and mortality. Mary, written about in the previous section, fulfilled her own spiritual needs through attending chapel, though it wasn't always possible for her to achieve this need because someone had to organise this and accompany her.

Activity

How do you think Mary could have been enabled to attend chapel more regularly?

Gifts and giftedness

Assessment in the care planning process considers 'gifts' as part of looking at needs. Gifts in this context, refer not to exceptional talents such as singing well for example, but to the recognition that every individual is unique, has a personality, a presence and characteristics which distinguish him or her from everyone else. These gifts need to be recognised so that they can be used and built upon in care planning. Judith Snow in Sanderson et al (1997) has written beautifully about how giftedness can be seen as based upon presence and difference. A passage from her work is quoted below:

But ... everyone has gifts – countless ordinary and extraordinary gifts. A gift is anything that one is or has or does that creates an opportunity for meaningful interaction with at least one other person. Gifts are the fundamental characteristics of our human life and community.

There are two simple gifts that all people have and that every other gift depends on. The first is presence. Since you are here you are embodying the possibility of meaningful interaction with someone else.

Secondly you are different from everyone else – in countless ways. Difference is required to make meaning possible ... human interaction arises from presence and difference. You are different from the next person in hundreds, perhaps thousands of ways – in your body, your thinking, your experience, your culture, your interests, tastes and desires, your possessions, your relationships, and more. Therefore you are a bundle of hundreds, perhaps thousands of gifts. So is everyone else.

Mary, discussed above, has a lot of gifts. She is witty, she smiles a lot and makes other people feel comfortable in her presence, she is warm and affectionate, she is very firm in her religious faith, she is absolutely truthful, she has a good sense of colour, she is a good cook and she is a good friend to Jean.

Dreams and nightmares

Everyone has dreams, things which they would really like to do, to be, places they would like to go, people they would like to see and spend time with; and nightmares, things which they definitely do not want to happen, places they certainly do not want to be or to go, people they would rather not see. Here are some of Mary's dreams and nightmares:

Dreams	Nightmares
To share a flat with Jean	To go back to the hospital
To walk	To live by myself
To go to the pictures every week	To be left outside alone in my wheelchair
To go on holiday to Greece	To lose my friendship with Jean
To use a computer to write letters	To be bored all day
To see my sister in Australia	Never to go out or to travel
To have a job	To be forced to eat things I don't like

Opportunities

Opportunities are things which can be used to produce a favourable outcome. They may exist already or they may have to be created. They may be the gifts and qualities of an individual as outlined above or they may exist outside the person in the form of resources; they may be here within this agency or they may be outside in the wider community. They are important in assessment and care planning because they present the means by which the plan can be put into action. A care worker needs to build up a picture of what these opportunities are, what needs to be done to access them or create them or fight for them. Resources refer to anything which can be helpful: money, people, services in the statutory, voluntary and private sectors including day centres, educational opportunities and respite care. The assessment and care planning focus should be needs led but must also be realistic in terms of what may be possible. This doesn't mean abandoning dreams, which should be fought for, but it does mean that a worker has to be honest both with herself and with the service user about what opportunities exist or are likely to exist. The one great resource which a good care worker needs to develop is imagination, since many care plans can be implemented using all available resources imaginatively. Befrienders, volunteers, shared carers, everyday facilities in the community such as coffee shops and pubs, family members, friends, can all be useful resources providing opportunities for fulfilling many needs.

TOOLS OF ASSESSMENT

Assessment builds up a picture of needs, gifts, dreams and nightmares. There are available to the care worker some tools which can help in building this picture over a period of time, some of which are a necessary requirement of the agency, some of which can make the process enjoyable rather than a chore. The emphasis is upon building relationships as a prerequisite to good assessment and upon taking time, rather than attempting to complete an assessment and plan in one short meeting. Below is an account of some of these tools, which are examined in terms of their merits and disadvantages.

Assessment meetings

An assessment meeting can take many forms. In person-centred planning (see page 000) for example, the service user can invite those people whom he or she chooses, to a meeting or, if necessary meetings, at which needs, dreams and people who are to be part of implementation are discussed with an aim of making a plan which is truly focused upon **this** individual. Another form of meeting is a multi-disciplinary one which is attended by the service user and as many people involved in his or her care as possible. Meetings need to be as non-threatening as possible, to be relaxed so that everyone feels confident enough to make a contribution. Meetings have the advantage of bringing many people together but are only one aspect of the assessment/care planning process. They can be rather formal occasions unless a conscious effort is made to avoid this.

At one assessment meeting I attended recently the chair of the meeting began by taking this opportunity to discipline the service user. Why do you think this defeated the purpose for which the meeting was called? The service user was immediately put on the defensive, his mother was furious, other people at the meeting felt extremely uncomfortable and were completely taken by surprise by this approach. Although efforts were made to rescue the situation, the participation of the service user and his mother was effectively lost. When you read the section on person-centred planning you will see an emphasis upon meetings being facilitated rather than chaired, with a facilitator representing and advocating for the service user where necessary. Some situations may require both some formal structure and a degree of advocacy, for example when assessment and planning are taking place with a child at risk.

Assessment forms

Assessment forms have their uses but should never be the be all and end all of the assessment and care planning process. Most local authorities have a Community Care Assessment form of some description which summarises useful information usually under such headings as: personal details; family members and contact with these; housing situation; physical and psychological health; dependencies e.g. upon drugs or alcohol; informal support received e.g. from family members; formal support/services received; service user's views; carer's views; any disagreements between the two; people contacted as part of the assessment process; a summary of needs; a summary of areas to be carried forward to the care plan.

These forms are often used as a way of arguing for resources and often don't contain the kind of information which a residential or day centre worker needs to know about everyday life. For this reason many agencies also have their own forms asking for the kind of information they need for work on a day-to-day basis. The Archdiocese of Glasgow, for example, has a respite care assessment form which details likes and dislikes, medication, how to respond if a particular emergency should arise, contact numbers and a photograph. Information written on the assessment form can be gleaned through the use of other tools of assessment. The form is only the written account of a process which should be personal, built upon thorough knowledge and relationships. Forms have the advantage of providing a written summary but are limited by the questions asked which may not always be the most appropriate ones.

Checklists

Checklists are often used in care practice to establish what a service user can do in relation to a set of tasks, as a way of planning what needs to be achieved to make progress. They are often used with people with learning disability to establish a baseline from which a plan can be made. These checklists go under such names as 'Irabeena' and 'Copeland' and have many of the advantages and pitfalls which have already been seen to apply to forms. They are only as good as the questions asked and there is a danger that they can become the main focus of work when they are only one tool in the care planning and helping process.

Observation and asking questions

These are two sociological research methods which were outlined in Chapter 5 and which are also useful to the care worker in assessment. Observation doesn't mean that a person's every move and action needs to be watched and recorded but that a care worker's and other's observations of the service user can be of relevance in the assessment process, especially in situations where the service user has difficulty in communication. Observed changes in behaviour, difficulties in relating to some people more than others, observations of likes and dislikes can all be important aspects of assessment. If, for example, you are working with a child with a learning disability whom you observe to become very agitated and to exhibit challenging behaviour when there is a lot of noise, you may build into the care plan opportunities to have quiet times away from other service users. As with observation, asking questions is a very straightforward way of obtaining information if the service user or those being asked have the communication skills to provide adequate answers. This method is quick and is a very good way of obtaining factual data. Wheal (1994) lists areas about which 'looked after' children answer a set of questions: health, education, identity, family and social relationships, emotional and behavioural development and self care skills. Asking questions can, however, be seen as rather threatening and sometimes people give the answer they think you would like to hear rather than what is really concerning them. Other information is just as well gained through one of the other more informal ways set out below which may, in the end, produce a more accurate picture.

Diaries and scrapbooks

Diaries record day-to-day events of significance. A care worker can suggest to a service user that he or she keeps a diary for perhaps a period of two weeks, writing down (with help, if necessary), all of the things which are important during that time: activities, people, classes, outings and so on. In this way a picture of the service user's everyday life and the network of people who are important to him/her can be built up as a basis for assessing need and looking at things which should and should not happen in the plan of care. One care worker worked on a diary with Stephen, a boy of thirteen resident in a care and education centre. Stephen enjoyed going over his day and the care worker realised from the diary just how important routine was to Stephen. One of the most vital parts of the day was a morning shower without which Stephen felt very uncomfortable. Keeping the diary not only enabled the care worker and Stephen to identify needs and things which should be incorporated in the care plan, but as a spin-off improved their relationship with one another and gave Stephen the opportunity to improve his literacy skills in an enjoyable way.

A diary may also be a useful tool for the care worker to keep, recording events in relation to a specific service user over a set period of time. In this way it may be possible to identify patterns of behaviour, triggers to challenging behaviour, issues which are of importance, social contacts, likes, dislikes and needs which have not previously been evident. Carers too, for example family members or carers in shared care situations, can facilitate the assessment process through the use of diaries from which needs can be identified.

Where communication, especially written communication, is difficult, a scrapbook of pictures could be built up as a shared exercise enabling the service user to identify needs and people of importance through photographs and magazine pictures.

Activity

Use one of the above (diary or scrapbook) over a period of two weeks with a service user as a means of identifying needs.

Shared activities

Sometimes needs can be identified when the focus isn't on assessment at all but upon an enjoyable activity which is shared between service user and worker. When Linda and her care worker went to the cinema together they had a good chat afterwards about the film and about all sorts of other things too. Linda talked about her family, about how she wished she could see her sister more often, about her great love of the cinema and going bowling and swimming, she mentioned her keyworker several times and expressed a dislike of one particular night shift worker. All of this contributed to building up a picture of her needs which could subsequently help in developing her care plan.

The above are not the only ways in which information for an assessment can be gained. You may be able to think of others which work just as well. They do, however, provide a start and a basis upon which a plan of care can be formulated.

THE CARE PLAN

The Social Care Association in 'An Introduction to Care Planning' (1994) says the following about a care plan:

A care plan is an action plan in working with service users. As plans are written down and shared with users, they emphasise the contractual nature of the service provided.

Planning is a practical activity that:
- *gives a sense of purpose to meeting needs;*
- *takes action in advance of any problems;*
- *ensures that service users do not get overlooked.*

Plans can be staged according to which needs are to be met in what time scale. For example, there will be some needs to be met immediately, some in one month, some in three months, some by next year and some which will be worked towards at some point in the future. The essential features of a care plan, from the above definition and the preceding discussion of assessment, are that:
- it is the basis for **action** (not just a paper exercise);
- it is **written down**;
- it is **shared with** the service user;
- it is a **contract** – providers and users agree about what is to be done by whom;
- it is a **practical activity**;
- all team members should be working to **this** plan which is the **service user's**, not theirs;
- the plan should state **specifically what** is to happen, **who** should be doing what and in what **time scale**;
- **monitoring and review** of the plan should be built into the planning process (see page 294);

- the plan should clearly identify any **statutory/legal** requirements, implications or **constraints**. For example, some care plans for children incorporate a supervision requirement which is legally enforced by the children's panel or the courts. Any other likely constraints which may affect the care plan should be detailed.

Models used in the care planning process

The above discussion has drawn heavily upon two models of planning: the **exchange model** and **person-centred planning**. Both of these emphasise the importance of placing the service user at the centre of the planning process. However, person-centred planning goes much further than this and presents exciting possibilities for the service user to make supported choices ranging from who attends planning meetings to how the future is to be lived.

The exchange model

The exchange model is described in Coulshed and Orme (1998) and emphasises an exchange among service users, carers and workers of their knowledge and skills, including knowledge of methods of helping and of resources and skills in the process of problem-solving. The model recognises that people with needs and those in their network know **more** about their problems than any worker who comes along to help them, though workers have their own areas of expertise. The process of producing a plan is an exchange among everyone involved and should be multi-disciplinary in nature. A plan emerges which is a balance-sheet of everything which has been presented. One person, usually a keyworker or social worker coordinates the plan and negotiates agreements about who is to do what for whom in what time scale. The focus is upon the social situation and everyone in the service user's network. Smale (1993) summarises the main tasks of this model as follows:

- *facilitate full participation in the process of decision making;*
- *make a 'holistic' assessment of the social situation, and not just of the referred individual;*
- *help create and maintain the flexible set of human relationships which make up a 'package of care';*
- *facilitate negotiations within personal networks about conflicts of choices and needs;*
- *create sufficient trust for full participation and open negotiations to actually take place; and*
- *change the approach to all these broad tasks as the situation itself changes over time.*

Person-centred planning

(Most of the following section is produced with permission from SHS Ltd., Edinburgh.)

Person-centred planning creates
a compelling image of a desirable future
and invites people to join with
the person to make it happen.

(O'Brien and Lovett in Sanderson et al, 1997)

Person-centred planning is a way of helping people who may wish to make some changes in their life. It is an empowering approach to helping people plan their future and organise the supports and services they need. It seeks to mirror the ways in which 'ordinary people' make plans.

(Sanderson et al, 1997)

Person-centred planning has developed from ideas presented by O'Brien and Lovett (1992), mainly in relation to people with learning disability who are now beginning to find a place 'in the community', often after spending many years in hospital. Some of its central ideas, however, can be transferred to care planning in general and can be useful with any service user who **wants** and is in a position to make changes in his or her life. It is an exciting advance upon traditional models of care planning, moving away from professionals organising the process, towards placing as much control and decision-making in the hands of the service user as possible. Various forms of care planning are based upon the person centred approach, including **personal futures planning** and **essential lifestyle planning** and many agencies, among them the Outlook project in East Dunbartonshire and Richmond Fellowship, Scotland, are embracing person-centred planning as central to their work. The potential of this approach for empowering service users is enormous and exciting and for this reason it is given considerable space in this section of the book. Unlike the exchange model, the focus is well and truly upon **this** service user, rather than a social situation and a plan which must account for the needs of many people. The roots of person-centred planning are illustrated in Figure 7.2.

Person-centred planning is often very visual, using diagrams and charts to assist in building a plan. Figures 7.3, 7.4 and 7.5 below show some of the ways in which visual material is used in the planning process, illustrating 'building a shared understanding', 'relationship circles' and 'when a meeting is needed'. These are reproduced with the permission of SHS, Edinburgh.

The roots of person-centred planning have now been explored. Three ways of working which are essential to the person-centred planning process are now considered. These are:

- sharing power;
- building a shared picture;
- building a capacity for change.

Sharing power is not always easy, especially when service users have experienced many years of powerlessness in institutional settings. For this reason planning may have an educational element, showing and informing the person about what is possible. It may also require enormous patience and a very positive belief that the person **is** capable of growth and participation. The use of visual materials is one of the ways in which people are both empowered and can begin to build a shared picture of their future. Building a capacity for change may involve investigating and utilising community resources in creative and new ways. Here are some ways in which agencies share power and build up a shared picture. Outlook (Kirkintilloch) asks the service user **who** he or she wishes to invite to a planning meeting, and the meeting is at the user's and not anyone else's pace. SHS Ltd. looks at the best possible day and the worst possible day for the person, going right through a 24-hour period and looking at every detail. The important thing about this is that it focuses attention upon the small details of life, such as what this individual likes for breakfast.

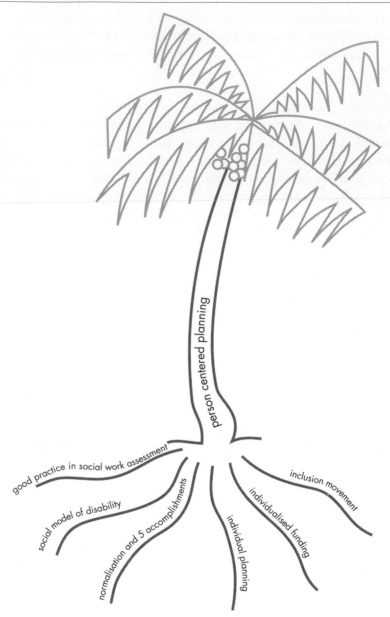

Figure 7.2 The roots of person – centred planning (reproduced with permission of SHS Ltd, Edinburgh)

Person-centred planning is a comprehensive way of planning for people. There may still be some formalities to be completed in order to access some aspects of the care plan. It will probably still be necessary, for example, to complete a community care assessment form, but the process of getting there in person-centred planning is unique to **this** service user who is being empowered to make **these** changes in his or her life.

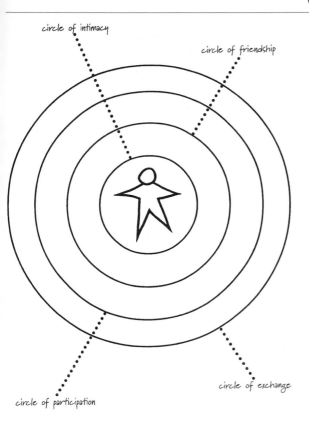

circle of intimacy

circle of friendship

circle of participation

circle of exchange

Figure 7.3 Relationship Circles (reproduced with permission of SHS Ltd, Edinburgh)

Below is a summary of what person-centred planning is moving from and towards.

Moving from		Moving towards
clinical descriptions of people	→	seeing people as human beings
professionals being in charge	→	sharing power
professionals inviting people	→	the person choosing who attends meetings
meetings in offices at times convenient to staff	→	meetings in a venue chosen by the person, when it suits her/him
meetings being chaired	→	meetings being facilitated
not asking what person wants	→	encouraging person to dream
assuming inability	→	looking for gifts in people
filing plans away	→	giving the plan to the person
writing notes of meetings	→	graphic facilitation of meetings
professionals putting plan into action	→	all team members having some responsibility for implementing plan

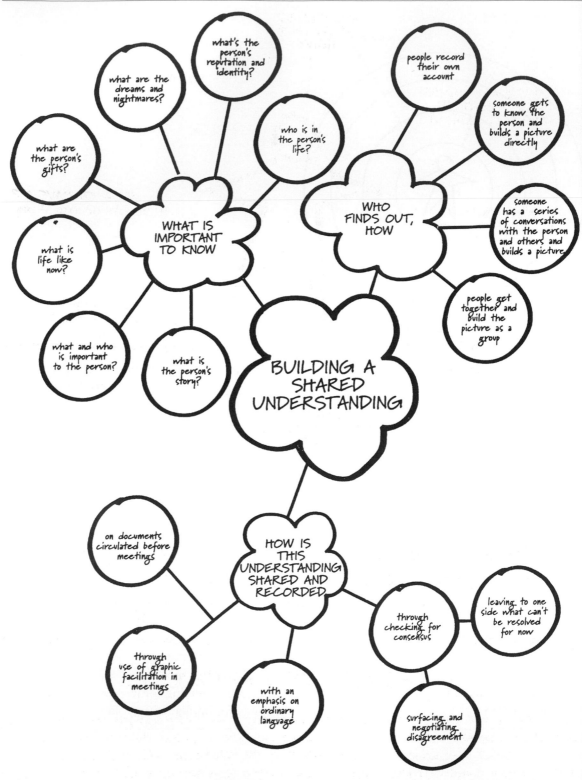

Figure 7.4 Building a shared understanding (reproduced by permission of SHS Ltd, Edinburgh)

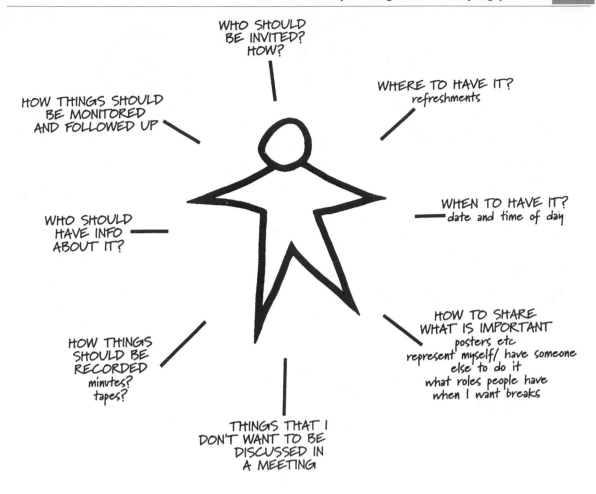

WHO SHOULD
BE INVITED?
HOW?

WHERE TO HAVE IT?
refreshments

HOW THINGS SHOULD
BE MONITORED
AND FOLLOWED UP

WHEN TO HAVE IT?
date and time of day

WHO SHOULD
HAVE INFO
ABOUT IT?

HOW TO SHARE
WHAT IS IMPORTANT
posters etc
represent myself/ have someone
else to do it
what roles people have
when I want breaks

HOW THINGS
SHOULD BE
RECORDED
minutes?
tapes?

THINGS THAT I
DON'T WANT TO BE
DISCUSSED IN
A MEETING

We need to look creatively at these issues
with the person and think about how decisions
can be made in the most empowering way.

Figure 7.5 When a meeting is needed . . . (reproduced by permission of SHS Ltd, Edinburgh)

THE HELPING PROCESS

The helping process aims to **implement** the care plan in ways which respect worth and dignity, empower the person and promote rights and welfare. A lot of people think of helping as a very active process of doing things for other people. From the value base, skills and qualities explained in the previous chapter, you will have realised, however, that helping is really about empowering and enabling people to do as much as possible for themselves, empowering them to have opportunities which are available to most other people. This should always be considered in order that helping does not become patronising, discriminating or demeaning. With these factors in mind, some useful skills and methods, which aim to improve the service user's quality of life and put into action aspects of the care plan, are set out in the following section. Before reading this, it is useful for you to think about the skills which you already have. These are some of the suggestions made by a group of care students on placement when asked what skills and methods they used to implement plans:

- *I use empathy when I'm helping people, just imagining what they would want and how they're probably feeling.*
- *I always demonstrate respect so that people aren't embarrassed when they need help.*
- *I talk to the young people, get to know them first.*
- *I try to motivate the older adults I work with by providing some interesting activities and a choice of things to do.*
- *I play with the young people and try to help with their socialisation and their education plan.*
- *Communication, communication, communication – verbal and non-verbal; anything that works.*
- *I assist people to the toilet and with bathing, always being careful to find out how much they can do for themselves first, and I always talk to them and ask how their son or daughter is or whoever is important to them.*
- *I write up notes in the log at the end of the day and attend the handover meetings so that I know what is being achieved in the care plans and others have an idea about what has happened during my shift.*
- *I take one lady shopping. It sometimes takes us an hour to get out of the house because she's quite slow at getting ready and the other care staff seem to think this isn't relevant work. I think this is what the job is all about. We go to the post office and collect her pension, then we'll go for a coffee and take our time, then a walk back in time for lunch. Admittedly you can't do that every day, but it's an important part of care work.*
- *I've been helping a group of children with life story books so that they have a reminder about who has been important to them and important places, holidays and so on.*
- *I've been doing something similar with some older adults, making a scrap book to represent old times. We have some amazing conversations about some of the pictures. Some people in their 90s remember the first world war.*
- *I used to be a hairdresser and when we're going on an outing I ask if anyone wants their hair done. Lots of them do. While you're doing their hair or their nails you talk to them and they tell you all sorts of things they never would usually, because they're so relaxed.*

Activity

In the examples above identify the needs which are being met, in terms of PROCCCESS needs.

What else do you notice about the above examples? Most of them illustrate skills which are part of everyday life: talking to people, playing with children, making scrapbooks, going shopping. The importance of communication is emphasised again and again and is an essential part of all care work. Some useful skills and ways of working, which has communication at the beginning and includes many of the suggestions made by students above, is now set out under the following headings:

1. Developing communication skills; on-the-spot counselling; the work of Carl Rogers (1991) and Gerard Egan (1986).
2. Working as a member of a team.
3. Organising the worker's shift/managing work and time in order to provide a quality service.
4. Developing practical skills, e.g. skills which meet physical needs, safe moving and handling, first aid and emergency procedures, health and safety.
5. Dealing with critical incidents and challenging behaviour – a summary.
6. Promoting activities, including life story books.
7. Developing networks.
8. Advocacy skills.
9. Transferring skills which you already have to the helping situation.
10. Developing group work skills.
11. Providing a 'good' environment for care.
12. Keeping records and report writing.
13. Keyworking (this is dealt with in Chapter 6, page 247).

This is not, by any means, a comprehensive list and, as you progress through your career, it is likely that you will develop other methods and skills relevant to the service users with whom you work.

1. Developing communication skills; on-the-spot counselling

Communication skills are at the heart of the helping process. These have already been discussed very thoroughly in Chapter 6. In this chapter the contribution which ideas from counselling can make to enhancing these skills is considered. To become a trained counsellor takes a long time and special training, but the counselling literature provides care workers with some fairly straightforward skills which can prove useful in what are called on-the-spot counselling situations. These are natural, everyday occurrences, often short in time and frequently emotionally charged, which can provide opportunities for helping the individual through effective communication and can prevent the development of much more complex and serious problems if handled sensitively. Examples of such situations include Bill, an elderly man, who spills his cup of tea and becomes excessively upset by this; Mary who has cerebral palsy and becomes extremely depressed when an outing is cancelled; Julie, who has a learning disability and is found one morning sobbing her heart out over a photograph of her mother who died last year. A worker who fobs off these people with a comment like 'never mind, tomorrow will be a better day', often loses an opportunity to develop a meaningful relationship and to help through on-the-spot counselling.

Carl Rogers' work

The work of Carl Rogers (1991) provides a good starting point here. Rogers emphasised that there are three core conditions to promoting a good helping relationship. These core conditions are **empathy**, **unconditional positive regard** (warmth, acceptance and respect), and **congruence** (genuineness), all of which received consideration in Chapter 6. Once these core conditions are established and the counsellor is prepared to listen actively to the service user Rogers believed that people could begin to solve their own problems, to make their own choices and to move towards self-actualisation. This doesn't mean that the counsellor doesn't do anything, since providing these core conditions and listening actively can be very hard work, but it is not the counsellor who solves the problem, it is the individual who is enabled to do so him/herself. Giving advice and active guidance are **not** part of the counselling process; active listening and enabling the individual to explore the problem are. The skills of on-the-spot counselling are thus not particularly distinguishable from social, communication and interpersonal skills. The main skills, once the core conditions are established, are considered in a little more detail below:

Listening/active listening. Are you able to let a person finish talking without reacting? Are you able to listen without interrupting? Listening, really listening, isn't easy and sometimes it is necessary to stop yourself from barging in and solving a problem on someone else's behalf when all they need or want from you is a listening ear. Often people can solve their own problems, have virtually decided what to do, and only need reassurance and encouragement from someone else to go ahead. There isn't always time to listen for very long but the care worker who misses opportunities to listen to service users often loses the opportunity to achieve a lot in a short period of time. A little listening can go a very long way. It can give reassurance, comfort, warmth, a sense of worth and the support needed to move forward towards problem resolution. If much fuller discussion appears to be needed and the worker cannot give time **now**, then an honest response about this should be provided with an acknowledgement that the service user has been heard and the situation has been taken seriously.

Active listening can be taken further than this through the use of the skills of **paraphrasing**, **reflective responding**, **summarising** and **asking open questions**. **Paraphrasing** involves letting a person know that you have heard and understood what has been said by saying it back to them in your own words. This is quite a skill and requires a lot of practice. **Reflective responding** reads the music behind the words, reflects a grasp of how the person is probably feeling as well as what they are saying through empathising with body language, tone of voice and other non-verbal cues. **Summarising** feeds back to the person a shortened version of what has been presented, emphasising the main points. It is another way of checking that you have heard accurately and also keeps the main strands of discussion in mind. **Open questions** keep a discussion moving forward and elicit more information than the alternative closed question. A closed question is one to which you can answer 'yes', 'no' or give a one word reply. 'Do you like tea?' is a closed question. 'What do you like to drink?' is an open question. 'How many brothers have you got?' is a closed question. 'What is your family like?' is an open question.

Gerard Egan's three stage skills model

All of the skills above can be applied in Egan's three stage skills model of helping, which provides a framework for assisting people to deal with their difficulties. Like Rogers, Egan (1986) believed that helping works best when people take ultimate responsibility for seeing solutions to their difficulties. If the person is helped to develop a sense of personal responsibility and self-reliance he or she is more likely to benefit in the long term. Egan divided the helping process into the three stages of **exploration, developing new understanding and action**. The explanation of his theory below is based upon an account by Carol Sallows, a counsellor with the Women's Counselling and Resource Service in Glasgow and is adapted from Miller, J. (1996).

Stage 1: Exploration. This involves the helper/worker in assisting the person to explore areas of concern so that they become clear. Often people know that they need help but haven't yet clarified why. The task of the worker during this phase is to explore problem areas in order that the person gains a clear picture of what the problems are. The worker builds up a relationship using empathy, congruence and unconditional positive regard and develops understanding through such skills as active listening, paraphrasing, reflecting, using open questions and summarising. Demonstration of the above skills should make the person feel comfortable so that he or she can move forward. Noticing people's body language will help the worker to be more in tune with them and their feelings. It is also important that the worker is aware of his or her own body language.

Stage 2: Developing new understanding. In stage 2 the helper's role is to enable the person to see him/herself from new perspectives and to develop deeper understanding. This allows the person to decide what may be done about the area of concern, leading to setting specific goals and objectives. By the end of this stage, the problem should be seen by the person in new ways and stated in different terms. People often have their own interpretation and explanation for difficulty which may stem from a lack of self esteem. They may blame themselves for their difficulties and the helper can assist them to examine this in a new light. Seeing things from a fresh angle can often help to replace the lethargy and depression which arises from feelings of helplessness, with new energy and willingness to take action. At this stage all of the skills of stage 1 remain relevant, but there is a shift in emphasis towards challenging the person so that he or she can move forward. These skills are sometimes known as challenging skills and include summarising, appropriate sharing about self, offering information, immediacy (what is happening here and now between helper and person) and goal setting.

Summarising has been looked at above. Self disclosure is the process of communicating thoughts and feelings about one's own attitudes. It means knowing at what point and to what extent the helper should offer information about him/herself. Positive self disclosure can be effective in initiating and maintaining warm, genuine and empathic relationships and can be communicated by facial expressions, gestures, body language and tone of voice. In this stage the helper can risk hunches, pick out themes, put two and two together, make the implicit explicit, and identify the meaning behind the words. It is essential at this stage to provide the correct balance between challenge and support for the person, and any form of challenge should be done in a way which indicates the helper's sense of caring for the person.

Stage 3: Action. In the third stage, the helper's role is to assist the person to translate the goals previously identified into specific action plans. This is done by examining different ways of achieving the goals. In this process, the helper enables the person to identify personal resources and assets. At this stage, all of the skills of stage 2 remain relevant, as well as the skills of creative thinking, problem-solving and decision-making. By the end of this stage, the problem should have been managed. It is important however that the goals the person sets are realistic and within the person's control.

Activity

1. Work in a group of three in which one person takes on the role of service user with a problem, another takes on the role of helper and a third person is an observer. The service user should talk for a maximum of five minutes (three minutes is usually enough) about a problem, real or imagined. The helper should use as many of the above skills as seems appropriate but must paraphrase at intervals and summarise at the end. It is not necessary to reach any kind of resolution to the problem. The observer should give feedback about the service user's skills and the service user should relate how he or she felt about the helper. Did the helper try to solve the problem? Was he or she able to listen without interrupting? Were there too many questions? This activity should be practised several times.

2. How do you think the three service users, Bill, Mary and Julie, introduced earlier in the chapter, can be helped through on-the-spot counselling? The example of Julie is expanded upon below and you are asked to describe possible work which could be achieved with Bill and Mary in a similar way.

Here's Julie crying over her Mum's photograph. What are you going to do? Will you walk out and let her finish crying before you go back? Will you take the photograph off her and tell her not to be silly? Or will you see this an opportunity to help Julie to explore her feelings and to work through the loss of her Mum? Many people, even a long time after a loss, can experience grief and sadness. If this grief is constantly suppressed it can give rise to a serious inability to cope with everyday life. Here the worker can just stop for a while, ask Julie some open questions about her Mum. Do you want to tell me what she was like, Julie? This can then be paraphrased back to Julie. 'So you're saying that she was a very kind person. You used to enjoy a laugh and now you really miss those times together.' This gives Julie the encouragement to go on and remember what they used to laugh about and to express her sadness at missing her mother. You will probably find that Julie feels much better after she has talked to you and you have listened and shown her empathy, genuineness and unconditional positive regard. She probably won't exhibit some of the challenging behaviour which she may otherwise have shown and her week will be a much better one because you stopped to listen. It may only have taken ten or fifteen minutes to save yourself and other workers hours of the much more demanding task of coping with a destructive emotional outburst. Also the outcome is considerably more positive in terms of Julie's self esteem and self actualisation. Here the ideas of Rogers have been used together with a very condensed version of Egan. The problem has been briefly explored and Julie, even in this short time, has begun to see it in a new light and is able to get on with her day.

2. Working as a member of a team

. . . team work should never be regarded as an optional extra in this sort of work: it is the heart of the matter.

(Ward, 1993)

The care **team** is a vital ingredient of good care practice, and good team work requires the ability to co-operate and work together to achieve the aims of the agency in which you work. A group of people working in the same organisation do not necessarily form a team. They only do so if they are working **together** towards the same **philosophy** and **goals**. This doesn't mean that everyone has to agree but it does mean that sometimes individual preferences have to be laid aside for what has been agreed among team members. A good team leader can often promote a positive feeling among team members. To do this he or she needs to show team members that their work and their views are valued and to emphasise that only through working together can the aims of the team be achieved. All team members should be enabled to contribute their views and ideas at team meetings and at other times during the working week. Good teamwork requires people to **feel** like a team, to **think** like a team and to **act** like a team.

Activity
What skills do you think are useful in enabling you to work as a team member?

While completing the activity above you may have thought of **communication skills**. These are just as useful in teamwork as in any other form of work. In addition to all of those communication skills discussed already, the good team member needs to develop **confidence** in expressing his or her ideas in front of others and **advocating** on the service user's behalf where this seems necessary. These skills can be developed through role playing team meetings, for example, and practising ways of communicating views in front of others. This often requires courage and confidence, taking the bull by the horns and speaking up when perhaps normally you wouldn't do so. Remember that if you do not contribute it is often the service user who receives a poorer service. When Joan attended a meeting at which she sensed that a service user's request for a single room was about to be turned down, she spoke about all the reasons why the request should be granted with a force and clarity which she would not previously have thought possible. She had prepared a speech in her mind before the meeting and was very glad of this when the request was granted.

Communication skills are also needed in the resolution of differences in the team. When expressing any grievance or difference with another individual or group of colleagues it is useful to try the following (adapted from Strathclyde Regional Council's training package in residential child care, 1993):

- try to be as specific as you can, e.g. 'I want to speak to you about the way you handled that situation yesterday', not 'I think the way you handle situations is pretty awful';
- try to state your feelings, e.g. 'I am angry about . . .' rather than 'you are a real pain in the neck'. The first is an indisputable fact; you may think the second is too but it is only an opinion and expressing it may lead to further problems!
- listen to what others have to say and be clear about what your grievance or difference is all about;
- address yourself to the issue, not to the person. Once an issue becomes a 'personality clash' it gets more difficult to solve, because it gets confused with feelings and attitudes;
- if possible, talk **to** the person involved not **about** them to others. It is all too possible to develop and pass on opinions that become rumours, without ever checking the facts.

You may also have come up with **flexibility**. Good teamwork depends upon a willingness to change, to be adaptable, open-minded and to learn from the skills of others. Sometimes workers who have been in the job for a long time lose their flexibility, assuming that they have done the job for so long that they know everything there is to know about it. Have you ever heard people emphasising how long they have been doing this or that, implying at the same time that they therefore know best how to do it. The two do not necessarily go hand in hand and the good care worker should always be flexible enough to change in the light of new knowledge or the opportunity to acquire new skills.

Another skill to mention is **negotiation**. This is a need and willingness to discuss issues, consult service users, colleagues and management in reaching optimum solutions to problems and issues. Sometimes it involves compromise or confrontation, as well as collaboration. In order to negotiate with other team members or with management, the team member needs to be clear in advance about the aim of the negotiation, to keep her temper and maintain a climate of goodwill even when there is disagreement, and be prepared to compromise if there isn't an alternative. The example of Joan's request for a single room on behalf of a service user in the section above on communication is also a good example of negotiation.

Activity

Imagine that you are a keyworker to a service user who has asked you to negotiate with management about moving from hospital into a community house. How will you go about this?

Another key skill is **partnership**. Partnership involves all of the preceding skills of communication, flexibility and negotiation in working together with others, especially service users and colleagues, to share ideas, work practices and information. Sharing implies that this should be done without feeling threatened by others encroaching upon 'your' territory, and that territorial and possessive feelings about a particular piece of work or service users are unhealthy to the pursuit of effective teamwork.

Evaluation is a vital skill too. Opportunities for the evaluation of team work include the worker's own reflections upon practice which can be presented in the form of a work log or diary, discussion with a supervisor or discussion in team meetings. The benefit which accrues from this is to ensure that your own contribution to team work is as good as it can be. Sometimes evaluation can point the way to more effective team work, sometimes it may mean coming to terms with a less than perfect situation over which you have exercised as much control and ingenuity as possible. This should not result in depression or throwing ideals out of the window and is more about accepting that sometimes you just have to get on with the job as well as you possibly can given the circumstances, until eventually you can be in a position to promote positive change.

Finally, there is **commitment**. Members of the team need to be committed to the ideal of a team and to the team's goals. This commitment involves a willingness to get to know your role in terms of individual care plans and to play your part in order that all team members are pulling together, rather than competing or conflicting with one another. It means consulting with others if you are planning activities or outings so that they can be seen in the whole team context. One care student couldn't understand why staff were annoyed when she took a service user on an outing without consulting other staff members. What do you think could be the possible consequences of this for the work of the team? If staff are not committed to the team service users often sense this. This can affect the well-being and sense of belonging of service users and the ability of workers and users to achieve goals they have set for themselves.

3. Organising the worker's shift

When arriving on shift the worker needs a combination of organised time and flexibility in order to meet the needs of service users. Helping is full of the unexpected, and unless a worker can stop for a chat or some on-the-spot counselling here, attention to a physical need or an answer to a question there, the task is not going to fulfil either the needs of the service user or the demands of the job. On the other hand the care worker needs to carry some idea of what is to be achieved during the course of the shift, a rough plan which has tasks which must be achieved and others which it would be desirable to achieve. In this way care plans can be brought to fruition and the worker and service user can experience a sense of achievement that aims and objectives have been achieved. At one home for elderly people workers were given a slip of paper at the beginning of each shift on which was written one activity to be done in addition to the usual routine of the day. This could be providing manicures or a reminiscence activity, for example. The list had been drawn up in consultation with service users so that everyone felt that they had played a part in how shifts were organised.

4. Developing practical skills

A lot of care work consists of balancing the meeting of many kinds of need, including meeting physical needs. In the words of the Social Care Association:

A characteristic of good . . . care practice is the ability to meet physical needs at the same time as respecting the feelings of others and addressing social, intellectual, emotional and cultural needs, responding to strong emotions and dealing with difficulties in behaviour and relationships.

(SCA, 1993)

The meeting of physical needs requires the development of some very practical skills. It is recognised that not all practical skills are directed at meeting only physical needs, though this section emphasises this aspect of care work. Meeting physical needs often involves doing some rather unpleasant tasks with a smile and 'oomph', maximising respect for the individual by maintaining privacy, asking how a person wishes to be treated, finding out how much an individual can do for herself and providing the means (aids, adaptations, access etc.) for the individual to maximise independence and doing things in ways which are as 'normal' as possible. Care workers are often thrown in at the deep end and are expected to assist with individuals with very complex needs from the first day. Supervision and guidance are often minimal and the way things are done is often gained from a worker or workers who were similarly thrown in at the deep end and have had to fend for themselves. This, fortunately, is not always the scenario, but it is so often enough. It is therefore important to ask yourself these questions: is this the best way to do this? Does it follow the principles of good practice? Is there a care plan, what does it say? If you are assisting someone to the toilet, for example, are privacy, choice and independence maximised? Sometimes an occupational therapist can suggest aids (a walking aid, for example) or adaptations (a hand rail on the wall) which would maintain the dignity of the individual so much more effectively than complicated assistance.

Empathy is as important in meeting physical needs as in any other area of work. One care worker told me how she absolutely detests cleaning up vomit (who doesn't?) but when she puts herself in the shoes of the person who has been sick she manages the task much better because she realises that it can't have been pleasant to be sick and to have to depend upon someone else to clean it up.

Other practical skills are acquired through special training in relation to safe moving and handling, first aid and emergency procedures and health and safety requirements.

5. Dealing with critical incidents and challenging behaviour – a summary

Care work is not, unfortunately, without its periods of disruption, though these can be minimised if a unit has a well-planned and prepared, varied and sufficiently stimulating and/or interesting pattern of life and activities. Even in the best run units, though, there will sometimes be what are called 'critical incidents' when the normal pattern of life is disrupted. This is in the nature of some settings which care for people who may lack socialisation and internal controls over their behaviour or who may have experienced mental ill health or who have dementia. Any form of group living also has stresses and strains and these may build up to a critical incident involving challenging behaviour from one or a number of service users. There are no absolutely fool-proof solutions to these situations which will guarantee that calm will be restored, but there are a number of things you can do to minimise the effects. These are summarised below:

If a serious incident is occurring, then act decisively to disrupt the pattern of activity which is taking place. This is achieved by breaking up the action (using a variety of tactics appropriate to the situation) and diverting attention and energy elsewhere. The sooner the heat can be taken from the situation, the better. Do not inflame the situation by adding fuel (i.e. your own emotions) to the fire. Keep calm, act firmly and decisively and, especially when you are only recently in post, do not hesitate to seek help when needed.

(SRC, 1993)

There are, in addition to the above guidelines, some special techniques which can be learned through special training, including therapeutic crisis intervention, behavioural therapy and gentle teaching.

6. Promoting activities

Activities can range from going out for a cup of coffee to going on holiday, from playing a game to going to the cinema, from working on a life story book to playing computer games, from doing something with to arranging something on behalf of an individual or a group. Activities can meet a number of needs set out in the section on PROCCCESS, including physical, cultural, cognitive/intellectual, emotional and social needs and can utilise many of the skills set out in the section on teamwork. Activities should be seen as a way of implementing some aspects of the care plan and often involve balancing the benefits to be gained against the risks involved. They can be used to develop skills, including communication and practical skills, to relieve stress, to raise self esteem, and can have spin-offs in other areas of life.

One example of an activity is a **holiday**. Holidays can perform many functions in the helping process. They can be occasions for both meeting needs and achieving dreams. A holiday in Ireland for Mary and other residents of 'the house' achieved the following (in brackets are the areas of need also fulfilled):

- enhanced skills of planning (cognitive);
- enhanced choice and ability to make decisions (emotional, cognitive);
- led to new experiences (cognitive, social, cultural, emotional);
- enhanced relationships and sharing (emotional, social);
- enhanced relationships between service users and staff (emotional, social, organisational);
- provided memories which gave a sense of bonding amongst those who participated (emotional, social).

Life story books can be used with any service user as a way of developing and keeping a record of past and present experiences and of important people and places. They are usually a visual and written record of things which are important in the service user's life and are compiled jointly with a care worker, sometimes but not necessarily the keyworker. This is a task which a student may have the time to do on a placement where other members of staff are under a lot of pressure. Life story books are often made with 'looked after' children who are separated from their families for periods of time, but are equally relevant to people with a learning disability, to older adults, to any service user. Such a book may serve the purpose of enhancing the service user's sense of identity, of raising self esteem, of keeping memories alive of important family members, friends and other significant people and of enhancing the relationship between worker and service user through sharing an enjoyable and meaningful activity.

Activity

Plan and implement an activity with an individual or group of individuals. Say which needs you hope to achieve before the activity and which needs were achieved as a result of the activity.

7. Developing networks

Networks were useful in the assessment process but can now be developed as part of the helping process to meet many kinds of need. The individual's network of contacts, a picture of which may have been built up through observation, diaries, conversations and questions, can be examined with the service user to see if there is potential for improvement or development. A network sets out the links which an individual has, their nature and frequency.

Activity

If you examine Jim's network in Figures 7.6 and 7.7 you can see how it was developed over a 6 month period. Now examine Ted's network in Figure 7.8. Do you see any areas which could be explored with him? Draw a network diagram which may give Ted a more fulfilled life.

8. Advocacy skills

Advocacy means representing another person as if you are that person. It is needed when someone is unable to represent their own views and applies particularly to vulnerable groups such as people with learning disabilities, sensory disabilities, mental health problems, elderly people with dementia and very young children. Some members of these groups are perfectly able to advocate for themselves and should be encouraged to do so. Others will need the support of someone to advocate on their behalf. Advocacy can be seen as a form of empowerment and utilises all of the skills detailed in the section on team work, especially communication and negotiation. It can be about small issues of everyday life or big events such as moving from hospital to a house in the community. Here is an example. A care worker in a home for older adults which provided no interesting activities at all empathised with the residents, imagining herself in their shoes with no opportunities to do anything except sit, eat, sleep and watch television. Although most of the residents had a level of dementia and many had mobility problems she asked them what they used to like doing

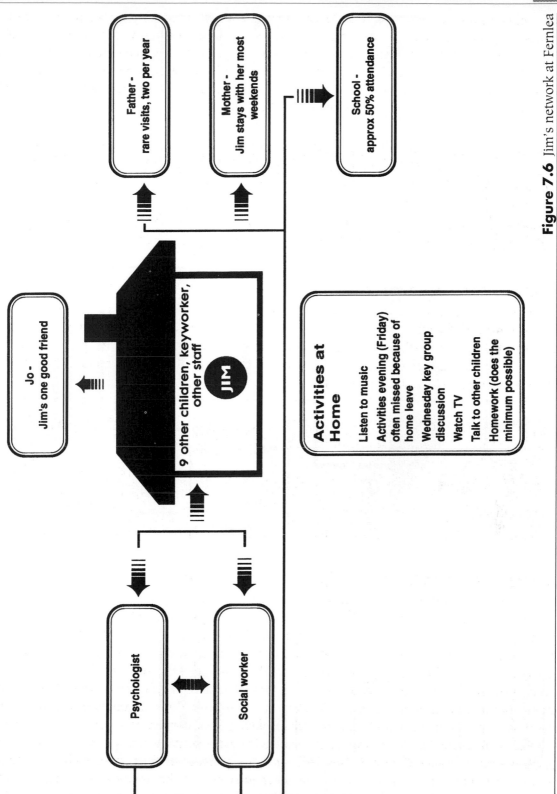

Figure 7.6 Jim's network at Fernlea

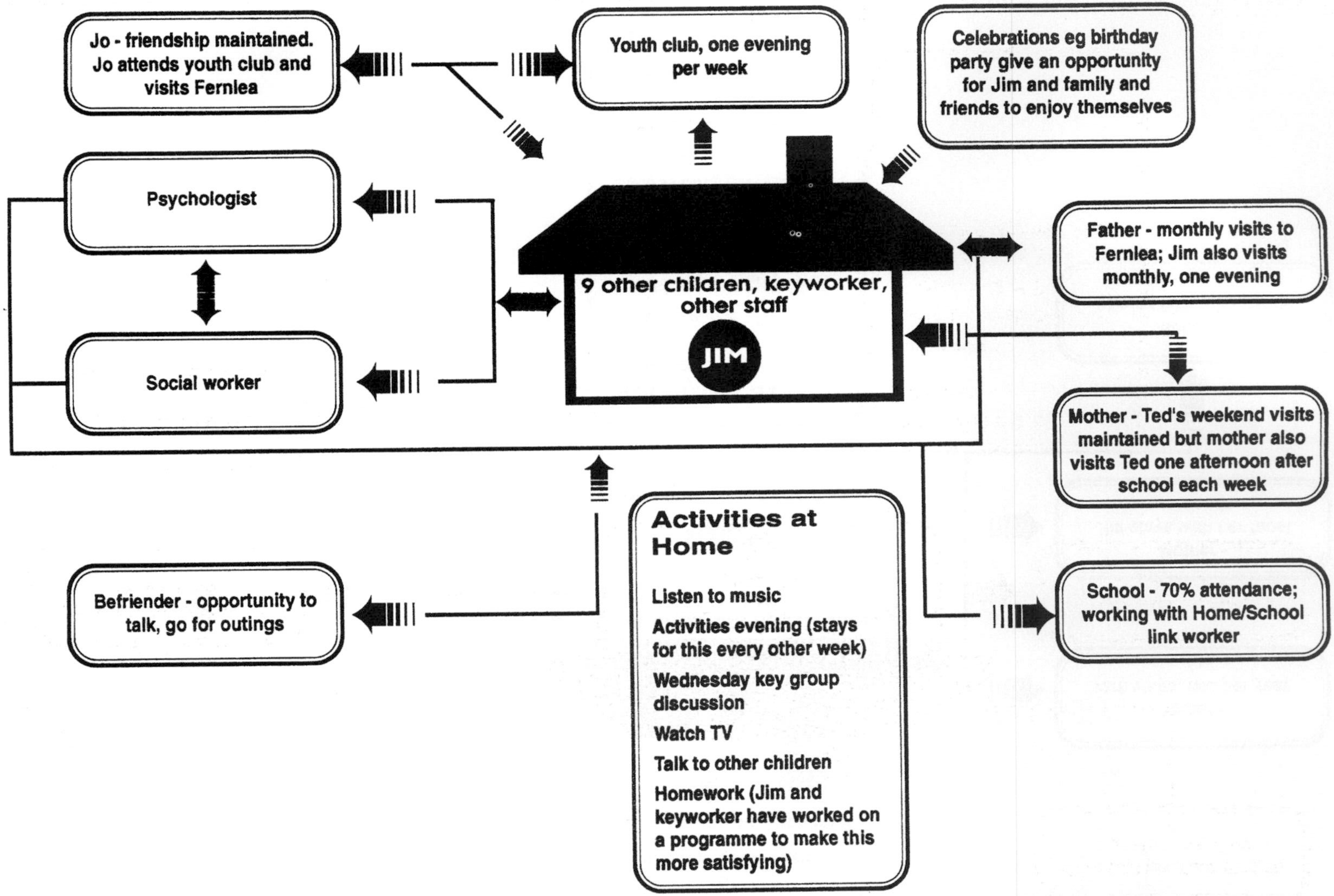

Celebrations eg birthday party give an opportunity for Jim and family and friends to enjoy themselves

Father - monthly visits to Fernlea; Jim also visits monthly, one evening

Mother - Ted's weekend visits maintained but mother also visits Ted one afternoon after school each week

School - 70% attendance; working with Home/School link worker

Youth club, one evening per week

9 other children, keyworker, other staff

JIM

Activities at Home

Listen to music

Activities evening (stays for this every other week)

Wednesday key group discussion

Watch TV

Talk to other children

Homework (Jim and keyworker have worked on a programme to make this more satisfying)

Jo - friendship maintained. Jo attends youth club and visits Fernlea

Psychologist

Social worker

Befriender - opportunity to talk, go for outings

Figure 7.7 Jim's network after six months at Fernlea

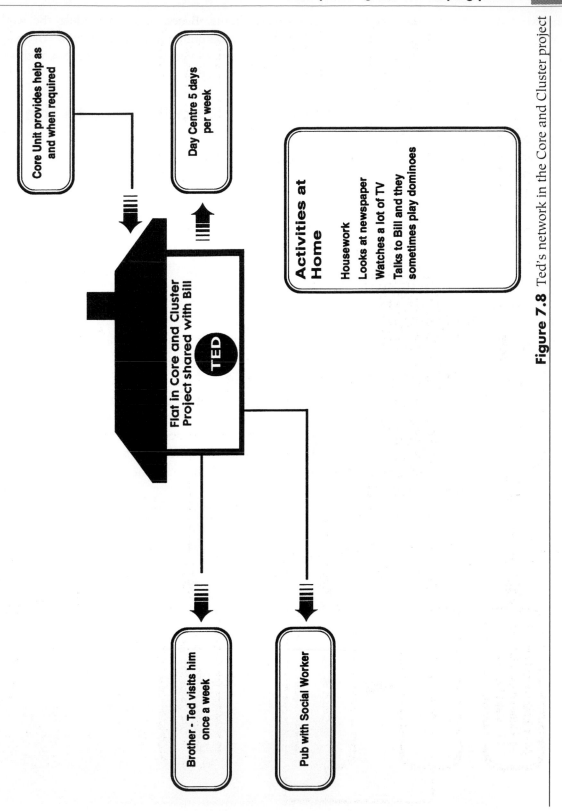

Figure 7.8 Ted's network in the Core and Cluster project

and what they thought they might like to do in the home. Based upon their ideas the worker advocated the introduction of an activities and outings programme at a team meeting. In spite of opposition from some members of staff this was introduced and proved a great success, with spin-offs in other areas of life such as health, friendship and mobility.

9. Transferring skills which you already have to the helping situation

Many care workers come to their posts already in possession of life, interest and professional skills. Some have been engineers, some have been hairdressers, some do woodwork in their spare time, some can draw and paint, others can cook, do first aid, swim, teach exercises or have a knowledge of aromatherapy. Others are marvellous conversationalists and bring cheerfulness with them. Whatever you bring to the care situation can provide interest and variety for service users. One care worker used her aromatherapy skills to relax a very anxious woman with a learning disability, another worker in a home for older people had artistic skills and introduced wax drawings using heat from an iron to melt the wax and make interesting patterns. The service users produced some wonderful pictures and were very proud of their creations. Other workers have wonderful personal qualities. They can just make people feel better by being there. Whatever gifts and skills you have, bring them with you – and it's never too late to develop a few more.

10. Developing groupwork skills

Many care situations are group situations where you are working not just with one individual but with a group of people. In order to enable people to get the best out of these group situations it is useful to understand some things about groups, the ways they function and how people behave when they are in groups. A group may be defined as a collection of people who have some reason for being together. A useful beginning in examining groups is to look at how **you** behave in group situations.

Activity

Choose one group to which you belong and say whether the word **'rarely, 'sometimes' or 'often'** is the most appropriate one in relation to each of the statements below, bearing in mind that there are no 'correct' answers:

■ I make suggestions which are relevant to the group task;

■ I initiate activities relevant to the group;

■ I share ideas and resources;

■ I try to keep members on the subject of the group;

■ I'm good at summarising where we are;

■ I try to be honest about my thoughts and feelings;

■ I think before I speak;

■ I only speak when I think I've got something really important to say;

■ I try to support participants who appear to be having difficulty in the group;

■ I empathise with other people's needs in the group situation and try to build up their self esteem;

■ I make sure everyone is aware of my point of view;

■ I like to feel in control of the group;

■ I feel responsible for the group;

■ I try to find ways to cope with difficult group members;

■ I always seem to get the blame for everyone's shortcomings;

■ I don't like groups very much and say and do as little as possible;

■ when things seem to be getting too serious I lighten things up with a joke.

On the basis of your responses to these statements look at the following roles which are often present in group situations and decide which, if any, apply to you:

■ a dominant member;

■ an active member;

■ a passive member;

■ an isolated member;

■ a joker;

■ a scapegoat;

■ a rejected member;

■ a leader;

■ a follower;

■ a monopoliser.

Awareness of yourself in groups provides a beginning to being able to use group situations as a way of enhancing life for some service users. Tom Douglas (1978) is a group worker and writer who has promoted working with groups as a valuable way of helping people through problem situations. I will use the example of a group for young people in a children's home, set up with the aim of enhancing decision making skills, to illustrate some of Tom Douglas's main points. Here are some of his statements followed by their relevance in relation to the young people's group:

■ *the more a person needs a group the more pressure it can bring to bear.* The young people were highly motivated to take control of their lives and the group was seen as an important component in this process;

- groups can begin to repair the deficiencies of naturally occurring groups. Many of the young people had had little opportunity to talk through problems in family or friend-ship situations;

- *a group worker takes the interactions of people in a group to improve the quality of their lives.* The group worker looks at the behaviour and roles of the young people in the group, attempts to enable all members to participate, builds upon the strengths of group members and prevents some members from becoming too dominant and others from remaining too passive;

- *a group worker can highlight for people what their behaviour is and the consequences of it.* Within the group there is one member who is always playing the fool. The group worker encourages this when it is really helpful and discourages it when it is inappro-priate, without posing a threat to the young person;

- *a group possesses more resources than individuals.* The group discussed what decisions they thought they should be able to make in the home and produced suggestions about meals, outings and holidays which were taken on board by care workers. If they had done this individually their suggestions would have carried less force and they may not have been able to see the potential for change;

- *the group worker enables people to feel safe to express themselves.* The group worker gained the respect of the young people by being there every week at the agreed time, by being fair to participants in ensuring that everyone had a say, by handling outbursts of temper calmly and firmly, by emphasising the confidentiality of things said in the group. In this way group members felt safe to express themselves;

- *a group is like a small society with its own rules and its own behaviour patterns.* Over a period of weeks members began to look forward to group meetings because they had a sense of belonging to something which was having a positive effect upon their lives. They established a few group rituals, always beginning with a few jokes and ending with crisps and a drink; different members had different roles in the group and each person had a niche which the others respected. Outside the group members started to feel more positive about themselves.

Douglas emphasised that working with groups is not easy and that anyone working with groups should try to gain some supervised practice, run a group alongside someone who is already experienced and skilled in this work and should gain feedback from the group. He sug-gested that the worker should keep a record of group work, of things which were successful, of thoughts about why some things were effective, other things weren't, as a means of building up a group work data bank.

Some of the ideas of **Bion** (1968) a psychoanalyst writing before Tom Douglas and prob-ably influential upon his thinking, are also interesting in relation to groupwork. Bion contributed to the development of the use of group therapy in psychiatric hospitals and was very interested in the functions and the dynamics of groups, i.e. what groups achieve and how they work. He advocated the use of groups in creating a living-learning environment. This was a way of getting away from a medical model of health in which staff were the experts and patients the sick, passive recipients of treatment. Bion's emphasis was to use groups to encourage **participation** by everyone in performing the essential tasks of living. In examining the dynamics of group situations Bion drew attention to many issues, four of which are:

- ■ **the unconscious life of the group** and the members' need for psychological security. Like Douglas, Bion found that the most successful groups were those which individual's needed for their own well-being, needs being at both a conscious and an unconscious level.

- ■ The notion that individuals carry and express feelings in group situations, not only for themselves but also for the group; also that what is often seen as **individual pathology may be a collective problem**. Individuals can be scapegoated for problems present in a group, a family or an organisation. This is also part of the unconscious life of the group.

- ■ Groups have a tendency towards **fight/flight** in the face of difficult issues. This is a process whereby, through what Bion calls groupthink, groups refuse to face difficult issues. They prefer to take the easy route of lightening the conversation, unless an effective group worker can encourage confrontation of issues and a recognition of what cannot as well as what can be changed.

- ■ The effective group worker creates a **group climate** which is safe and which reinforces the group task; this climate needs to encourage individuals, particularly those who are more shy, to assert their opinions in the face of more dominant people.

Activity

Apply each of the above ideas of Bion to the young people's group used in examining Douglas' ideas.

11. Providing a 'good' environment for care

In the House in the Hollow they were allowed opportunities for regression, indulging in play and fantasy, which for many of them was sadly a novelty. They were offered acceptance and love . . . and . . . enjoyed the benefits of childhood which had hitherto been denied them . . . The House in the Hollow was not just a short-stay residential establishment or an intermediate treatment centre, it was a home where young people, staff and children, lived together and enjoyed life . . .

(Donohue, 1985)

The above description emphasises that the feeling which people have about a care establishment is a very important part of the care process. If people are living there the place should feel like home, people should feel accepted, should be given opportunities to enjoy themselves, should feel loved and wanted. Kahan (1994) in her writings about childcare emphasised that not only are these factors important but the physical environment is part of creating this homely feeling. If people are accommodated in shabby, run-down buildings with a lack of privacy in bathrooms and bedrooms they feel undervalued and that their needs are not being met. This can have adverse consequences in all areas of health and development.

Davies (1992), in a long professional career in caring, emphasised the importance of making provision for the five senses in care settings: **sight** (the place should look nice); **smell** (there should be pleasant smells, not strong smells of urine, polish, disinfectant and stale cooking); **hearing** (the place should respond to the needs of people for both peaceful sounds, stimulating sounds, not constant loud noise and lack of consideration. If people are unable to hear there should be attention paid to compensating for this); **taste** (this is coupled with food and the need to accommodate people's differing tastes and cultural food needs); **touch** (the importance of physical contact with other human beings). This is a subject surrounded by much controversy which needs to be aired in each setting without being excessively discouraged; also the feel of things like fabrics, cups and plates (do **you** like drinking out of plastic cups?). The care worker can influence all of these things.

A 'good' care environment is also one which maintains and fosters as many links as possible with the wider community and promotes participation in activities and services which are available to others, e.g. libraries, education centres, health centres, hairdressers, cinemas, cafés, pubs. Clough (1987) showed that poor practice and institutionalisation are often associated with isolation, few visits form outsiders and a lack of community links.

Activity

Choose a client group and imagine that you have been asked to make suggestions for the improvement of a very old, run-down residential setting for this group. What factors will you take into account and what are your suggestions?

12. Keeping records and reports

Record keeping is *about providing a better and more accountable service for clients . . .*

Patrick McCurry, *Community Care Magazine*, 14.1.99)

Care workers, whether they like it or not, need to be involved in keeping records and sometimes writing reports about the people with whom they work. These can serve many purposes. Writing in the 'Day' book ensures that staff from one shift know what has gone on during other shifts, the incident book records incidents which have occurred and how these were dealt with, service user records and care plans relate work in relation to specific people and ensure that the care plan is being followed by all staff, review reports are useful in summarising work over a period of time and ensuring that relevant information is heard at the review. Whatever the nature of the recording it is important that it is done and that it is done as well as possible. Practice is the best possible way to learn, bearing in mind some essential guidelines:

- keep to the point and do not provide irrelevant detail;
- be accurate; write down dates and times;
- maintain confidentiality by keeping confidential records in a secure place;
- write in a way which is easily understandable to others, avoiding jargon;
- pay attention to grammar and spelling as a way of enhancing your respect for the service user;

- distinguish opinions from facts and avoid unnecessary labels and judgements;
- remember the value base and the need for anti-discriminatory practice;
- enable people to present their own perspectives;
- address culture in a constructive way.

Activity

1. Write an account, real or imagined, which details the main points about a shift at a residential home, which will be helpful to people who will be on the next shift.

2. Keep a diary of the work you do, using the guidelines above.

13. Keyworking

Keyworking could also be relevantly discussed at this point but has been considered already in Chapter 6. It is worth reading the account again on page 247 at this point.

BOUNDARY ISSUES

Care practice is not self contained, but is part of many systems and links with many others. This raises the subject of boundaries with these other systems and how these boundaries are to be dealt with. 'Systems theory' has given a framework for understanding a little about boundaries and, without going into too much detail about this theory, it provides a useful way to begin to think about boundary issues. A **system** is an entity with boundaries. If there is no interchange across the boundaries, the system is a **closed system**. A total institution (see Goffman on page 213) is virtually a closed system. An **open system**, on the other hand, has exchange across the boundary. Payne (1991) suggested that it's rather like a tea bag in a cup of hot water which lets water in and tea out but keeps the tea leaves inside. This isn't a wonderful analogy since the tea in the tea bag loses flavour and that's not quite what should happen in care practice, but it does give an idea about the permeability of the boundaries of an open system.

Below are some areas for discussion in terms of boundary issues, i.e. issues which relate specifically to the boundary, rather than to the things on either side of it which are considered elsewhere. There are no absolute answers to these issues but they should be discussed among care workers because the ways they are dealt with can affect the quality of life of service users. Here are some of the issues; you may think of others in relation to your own work:

- the boundary between a personal and a professional relationship;
- the boundary between an agency and the family;
- the boundary between different services, e.g. health and social work;
- the boundary between a residential or day care centre and the wider community;
- the boundary between a private trouble and public issues;
- the boundaries between management, workers and service users;
- the boundary between workers on different shifts.

Health promotion and the helping process

Most of the above discussion about the helping process and boundary issues is relevant to health promotion. Of the issues discussed above the following are particularly relevant in health promotion and should be read as part of that higher unit as well as for the unit Interpersonal Skills for Care: communication skills; working as a member of a team; organising the worker's shift; promoting activities; developing networks; developing groupwork skills; keeping records and reports; boundary issues.

Evaluation – monitoring and reviewing

The final link in the care planning and helping process and in health promotion is to evaluate all of the work which has been done. This involves looking at the process and at the outcomes of the work done. It should be achieved on an on-going basis (monitoring) and at regular, scheduled intervals e.g. every six months, usually through a review meeting. The aim of evaluation is to determine whether the plan is being implemented, how far needs are being met, whether the plan is still appropriate or needs to be changed in the light of changed needs or circumstances. Evaluation can also be used to improve your practice in the future, help others to improve their practice, justify the use of any resources which were used, and to identify any unexpected or unplanned outcomes.

The evaluation should not be the task of one person, since it needs to be as objective as possible and to include the views of those who participated. **In care practice**, as with all other aspects of the helping process, evaluation should focus upon the service user and be done with the service user. The service user, relevant family members and friends, care staff and professionals across a multi-disciplinary spectrum are among those who can play a part in the review process. Participants should come prepared, with a review of their own work and role, in order that a comprehensive picture of all aspects of the helping process can be achieved.

In health promotion evaluation may focus upon particular areas of change and involve some results from the use of research methods discussed in Chapter 9. A health promotion project may have sought change in some of the following areas and evaluation will involve looking at the value of these: changes in health awareness; changes in knowledge or attitude; behaviour change; policy change; change to the physical environment; change in health status. The care worker may also have been working towards change in some of these areas.

SUMMARY

This chapter has introduced you to a model of care practice based upon assessment, planning, implementation and evaluation. The usefulness of this model to health promotion has also been considered. The importance of the assessment of need has been emphasised. Need was considered from several perspectives including a return to Maslow's hierarchy, PIES (physical, intellectual/cognitive, emotional and social), Bradshaw's taxonomy and PROCCCESS needs. Assessment is built upon a consideration of need and plans are built upon assessment. Tools of assessment were described, together with two models of care planning: the exchange model and the person-centred model. Several skills needed to implement plans were examined including communication and on-the-spot counselling (Rogers and Egan's models of helping), teamwork and groupwork. The importance of evaluation and building this into the helping process were emphasised. Wherever relevant, links were made with health promotion.

Activity – The care planning process

1. Imagine that you are Mary's keyworker and are assisting her to implement her plan of care. What skills and methods of 'helping' might be useful? How will you evaluate the helping process? (For a description of Mary see page 262).

2. In the case study in Chapter 10 of this book imagine that you are asked to assess the needs of Nabeil Ahmed. State what you think could be a) the tools of assessment; b) the needs of the service user; c) the care plan; d) the ways in which the care plan may be implemented and evaluated.

Activity – Planning and health promotion

Once you have read the chapter on health promotion as well as this one, choose a health promotion aim (e.g. to reduce smoking among twelve year-olds in care settings) and set out the process which you will need to pursue in order to achieve this aim. Be as detailed as you can.

SELECTED BIBLIOGRAPHY

Brown, A. and Clough, R. (eds.) (1989). *Groups and Groupings.* London: Tavistock/Routledge.
A book of readings about life and work in day and residential settings.

Miller, J. (1996). *Social Care Practice.* London: Hodder and Stoughton.
Examines many of the issues raised in this chapter in greater depth.

Sanderson, H. et al (1997). *People, Plans and Possibilities.* Edinburgh: SHS Ltd.
An interesting and well-illustrated exploration of person-centred planning.

Ward, A. (1993). *Working in Group Care.* Birmingham: Venture Press.
Provides a framework for looking at work in residential and day care settings based upon 'the client's stay', 'the worker's shift' and 'the team and its task'.

CHAPTER 8
Health promotion

Sadie Hollis

Good health helps us each to live life to the full. It is worth investing in for that alone. But a healthy population is also crucial to our national prosperity and well-being. Our attitudes and lifestyles have a vital bearing on our health. So, too, do the circumstances in which we live. Poverty, unemployment, housing and the environment around us are all inextricably linked with health. Only by tackling these vital issues will we achieve the sustained health improvement we need . . .

(The Scottish Office, 1998)

INTRODUCTION

In Part 1 of this chapter, you are introduced to the concept of health. Health is more than the absence of illness or disease, and explored in the chapter are factors which influence health such as family, culture, heredity, behaviour, socioeconomic factors, gender and ethnicity. Factors which can influence access to health provision and which may influence an individual's concept of health are also considered. There is also reference to core values and principles relating to health promotion, though values and principles are more fully discussed in Chapter 6. Health promotion is introduced and elements of health promotion explained, including health education, health protection and prevention. Relationships among these are studied. The chapter includes an analysis of the different media used for promoting health and the effects of legislation and policy on health promotion. The information and activities in this section are at Intermediate II level.

In Part 2 of the chapter, the theoretical models of health promotion will be presented and evaluated. These include the medical, educational, community development, marketing, political, and client-centred models. Examples of how these models are used in health promotion strategies are included. Reference is made to skills required to promote health and well-being to others, and the application of these to assessing, planning and managing health promotion situations. More detailed consideration of these subjects, together with a consideration of investigation and research in relation to health promotion is, however, contained elsewhere in the book. The application of criteria for analysing the effectiveness of a health promotion campaign is explained and this includes whether the message is acceptable to the service user to enable him or her to have control over the decisions affecting his or her health. The information and activities in Part 2 are at Higher level.

As indicated above, you will find that a lot of material discussed elsewhere in the book is relevant also to a discussion of health promotion. A knowledge of developmental psychology and sociology, core values and principles, interpersonal skills and research methods all play an important part in an understanding of health promotion. At the end of the chapter references to other relevant topics are given to enable you to integrate this chapter with others.

Example of health promotion poster from Greater Glasgow Health Board

Part 1 – An introduction to health promotion

WHAT IS HEALTH?

The concept of health changes with the acquisition of knowledge and changing cultural expectations. The most well-known definition is that of the World Health Organisation (1946) which defines health as '... a state of complete physical, mental and social well-being and not merely the absence of disease or infirmity'. Underlying this definition is the assumption that to be healthy means much more than not having an illness – indeed it promotes an holistic view, implying that it is necessary to look at the whole person and their situation. It might be a bit unrealistic, however, to think that it would be possible to achieve complete physical, mental and social well-being.

The word health itself comes from an old English word meaning whole. Increasingly over the past 30 years health has not only been viewed from an individual perspective. It is also recognised that an individual's health is influenced by social and economic factors and how they can adapt and cope with the challenges throughout a lifetime. Of course, being healthy means different things to different people. A person's state of health changes more for some people than others and can affect everything else they do. Poor health, whether it is physical or mental, can lead to an inability to hold down a job, which in turn affects the lifestyle not only of that person but also of their family. Being healthy is not just a physical matter, for example a young mother may have to spend time in hospital because she has broken her leg, but this will also cause her to be stressed as she cannot care for her family.

Activity

Everyone has differing views about what factors are needed to remain healthy. Below is a list of twelve, some of which you will regard as more important to your health than others. Working in small groups, place these factors in order of priority.

Home	Family
Friends	Money
Job	Feel good about yourself
Partner	Education
Recreation	Diet
Doctor	Love

Was it easy to get agreement in your group? Did your group have similar answers to the other groups?

An individual may be very well aware of the risks to health, e.g. smoking, but may still continue to do it.

Activity

List some reasons why people would not choose to live a healthier lifestyle.

What affects health?

In 1980 the Black Report on inequalities in health was published. It stated:

There are marked inequalities in health between the social classes in Britain. ... Mortality tends to rise inversely with falling occupational rank or status for both sexes and at all ages. At birth and in the first month of life, twice as many babies of unskilled manual parents, as of professional parents, die and in the next eleven months of life nearly three times as many boys and more than three times as many girls respectively die. In later years of childhood, the ratio of deaths in the poorest class falls to between one and a half and two times that of the wealthiest class, but increases again in early adulthood before falling again in middle and old age.

It proposed that better child benefits and better housing programmes could alleviate poverty.

However, when the green paper 'Working Together for a Healthier Scotland' was published in 1998, it found that there is still a remarkable difference between the health experiences of those in the highest and lowest social classes.

Scotland carries a greater burden of ill health than other developed countries, with the problem being greatest among low income groups.

The green paper proposes:

Tackling Scotland's health problems is not just about confronting major diseases and illness.

It is also about recognising and attacking the health inequalities which have increasingly seen the more affluent enjoy much better health than people who are less well off.

Many groups in society, such as elderly people, single parents and people belonging to ethnic minorities find themselves constrained from making choices about their health. Social structures may result in them not having the knowledge or understanding to empower themselves. Instead, the individual often feels you should just get on with life because you cannot change your circumstances. Parents who live in damp housing and whose children are asthmatic wish for a dry home to improve the health of their children, but may have difficulty in obtaining this. These same parents may also smoke and have been told that this factor exacerbates their children's asthma. However, they may feel that this is their only luxury and it enables them to cope with the worry over their children. The culture in which you live also influences your view on health choices. In the following section several factors which influence health are discussed more fully. These factors are:

- family and culture, heredity and behaviour;
- social class/socioeconomic status;
- gender;
- ethnicity and culture.

Factors which can influence health
Family and culture, heredity and behaviour

The family in which an individual develops is one major determinant of health status. The family determines initial socioeconomic status. It is an agent of socialisation and therefore is the individual's first experience of the culture of the society in which he or she lives. All of these factors are discussed later in the section as major influences upon health.

Although children do not always grow up with their birth parents, these parents do determine the genetic heredity of the individual child. As discussed in Chapter 3, both nature (genetic heredity) and nurture play a part in development and behaviour. They also both play an important part in health. Some illnesses, for example, are inherited. These include cystic fibrosis and haemophilia. A propensity towards good health or poor health, a short life or a long one, are also influenced by heredity as well as environmental factors.

Most behaviour is learned and it is within the family that a lot of behaviour in relation to health is acquired. Diet, whether or not to breast feed, amount of exercise, are all influenced by the family in which the individual develops, and all in turn influence health.

Social class/Socioeconomic status

Social class was discussed in Chapter 5. This provides a means of assessing people's socioeconomic status and the influence this may have upon their health. One way in which people are allocated to a social class is by occupation. In the Registrar General's scale, there are five different occupational classes. These range from professional occupations in class one to unskilled occupations in class five. What class does is give an insight into the lifestyle, living standards and

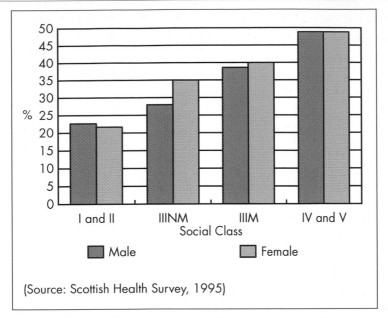

Figure 8.1 Percentage of people who smoke cigarettes by social class

culture of the different groups. There are many differences in lifestyle and culture among different socioeconomic groups, for example levels of smoking are associated with class. In social classes one and two, fewer than 25 per cent smoke whereas in classes four and five, 50 per cent smoke. Smoking is linked to the main causes of mortality in Scotland – cancer and heart disease (see Figure 8.1).

People from lower social classes also suffer more sickness and ill-health. In fact, these inequalities begin even before birth. Children in the lower socioeconomic groups are more likely to be born prematurely and have a lower birth weight. There is also a difference in the perinatal mortality rate (see Figure 8.2) – in social class five, it is 11.1 per 1000 compared with 7.1 per 1000 for social class one (Scottish Health Statistics, 1996, HMSO, 1998).

Working Together for a Healthier Scotland (1998) states that:

. . . the gap in health between living in the most affluent and most deprived areas has widened during the 1980s.

The all ages mortality rate shows a marked relationship with deprivation – in the most deprived areas, mortality rates are some 60 per cent higher than in the most affluent areas.

Linked to social class is diet. Everyone needs a balanced diet which is appropriate to their age and stage of life. In 1983 the National Advisory Committee for Nutrition Education published a report on recommendations for a healthy diet. It advised reducing the dietary intake of fat, sugar and salt and increasing the intake of fibre, fruit and vegetables.

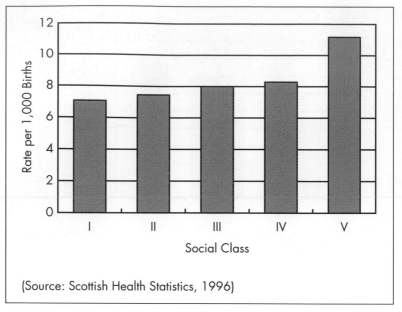

(Source: Scottish Health Statistics, 1996)

Figure 8.2 Perintal mortality rates by social class 1999

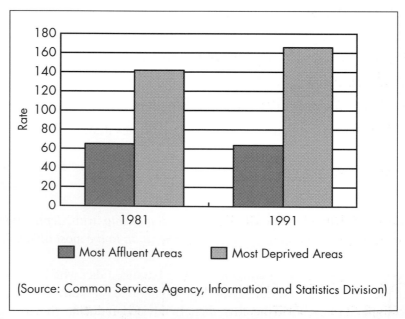

(Source: Common Services Agency, Information and Statistics Division)

Figure 8.3 Standardised mortality rates among people under 65 in 1981 and 1991

Activity

Recently there have been many programmes on television about the importance of diet and exercise on health. Find educational material which gives you information about the importance of eating a balanced diet. Which section of the population is it aimed at? Does it include any statistical evidence to show those groups that they are at risk?

Figure 8.4 gives an example of educational material from Greater Glasgow Health Board. The James Report (1993) on Scotland's diet confirmed that the average diet contains too much saturated fat, sugar and salt. Many children never eat fruit or vegetables. The percentage of people who eat fresh fruit or vegetables once a week or less varies considerably between the social classes, as shown in Figure 8.5.

Look after your heart:
EATING HEALTHILY

- Contributes to a healthy pregnancy and helps to protect your baby from heart disease in later life
- Contributes to reducing your risk of heart disease and strokes by helping lower blood pressure and cholesterol levels
- Helps control weight
- Helps reduce the risk of many types of cancers
- Prevents constipation and is good for the digestive system.

Figure 8.4 Educational material from Greater Glasgow Health Board

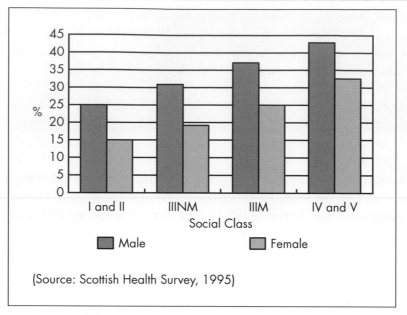

Figure 8.5 Percentage of the population eating fresh fruit once a week or less by social class

The rate of breast-feeding by Scottish women is also very low, despite the fact that breast milk provides a healthy start to life. In Glasgow, there is a breast-feeding initiative to encourage as many women as possible to breast-feed. It is funded by the NHS Trust and Health Promotion and to date 119 GPs have purchased its services. Although it has only been established for two years, this initiative is proving to be successful. It works by providing peer support from lay volunteers. Each mother is given the opportunity to have ten hours of breast-feeding support from a volunteer if she wishes it. This initiative will continue to target areas by postcode.

Activity

Why do you think more women do not breast-feed in Scotland? Do you think there is a difference between the social classes? What role do the media have in influencing this decision?

Although it is 50 years since the inception of the National Health Service and the many advances in healthcare, people in Scotland have a lower life expectancy than most other Western countries. Coronary heart disease, stroke and cancer, all of which are partly attributable to inadequate dietary intake, will continue to cause high rates of mortality and disability.

Gender

Women live longer than men. They are also more likely to consult their doctor when ill. Why do you think this is? You may have suggested that this could be due to the fact that they are less likely to be in full-time employment and so are more able to visit a doctor; or that they take better care of their health. Another explanation is that women are socialised to acknowledge and talk about their illness whereas men are expected to put on a stiff upper lip; or are women expected to be passive and 'sick' partly because of their genetic make-up? Female hormones are constantly blamed as the cause of much of women's physical and mental ill health.

The medical profession is male dominated and this may have an effect on women's health experiences. Although nearly 80 per cent of health service employees are female, only 25 per cent of doctors are female (O'Donnell, 1997). Women are more likely to be labelled as ill than men and O'Donnell says that women are over 50 per cent more likely to be labelled as having mental problems than men. This male domination can also lead women to be unaware of their rights and choices. One example of this is what Ann Oakley (1993) calls the medicalisation of childbirth, where there is often unnecessary medical intervention and the woman feels she has little control over events.

Although there are more women in the workforce than men, on average a woman's salary is less. They are more likely to be working part-time with fewer benefits. Women who work outside the home can become very stressed because they often have to combine this with the role of carer and housekeeper. There is a difference in the health of those women who live in social classes one and two from those in social classes four and five. Those in the higher social classes have much less morbidity than those in the lower social classes. An example of this is the rise in health problems related to smoking. At present lung cancer kills more women than breast cancer. This was highlighted in the *Glasgow Herald*, in February 1999:

Anti-smoking campaigners are demanding long-term investment from the Government to help women on low incomes to kick the habit. Scotland has one of the highest rates of tobacco-related deaths in the world, with women on low incomes most likely to take up smoking and least able to give up the habit.

A three-year project by Action on Smoking and Health (Scotland) on women, smoking and low income, found a 'disturbing' lack of support services for those in deprived areas. Findings revealed that many women felt let down by health workers who did little to help them give up smoking. A majority believed that they would benefit from nicotine replacement therapy – if it was available on prescription. Mrs Maureen Moore, chief executive of ASH in Scotland, said:

Smoking is now concentrated amongst the poorest groups yet our findings reveal that services aimed at women on low incomes are piecemeal and underfunded. Long-term funding is necessary for initiatives which support the reduction of smoking amongst women at community level.

Ethnicity and culture

Cultural explanations tend to interpret health inequalities in terms of the culture of 'a given' group, but there are differences in the mortality and morbidity rates between the different ethnic groupings in our society. It is very important that all ethnic minorities are not grouped together. For years health education practice has focused on clinical pathology – that is, the small number of people who are affected by genetically acquired disease, for example sickle cell anaemia or tha-lassaemia. There is very little research into the health problems of people from different ethnic minority groups. Health education campaigns have tended to emphasise the need for those people of ethnic origin to adapt to British culture to improve health. This has diverted attention from the socioeconomic effects on health and illness. According to the Rowntree Report (1995):

The incomes of certain ethnic minority groups are well below the national average and a large pro-portion of their population live in areas ranked highly by indicators of deprivation.

They face a huge range of problems which could adversely affect their health, for example housing, unemployment, language barriers and discrimination. When communication is a problem, people from different ethnic groups may feel powerless when dealing with health profes-sionals and so do not have the ability to use any services to their full capacity. Therefore it is important that policies are established to assess and meet the needs of each ethnic grouping.

Activity

Investigate:

1. How people from different ethnic minority groups view the concepts of health and illness/disease.

2. Has there been any contact with health services and if so, has it been a positive or negative experience?

Factors which influence access to health provision

Many of the factors which influence health are also factors which influence **access** to health pro-vision. Culture, gender and social class, for example, influence not only your health but the access you may have to health provision. In turn, access to health provision itself affects health. In this section the following factors are considered as influencing access to health provision. These factors, although discussed separately, are linked and overlap in many ways:

- discrimination;
- attitudes;
- social class/socioeconomic factors;
- geographical location;
- education;
- legislation.

Discrimination

A detailed discussion of discrimination and its effects is provided in Chapter 2. It is therefore a good idea at this point to re-read the first sections of that chapter. Discrimination is seen as unequal or unfair treatment of an individual or group. In theory the National Health Service aims to iron out inequalities in the provision of health but in practice this has not occurred.

Activity

In what ways do you think discrimination may affect access to health care?

Discrimination works in many different ways, but in examining its effects some examples are taken from Chapter 2.

A person with learning difficulties is frightened to walk down the street because they are being taunted and bullied.

In terms of access to health provision this may mean that the person doesn't like going to the doctor's surgery because of a fear of being bullied on the way or stared at in the surgery.

A gay person.

A person who is gay may fear that the attitudes of health care providers may reflect those of others in society. **Fear** of discrimination or **actual** discrimination often prevents people from seeking the services they need.

Thompson, H. et al (1995) provides some examples which indicate that racial discrimination has an impact on access to health care for some groups. She states:

Compulsory detention under the Mental Health Act is twenty five times more likely for 16–25 year old blacks than for whites.

(*Observer*, 1 January 1998)

Thirteen of every 1000 Asian babies born die before their first year, compared with the national rate of five out of 1000.

('Race through the 90s', CRE and BBC, 1992)

Activity

In the above examples what discriminatory factors do you think may have played a part?

You may have thought of:

■ direct discrimination by workers;

■ direct discrimination by other members of society leading to fear of seeking help;

■ lack of personnel able to communicate or empathise with these groups;

■ lack of understanding of cultural factors by providers of health care;

■ a fear of discrimination by service users;

■ a lack of knowledge of services available because of some of the above factors.

All of these constitute discrimination.

Attitudes

An attitude can be seen as 'settled behaviour or manner of acting, as representative of feeling or opinion; habitual mode of regarding anything' (Oxford English Dictionary). Attitudes rest upon feelings or opinions, they are usually fairly stable though not necessarily fixed. They do change and can be changed. They also affect the way people behave and are central to understanding people's behaviour. Attitudes are gained from experience. Socialisation is important in the formation of individual attitudes. It is vital to consider the main agents of socialisation, both primary (the family), and secondary (school, peer group etc.) in examining attitudes.

Activity

Why do you think it is important to look at attitudes when considering access to health provision?

You may have thought of:

■ attitudes to health and health provision determine to some extent the uptake of provision;

■ attitudes of health providers influence who benefits most and what are health priorities;

■ attitudes can be changed and it is important to look at what people's attitudes are in deciding how to tackle issues relating to their health;

■ some attitudes are gained through the socialisation process and it is necessary to work in this area if access to health provision is to be improved;

■ or you may have thought of different reasons.

In the promotion of access to health provision it is essential that those for whom services are provided gain positive attitudes towards the aims and objectives of such services. If services are seen in a negative light this diminishes access. The principles guiding provision (anti-discriminatory practice, choice, empowerment, privacy etc.) are very important in promoting positive attitudes to provision.

Socioeconomic factors / social class

This topic received attention in the consideration of factors affecting health. It is also part of a consideration of access to health provision. Many factors affecting access to health provision concern money. Transport to and from health services can present very real problems to people in lower socioeconomic groups because it is expensive. Earthrowl and Stacey (in Black, N., 1984) examined reported difficulties in obtaining transport to hospital and paying for it, in terms of social class: 3 per cent of patients in social classes 1 and 2 had difficulty in obtaining transport compared to 25 per cent in class 5; 7 per cent in social classes 1 and 2 had difficulty in paying for transport, compared with 46 per cent in social class 5. In rural Scotland these problems are exacerbated by large distances involved in travelling to and from specialist services. The lower socioeconomic groups have fewer cars, greater difficulty in obtaining and paying for transport and are more likely to experience a loss of income if a working family member has to take time off work. They are also restricted in their choice of service, since the choice to pay privately for care is rarely available to them.

Single parents are over-represented in social class 5, and as well as economic difficulties they often experience discrimination. Bob Holman (1998) has put together a book of writing by residents of Easterhouse in Glasgow. Here is a quote from one single parent:

I felt I never had a chance to be alone with my baby. I felt that decisions were being made above me because I was a single parent.

All of the above factors are increased for people who are homeless. People become homeless for a variety of reasons, from marital breakdown to domestic abuse, from mental health problems to a lack of support upon leaving care, from social exclusion because of difference to a shortfall in affordable housing. Homeless people are rarely registered with a GP and so receive little preventative care. They experience poor access to health provision for many other reasons ranging from lack of money to get to services to discrimination. There is also a lack of services to meet their particular needs.

Culture, ethnicity and gender

From discussion of these issues in the sections on factors affecting health, it can be concluded that they also affect access to health provision. Culture, seen as the way of life of society's members, includes values, beliefs and customs. Culture affects attitudes and so the previous discussion of attitudes is also relevant here. The perception of what constitutes health provision may vary form culture to culture as may the perception of what constitutes health. Culture is likely to affect access most when people see themselves as culturally different from those making provision. Culture may affect the experience of discrimination which has already been shown to affect access. The availability of information about health services is often culturally blind, aimed at an 'average person' or the largest service user group frequently with visual material which only shows white people or which is available only in English. Although there is an increasing awareness of these issues, access if often still impeded by cultural and ethnic insensitivity. Similarly gender may affect access when there is discrimination and/or a misuse of power in the service

Don't think of it as a box son, think of it as a single person, self contained, open plan accomodation Unit.

Figure 8.6 The homeless are particularly disadvantaged

provided. Earlier discussion by Oakley of the medicalisation of childbirth is an example of this. The kind of misuse of power sometimes shown by the medical profession was demonstrated in two quotations below from Philips and Rakusen (1978). One is a comment from a woman who had a baby in Hackney.

I asked for the father to be with me at the time of confinement. A sister told me, 'we do not allow the father of the child to be there or just in special cases. Besides you are unmarried and foreign . . .

The second example is from a woman suffering from a severe drug reaction.

Group gathers at end of bed – consultant surrounded by registrars, students, ward sister etc. I am not consulted. 'How old is she?' – to sister – 'Get that thing off her' (my nightie) . . . 'no wonder she's got a rash', and so on . . . – Why not ask me? . . . I knew what caused the reaction.

Although the last 20 years have seen immense improvements in attitudes towards women in their access to healthcare it is still not unusual for women to complain of the entrenched conservatism and elitism of the medical profession. Only last year one of the contributors to this book accompanied a female psychiatric patient to casualty after she had harmed herself. She was appalled at the lack of basic respect and understanding.

Geographical location

Some of the implications of geographical location have already been mentioned in the section on socioeconomic factors. The cost of transport to specialist services may be prohibitive for some people in remote areas. People on income support can often claim some expenses, though not usually in terms of their true cost in terms of either money or time. People on low incomes but who fall outside benefit levels may find transport costs prohibitive, especially when they are added to loss of income. People in the large centres of population (Glasgow, Edinburgh, Aberdeen and Dundee for example) have reasonably close access to specialist healthcare, but outside these areas access to specialist health provision may be extremely difficult. Even within the large cities access is becoming increasingly difficult for people without their own transport as small local hospitals close and specialist services are increasingly concentrated in 'centres of excellence'. Geographical factors, especially in combination with poor socioeconomic status, can further exacerbate problems of access.

Education

Access to health care provision is affected by three aspects of education:

- education through socialisation;
- formal education (school/college);
- education specifically related to health.

The role of education is more fully considered in the section on health promotion. Here a few points are made specifically in relation to access. Education through socialisation begins with the family. Families pass on knowledge, practices and attitudes about health and seeking healthcare. If families lack knowledge or view the health service negatively this is likely to affect the access of their children to health provision. Some negative aspects of this can be remedied through formal education or specific health education, but the effect of these is likely to be diminished if it is not reinforced by the family or other agents of socialisation such as the peer group. Education about access to health provision is closely linked with education about health and needs to be directed at those family members who influence others through the socialisation process. Whatever the nature of the education, it is likely to work best if the following conditions are achieved:

- education should be participatory with two-way communication between 'the educator' and recipients;

- educators should show an appreciation of and acknowledge socioeconomic and other life factors;
- the advantages of accessing health provision should be presented in terms of positive and enjoyable gains.

Legislation

Legislation can affect access to health provision both directly and indirectly. The National Health Service (Scotland) Act of 1947, for example, directly affected access by making health service free to everyone. The Abortion Act of 1967 enabled women in certain circumstances with certain specific conditions to obtain an abortion on the NHS. In legalising abortion in this way it also opened the way for women to pay for abortions privately (if they could afford it). Anti-discriminatory legislation, e.g. The Race Relations Acts, The Sex Discrimination Act, the Disability Discrimination Act, both directly and indirectly affect access on the grounds of race, sex or disability. There is more coverage of legislation in Chapter 2.

Factors which may influence an individual's concept of health

Rather than write a list of factors, discussing each one in turn, this section presents you with an activity. It then goes on to discuss factors which may influence an individual's concept of health through the use of one example, that of Andy MacDonald from the case study in Chapter 10. A list of possible factors is then presented at the end of the section, and you are asked to apply this yourself, to a particular individual. Before you read further, you may wish to look back at the first activity in this chapter which related to individual perceptions of what factors are needed to remain healthy. These factors reflect individual concepts of health.

CASE STUDY

Andy MacDonald (see Chapter 10) is sixteen years old and lives at home with his mother and sister (who has cerebral palsy). What factors are likely to have affected his individual concept of health?

He is 16. How does this affect his concept of health? He wants to be like other sixteen year-olds he knows; most of them play football which is healthy; most of them smoke, which isn't; most of them like to go to MacDonald's after school and to drink alcohol when they can get away with it.

He is male. His view of males is that they are physically strong and healthy, don't give way to illness and don't talk much about health.

He is working class. Andy may belong to the socioeconomic class 4/5 but he wants to be rich. His class position, though, limits the amount of **money** he has. He can't afford to belong to a private sports centre, obtain private medical care if he's ill and his concept of health is rather fatalistic. He believes that if you're going to be ill you're going to be ill and there's not much you can do about it.

He lives in reasonably good housing with a bath and shower and plenty of hot water. There is a park locally where he goes to play football. It's not a bad environment for the city.

He attends the local secondary school which has a very mixed population in terms of class and ethnicity. The teachers are very committed but devote most of their efforts to pupils who they think are going to be successful. This doesn't include Andy, who often misses school if he doesn't feel well enough to go. Andy doesn't believe in pushing himself to do things when he's feeling a bit under the weather.

He watches a lot of TV, mostly soaps and detective films, and listens to popular music. He and his friends model themselves on some of their favourite male singers, some of whom take drugs.

He isn't a great conversationalist but likes to ridicule adults, including his Mum (though he does secretly respect her too, for working so hard and caring for his sister). If he's told to do something he usually doesn't, but he enjoys the discussions they have at school about different cultures and current issues. He feels he gets picked on at school because of where he lives, his broad accent and his family circumstances. He doesn't' know what discrimination means but he probably experiences it. It makes him reluctant to approach any public service, including the doctor.

He is registered with a local doctor at the health centre down the road, but it's always difficult to get an appointment. He only goes there if he feels really ill and never feels comfortable talking to the GP. If he needed to go to hospital for an out-patient's appointment, he'd have to get a bus or get his Mum to take him in the car when she wasn't working or looking after his sister.

He is Scottish and this, together with his working class position, is the basis of his culture. He shares the values and ways of life of other people of his age who are Scottish and working class. They don't discuss health very much, but they do believe in staying healthy, as long as this doesn't mean giving up drinking and smoking.

He has had to do a lot of looking after himself because his Mum works, his Dad isn't there and his sister needs a lot of help. If he's left to himself to get a meal he usually heats up a ready meal from the freezer. He hardly ever eats fresh green vegetables or fresh fruit.

From this account, what factors do you identify as possibly influencing Andy's concept of health? You may have mentioned:

- age (16)
- gender (male)
- social class (working class)
- finance (not much money)
- beliefs (fatalistic)
- housing/environment (reasonably good)
- education (local secondary school)
- media (TV, music)
- communication (conversation/discussion)
- discrimination ('picked on' at school)
- availability of health care (local health centre)
- transport (bus or car)
- culture/values (Scottish/working class)
- coping skills (looking after himself)
- expectations (wants to be rich, but doesn't really expect to be)

Activity

Take one person from the Ahmed family case study (Chapter 10) and list the factors which may influence their concept of health. Explain how you think that four of these factors may affect this concept.

Health promotion

In the previous sections it has been shown that socioeconomic and environmental factors play a large part in health and access to health provision. Individuals often feel powerless to do much about these factors, which is where health promotion has a part to play. One of the major aims of health promotion is to empower people to have control over those parts of their lives which affect their health. Downie et al sum this up in the following quotation:

In the film Educating Rita, *Rita, having begun her education, goes back to the pub with her parents and listens to the singing. She is dissatisfied with it and says: 'There must be better tunes'. Health promotion seems to us to be committed to the belief that indeed there are better tunes – better and worse lifestyles.*

(Downie, R., et al (1997)

There is quite a lot of controversy surrounding what constitutes health promotion and in defining the term. Two definitions which complement one another are used here and explored more fully as the chapter progresses. The World Health Organisation's definition is as follows:

Health promotion is the process of enabling people to increase control over, and to improve, their health.

Downie et al (1997) provided the following definition:

Health promotion comprises efforts to enhance positive health and reduce the risk of ill health, through the overlapping spheres of health education, prevention and health protection.

The World Health Organisation (O'Hara Charter, 1996) suggested that key factors to promoting health are **equity, empowerment and community participation**.

Equity

This means that everyone should have equality of access to, and should get the same benefit from the services. Everyone, therefore, should have the same opportunity to enjoy good health. In order to achieve equity, influences on health, including poverty, self-esteem, housing and employment should be assessed and needs met.

Empowerment

People are enabled to identify their health needs and then encouraged to develop skills to meet these needs. In other words, service users take control over their lives.

Community participation

The O'Hara Charter states that

people have a right and duty to participate in the planning of their health care . . .

but

making an impact on public health means acting on the life circumstances that underlie poor health, including a worthwhile job, a decent home, a good education and a clean environment.

In order to achieve this, it recommended that there should be strong links between health services and other organisations, and this should be backed by legislation making good health available to all. This means that workplaces, community settings, schools, colleges and health services should all be targeted to promote health.

Core values and principles of good practice

As well as the three factors of equity, empowerment and community participation, the Care Sector Consortium (HMSO, 1997) has presented a set of values and principles for professional activity in health promotion and care, reproduced in Figure 8.8 below. There is full discussion of values and principles in Chapter 6.

The following *Principles of Practice* have been produced by the Society of Health Education and Health Promotion Specialists (SHEPS). SHEPS intend them for use by Health

Figure 8.7 Be in the right frame of mind for moving and handling training

Education/Promotion Specialists and others working in the fields of health education, health promotion and public health, as they cover areas which all health promoters may find helpful to consider. They consider similar issues to those in the National Occupational Standards, but focus more specifically on health promotion activities (see pages 318–319).

Legislation, Policies and Charters

Legislation, policies and charters relating to rights to health care and health promotion are intended to make health choices easier and to give individual rights. In the workplace, the **Health and Safety at Work Act** (1974 and 1983) and more recently, the **Manual Handling Operations Regulations Act** (1992) impose mandatory safe practices on both the workplace and the worker, and so reduce the incidence of injury and illness. Health promotion has been peripheral to many employers, for whom it has been easier to focus on individual problems or blame workers for carelessness. In Scotland, there is a national award scheme for promoting health in the workplace. It aims to encourage employers to promote practices which will 'build a healthy workplace and a healthy organisation'. Some of the benefits of this scheme for employers are set out as:

■ *a healthier happier workforce;*
■ *a motivated team with high morale;*
■ *good management/employee relations;*
■ *less sickness absence;*
■ *a lower staff turnover.,*

Benefits for employees include:

■ *healthy working conditions;*
■ *health information at work;*
■ *practical help to be healthy;*

- *a boost to morale and motivation;*
- *good management\employee relations;*
- *the benefits of working for a good employer.*

Of prime importance in health promotion is identifying and meeting the needs of the people who live in the local area. People should feel valued and this is achieved by giving them control over their lives. This includes having sufficient information to take decisions and risks about their health and to enable them to access services quickly, as stated in *The Patient's Charter* (The Scottish Office, 1991) and in *Scotland's Health: A Challenge to Us All* (HMSO, 1992). It also means ensuring that everyone receives opportunities for screening and treatment as well as enabling individuals and families to act on increased knowledge about health.

The National Health Service and Community Care Act (1990), discussed in Chapters 1 and 2, sets out a community care policy giving people in need the right to an assessment and promoting community care through a mixed economy. Section 12 of the **Social Work (Scotland) Act (1968)** remains in force, imposing an overall duty upon local authorities to promote social welfare.

The Citizen's Charter outlines a charter for all citizens. Many other charters have been drawn up based upon the general guidelines and principles of the Citizen's Charter, including The Patient's Charter and charters for individual local authority Social Work Departments.

The Patient's Charter is examined in further detail since it has a very direct impact upon health and health promotion. There is a Patient's Charter specifically for Scotland (The Scottish Office, 1991) which sets out in broad terms what can be expected from the National Health Service. Ian Lang, in his Foreword to the Charter sets out the main commitments of the government in relation to the NHS in Scotland. The Government are committed:

- *to improving QUALITY at all levels;*
- *to increasing CHOICE to the consumer;*
- *to publishing NHS STANDARDS of performance and making it easier to complain when these standards are not achieved;*
- *and by improving quality, to improving VALUE FOR MONEY.*

The Charter itself sets out what you or any other citizen can expect from the NHS. Among the points made are the following:

- you are entitled to information and practical help towards healthier living;
- you are entitled to expect the staff of the NHS to set a good example;
- everyone should have access to suitable NHS health care, irrespective of special needs or disabilities;
- you are entitled to know how long you are likely to have to wait for an out-patient appointment;
- you are entitled to expect that any comment you may have will be taken seriously, and that any complaints will be treated fairly and quickly;
- you are entitled to clear information about the specific services offered by each GP practice.

BOX 3.1 NATIONAL OCCUPATIONAL STANDARDS FOR PROFESSIONAL ACTIVITY IN HEALTH PROMOTION AND CARE. JULY 1997

Values and Principles of Good Practice

Professional standards from a number of different professional bodies were analysed to identify the values and principles on which the national occupational standards for professional activity in health promotion and care should be based. The *values* identified are respect for:

- the human condition and its complexity;
- our essential humanity;
- the wealth of human experience;
- the holistic nature of health and social well-being;
- diversity.

The National Occupational Standards for Professional Activity in Health Promotion and Care have been built on ten *Principles of Good Practice*:

1. Balancing people's rights with their responsibilities to others and to wider society and challenging those which affect the rights of others.
2. Promoting values of equality and diversity, acknowledging the personal beliefs and preferences of others and promoting anti-discriminatory practice.
3. Maintaining the confidentiality of information provided that this does not place others at risk.
4. Recognizing the effect of the wider social, political and economic context on health and social well-being and on people's development.
5. Enabling people to develop to their full potential, to be as autonomous and self-managing as possible and to have a voice and be heard.
6. Recognizing and promoting health and social well-being as a positive concept.
7. Balancing the needs of people who use services with the resources available and exercising financial probity.
8. Developing and maintaining effective relationships with people and maintaining the integrity of these relationships through setting appropriate role boundaries.
9. Developing oneself and one's own practice to improve the quality of services offered.
10. Working within statutory and organizational frameworks.

BOX 3.2 SOCIETY OF HEALTH EDUCATION AND HEALTH PROMOTION SPECIALISTS PRINCIPLES OF PRACTICE. JULY 1997

Relationship to Client/Recipient

1. Adequate needs assessment, consultation with and involvement of the client or target group is essential to the effective planning, implementation and reviewing of health promotion activities.
2. The promotion of self-esteem and autonomy amongst client groups/recipients should be an underlying principle of all health promotion practice.
3. Health promotion should encourage people to value others whatever their gender, age, race, class, religion, culture, sexuality, ability or health status, and attempt to counter prejudice and discrimination wherever it occurs.

Social and environmental influences

4. Health promotion programmes should be relevant and sensitive to the nature of the intended client group, for example, the social, economic and cultural framework of the group.
5. Health promotion work should include recognition of and action focused on the social, economic and environmental determinants of health.
6. Health promotion work should aim to empower and enable people to exercise informed choice and influence structures and systems that have an impact on health.
7. Health promotion programmes which focus on specific issues should always be set in the wider political, social, economic, geographical, psychological and environmental context which has a bearing on health.
8. The sustainability of health promotion interventions needs to be considered within the context of the aims of any programme of activity. Health promotion interventions should aim to have a positive impact on both the immediate recipients and future generations of people.

Health promotion practice

A. An aim of health promotion practice is to bring about change in the social and economic environment to improve health and to reduce or eliminate inequalities in health at a local, national and international level.
B. Appropriate research and evaluation is an essential component of health promotion activity. Practitioners should endeavour to disseminate results and findings.
C. Practitioners have a responsibility for ensuring an accurate and appropriate information flow between the public, professionals, local and national agencies, and for taking the initiative and responding accordingly.

Box 3.2 – *continued*

D. Practitioners will endeavour to provide services or information that they have at their disposal that would, in the light of current theory and/or evidence, maintain and promote health. They will endeavour to keep their knowledge of current developments in health promotion up to date.

E. Practitioners will have due regard to the confidentiality of information to which they have access, bearing in mind the requirements of the law.

F. Health promotion work should encourage all services and organizations to develop their health promotion role and to adopt the above principles of practice.

G. Health promotion activity is by its nature a collaborative endeavour. Practitioners should seek to actively collaborate with colleagues and others to promote health.

H. The methods and process of health promotion should be health promoting.

Figure 8.8 Values and principles of good practice

Individual Health Boards and hospitals have produced their own charters based upon these commitments, setting their own targets for the delivery of services. For example, Greater Glasgow Health Board brought out its own charter 'Yours for Life' in 1993.

Local Health Councils are independent consumer organisations set up within the National Health Service to represent the interests of the public in the NHS. Members are all local unpaid volunteers, appointed following public advertisements, though councils do also have paid staff members to administer the service. There are regular meetings of members to consider a variety of issues, including legislation, length of waiting lists and standards of service. Health Councils have the right to visit NHS premises on behalf of the public to monitor services and to talk to both staff and patients. Full reports of the visits are produced, which are available to the public. Local Health Councils also provide advice and information, produce publications, research consumer opinion and liaise with various local groups, hospital trusts and the local Health Board. Health Boards **must** consult with the local Health Council before making changes in the provision of health services (e.g. proposed hospital closures).

(Much of the above information was provided by Greater Glasgow Council in their leaflet, *Patient's Guide No. 1 Your Local Health Council*, July 1996.)

GP Contracts are agreements between the government and General Medical Practitioners that payments will be made if certain services are provided. In April 1990 a new contract was introduced which encouraged GPs, through financial incentives, to increase their provision of screening and health promotion activities. For example, target payments were set for cervical cytology (smear tests), for childhood immunisations and pre-school boosters, for working with patients in areas with high levels of deprivation, for child health surveillance and for working with patients of 75 and over.

Activity

Investigate the implementation of at least two policies which affect health and health promotion. You could, for example:

a) obtain a copy of the patients' charter of a local hospital and list the entitlements identified;

b) obtain a charter of rights from the local social work department and list the rights identified;

c) find out the composition of the Local Health Council and what it is currently working on;

d) find out about the targets which GPs need to meet in relation to two preventative measures in order to satisfy criteria for additional payments.

Elements of health promotion

From the definition of health promotion provided by Downie et al (1997) at the beginning of this section it can be seen that health promotion has three overlapping spheres or elements:

- health education;
- prevention;
- health protection.

These three elements are considered in turn before combining them into a single model.

HEALTH EDUCATION

This is an integral part of health promotion and is the process by which the individual acquires knowledge about health. It is designed to enable people to have the necessary understanding to make informed choices about how their behaviour may affect their health. Health education is based on the premise that if you increase an individual's knowledge it will lead to a change in behaviour. It must take into account attitudes, values and beliefs, and be aware that the individual has freedom of choice to respond to the advice given. Health education is often aimed at preventing specific diseases such as the campaign to prevent the spread of HIV/AIDS, and high risk groups are targeted. Any information on health must be useful and relevant to its audience. It is important to remember that it is necessary to target all age groups when providing health education. The stages of development and the needs of each group will vary. The target group will affect the language used, the presentation of the information and the emphasis and content of the information. The method of presentation can easily influence how well the message is understood, for example in promotions aimed at children or adolescents the use of pictures, cartoons or diagrams can make the information more effective. The language used should be straightforward because jargon can make the audience feel stupid and worthless.

Figure 8.9 Recent anti-smoking campaign posters

Poster campaigns can also be effective if they are attractive and have similarities to the group which is being targeted for health education. The media enable information to be passed on to vast numbers of people. This includes television, which is usually available to most of the population including those who have low levels of literacy and few material resources.

Activity

Have you seen any campaigns on television about the repercussions of smoking? What impact did they have on you?

The media are widely used for promoting health. The media include TV, radio, posters, newspapers, the internet, magazines, books, displays, leaflets and videos. According to Naidoo and Wills (1997) it is now accepted that the mass media can:

- raise consciousness about health issues;
- help place health on the public agenda;
- convey simple information;
- change behaviour if other enabling factors are present.

However the media do have their limitations. They cannot change people's fixed patterns of belief or teach new coping skills. Motivation and supportive circumstances are crucial if there is to be behaviour change. Newspaper campaigns are not always available to all of the population either because of literacy or language barriers. Videos and the internet are, however, areas which can now be more fully utilised. The media in combination with a community participation approach do have the capacity to produce change.

Prevention

The aim of prevention is to reduce the risk of disease or disability. Health prevention can be primary, secondary or tertiary. **Primary** prevention is aimed at preventing ill-health from occurring. Examples of primary prevention include information on immunisations, hygiene and nutrition. Doctors are funded to promote immunisation programmes in babies to protect against the following diseases:

Diphtheria	*Measles*
Whooping cough	*Mumps*
Tetanus	*Rubella*
Polio	*Meningitis*
Tuberculosis	

Some parents are concerned about the possible side effects of immunisation. However this is a very small risk compared to the complications of the diseases.

Secondary prevention aims at restoring people to their former state of health following a

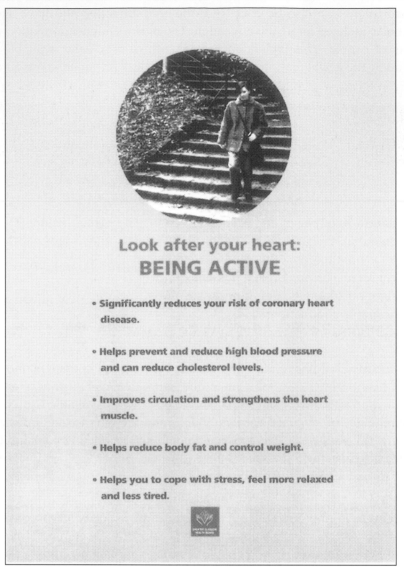

Look after your heart:
BEING ACTIVE

• Significantly reduces your risk of coronary heart
  disease.

• Helps prevent and reduce high blood pressure
  and can reduce cholesterol levels.

• Improves circulation and strengthens the heart
  muscle.

• Helps reduce body fat and control weight.

• Helps you to cope with stress, feel more relaxed
  and less tired.

Figure 8.10 Information for cardiac patients

bout of illness and prevention of a disease from progressing any further. Examples are information on smoking and exercise for someone who has had a cardiac problem.

Coronary heart disease was responsible for a quarter of all deaths in Scotland in 1996 and so has been identified as a priority for health prevention.

Tertiary prevention is aimed at reducing the limitations of a disability when the person will not return to full health. This can often include the use of mobility aids following a cerebro-vascular accident or stroke.

Of course within the realm of health prevention there is a remit for health education, for example when children have their teeth fissure sealed they are also given advice about reducing their sugar intake.

Health protection

The following definition of health protection is provided by Downie et al (1996):

> *Health protection comprises legal or fiscal controls, other regulations and policies, and voluntary codes of practice, aimed at the enhancement of positive health and the prevention of ill-health.*

The legislation, policies and charters considered on pages 316–317, including Health and Safety at Work legislation, can be seen as health protection. Other relevant legislation relates to the wearing of seat belts, the sale of alcohol and tobacco to minors and the control of communicable diseases, such as HIV/AIDS.

Fiscal or tax control is rather inconsistently applied in relation to health promotion. For example, tax on tobacco has been considerably increased in recent years, whilst tax on alcohol has remained fairly stable. ASH et al (1988) have shown that raising the tax on tobacco does work and is positively correlated with a reduction in smoking.

Health protection can also be provided through workplace 'No Smoking' policies, workplace health days and the commitment of public funds to leisure centres and sports facilities which are easily and cheaply accessible to all members of the population.

A model of health promotion

The elements of health promotion have now been examined. Downie et al (1996) present Tannahill's model of health promotion which integrates these elements, as shown in Figure 8.11 overleaf.

Seven domains (numbered in the diagram) may be distinguished within health promotion:
1. Preventative measures, e.g. immunisation, cervical screening, hypertension case-finding, screening for congenital disorders, use of nicotine chewing gum.
2. Education to prevent ill-health, e.g. anti-smoking campaign.
3. Preventative health protection e.g. fluoridisation of public water supplies.
4. Health education of policy makers.

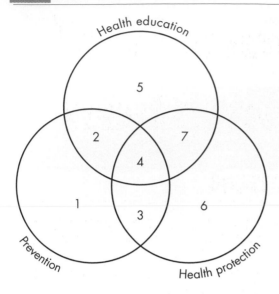

Figure 8.11 Tannahill model of health promotion

5. Positive health education, e.g. encouraging a productive use of leisure time in the interests of fitness and well-being.
6. Positive health protection, e.g. implementation of a workplace no-smoking policy.
7. Raising awareness and securing support for positive health protection measures.

This model describes what happens in the practice of health promotion, and it shows how different approaches relate to each other.

Activity

Choose one target group for health promotion, e.g. adolescents, and name one measure for each of the seven domains of Tannahill's model which could be used to promote health.

SUMMARY OF PART 1

Part 1 of this chapter has covered material at Intermediate II level, though much of it is also relevant to the Higher syllabus. It has also covered a great deal of Intermediate 1 as introductory material, relating to the meaning of health and influences upon health. Health was examined in an holistic way, emphasising that it has physical, psychological and social dimensions. Factors influencing health, access to health provision and an individual's concept of health were explored with an emphasis upon hereditary, environmental and socio-cultural factors. Elements of health promotion – health education, prevention and health protection – were examined separately and as constituents in an integrated model. At various points in the text consideration was given to values and principles, legislation and policy and the media.

Part 2 – Models of health promotion

INTRODUCTION

In Part 1 of the chapter, you discovered that there are many factors which influence health – social, environmental, genetic and cultural – and that there are inequalities in the health status of groups of people. These can be due to gender, social class and cultural differences. People also differ in their perceptions of health. Just as there are different perceptions of health, so there are also different models of health promotion. This is partly because health promoters come from different backgrounds and have different beliefs about how to promote health. The models explored in this chapter are the medical, educational, community development, marketing, political and client-centred. Once the models of health promotion have been looked at, strategies for analysing the effectiveness of health promotion campaigns are examined. Consideration is then given to skills to promote health and well-being to others, including management skills and presentation skills. The information and activities in Part 2 are at Higher level and relate predominantly to Outcomes 1 and 2 of the Higher Health Promotion Unit.

Activity

Make a list of the people and agencies which have affected your health either directly or indirectly. As you read through the chapter try to identify which models of health promotion most closely accord with their approach.

MODELS OF HEALTH PROMOTION

One model of health promotion has already been presented in Part 1 (Tannahill in Downie, 1996). This model describes what happens in the practice of health promotion and it shows how different approaches (health education, prevention and health protection) relate to each other. The concept of health and influences on health are so diverse that a number of other theoretical models are used. In Part 2 of this chapter, the following models will be discussed:

■ medical;
■ educational;
■ community development;
■ marketing;
■ political;
■ client-centred.

These models will be evaluated in terms of strategies for promoting health.

Medical model

The emphasis of this model is upon the detection and prevention of disease resulting in a reduction of morbidity and early mortality.

Morbidity

Morbidity is the effect of illness and disease on the individual. This does not only mean physical symptoms manifested, but also mental health or emotional problems which may be long- or short-term in their effect.

Mortality

The incidence of death from a given disease or illness.

Prevention and detection of disease is much cheaper than caring for those who have become ill and this is achieved by medical intervention. Health professionals aim to encourage the general public to use their interventions to prevent the disease process. The medical model targets high risk groups or whole populations and most preventative work is carried out by health visitors and community nurses. Examples of this are immunisation and vaccination. Indeed, smallpox has been eradicated worldwide as a result of mass vaccination uptake. Other examples are well-men clinics and three-yearly cervical screening of women over twenty years. The latter has reduced the incidence of invasive cancers by 30 per cent.

Based on reduction of disease and mortality, the medical approach is not always successful because it depends on the level of uptake for efficacy. This model creates dependency on the medical profession. Many people feel threatened by medical authority and so, rather than discuss their feelings, tend to ignore the advice given. This model does not necessarily take social and environmental factors affecting health into account. Since 1990 there has been much more emphasis on health promotion in primary health care. This in part may be due to the fact that GPs have been paid according to their targets for cervical screening and immunisation. No matter how many health promotion clinics there are, they need to be flexible and accessible if they are to encourage service users to attend. A young mother who is pregnant and has two small children under five years will have difficulty in attending an ante-natal clinic which is situated far from her home if she has to rely on public transport. Instead, she would use the health services should they be provided in her local community.

Educational model

This model is based on the premise that if the individual is given sufficient knowledge about a health topic, it will enable him or her to make an informed decision about their behaviour. There is an assumption that extra information will lead to the person challenging their attitudes and so their behaviour. Education can be provided on a group basis where there can be an exchange of views and the group members can support one another. Information can also be given to larger audiences using the media. One example of this is the anti-smoking advertisements on television and in the newspapers.

The Health Education Board for Scotland in its Strategic Plan 1997 to 2002 is aiming to reduce smoking by 30 per cent in ages 12 to 24 and by 20 per cent in those aged 25 to 65. However giving of information on its own is insufficient to enable people to change their behaviour. Information must be given in a manner which captures the targeted audience's attention. A credible presenter with whom the audience can identify adds impact and so do novel means of presentation. The audience must be able to understand any health promotion message. It should therefore be simple and the positive aspects of change should be emphasised. It must be remembered that not everyone is literate, therefore visual images are also important. As our community is multi-cultural, information should be presented in a variety of languages to enable the widest audience possible to be reached. The subject of presentation skills is more fully developed on pages 341–343 in the section 'Skills to Promote Health and Well-Being to Others'.

Community development

In 'Working Together for a Healthier Scotland' (HMSO, 1998), the Scottish Office states that 'community involvement is a key component' in promoting health and there has been considerable growth in this area. A community is generally identified as a discrete group of people living within a geographical area. There is an underlying assumption that the social class, environmental factors and attitudes of this group of people will be similar. This in turn is an index for the health status of the group.

The key principle of community development is empowerment. The needs of the community are identified by the community and the emphasis is on the holistic approach to health, which means focusing on the whole person and not only on the symptoms of ill-health. Instead of blaming individuals for their ill-health, the focus is upon addressing social and environmental factors and enabling people to take control of their lives. This leads to a rise in self esteem which in itself is a health promotion issue. Community development deals with both specific health issues and more general issues and generally the uptake for these activities is very high, with the majority of participants being female. Why do you think this may be? Eastbank Health Promotion Centre 'was designed to become a focus for health activity information and education in the east end of Glasgow'. It has a range of free activities on offer. These include aromatherapy, stress management, tai chi, slow time, yoga and line dancing. They have recently introduced a men's class on cardiovascular workout, but to date the uptake has been poor. In its first annual report (1997), the Centre reported that in its December 1996 survey 75 per cent of users reported positive changes in their health or lifestyle. Of these users, 30 per cent cite convenience of access and free service as prime motivators, 36 per cent attend because of enjoyment and 26 per cent for the company and friendship.

Community development can also facilitate support groups, and at Eastbank there is a Women's Support group, a pain association group, a cancer support group and a deaf/blind support group.

Community development is very popular with both health promotion professionals and the public. On-going evaluation of a project enables it constantly to modify its provision and assess the project's impact. It raises feelings of autonomy and self esteem within the community and seeks to deal with the underlying factors which affect health. As with many projects, its main problem is lack of funding.

Marketing model

The society in which we live is heavily influenced by marketing techniques which have proved to be very lucrative. Consumers are provided with information about a range of products which can transform your life – or so you are encouraged to believe.

If health is viewed as a product which it is desirable to own, then surely health promoters can use marketing techniques to sell health?

The key to marketing is to provide the audience with a product which satisfies their needs, therefore the needs of the audience must be researched and planned. It is important that research is carried out to explore the public's perception of health, as attitudes to health will influence whether a person is ready to change his or her behaviour. In a recent study, for instance, it was discovered that one of the main reasons for young girls taking up smoking was the belief that it enabled them to remain thin. This view is perpetuated by the media. There is tremendous media pressure on young people that it is glamorous to be thin. In this case it is insufficient to give information about the dangers of smoking or that you will feel healthier/cleaner etc. when you stop.

The message of health must appeal to its target audience and must be credible. Credibility relies on the person presenting the message being someone the audience can identify with either as a role model or specialist. Media personalities or sports personalities can be used to spearhead health campaigns as people will copy the behaviour of those they admire. The message must be relevant to its target group to motivate change, e.g. a drugs awareness campaign aimed at adolescents may use slang names to make the message more effective. A variety of media from posters to newspapers or television campaigns may be used for presentation. Thus a wide audience can be reached. Marketing therefore does provide useful techniques for health promotion but it does have its limitations. It does not take into account the fact that not everyone sees health as a valuable asset and indeed may cause anxiety or guilt which only results in stress to the individual, e.g. many people know the importance of providing a balanced diet for their children but are prevented from doing so because of financial constraints. The information presented may be limited and it is difficult to get feedback from the target audience about the efficacy of the message.

Political model

When the National Health Service was founded just over 50 years ago as part of a welfare state, all political parties were united in the promotion of a free service for all. Due to the economic recession in the 1970s there was high unemployment. At the same time demographic changes led to a fall in the birth rate and a rise of those who were over 65 years. This led to rising costs in the welfare state. A change in government to the Thatcher government of 1979 onwards led to new policies, which changed the emphasis of the welfare state on paternalism to the idea that there should be minimum state intervention with individuals taking responsibility for their actions. According to that government the welfare state merely results in dependency and raised unrealistic expectations.

As the policy makers, this of course has influenced health promotion activity. There has been a rise in health promotion over the last 20 years partly as a result of the 1976 publication 'Prevention and Health – Everybody's Business'. This publication emphasised that ill-health should be prevented because it is very expensive. As a result, the National Health Service was regarded as the natural place for health promotion. The medical model influenced health promotion activity with the professionals giving education and advice to the service users. They expected these service users to adopt healthy behaviour patterns as a result of this advice. It is difficult to influence other factors within this model. Other policy changes have been the introduction of the National Health Service and Community Care Act (1990), whereby health authorities have become both purchasers and providers of care – the role of the purchaser being to determine health needs. The primary care role rests with GPs whose funding is linked to the degree of health promotion activities presented. Again this tends to focus on individual lifestyles as opposed to population level interventions, e.g. banning tobacco advertising and sponsorship and increasing taxation on tobacco products. Of course governments are also influenced in policy-making by powerful companies whose interests are economic and who may oppose pro-health policies.

Following their election in 1997, the Labour government published the 1998 Green Paper 'Working Together for a Healthier Scotland' (HMSO, 1998). It states that 'Scotland carries a greater burden of ill-health than other developed countries with the problem being greatest among low income groups'. The priority health topics identified in this document are coronary heart disease and stroke, cancer, mental health, sexual health, dental and oral health and accidents and safety.

This document takes into account the effect of poverty and disadvantage on ill-health.

Improving lifestyles must continue to be rigorously tackled but within a framework which recognises and focuses on the underlying social, economic and environmental circumstances which influence health.

However first level action will again be on the prevention of illness. The emphasis is on education where people will change their lifestyles as a result of information, e.g. NO SMOKING DAY, but other areas of policy such as better provision of housing, nursery places or maternity benefits are not addressed. Health promotion is linked to politics because prevailing policy determines the strategies of promotion provided by funding the preferred options. The emphasis is still on preventing ill-health rather than addressing the promotion of positive health.

Client-centred model

All models of health promotion should be client-centred. This model however emphasises the role of clients or service users in taking action on their own behalf. It has many similarities with the community development model, and some similarities to person-centred planning discussed in Chapter 7. The health promoter's role is that of facilitator, enabling people to gain the knowledge and skills which they need to achieve change. Empowerment is central to this model with service users seen as the main change agents, more than equal partners in the health promotion process. The right of individuals to control their own lives is paramount. In this approach, smoking would only be regarded as an issue if, once information and knowledge had been provided, service users raised it as an issue. They would identify what else, if anything, they wanted to know and to do about it.

STRATEGIES FOR ANALYSING THE EFFECTIVENESS OF HEALTH PROMOTION CAMPAIGNS

Different methodologies and criteria must be applied when defining what is effective, because health promotion covers such a wide remit. Health promotion practitioners work within financial constraints, vying for resources. It is therefore important to present evidence that health promotion does work. Many agencies, including the Health Education Board for Scotland, are carrying out research to evaluate health promotion strategies. Naidoo and Wills (1998) believe health promotion can be assessed according to effectiveness, efficiency, appropriateness, acceptability and equity. When analysing whether a health promotion campaign has been effective, you have to take into account the model used and whether the objectives have been met. Therefore different research methodologies need to be used including surveys, questionnaires, observation, case studies and the methods of epidemiology. These are discussed in full in the following chapter. When evaluating the effectiveness of a campaign, according to Moonie et al (1996), you firstly have to identify the target group and its needs. These needs may be broad, such as information about nutrition and health, or specific, like the effect of poor diet on pregnancy. This leads to the identification of the aims and objectives (see pages 337–338) which should be clear and connected to improving health. The methods used in the campaign should be analysed. These depend on the material available which must be appropriate for the audience and on the facilities available. The effectiveness of any campaign should be assessed by researching the audience.

The medical model of health promotion aims to prevent disease and increase life expectancy. Indications of effectiveness measured are, for example, the uptake of immunisation or screening programmes. These give quantitative evidence of long-term outcomes. Another way is to assess the cost-effectiveness which compares which interventions differ in their success and cost. Marketing health as a desirable product can be used by health promoters to reach a wide audience, providing it promotes a credible message.

The community development model has as its focus the social and environmental factors of its members. It enables the community to identify its needs and find the resources to meet these needs. It is very popular and empowers the community constantly to evaluate and modify its provision.

The educational model provides information about health issues, either through a media campaign or in a classroom setting. However, the onus to change behaviour is placed on the person as a result of the information given and sometimes the information could be difficult to understand. Here knowledge of health issues by the presenter and skills of presentation are very important. Changes produced can be analysed through looking at changes in knowledge and perceptions, attitudes and behaviour, or in health status of the individuals concerned. Research using a variety of the methods discussed in Chapter 9 (e.g. surveys, questionnaires and observation) will enable you to analyse the effectiveness of a health promotion campaign, whether it is based upon an educational or any other model.

Politics influences health promotion because it proposes legislation and makes policy which influences all areas of health. A good example of this is the legislation about wearing seatbelts which has cut down mortality rates in road traffic accidents. However, because the emphasis has been mostly on the individual it has not been effective because not everyone has equal resources or motivation.

Health promotion benefits tend to be long-term and therefore difficult to analyse economically. However, in the workplace, reduced levels of sickness and a low staff turnover are benefits which can result from a health promotion programme. This leads to increased productivity for the company and so may be deemed to be economically effective. This is what Scotland's Health at Work Scheme is promoting. For many health promoters, equity and empowerment are the most important outcomes of health promotion and so quantitative data are insufficient. Rather it is the benefits accrued to the service user of feelings of raised self esteem and the feeling that you can have control over your life which are important. It is difficult to analyse this type of data scientifically but the community development model can provide figures for increased participation and social interaction such as in the Eastbank Resource Centre. Qualitative research methods (see page 347) can demonstrate how service users feel about services provided.

It would appear therefore that a variety of methods should be used. The strategies used by health promoters will result from research into the audience, what activity is flexible enough to meet their needs and result in the individual having a better quality of life. This means not only an absence of disease, but tackling the social, economic and environmental factors which influence health.

SKILLS TO PROMOTE HEALTH AND WELL-BEING TO OTHERS

Many of the skills of care are also the skills of health promotion. To promote health requires the skills of assessment, planning implementation and evaluation explained in Chapter 7. The communication and interpersonal skills described and explained in Chapter 6 are as relevant to health promotion as to any form of helping. There are some other skills which, although transferable form other areas of helping, require a different emphasis in relation to health promotion. It is these skills which are explained in this section. They are:

- management skills, including skills in setting objectives;
- presentation skills.

Management skills

Although you may not be a manager or have any intention of becoming one, the skills of management can be useful to anyone organising a health promotion programme. As with counselling skills which are useful to care workers in developing communication ability, so management skills can be useful in health promotion where a project needs to be set up and organised. Which management skills are being discussed here? The main ones relate to **managing information, managing time, managing project work, skills in setting aims, objectives and targets, managing change and striving for quality**.

Managing information

Any worker can easily get buried under mounds of needless paper. One of the secrets of being organised is to:

- keep only information which is necessary;
- ensure that information is easy to retrieve and is stored in the most efficient and accessible way possible; use computers if available;
- ensure the administrative staff are involved in organisational aspects of the job and keep information which is for the use of all team members;
- ensure that the system of keeping information can be understood by everyone who needs to use it; keep it simple.

Another aspect of managing information is writing reports. In Chapter 9 criteria are set out for writing research reports. These apply to any kind of report writing. Don't forget to define the purpose of written material, define who is likely to read it, structure it logically with all relevant information and get someone to check it if you can. Look back at page 292 for more guidance.

Managing time

It's easy to make pronouncements about managing time and difficult to actually put them into practice. Here are a few guidelines and a rather simple chart to help you. Remember the three Ps: Plan, Prioritise and Practise. **Plan** your time by writing down everything which needs to be done, how long each task is likely to take and when you are going to do what. **Prioritise** the tasks to be done so that tasks which are really important do get done. At the same time, you need to build in time for such things as research and development work and ensure that you use it for these purposes. This doesn't mean that you have to be absolutely inflexible about time, but without planning and prioritising you certainly won't use it effectively – and it is a very precious and rare resource. **Practise** time management consistently, not just when the unit manager is in the office or the inspectors are coming. Part of practising time management is taking time out every now and then to evaluate your use of time.

The following chart, called a Gantt chart after its alleged inventor, is a useful chart in planning time and managing project work or any kind of long-term work for that matter. The example used is the setting up of a support group for bereaved people who attend a health centre. GPs have for a long time felt that many health problems are exacerbated by bereavement. Research (Worden et al) supports this finding, and working with groups can be a very useful source of help.

Managing project work

Here are some examples of project work, some of which have already been mentioned in this chapter:

- setting up a scheme to encourage breast-feeding among young mothers;
- setting up an information service for hospital out-patients;
- encouraging teenagers to think carefully about smoking.

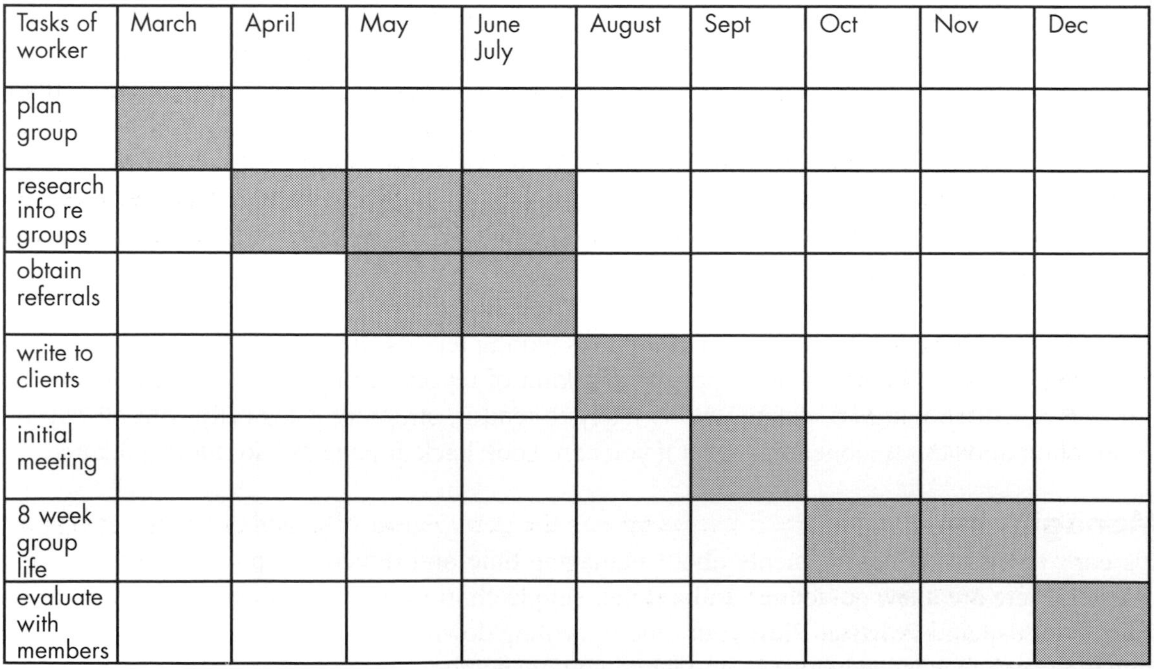

Tasks of worker	March	April	May	June July	August	Sept	Oct	Nov	Dec
plan group	▨								
research info re groups		▨	▨	▨					
obtain referrals			▨	▨					
write to clients					▨				
initial meeting						▨			
8 week group life							▨	▨	
evaluate with members									▨

Figure 8.12 Gantt chart: Support groups for bereaved people

Activity

Skills described elsewhere in the book are very useful in managing such project work. Make a list of the skills which you can transfer to setting up and managing one of the above projects.

You may have mentioned the following skills more fully discussed in Chapter 7:

■ assessment of need;

■ planning;

■ implementation;

■ evaluation.

Once the planning has been achieved a project is implemented. The start of the project is very important and much of what happens subsequently rests upon the firm foundations laid at the beginning. It is important that aims and objectives are clear and understood by everyone involved (see the next section), that there are adequate time and resources allocated to the task, and that roles and responsibilities are clear. The way in which the project is to be evaluated should be set out clearly at this stage. Planning the project can make use of the Gantt chart discussed in the section on time management.

Skills in setting aims, objectives and targets

The setting of aims and objectives in health promotion has already been mentioned in Chapter 7 as part of the planning process. Here more detailed consideration is given to this, since clarity in aims and objectives equates with clarity in what you are trying to achieve. Aims can be considered as stating what you are trying to achieve in general terms, e.g. to reduce the incidence of heart disease. Objectives are more specific and describe the desired result or outcome. For example, Greater Glasgow Health Board set out five objectives in relation to the aim of reducing the incidence of heart disease:

■ reducing stress;
■ drinking responsibly;
■ eating healthily;
■ exercising regularly;
■ not smoking.

The Europe against Cancer campaign has the general aim of avoiding cancer. It sets out the following ten objectives:

1. Smokers, stop as quickly as possible.
2. Go easy on alcohol.
3. Avoid being overweight.
4. Take care in the sun.

5. Observe Health and Safety Regulations at work.
6. Cut down on fatty foods.
7. Eat plenty of fresh fruit and vegetables and other foods containing fibre.
8. See your doctor if there is any unexplained change in your normal health which lasts for more than two weeks.

Especially for women:

9. Have a regular cervical smear test.
10. Examine your breasts monthly.

Each of the above objectives can be tackled on its own with its own set of objectives, though it is pursuing all of them in combination that promotes maximum avoidance of cancer. **Targets** are also often set alongside objectives. These state how the objective will be achieved in terms of quantity, time and/or quality. The Europe against Cancer campaign has the target of reducing the number of deaths from cancer by 15 per cent.

Objectives and targets should be:

■ **attainable.** It is no good setting objectives which are unrealistic and which it is virtually impossible to achieve;

■ **relevant.** Objectives should be relevant to your job and to the individuals with whom you are working;

■ **challenging, but not unrealistically challenging.** Objectives should provide you and those with whom you are working with something worthwhile to work towards;

■ **as measurable as possible**, though difficulties of measurement should not prevent you from setting objectives. Measurements can be in terms of quantity (e.g. reduction in the number of cigarettes smoked), time (e.g. in one year), and quality (e.g. changes in health/feelings of well-being).

Setting aims and objectives is influenced by the health promotion model or models from which you are working. For example, if you are working from an educational model you may provide participant presentations about cigarette smoking as well as information and advice. A client-centred model promotes maximum participation by and empowerment of service users from the stage of setting aims and objectives, through to planning, implementation and evaluation.

Activity

Identify a health promotion aim that would be relevant to at least two of the people identified in the case study in Chapter 10. Plan a project in relation to this clearly stating your aim(s), objectives, targets and the models of health promotion that you would use.

Managing change

Change is quite a threatening thing. Most people think carefully about making changes in their lives. Even when there seem to be (to us) blatantly obvious reasons why people should make changes, they often don't. Why do you think this is?

The changes discussed in this chapter are those that a health promotion project may encourage. There are some ways in which change can be facilitated and some circumstances that can be created to make desirable changes more likely to occur. Reasons for change need to be clearly given and targets for change need to be achievable; the benefits of change need to be clearly explained; people feel better about change if they have had maximum participation in the process of change and can see an easily attained first step to change. Ewles and Simnett (1999) set out four factors important in a consideration of change, which together make the change equation. These four factors are:

A – *the level of dissatisfaction with the present state of affairs;*
B – *a shared vision of a better future;*
C – *the existence of an acceptable **first step**;*
D – *the costs (of all kinds, not just financial).*

Change is likely to be viewed positively, and be implemented successfully, if: A + B + C is greater than D.

(Ewles and Simnett, 1999)

Prochaska and Di Clemente (1984) developed a model to show that people go through a number of stages when acquiring new behaviour. These stages are:

Pre-contemplation
The person has not considered their behaviour or become aware of any potential risks in their health behaviour.

Contemplation
Although the individual is aware of the benefits of change, they are not yet ready and may be seeking information or help to make that decision. This stage may last a short while or several years.

Preparing to change
When the perceived benefits seem to outweigh the costs and when the change seems possible as well as worthwhile, the individual may be ready to change, perhaps seeking some extra support.

Making the change
The early days of change require positive decisions by the individual to do things differently. A clear goal, a realistic plan, support and rewards are features of this stage.

Maintenance
The new behaviour is sustained and the person moves into a healthier lifestyle.

Of course, there can be many relapses on the way to change, and motivation is probably the most crucial factor involved for change to become effective. Some health promotion campaigns attempt to motivate people through fear or guilt, e.g. the drink/drive campaigns at Christmas showing the effect of road deaths on families. This certainly does increase awareness, but Naidoo and Wills contend that any change may disappear over time. In order for change of behaviour to be maintained it is important that health promoters recognise that people will only change their behaviour if they want to. Changing behaviour can be very stressful and so support, especially that of peers as in the breast-feeding campaign in Glasgow, can reinforce the behaviour and ensure it remains.

Striving for quality
On page 333 evaluating the effectiveness of a health promotion campaign was considered and the criteria of effectiveness, efficiency, appropriateness, acceptability and equity were identified. These are criteria that are also quality indicators. As an illustration of this take the breast-feeding initiative described in the first half of this chapter. There breast-feeding was being promoted for and by members of the local community as an effective way of getting the message across that breast-feeding is the healthiest option for babies.

The message is **appropriate**, because breast-feeding really does improve the health of babies.

It is made **acceptable** by people within the community who have experienced the benefits of breast-feeding, passing on the message to others.

Equity is promoted through giving everyone an equal opportunity to put this health message into practice through community support mechanisms.

Using community resources is an **efficient** and **effective** way of putting the message across. It achieves the aims and objectives of the project (i.e. effective – to increase the uptake of breast-feeding) and makes the best possible use of resources (efficient).

Activity

Look at a health promotion campaign, e.g. an anti-smoking poster campaign, and analyse its effectiveness, efficiency, appropriateness, acceptability and equity. Write a sentence about each of the criteria.

Presentation skills

I know I cannot teach anyone anything. I can only provide an environment in which he can learn.

(Carl Rogers, 1969)

Among the many skills that someone promoting health needs to develop is the skill of presenting information to others. This has been briefly discussed and equates with many of the skills associated with educating.

Activity

Think of educational experiences when you were taught or went to a lecture or a presentation. Identify the characteristics of: a) a good educational experience; b) a poor educational experience, to do with:

i) the environment (comfortable/uncomfortable; hot/cold);

ii) the qualities of the presenter (lively/apathetic; honest/insincere; interested/bored);

iii) the presentation itself (interesting/boring; long/just right; clear/muddled; used OHPs effectively/no visual assistance etc.).

Complete the chart below to summarise your answers.

Factors	Good experience	Poor experience
Environment		
Qualities of presenter		
Presentation		

Imagine that you are going to present a session on how to deal with a health emergency to a group of SVQ (Scottish Vocational Qualification) candidates. Before the session, what needs to be done? You need to ensure that you have a room where you can seat everyone comfortably, have equipment that you need (e.g. overhead projector, a dummy upon which you can demonstrate CPR (cardio-pulmonary resuscitation/mouth to mouth) and you need to **plan** how you will present your material. Even if you know your subject very well you still need to plan. This doesn't mean writing down every single word you are going to say. One way to plan is to use file cards on which you write triggers and main points: ask group members what they know already; describe a health emergency; make main points about assessing danger and response; demonstrate using a dummy; ask group members to demonstrate etc.

Once the day has arrived, your planning is done and there is the group ready and waiting for your presentation, how do you go about it? There is no one right way of doing this and the more you do, the more you discover both what works and your own personal strengths. Below are just a few pointers.

- Introduce the session by stating what it is about and why it is being looked at.
- Always try to provide something positive, interesting, relevant and short at the beginning.
- Don't be afraid to refer to your notes – at least the group will appreciate that you made some and you won't lose your way.
- Ask questions at frequent intervals. This will establish what the group members already know and will also enable you to check learning at key points.
- Try to give group members the opportunity to come to their own conclusions by guiding them towards the 'correct' answers. Involve them in the presentation as much as possible.
- Use some means of recording points made, e.g. a flip chart/blackboard/whiteboard, in conjunction with other media (usually an overhead projector with prepared overheads). If you use prepared overheads, make just a few points in large writing on each one, so that the message is clear and not lost.
- Remember that people in general have a fairly short attention span (about 20 minutes) and can only absorb limited quantities of information at a time. Vary how you present material, provide opportunities for practice and/or discussion and don't try to include too much. It is much better to make a few points well, clearly and thoroughly than lots of points in a rushed and monotonous way. In a session that introduces dealing with health emergencies don't try to look at every single health emergency – make points which apply to all and deal with one or two, e.g. drowning and electrocution, in detail.
- Bring the session to a conclusion by providing a summary of what has been covered: the key points. Remind members of the aims of the session and try to recognise what they have contributed.
- Think about how you will evaluate the extent to which the aims and objectives of your presentation were achieved, e.g. through an evaluation questionnaire, achievement and comment of participants, feedback from colleagues who attended etc.

From the above list of dos there emerge a few don'ts. Don't:

■ try to do too much;
■ read directly from a prepared script, word for word;
■ go on for too long;
■ appear bored by the subject.

SUMMARY

This chapter has identified the many factors which influence health and access to health provision. People's perception of health depends on such things as their knowledge and socioeconomic circumstances and on many occasions they feel constrained from making healthy choices about their lifestyle. It has also provided a definition of health promotion activities and an examination of the theoretical models used in health promotion campaigns. The criteria for effectively analysing a health promotion strategy are discussed in relation to the models to promote health and well-being to others, though a much fuller discussion of methods of investigation is contained in Chapter 9. The chapter ends with a consideration of skills to promote health and well-being to others, including management and presentation skills. A detailed consideration of different health conditions, illnesses and diseases is beyond the scope of this book, though an activity in relation to this background knowledge, part of the health promoter's knowledge base, is presented at the end of the chapter. Other information relevant to health promotion is provided in Chapter 6, Chapter 7 and Chapter 9.

Activity (Part 2 – Higher)

1. Plan (and if possible, implement) a short presentation (about 10 to 20 minutes) about a health promotion topic of your choice. Write down all of the things you will do before the presentation, how you will present your material and how you will involve participants.

2. Choose a target audience and produce a campaign to promote the message that exercise or good diet promote a healthy lifestyle. You may choose one or more theoretical models to help you meet your aims and you must evaluate the effectiveness of your material.

3. Choose one health promotion campaign with which you are familiar and evaluate it in depth. You can choose a campaign feature in newspapers, magazines or on television or use either a presentation which you have attended or leaflets and posters. If possible use a campaign which uses a variety of methods to put its message across. You must also analyse how effective the campaign has been.

4. Although the provision of factual knowledge about illness and health topics has been beyond the scope of this book, such knowledge does nevertheless provide a background to health promotion. As a final activity you are asked to research three health/ill-health conditions and write or present a short account of each one. Some suggestions are:

- coronary heart disease;
- lung cancer;
- diabetes;
- HIV/AIDS.

SELECTED BIBLIOGRAPHY

Naidoo, J. and Wills, J. (1994). *Health Promotion: Foundations for Practice.* London: Balliere and Tindall.
This book examines the concepts of health, health promotion and health education. It also explains the dilemmas facing health promoters and evaluates the effectiveness of health promotion in practice.

Naidoo, J. and Wills, J. (1998). *Practising Health Promotion: Dilemmas and Challenges.* London: Balliere and Tindall.
The theory underpinning health promotion is explored using practice-based examples in this book. It is written for health promotion practitioners to enable them to be reflective in their practice.

Downie, R., Tannahill, C. and Tannahill, A. (1996). *Health Promotion: Models and Values.* Oxford: Oxford University Press.
Various health promotion models are evaluated in this book. It also presents an overview of the health promotion movement and stresses the socioeconomic factors affecting health.

CHAPTER 9
Research and gathering evidence

Janet Miller

Life with the gang was not all violence, sex and petty delinquency. Far from it. One of the foremost sensations that remains with me is the feeling of unending boredom, or crushing tedium, of listening hour after hour at street corners to desultory conversation and indiscriminate grumbling.

(Patrick, J., 1973, *A Glasgow Gang Observed*)

The two most common causes of death in Scotland are coronary heart disease (CHD) and cancer, each of which accounted for approximately a quarter of all deaths in 1996. In the same year, among people aged under 65, cancer was responsible for almost one third of deaths, and CHD for just under a fifth. Stroke is the third largest killer, and the three diseases are increasingly referred to as **'Scotland's Big 3'** ...

(The Scottish Office, 1998)

INTRODUCTION

This chapter aims to introduce you to different approaches to research, which can be used both in small-scale and large-scale studies. Research is used in all of the subjects of this book: in psychology; in sociology; in health promotion; in evaluating the effectiveness of practice. It is particularly relevant to the higher units Health Promotion (Outcome 3) and Human Development and Behaviour. The subjects dealt with in the chapter include: research and data, both quantitative and qualitative; sampling, including random sampling and quota sampling; methods of research including questionnaires, interviews and observation; epidemiology and health promotion; ethical considerations; using secondary sources including government reports and other published research; the application of research methods to health promotion; presentation of research findings.

By the end of the chapter you should be able to:
- understand the difference between quantitative and qualitative research;
- sample populations for research purposes;
- apply different methods appropriately to research subjects;
- understand the relationship between epidemiology and health promotion;
- understand some of the ethical implications of research;
- use secondary sources such as government statistics and historical documents;
- apply your knowledge to setting up a piece of small-scale research in sociology, psychology, care practice or health promotion;
- present your research findings clearly and effectively;
- understand the relationship between health promotion, models of health promotion and research.

THE RESEARCH PROCESS

The quotations at the beginning of the chapter both result from research, but the researchers have used different methods to obtain their information. The first results from an approach known as participant observation (explained on page 358) and the second from a statistical survey by the Scottish Office. They give some idea of the range of material which is covered in a chapter about research. The many disciplines which contribute to this book and to the process of care practice all benefit from and achieve progress through research. The Oxford English Dictionary defines research as:

An investigation directed to the discovery of some fact by careful study of a subject; a course of critical or scientific inquiry.

Research involves finding out about things and this involves gathering evidence of one kind or another, or of several different kinds. The approach used in research depends very much upon the **purpose** of the research. It also depends to some extent upon the **discipline** (e.g. psychology, sociology or health promotion) to which the research is likely to contribute and to the **perspective** of the researchers designing and conducting the research. This chapter focuses on providing an array of research methods which can be used separately or in combination to provide useful information. If you tackle any research yourself you will need to decide which of these research methods are appropriate to your purpose, discipline and perspective.

Research and data

Data is information. It consists of the information generated from research and can be quantitative or qualitative and gained from primary or secondary sources. These terms are explained below.

Quantitative data refers to quantities or numbers and is usually presented as a series of statistics, graphs, holograms or tables. The data published annually by the government in *Social Trends* and the *Scottish Statistical Survey* provide a lot of numerical information about the population, birth rates, divorce rates and so on. You will find examples of such data in the form of graphs in Chapter 1 and Chapter 8.

Here is some quantitative data about Scotland in 1995:
- The population of Scotland at 30 June 1995 was 5 136 600, an increase of 4200 since mid-1994.
- There were 60 051 live births in 1995, the lowest number recorded since civil registration was introduced in 1855.

Qualitative data is, as the title implies, about the quality of interactions, of social behaviour. It deals directly with meanings which people give to their situations and interactions. This data comes from in-depth interviews and from observation of behaviour in social situations (see pages 357–358). James Patrick's description of a Glasgow gang at the beginning of the chapter is an example of qualitative data.

Primary data means information produced by the researcher him or herself through his or her own research. It is original research which can be qualitative or quantitative or a mixture of the two. If **you** are conducting a piece of research the data which you generate is primary data.

Secondary data is any other data used. This can range from official statistics, newspaper and magazine articles, information from the internet, to historical documents, other published research and personal documents such as diaries, letters, photographs and autobiographies.

Choosing a research topic

The first decision which the researcher has to make is the topic which is to be researched. You may, for example, be interested to know more about drug abuse in the area in which you live or in the interactions of people in clubs or residential homes or in equality of opportunity in education. Once you have decided upon a broad area of study you could draw a thought explosion diagram like the one in Figure 9.2 overleaf, which asks lots of questions which you could pursue in your research.

From Figure 9.2 you may conclude that there are some aspects of the subject which you wish to know more about and these can form the basis of your research topic. There are some general considerations which should be taken into account at this early stage:

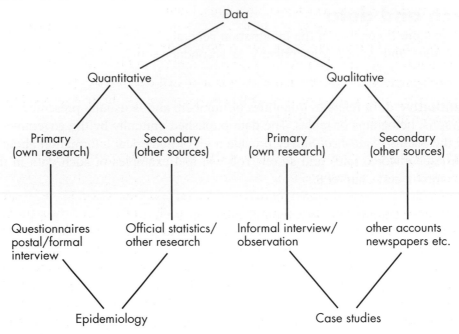

Figure 9.1 Diagram to show different methods of data collection and associated research methods

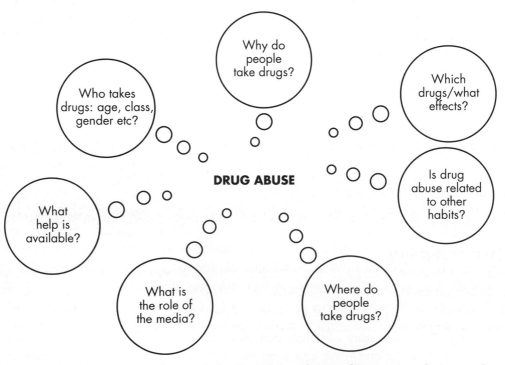

Figure 9.2 Thought explosion diagram in relation to drug abuse

- choose something in which you have a real interest;
- don't try to achieve too much in your research – narrow the research topic down to something which you think you can manage in the time you have available;
- once you have read the next sections on sampling and research methods, decide what your sample is going to be and what research methods you are going to use;
- keep a log book of your research, all of the steps you go through to decide your subject and obtain your data, with dates.

Choosing a sample – who is to be researched

It would be difficult and often impossible for researchers to investigate the whole of a relevant population in relation to their research topic. The expense and time alone would be quite prohibitive and often unnecessary. For such reasons data is usually gained from **samples** of the population, i.e. smaller numbers than the whole, often a percentage of the total relevant population. For example, in order to study voting intentions before an election a sample of .01 per cent of the population might be asked their voting intentions. From this sample generalisations can be made about how the whole population is likely to vote. Although this is unlikely to be 100 per cent accurate it gives a good idea and is a practical and affordable way of gaining information. Similarly, in health promotion research a sample of the population registered at a census may be asked about smoking or alcohol consumption. This will give some indication about these issues among the whole population.

Sampling may be one of six different kinds: random, stratified random, quota, multi-stage, snowball and non-representative. In addition there are two other ways in which a research population or subject may be chosen. These are case histories and life histories. To begin sampling a population is needed and this is termed the **sampling frame**. Examples of sampling frames are:

- the electoral register which lists all registered voters;
- a list of students registered in a school or college;
- a list of members of an organisation e.g. a political party;
- a list of the patients registered at a health centre.

Activity

Suggest three other sampling frames which might be useful in the fields of care and health promotion.

Random sampling

If the Electoral Register is taken as the sampling frame a **random sample** would give everyone on the register an equal chance of being selected. This could be achieved by selecting every 10th name for example, or by picking a 10 per cent sample out of a hat or by using tables of random numbers, selecting those on the register whose number coincides with those on the table.

Stratified random sampling

A stratified random sample is one which samples particular groups according to their representation in the sampling frame. If, for example, the sampling frame is all of the patients in a particular hospital and you wish your sample to be representative of the distribution of men and women in the hospital, your sample should have in it the same proportions of men and women as the sampling frame. If the sampling frame has 60 per cent women and 40 per cent men you will take separate random samples of all of the women and all of the men, giving a sample distribution of 60 per cent women and 40 per cent men.

The following is an example of stratified random sampling:

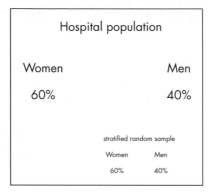

Figure 9.3 Stratified random sampling

The sample has the same proportion of men and women but is only 1/10th of the size.

Activity

This is a fairly straightforward sample but can you suggest any stratified random samples which could present difficulties to the researcher? What difficulties may you experience if you wish for a stratified random sample based upon social class?

You may have thought of the controversy over the definition of social class. Are you going to ask people to put themselves in a social class or are you going to do it? What difference would it make? Now try a similar analysis based upon ethnicity.

Quota sampling

Quota sampling is probably something which you have come across in the street without realising it. How many times have you passed a researcher on the high street armed with a clipboard evidently seeking out particular individuals? He or she may have been asked to interview 25 men and 25 women in each of the age categories 18–24, 25–30, 31–35, for example. Towards the end of the day he or she may be desperate to interview an elusive 25–30 year-old to complete the quota for each age group. This is quota sampling in action. It doesn't necessarily require a sampling frame but researches the views, attitudes or behaviours of particular kinds of individual.

Activity

Can you see any possible problems with quota sampling in terms of the representativeness of the sample?

You may have suggested that the time of day might mean that more non-working than working people are out and about. Think of a shopping street which you know and suggest what factors may influence who is around at a particular time.

Multi-stage random sampling

This method of sampling involves taking a sample of a sample. If, for example, you wanted to undertake a study of care in residential homes for older adults in Dundee you may find that it is far too costly and time-consuming to interview people in all of the homes even if you only interview a sample of people. You may therefore decide to sample 20 per cent of homes and then take a further sample of 20 per cent of people in those homes as subjects of your study. This would be a multi-stage sample since you have gone through more than one stage in the sampling process. You may decide to refine your study by initially taking a stratified random sample based upon a division of homes into private, voluntary and Local Authority run homes. Why may this improve the validity of your study?

Non-random sampling

The people studied may not be selected according to any of the above criteria but may be chosen for other reasons than their representativeness. In these cases the sample is a non-random one. **Snowball sampling** is one form of non-random sampling. Here the researcher obtains a sample beginning with one known contact who then suggests others who could be contacted who then suggest others and so on, rather like a snowball gathering snow as it is rolled along the ground. This method is useful if the subjects of the study are likely to be rather difficult to find or identify in a random sample. Can you think of examples of such people? Professional criminals are one such group and Taylor, L. (1984) began a study of professional crime in London through one initial contact who introduced him to others who introduced him to others. Although such a sample is not representative the information acquired in the study provides useful insights into an otherwise hidden world.

Another form of non-random sampling is **opportunity sampling**. Here the researcher studies certain people because they fulfil a particular requirement and are available to be studied. James Patrick's study of a Glasgow gang is one such example; Colin Lacey's *Hightown Grammar*, based upon the study of one school, is another. **Case studies** are a very specialised form of non-random sample where one person or a group of people are studied in depth in order to gain insights into their behaviour. These insights may be of interest in themselves but may also serve to generate new hypotheses and/or to disprove general theories (e.g. Murdock (1949) argued that the family is universal whereas a study by Gough (1959) of Nayor society showed that family structures based upon a marital bond are not universal).

Validity, reliability and pilot studies

Once a sample or population to be researched has been selected the next step is to decide how information is to be obtained. Two issues are important here before a decision is made. The first is **validity**. Do the research methods chosen or the questions asked actually produce information which is as accurate as possible about what is being studied? The second is **reliability** which can be tested according to the consistency and repeatability of the research. In order to maximise validity and reliability the researcher can conduct a **pilot study** which is really a trial run of the research. For example, questions to be asked can be tested out on a small number of people to see if they are easily understood and understood in the same way by all people being questioned; also that information produced is valid to the research. Now to the research methods themselves . . .

Questionnaires

One way to obtain information is to produce a questionnaire. It's impossible to produce a questionnaire about a subject unless you know something about the issues which surround it. Here some **background research** of secondary sources is very useful (see page 347). Once you have a grasp of the issues, you can begin to formulate questions which will, as far as possible, produce valid and reliable data. You may formulate an hypothesis which you wish to test in your research. An hypothesis is an idea or theory about what you might find out in your research. Your hypothesis might be, for example, that people who smoke catch more colds than people who don't smoke. Or you may use your research results to develop theories or make generalisations. Whatever the purpose of a questionnaire it requires a lot of planning which can be divided into five main stages:

- what questions are to be asked;
- who will be asked (the sample);
- how will the questionnaire be administered (e.g. by post, in a structured interview, over the telephone);
- how will information be recorded;
- how will the results be presented;
- what will be done with the results.

What questions?

In all questionnaires the wording of questions is extremely important. As a preliminary exercise suggest four things you should take into account when wording questions. You may have thought of:

- questions should be clear and unambiguous (i.e. no double meanings or room for mis-interpretation);
- questions should be in language which is easy to understand;

- questions should not suggest or prompt a particular answer e.g. the environment suffers from car pollution. Do you agree? yes ... no ...
- questions should not use loaded or emotional language. In the example above the word 'suffers' is an emotive word;
- avoid writing double questions. Do you think that there should be a Scottish Parliament and that it should have the power to set taxation levels? That's a double question. What happens if you want to answer 'yes' to the first part and 'no' to the second and all you have is one yes or no option? Why else do you think this isn't a very good question? It does assume that you have an opinion about a Scottish Parliament and also that you understand something about taxation.

Two kinds of questions may be produced in a questionnaire. **Closed questions** are those which require a yes or no answer or a simple tick in a box for a particular category. This kind of question is ideal for questionnaires requiring very specific, quantifiable information. A closed question may be:

Do you eat meat?   Yes ...   No ...

Another kind of closed question is a closed-coded question which may be:

Please tick your age category
18–21 ...
22–25 ...
26–30 ...
etc.

(Note that in writing ages the researcher has been careful not to repeat numbers or create ambiguity. If he or she had written 18–21; 21–25; 25–30; which line would a 21 year-old or a 25 year-old have ticked?)

Open questions invite more detailed answers and/or give people the opportunity to express an opinion. They produce qualitative data which gives a much fuller picture than closed questions, but is much more difficult to analyse. An example of a closed question leading to an open question is as follows:

Do you see yourself as a healthy person? (closed question)
Why or Why not? (open question).

Qualitative data is more fully considered later in the chapter.

How will the questionnaire be administered?
Questionnaires can be administered in several ways all of which have their own advantages and disadvantages. They may be sent through the post (postal questionnaires), handed to a particular

group of people to complete by a certain time or date, used in an interview, or the questions can be asked over the phone. Before reading further write down what you think may be the advantages and disadvantages of each of these methods.

Postal questionnaires have the advantage of being easy to send out, there are no time-consuming and expensive visits or telephone calls, a wide geographical area can be covered and there is no interviewer bias (defined below). One of the greatest disadvantages of the postal questionnaire is the low response rate. Researchers have found that there is usually a response rate of between 25 per cent and 50 per cent. There is no way of knowing whether this percentage is representative of the whole or has some special characteristics which makes respondents more likely to complete the postal questionnaire. If the respondent has any questions about the questions there is noone to clarify matters.

A questionnaire which is **handed out** to potential respondents has more chance of being completed and the researcher may be able briefly to answer questions about the questionnaire. This method can only be used for relatively small numbers of people and the researcher must ensure that respondents do not discuss their answer with one another since this could have an effect upon their answers.

A questionnaire which is administered as **a structured interview** has the advantage of having a trained interviewer on hand to answer any queries about questions and to clear up any misunderstandings. The response rate is much higher than for postal questionnaires but the process is time-consuming, expensive and the availability of interviewers and money severely limits the number of people who can be interviewed. There is also a danger of interviewer bias which can be defined as the influence which is exerted consciously or unconsciously by the interviewer upon those being interviewed. In spite of these disadvantages structured interviews have provided a great deal of useful information about various groups in the population. Kinsey, R. used structured interviews in a study of young people in Edinburgh in the early 1990s. He was

Activity

Either:

a)   construct a short questionnaire which aims to find out whether young people have been involved in criminal activity. List five potential problems you should avoid in constructing your questionnaire.

or

b)   construct a questionnaire which aims to find out how satisfied hospital in-patients were with the information they received before they were admitted to hospital. List five potential problems you should avoid in constructing your questionnaire.

particularly interested in looking at crime and delinquency and one of the findings presented was that seven out of ten young people questioned said that they had recently – albeit occasionally – committed an offence. These offences were usually of a petty nature: graffiti, small-scale vandalism, minor shoplifting; only rarely were they more serious. Another interesting finding of the study was that the pattern of offending crossed boundaries of social class and neighbourhood without discrimination.

The final questionnaire method listed is the **telephone questionnaire**. This may be useful as a tool of market research and has the advantage over postal questionnaires that clarification of questions may be provided by the interviewer. There are, however, some severe limitations in using this method as a way of gaining information about behaviour. Many people regard unsolicited phone calls as a serious intrusion of their privacy and the response rate is as low as that of postal questionnaires. The sample is restricted to people who are on the telephone and respondents may not be representative of this group. Why do you think this might be the case? There is also the issue of interviewer bias which can arise in any interview situation. This is not a favoured method of sociologists or psychologists. It may however be useful if respondents are warned in advance of the survey and are sympathetic to its aims. A telephone interview with the group of in-patients in the above activity, once they have arrived home may, for example, elicit a favourable response rate.

EPIDEMIOLOGY AND HEALTH PROMOTION

All of the above methods of collecting data are as relevant in health promotion as in the subjects of sociology, psychology and care practice. Questionnaires and statistical surveys are particularly relevant in epidemiology, which in turn is especially relevant to the study of health promotion. Epidemiology is the study of the distribution and determinants of health in specific populations. As a result of epidemiological studies, the factors which affect disease can be identified, e.g. the effect of smoking and diet on the incidence of heart disease. Seven main uses of epidemiology in public health have been identified by Thomson and Manuel (1997):

1. *To study the history of disease*
   Epidemiology studies the trends of a disease.
2. *Community diagnosis*
   What are the diseases, conditions, injuries, disorders, disabilities or defects causing health problems or death in the community?
3. *To look at risks of individuals as they affect groups or populations*
   What are risk factors, problems and behaviours that affect groups?
4. *Assessment, evaluation and research*
   How well do public health and health services meet the problems and needs of the population or group?
5. *Completing the clinical picture*
   Identification and diagnostic processes to establish that a condition exists or that a person has a specific disease.
6. *The identification of syndromes*

Helps to establish and set criteria to define syndromes, e.g. Down's, fetal alcohol and sudden death in infants.

7. *To determine the causes and sources of disease*
   Epidemiological findings allow for the control, prevention and elimination of the causes of disease, injury, disability or death.

Activity

Coronary heart disease and cancer are the two main killers in Scotland. Research relevant epidemiological studies to find information about which groups are most at risk and identify the contributory factors.

Methods used by epidemiologists

The main methods used by epidemiologists are as follows:

Surveys/cross-sectional studies which look at the prevalence or patterns of conditions or behaviours in populations or groups at one point in time. A cross-section is a sample and an example is the Allied Dunbar National Fitness Survey, which found that 70 per cent of the population in 1990 do not take enough exercise at work or in their leisure time to benefit their health. Such studies usually utilise questionnaires. What other methods of collecting data do you think could be used?

Case-control studies which examine the causes of a condition by comparing a group with the condition with a control group without the condition, e.g. an investigation into spina bifida has the hypothesis that the diet of the mother is a contributory factor in causing spina bifida. One study in Wales (1980) looked at babies with spina bifida and a control group of babies born to the same mothers without spina bifida and asked mothers to recall their diets during the different pregnancies. Can you think of any disadvantages of such a study? One you may have thought of is that mothers were asked to **remember** what they ate. This may not have been a very accurate record of what they actually ate.

Longitudinal studies. A more detailed account of these is given below.

Randomised control trial which compares a group who experience an intervention with a similar control group who do not. Often volunteers are asked to try a new drug and are compared with a similar group of people who are not taking that drug. Other randomised control trials do ask for volunteers but they do not know whether they are taking the drug or a placebo (a harmless substance similar in appearance to the drug being tested). Others do not take anything at all. Can you think of any problems with this method of investigation. Some participants may miss out on a potential cure; or the drug in question may prove ineffective and/or have serious side-effects.

Epidemiology forms the basis of much, though certainly not all, health promotion work. It is at the scientific end of the research spectrum emphasising factual, usually quantifiable, evidence and the testing of hypotheses (informed guesses about the expected result, which may be confirmed or not by the research in question). Health promotion also utilises qualitative research at the other end of the research spectrum, which emphasises the importance of individual perceptions and feelings. Further consideration of the links between health promotion, models of health promotion and research are provided at the end of the chapter.

QUALITATIVE RESEARCH

Interviewing provides a bridge between qualitative and quantitative research with structured interviews being at the quantitative end of the spectrum and unstructured interviews, which are really conversations with no predetermined questions, at the other. Most interviews fall somewhere along this spectrum and even an unstructured interview will often have some open-ended questions to guide the course of the interview within certain parameters. In addition to interviews, observation is one of the most commonly used techniques for obtaining qualitative data and is the approach favoured by those with an interactionist perspective. More attention is given to this on page 000 but as an activity at this point state why you think that interactionists favour a research approach which relies upon observation.

Unstructured interviews

Many of the skills needed in an unstructured or semi-structured interview are those required of a care worker. You need to be a good listener, to pick up on non-verbal as well as verbal cues, it helps to build a relationship based upon trust, empathy and unconditional positive regard, you need to ensure that confidentiality is maintained. The novelist Sybille Bedford summarises some of the complex skills required in an unstructured interview when she says:

'... to tell the truth about any complex situation requires a certain attitude in the receiver.'

'What is required in the receiver?'

'I would say first of all a level of emotional intelligence.'

'Imagination?'

'Disciplined.'

'Sympathy? Attention? '

'And patience. '

'All of these. And a taste for the truth – an immense willingness to *see*.'

R.D. Laing (1970), a Scottish psychiatrist who rebelled against traditional psychiatric treatment methods, used in-depth interviews to study people diagnosed with schizophrenia and their families. He was especially interested in their communication patterns and found that informal, unstructured interview situations enabled him to gain useful information about their communication and to come to some conclusions about how communication may play a part in the development of schizophrenia. In his study of professional criminals in London Laurie Taylor (in Morrison, 1986) also used interviews. Direct observation of criminal activity could have proved rather difficult and in-depth interviews were the next best thing. Informal interviews have the advantage over other qualitative methods of being practical, relatively cheap and able to cover fairly large samples. They have some disadvantages though. They are not as likely as observation to provide accurate data and they don't produce quantifiable data which can be tested as in structured interviews. If this is translated into research language, unstructured interviews do not have as much validity as observed situations or as much reliability as structured questionnaires. Our old enemy, interviewer bias, may also affect the outcome of the unstructured interview. People may say what they think the interviewer wants to hear or they may be affected by the personality, gender, class or colour of the interviewer. In research conducted by William Labov he found that black children responded more favourably to black interviewers than to white interviewers. Interviewees may not always be entirely honest in the answers they give. Clancy Segal in an article in *The Guardian*, 1984, suggests that Laurie Taylor may have been misled by the criminals he interviewed:

But I don't believe for a moment that anyone was telling the truth. The crooks would have been crazy to trust Taylor, even on the say-so of McVicar.

What do you think? Do you think Laurie Taylor's interviews with professional criminals were useful? Was he being fooled?

In spite of some disadvantages unstructured interviews continue to be one useful and very rich source of research material. Conversations, which resemble unstructured interviews, are a part of every day life and as long as the researcher is aware of the possible pitfalls and disadvantages of unstructured interviews they can be used to enhance our understanding of behaviour and social situations.

Observation

Observation can be **direct** (otherwise known as non-participant) or **participant**. Participant observation can be **overt** (those being studied are aware of the reason for the researcher's presence) or **covert** (the researcher's true identity is not known to those being researched). Direct observation involves looking at the behaviour of people in chosen social situations as an outsider. The observer does not involve him or her self in the situations or participate in their activities. Participant observation, on the other hand, involves the researcher in becoming involved in the lives of those being studied. For example, when Goffman (1968) wanted to study psychiatric hospital life he took a job as a hospital orderly and observed what happened in the hospital on a day-to-day basis. This formed the research material upon which he later constructed his theories about institutionalisation.

Observation aims to uncover the meanings behind people's actions, their day-to-day experiences, and attempts to show the 'reality' of people's lives. It has the advantage of providing more depth than quantitative methods but it is extremely time-consuming and researchers run the risk of becoming so involved in their subject that their objectivity may be diminished. Observation is a skill and is not as straightforward as it may sound. What factors do you think should be taken into account when observing a group of people? You may have thought of:

- the effect the observer may have on the group (researcher effect);
- the effect of the observer's perspectives and values; this involves the researcher in being as aware as possible of the preconceptions and values which are brought to the research situation;
- the different degrees of alertness of the observer at different times;
- the feelings which the subject being assessed may raise for the observer;
- the researcher's ability to record accurately what has occurred; the researcher needs to rely on memory until an opportunity arises to write things down.

As with any other research method the researcher has to prepare how the research will be carried out; how will he or she gain access to the group to be studied? Will observation be direct or indirect, overt or covert? How will data be recorded and analysed? Are there questions which it is hoped that the research will tackle? What questions? Is observation to be combined with any other research methods? Finally, perhaps the best way to illustrate the use of observation is to look at a couple of examples (see the following pages).

Longitudinal research

A great deal of research consists of a project which looks at situations, conditions, attitudes, behaviours and/or views at one particular time or over a fairly short period of time. Sometimes, for example in health and health promotion research, there is a need to follow people over a long period of time to see what changes have taken place, collecting information at intervals and charting change. Such research is called longitudinal research. One example of such a study is *The Child Health and Education Survey*, which has attempted to follow the development of every child born in Britain between 3 and 9 March 1958. A second example is the Whitehall 2 study of 10 000 civil servants which examined the incidence of ill-health among different employment grades (Brunner, 1996). These longitudinal studies are generally fairly large-scale quantitative studies, though some qualitative studies have extended over quite long periods, e.g. Avril Taylor's study of women drug users extended over two years. These studies are not, in general, regarded as longitudinal since they are continuous rather than concerned with change charted at intervals. Longitudinal research relies upon research methods outlined above: surveys, questionnaires, interviews, sometimes in combination with some qualitative research of a sample of the research population.

In spite of disadvantages, longitudinal research is the only known way to research a population systematically over a period of time and is useful in planning and understanding. Care and health provision can therefore benefit from the findings of such studies.

Example of participant observation – A Glasgow gang

James Patrick in *A Glasgow Gang Observed* was quoted at the very beginning of this chapter. Patrick's method of study was participant observation. He gained his contact with the gang through a gang member 'Tim' whom he had met when teaching in what was then called an approved school. Patrick says of the study:

> *It does not purport to be an authoritative or exhaustive treatise on Glasgow's juvenile gangs, but is a descriptive account of a participant observation study of one such gang which I met on twelve occasions ... In all I spent just under 120 hours in the field, and as my involvement with the gang deepened, so the hours lengthened until towards the end of January I was in the company of the gang during one week-end from seven o'clock on Friday evening until six on Sunday morning.*

Patrick went to some lengths to fit in with the gang, to dress like them, talk like them, feel like them, in his attempts to interpret the world as it appeared to them. Here is what he wore for the first meeting:

> *I was dressed in a midnight blue suit, with a twelve-inch vent, three inch flaps over the side pockets and a light blue handkerchief with a white polka dot (to match my tie) in the top pocket. My hair, which I had allowed to grow long, was newly washed and combed into a parting just to the left of centre ...*

Sometimes the participant observer had to observe things he'd rather not see:

> *We had been walking for some time, 'jist dossin', when Tim had an idea. 'Let's get right intae that lib'ry,' he said pointing to one of Glasgow's Public Libraries. Running into the building ... Dan McDade and Billy Morton began setting fire to the newspapers on display, as Tim and the others pushed books off the tables and emptied shelves of encyclopaedias and reference books.*

Participant observation also involved seeing violence and escaping from the police on more than one occasion. The event below followed a fight which had started at a dance at a club.

> *'Right, get up', someone ordered. Before I could carry out the command I was dragged to my feet by a policeman in plain clothes ...*

One thing which Patrick showed through his observations was the tedium of much gang life and the fact that 'specifically delinquent activities occupied only a small fraction of their waking hours'. The intimate view which Patrick was able to describe could not have been gained through any form of quantitative study.

An example of participant observation – Women drug users

Avril Taylor's (1993) study was based upon fifteen months of participant observation of over 50 women injecting drug users and upon in-depth interviews with 26 women carried out at the end of this period. Eight of the women formed a core group of 'key informants'. For Taylor the advantages of this kind of research stemmed from providing a very colourful and vivid view of the experiences of those being researched. Here are some quotes from women in the study which illustrate this:

> One day I couldnae get any DFs, the guy I got them from got caught selling them. I said to my pal, 'Come and we'll get a tenner bag?' She said, 'Aye. But where do we get it from?' I said 'We go down the road and get it off Brian,' . . .

Attitudes to pregnancy and children are reflected in many conversations:

> I didnae want it at first, but I love it to death already. I need something in my life. The responsibility will be good for me. I've never had anything worthwhile to look forward to or to make an effort for.

Or alternatively:

> When I go in to have the wean you know I'm no' keeping the wean . . . Maybe if I wasnae on drugs at all it would have been a different story. Well I'd have been a different person obviously.

These quotations together with the way in which the study is structured in terms of issues which were important to the women themselves give the study a validity which would have been missing in a study based upon a quantitative method of research.

Activity

In order to appreciate some of the challenge, complexity and fascination of participant observation it is a good idea to try it out on a small scale. Choose a situation which is new to you but not too difficult to go to. Some suggestions are given below but you may wish to choose something completely different. Observe what happens, the inter-actions which take place, the meanings which actions have for the participants, the way they behave and any other aspects which seem relevant. Write a detailed account as soon afterwards as possible, noting all of these things. Review what you have written in terms of the knowledge which it provides and how this knowledge differs from, is better than or worse than knowledge which may have been gathered in other ways, e.g. from interviews or questionnaires. Discuss any ethical issues which you think arise (see discussion of these below).

Suggested research situations:

1. a hospital or health centre reception area;

2. the Sheriff Court;

3. a concert;

4. a betting shop;

5. a sports event;

6. a school or college dining room.

Activity

Longitudinal research has both advantages and disadvantages. List three possible advantages and three possible disadvantages of using such research.

You may have thought of:

Advantages

1. Gives a view of people at different points in time

2. Can be used to look at the effects of planned changes e.g. the effect of a health promotion programme (using controls).

3. They do not rely upon people's memories to remember past events.

Disadvantages

1. If the sample is voluntary it may be necessary to find people willing to participate over a long period of time.

2. Being part of a longitudinal survey may affect the behaviour of participants.

3. Some people are likely to drop out for various reasons. The ones who remain may not be representative of the original cohort.

Some ethical considerations of research

When conducting any piece of research, the researcher should be asking him/herself what the rights and wrongs are of this research, i.e. what ethical question does it raise? Does the research constitute an intrusion of individual privacy? Are people's rights adequately protected? One form of research, covert participant observation, raises these issues more extremely than other methods. Covert participant observation involves the researcher in a situation where his or her true identity is unknown. It does involve misleading people into thinking that you are one of them. Those researchers who have carried out such research justify this through the results of their findings. Sometimes they are able to demonstrate that there have been uninformed judgements made about particular groups which are shown through covert participant observation to be quite unfounded. For example Humphreys (1970) conducted a now famous study of homosexual behaviour by taking the role of 'voyeur' (someone who gains pleasure from watching homosexual acts) which was accepted in the homosexual milieu of 'tearooms' (public toilets). This study enabled Humphreys to gain insights into the activities of 'secret deviants'. They were secret in the sense that they were often not part of the gay scene but led otherwise 'normal' lives and often had a wife and children.

Activity

Set out ethical arguments for and against Humphreys' study and come to a conclusion about whether he was justified in using covert participant observation.

Randomised control trials also raise ethical issues since people are used in scientific experiments to test treatments or drugs. Although permission is sought from participants, they have little or no choice about which group they will belong to. Again ethical arguments are based upon the eventual benefits to large numbers of people if the treatment or drug proves to be successful. It is essential, though, in conducting any research, to build in safeguards which protect individual rights.

Using secondary sources

Secondary sources are any kinds of information used other than those gained from direct research. These can range from official statistics, newspaper and magazine articles, information from the Internet factsheets and previously conducted research to diaries, autobiographies and historical records. Although secondary sources can be extremely useful, especially in the initial stages of research when an attempt is being made to find out about a subject of interest and to place it in context, there are some difficulties in their use. Can **you** think of three difficulties associated with using secondary sources?

You may have thought of the following:

- secondary sources may have had a different purpose from the research being conducted and therefore will not be entirely relevant;

■ secondary sources may be biased;

■ secondary sources may be incomplete or only cover part of the problem being studied.

Some researchers have made the study of secondary sources the subject of their study looking, for example, at the way in which the media (TV, newspapers, etc.) cover such subjects as violence, child sexual abuse or industrial relations. This form of research is known as content analysis and is examined more fully below on page 000. Specific kinds of secondary source will now be looked at.

Official statistics

There is a vast array of such statistics available to the researcher ranging form the Census to regular issues of *Social Trends* and the Scottish Statistical Survey. **The Census** is a huge social survey conducted every ten years (1981, 1991, etc.) which is based on a questionnaire completed by every household in Britain. It not only records the number of people in Britain but provides a lot of other information about such subjects as age distribution, household size, employment, education and housing. **Social Trends**, published by HMSO (Her Majesty's Stationery Office), is a book published annually containing statistics about the British population and trends or changes which the statistics illustrate. The subjects covered are similar to those of the Census. **The Scottish Statistical Survey** contains similar information for Scotland and, again, is published annually. Other government reports are published at intervals, e.g. The Scottish Health Survey 1995, the Annual Report of the Registrar General for Scotland and the General Household Survey. If you look back at Chapter 1 you will see several examples of the use of the statistics contained in such reports. They have the advantage of being easily obtained, clearly laid out and often cover large samples or all of the population. Many arguments have, however, been levelled against the use of official statistics in isolation as reliable sources of information.

Activity

Can you suggest any possible problems in using published crime statistics to provide a picture of actual crimes committed?

Some problems you may have thought of are:

■ reported crime is not all crime;

■ of reported crimes only some are ever acted upon.

This can depend upon whether the 'crime' is considered sufficiently serious by the police or the procurator fiscal. Whether a crime is acted upon and how it is acted upon can be influenced by such variables as social class, sex, sexual orientation, colour or religion.

Activity

What disadvantages can you see in using official statistics of suicide to provide an actual picture of suicides committed? What factors may have influenced these statistics?

The mass media and content analysis

Newspapers and other media products (e.g. TV programmes, magazines) can provide useful secondary data for research purposes. These have the advantage of providing up-to-date information about many issues of current interest. Some disadvantages however should be taken into account. These sources were not produced for the purpose of your research and may be only partially relevant; they may be biased and/or attempt to influence the way you think. Newspapers sometimes purposely set out to sensationalise an issue in order to sell copies or may sometimes downplay an issue in co-operation with government or legal agencies. In *A Glasgow Gang Observed*, for example, James Patrick states that

> ... *the police had informed the press that publishing gang names only pandered to the 'mini-gangsters' craving for publicity. ... it has not always been apparent that the appeals were heeded.*

It is sometimes useful to use the media as **the** subject or part of the subject of your research. Here a research method called **content analysis** may be used. Content analysis involves looking at how a subject is treated by newspapers and/or other aspects of the media. It usually combines quantitative and qualitative methods by analysing how much space is devoted to it and what sort of coverage is given. The use of content analysis is demonstrated in the passage below based on research of the Glasgow University Media Group (GUMG) into coverage of child sexual abuse (CSA).

Activity

1. What issues do you think it is important to examine when carrying out a study of child sexual abuse?

2. What does the above quotation tell you about media coverage of child sexual abuse?

3. What reasons can you give for the way in which the newspapers and TV covered the subject of child sexual abuse?

4. Choose a subject of current media interest and conduct a small-scale content analysis of newspaper and TV coverage over a period of one week.

The content analysis of all press and TV news coverage of CSA which appeared during 1991 resulted in a comprehensive archive of 1668 press items and 149 TV news bulletins which covered this topic during that year. Initial findings from the content analysis reveal that 71 per cent of all the press coverage, and 83 per cent of all the TV news coverage was case based. In other words most reports focused on describing events around one particular incident or set of allegations, rather than discussing areas of general concern. The biggest single category of coverage (27 per cent for the press) was of the alleged organised sexual abuse in the Orkney Islands where several children were taken into care but later returned to their parents with no charges ever brought (see Asquith 1993 for a discussion of the case). The one exception to the case domination of reporting was that a significant proportion of coverage, approximately 9 per cent for both TV and press, concerned the general question about how best to intervene when abuse was suspected (what we termed the 'diagnosis and intervention' category).

Other documentary material and secondary data

There are many other sources of secondary data which should be approached with the same caution as those detailed above. These sources may include historical documents, case records, other relevant research, government reports, autobiographical and biographical information which can include letters, diaries and personal papers. Historical documents can be extremely useful in coming to an understanding of how present day patterns of social life or care provision have come about. One tremendous source of such material for the care worker is The Heatherbank Museum of Social Work located at Caledonian University. This museum, the only one of its kind in Europe, was founded by a social worker, Colin Harvey, who felt that as the whole field of social work and care practice was changing, vast sources of historical material could be lost. He set about collecting together books, artifacts, documents, photographs, films, journals, anything to do with the history of care practice and social work. He and his wife organised exhibits, all from their house, Heatherbank, in Milngavie. Sadly both Colin and Rosemary Harvey have died, but their collection lives on, has been moved to Caledonian University and is constantly being added to and utilised by people ranging from school and college students to researchers and teachers.

Case records can be useful sources of data about care practice but vary enormously in the quality and quantity of information which they provide. Cheetham et al (1992) point out that in case notes:

potentially relevant information (for research purposes) may be omitted, the assumptions underlying descriptions of clients and their problems may be unclear and the meanings attached by clients to the intervention are likely to be unrepresented. On a more practical level, the information contained in case records will often be incomplete, insufficient or inappropriate to the needs of the evaluative researcher.

In using case records the researcher must also ensure that confidentiality is maintained. McIvor (1989) used case materials in her study of Community Service by offenders in Scotland and although they contained much useful information, such as absences from work placements,

Figure 9.4 From the Heatherbank archives, circa 1900 – Quarries village and Eastpark Home

they were lacking in detail about intervention on behalf of clients. Case records usually need to be supplemented by research specifically aimed at whatever the research subject happens to be. The use of **other relevant research** meets with the same problem, though the student needs to be aware that a great deal of research material already exists, the results of which can save time and money and lack of repetition. For example the Social Work Research Centre at Stirling University, the University of Edinburgh's Scottish Young People's Survey, the Centre for Alcohol and Drug Studies at Paisley University and The Health Education Authority all produce research documents and research bibliographies useful to the student carrying out research into care practice.

Government reports provide the government with information about issues of concern. These reports are usually commissioned by the government of the day and their findings are inevitably coloured by the perspectives of those responsible for compiling them. They do, however, often contain a useful research component which can be used as background information for your own research. The Wagner Report, for example, looked at choice in residential care and produced a lot of evidence relating to good and poor practice. The Black Report (1980) into inequalities in health, a very controversial document which was not acted upon by the government of the day, brought out starkly the connections between poor health and poor housing, education, low income and generally the inequalities existing in society as a whole. The consultation paper, 'Working together for a Healthier Scotland' (HMSO, 1998) presented a lot of information about Scotland's health and the influences upon it.

Other more individual sources of information, diaries, letters, tombstones, pictures, give insights into social experience and can add a personal, exciting and interesting dimension to balance other quantitative and qualitative material. Here's a quotation from Jimmy Boyle who wrote an autobiographical account of his own experiences of Glasgow gang life.

Around this time the 'Wild Young Cumbie' were very active, getting involved in lots of heavy fighting scenes and getting the name of being the best fighting gang ever to come out of the Gorbals . . . Some of them were involved in a big fight that was reminiscent of a wild west saloon brawl . . . and there was a big court trial afterwards where John McCue, Artie Austin and three others were involved, and all given sentences . . . The Press made a big deal of it . . . All of us younger kids would pore over these newspapers and the press coverage only confirmed the years of adulation that we had given them. Being in the papers was a great thing to us.

Do you think the above account provides reliable data? What distinguishes this account from an account based upon research? You may have thought of the personal nature of this description, the fact that the writer was himself involved in the situation, that the writer is free to express opinion as well as fact, that there were no stated aims or objectives of the work apart from providing an interesting and vivid account, that the writer was relying on memory of events a long time in the past . . . or you may have thought of other factors.

Activity

1. Take any of the above secondary sources. Make two columns and on the left write down advantages of using that source and on the right list the disadvantages.

2. Choose a research topic and list the secondary sources which may be useful to you.

Combining several research methods

Many researchers do not just use one research method but emphasise that there is a need for different research methods to investigate different aspects of a problem or issue. The use of a combination of quantitative and qualitative methods is known as **triangulation**. Bryman, A. (1988) has suggested a number of ways in which this combination could be useful. Before reading the list below you should try to think of four ways in which you think a combination of qualitative and quantitative research methods may be beneficial. Bryman's suggestions are:

1. *Qualitative research can be used to check on the accuracy of the conclusion reached on the basis of each.*
2. *Qualitative research can be used to produce hypotheses which can then be checked using quantitative methods.*
3. *The two approaches can be used together so that a more complete picture of the social group being studied is produced.*
4. *Qualitative research may be used to illuminate why certain variables are statistically correlated.*

In their study of the occupational and educational aspirations and expectations of 13 year-olds in four contrasting Scottish towns, Furlong and Cartmel (1995) used a combination of formal questionnaires producing quantitative data, and short essays and interviews which produced qualitative material. The one form of evidence complemented the other and produced a much more complete picture than either could have produced alone.

Some of the quotes from young people are as follows:

I do not like school but it's worth going because it's the only way to get a job.

I think when I'm older I will hardly see my family because I think most people will have jobs in other places and not Steeltown and if there are some they are not good jobs.

I'll be working as a teacher in Clydemouth Primary.

I'm going to America and own my own hairdressing business.

Dry statistics are brought to life by the real-life statements of the young people.

Presenting research findings

The way in which research is written up and presented makes a tremendous difference to its usefulness. Partridge and Barnitt (1987) have presented some useful guidelines and the list below is adapted from their work. When writing up a piece of research try to present information about the following as clearly as possible:

- *a statement about the purpose of the research, the background to the study and the questions it is attempting to answer;*
- *the reasons for doing the research; research aims and objectives;*
- *a review of secondary sources / background information;*
- *the information which the research is designed to collect;*
- *methods used for collecting information and why these are used;*
- *a description of any pilot study which you conducted, its results and what was changed as a result;*
- *the findings of the research and all statistical data;*
- *a discussion of the findings;*
- *an account of difficulties encountered, how they were dealt with and whether they affected the results;*
- *a list of references, sources of help and any other relevant information.*

Research and health promotion: A summary

The value of epidemiology in studying the distribution and determinants of health has already been discussed. Below are some suggestions for methods which could be used to look at health promotion issues. You could choose one of these issues yourself and conduct some research using one or more methods, writing up your results as suggested above. You could research:

- **changes in health awareness** using questionnaires, an analysis of media coverage, interviews, observation etc.;
- **changes in knowledge or attitudes** using observation, interviews, questionnaires in before and after situations;
- **changes to the environment** using statistical measures, observation;
- **changes in behaviour** using observation, recording behaviour, questionnaires;
- **changes in policy** using secondary sources, observing organisational changes;
- **changes in health status** using statistical health indicators (weight, height, blood pressure etc.), surveys using questionnaires, analysis of published statistics.

The methods used and the nature of a piece of research are often influenced or determined by the model or models of health promotion which are used. Figure 9.5 shows the relationships among the models of health promotion discussed in Chapter 8 and the research methods discussed in this chapter.

SUMMARY

In this chapter you have been introduced to issues relating to research and to several research methods. The chapter began by looking at the research process and distinguishing between quan-

Model	What is measured/assessed	Research methods used
Medical	Impact of health promotion on preventing disease and increasing life expectancy.	Epidemiological methods: randomised control trial; longitudinal studies etc.
Educational	Changes in knowledge, attitudes and skills.	Pre and post testing of knowledge; questionnaires; observation.
Behavioural	Behaviour and changes in behaviour e.g. smoking.	Questionnaires, informal interview; observation.
Community Development	Empowerment of local population/social and environmental factors.	Questionnaires; observation; longitudinal studies.
Marketing	Changes in attitudes, beliefs and behaviours; success of marketing strategy.	Questionnaires, interviews, longitudinal studies.
Political	Changes in policy and legislation	Questionnaires, observation to monitor effects of political change e.g. on housing.
Client-centred	Beliefs; how people feel; whether empowerment/ equity are achieved.	Questionnaires and interviews; observation.

Figure 9.5 The relationship between models of health promotion and research

titative and qualitative research. Several ways of sampling research populations were described. Research methods were explained, including questionnaires, interviews, observation, epidemiology in health promotion, using the media and secondary sources. Activities gave you the opportunity to apply your learning to specific situations. Guidance was given about presenting research findings. Some specific suggestions were made in relation to researching health promotion topics, though the whole chapter is relevant to this subject.

Activity

1. Find one piece of written research relevant to your area of study or which is of particular interest to you. Analyse it in terms of the list of statements above under the heading 'presenting research findings' and write something about each item on the list, i.e. you should say something about the purpose of the research, the reasons for carrying it out, the methods used etc.

2. Design a short questionnaire to research one of the following among a small sample of people you know:

- smoking behaviour;
- attitudes to disability;
- family contacts.

SELECTED BIBLIOGRAPHY

Lewis, I. and Munn, P. (1997). *So you want to do research? A guide for teachers on how to formulate research questions.* Edinburgh: The Scottish Council for Research in Education.
This is a beautifully straightforward account of research methods; don't be put off by 'teachers' in the title.

Williams, L. (1994). *GCSE: Finding Out About Society.* London: Bell and Hyman.
Another clear, step-by-step account of how to do research.

Haralambos, M. and Holborn, M. (1995) *Sociology: Themes and Perspectives.* London: Collins Educational.
A more advanced, but very interesting, critical analysis of research methods and issues.

Ewles, L. and Simnett, I. (1999). *Promoting Health: a practical guide.* London: Balliere Tindall.
Examines research specifically in relation to health promotion.

Naidoo, J. and Wills, J. (1998). *Practising Health Promotion.* London: Balliere and Tindall.
Also examines research specifically in relation to health promotion, with clear examples and two relevant chapters: 'Research for health promotion' and 'Effectiveness and evidence-based practice in health promotion'.

CHAPTER 10

Integration and conclusions

Janet Miller

INTRODUCTION

The chapters of the book so far have separated related subjects for individual study. The task of this chapter is to weave the subjects together in order to enable you to begin to see the ways in which they are connected. This is achieved partly through reference to the case study, 'A tale of two families', and also through revisiting some of the subjects already discussed, relating them to one another. Human development is considered in relation to equality of opportunity. Both of these subjects are considered in relation to interpersonal skills and to health promotion. Some concepts, such as socialisation, need and institutionalisation, are seen as link words among the subjects of the book. Several activities enable you to make your own connections. At the end of the chapter some conclusions are presented together with guidelines for future study.

CASE STUDY – A TALE OF TWO FAMILIES

(Questions relating to this study appear at various points throughout the book.)

The MacDonald Family

Senga MacDonald and her children live in a rented five-apartment council house a few miles from the centre of Edinburgh. The area in which they live is one of a large 1950s housing scheme which has gained an air of reasonable respectability, with a mixture of houses and flats rented from the local authority and properties which have been purchased and are now owner-occupied. The scheme borders on tenement land which stands between it and the city centre. The tenements are a mixture of properties which are privately owned, rented from the council or privately rented, and the population is culturally diverse, with a mixture of religious and ethnic groups. It is here that the Ahmed family lives in a large, owner-occupied second floor tenement. **Joe MacDonald**, Senga's former husband, also lives in this area. The children of the MacDonald family and the Ahmed family attend the same schools, shop at the same shops and their teenage children sometimes hang about on the same streets.

The MacDonald family in 1999 consists of:

Senga MacDonald, aged 36, works part-time as a care assistant in a home for older adults. She has to work very hard and regrets that she didn't stay on at school or gain any qualifications. She tries to encourage her children with their school work. She has recently been trying to cut down on her smoking (about 10 cigarettes a day at the moment) and to lose weight. She was born and brought up in Edinburgh in the area in which her ex-husband now lives.

Joe MacDonald, aged 42, left the family home two years ago and lives in a tenement with his girlfriend, aged 29. He is unemployed but has occasional work as a driver for various home delivery Chinese and Indian restaurants. He says that he can't see the point of getting qualifications. He enjoys a drink and smokes about 20 cigarettes a day. Joe seems to have lost interest in his children since he and his girlfriend got a flat together, though his son, Andy, goes to visit him sometimes, especially if he needs money.

Andy MacDonald, aged 16, lives at home with his Mum, sister and brother. He is still at school taking some modules after gaining 4 Standard Grades at general level last year. He would rather have left school but couldn't see much chance of getting a job. He plans to go to the local FE College next year. He'd like to be rich and famous but is having such a struggle with his modules that he thinks there must be an easier way. Although he's very fond of his Mum and definitely doesn't want to end up like his Dad, he also wants to establish his independence from both of them. His friends at school encourage him to go drinking and clubbing at week-ends and sometimes evenings in between. His Mum despairs about this but Andy doesn't seem to take any notice of anything she says. He smokes about 10 cigarettes a day depending on how much money he has.

Linda MacDonald, 13, has cerebral palsy. She has difficulty with speech, a mild learning disability and is unable to walk. She attends a special school and goes there on the school bus each morning. She is still very dependent on her Mum who has to attend to all of her needs when she is at home. Linda and her family have a social worker who attends her reviews, supports the family when necessary and has arranged respite care for Linda on a rolling basis every six weeks. This provides her Mum with a much-needed break.

Joey McDonald is 5, a little clown with a great sense of humour and huge quantities of energy. He loves his toy building games and a toy garage. He is in P1 and loves it. He never seems to stop and Senga finds him quite exhausting, especially if she has had a hard day at work. He has just been allocated a male befriender by the Social Work Department and Senga hopes that this will provide him with a stabilising influence and will give her a break sometimes.

Senga's mother, Jean, aged 64, lives locally and offers support on an occasional basis, but she works in a shop and doesn't have a lot of spare time or energy. Her second husband (not Senga's father) died two years ago and her 86 year-old mother, Annie, is in a Local Authority residential home not far away. Jean visits Annie a couple of times a week after work and at least once at the week-end. Annie has severe arthritis, which limits her mobility, and mild dementia.

Senga's sister, Maureen, lives on a housing scheme a few miles from the city centre. She has three children and has had a very chequered life with a partner involved in both drink and drugs. Maureen has spent periods in a homeless unit and has now left her partner for good. Her oldest child, Alistair, is looked after by the Local Authority in a children's unit after committing a series of offences.

The Ahmed Family

The Ahmed family in 1999 consists of:

Hassan Ahmed, aged 45, is an accountant who qualified when he was in his early 30s. He set up his own practice in partnership with a fellow student. He works very long hours, spends less and less time with his family but is improving the business – he and his partner have almost doubled the number of clients in the past five years. He has some worrying health complaints and thinks he may have an ulcer, but hasn't got time to go to the doctor. He has gained quite a lot of weight recently. He is very determined that his children get a good start in life and stresses the importance of a sound education.

Aisha Bibi, Hassan's wife, is ten years younger than her husband, a very cheerful person most of the time, but recently she has become very concerned about her husband's health. She works part-time for a voluntary organisation, supervising a sheltered housing complex, and loves her work. She tries to encourage other Asian women to assert their independence but is viewed with some suspicion by many of their husbands and families. She also encourages her children to do well at school and helps them with their homework. Her own family viewed education as the key to success and Aisha attended Edinburgh University where she gained a Degree in Languages (French and Spanish).

Tanveer Ahmed, aged 15, attends the local secondary school. He is doing well there and is expected to achieve several credits in his Standard Grades and to continue at school to achieve Advanced Highers. He wants to be an engineer but for the time being works one or two evenings a week in his uncle's shop. He also is expected to help with his younger brother at the week-end. Tanveer has a great wish to be accepted by the boys in his class at school, who often tease him about his colour and his younger brother who has a disability. Whenever he gets the chance he lingers after school with a group of boys and goes to 'Mac-Donald's' with them for a laugh, a coffee and a cigarette. He tells his Mum he goes to the library.

Nabeil Ahmed, aged 11, was born with a severe heart condition which has necessitated several operations. After one major operation he had a stroke which affects his left side. He has delayed development, has great difficulty with speech and is unable to walk. His doctors think that he may eventually catch up intellectually and may gain some power of speech, though it is unlikely that he will ever walk. He faces the prospect of more heart operations in the future. He attends the same school as Linda MacDonald, though is in a different class. He is well-loved and supported by his family, though they took a long time to accept his illness and disability. His mother is especially concerned that he has all the opportunities possible to develop in the same ways as other children. Although the family has been reluctant to request outside help they have approached the Social Work Department to assist with day care for Nabeil during the summer so that Aisha can continue to work.

Hassan's older brother, Afzal, his sister-in-law Sira and their three children, Faisal, Asif and Nadia, live in another apartment in the same area. Hassan and Afzal originally set up in business together to run a shop but Afzal now owns the shop, whilst Hassan runs his accountancy business. The brothers do help one another out and attend the mosque together. Their mother, who speaks very little English, lives with Afzal and his wife. She is very helpful with housework and cooking but is a very domineering woman with rather traditional views. Sira resents her constant presence and her attempts to influence her children's behaviour. Tanveer gets on well with his grandmother whom he visits most days. She is always giving him little treats and telling him how she expects great things of him. Although this sometimes makes him uncomfortable, they have a good rapport which is without the stresses which his parents and aunt and uncle experience in her presence.

In the above study there are several members who require care both on an informal basis by family members and on a formal basis in care situations. These family members are: **Linda MacDonald** who goes for respite care at Ivy Unit; **Alistair McKay** who is looked after by the local authority children's unit at 16 Fir Street; **Nabeil Ahmed** who will attend Heron Day Centre during the summer; Hassan and Afzal's elderly **mother** who is due to go for a week of respite care at a home for older people, Queen's View.

Two family members work as care workers. **Senga MacDonald** works as a care assistant in a home for older adults. **Aishi Bibi** works for a voluntary organisation, supervising a sheltered housing complex.

Each of the units which the families use or will use is described below.

Ivy Unit is a twelve-bed, purpose-built voluntary organisation respite care unit for children with disabilities. Each of the 50 children who attends, comes for respite every six weeks (three nights Friday to Monday alternating with four nights Monday to Friday) and also for a one week summer holiday. There is a good staff ratio and a committed and trained staff team. Staff work well together, have regular meetings to discuss their work and aim to meet the needs of the children who attend through a combination of care and activities.

16 Fir Street is a small children's unit at present accommodating seven children in the age range twelve to sixteen who are looked after by the Local Authority. Most of the children attend local schools, though two of the children, including Alistair McKay, attend a care and education centre as day pupils. Here they are taught in small classes and their usual disruptive behaviour can be 'managed' by a trained and dedicated care and teaching team. There is a high rate of sickness among staff at Fir Street, so that there either aren't enough staff on duty or unfamiliar sessional staff cover for absence. Although the staff want to do a good job, only four out of eight have any kind of qualification at present. The Local Authority is hoping that all of the others will receive some training in the next couple of years.

Heron Day Centre is run by a voluntary organisation and accommodates ten children with moderate to severe disabilities during the summer months. A mixture of trained staff and untrained temporary staff are employed to work with the children, whose ages range from three to twelve. They assess the needs of each individual child through meetings with them, their families and other workers and devise a programme to meet these needs.

Queen's View home for older adults is a private home with 25 residential beds and five respite beds. Everyone has a single room with bathroom. Meals are eaten communally at set times. Very few of the staff have a formal qualification in care but the unit manager ensures that all staff have an induction training in the values and principles of care practice. There is a cheerful atmosphere in the home and people seem to enjoy living there. Some of the more active residents, however, regret the fact that there are not more opportunities for outings and activities.

The MacDonald and Ahmed families are referred to at various points in the text, especially in Chapters 3, 5, 7 and in this chapter. It is useful to look at them in terms of what they can illustrate about the content of the book. They can be used as the basis for activities which link the different strands with one another. Some ideas in relation to this are set out below and others you are expected to pursue yourself.

Links among the various strands of the book are set out in four sections below, though it is recognised that this exploration of links is not exhaustive. The four sections are:
- 1. the strands of human development and behaviour;
- 2. human development and behaviour and promoting equal opportunities in a care context;
- 3. human development and behaviour, promoting equal opportunities in a care context and interpersonal skills for care;
- 4. human development and behaviour, promoting equal opportunities in a care context and health promotion.

1. The strands of human development and behaviour – linking a developmental, life course perspective with other perspectives from developmental psychology and sociology

The study of human development and behaviour has been considered from a developmental life course perspective (Chapter 3), perspectives of developmental psychology (Chapter 4) and from sociological perspectives (Chapter 5). These chapters presented different viewpoints from which to look at many of the same things. Some themes, such as the nature/nurture debate and socialisation, ran through all of these chapters. It is perhaps useful at this point to recap the starting points from which these different strands begin as a way of beginning to pull them together.

Chapter 3 introduced **development** as a gradual unfolding, as an increase in complexity involving change and movement, and **behaviour** as the ways in which people conduct themselves. The chapter looked at influences upon development and behaviour (such as genetic, socioeconomic and cultural) and at strands of development (physical, intellectual, emotional and social) as they are manifested at different stages in the life cycle (0–2, 2–5 etc.). The chapter was fairly descriptive without much theory or presentation of different perspectives or ways of looking at things. This is where Chapters 4 and 5 come in useful. These two chapters present different perspectives or viewpoints from which to examine human development and behaviour in order that you can begin to develop a deeper understanding and broaden your ideas.

Developmental psychology is concerned with the study of how **individuals** develop – biologically, intellectually, socially and emotionally – over the period of their lives. In Chapter 4 several perspectives are presented including a Humanistic perspective (Rogers and Maslow) and a lifespan perspective (Erikson). Maslow's humanistic perspective presents a hierarchy of need. Through an understanding of this you can begin to associate some of the ideas acquired in Chapter 3, with developmental psychology. You can, for example, look at the different strands of development (physical, intellectual, emotional and social) in terms of Maslow's hierarchy, recognising that until some basic physical tasks have been accomplished through the meeting of basic physical needs, it is very difficult to proceed towards the fulfilment of the intellectual/cognitive tasks usually associated with progress towards self-actualisation. Almost all of the information presented in relation to development through the life cycle in Chapter 3 can be interpreted in terms of the perspectives presented in Chapter 4.

Activity

Choose a different perspective from Chapter 4 (i.e. not Maslow) and apply it to the interpretation of one aspect of development discussed in Chapter 3.

Developmental psychology and sociology

The perspectives of **developmental psychology** focus attention upon individual development. **Sociology** comes from a different direction and, whilst still interested in individuals, begins with society, its structures, institutions, cultures, and with social interactions. An understanding of human development and behaviour needs both of these disciplines. One way to examine the ways in which these two disciplines complement one another is to look at the ways in which each discipline studies concepts which are common to both. These concepts include socialisation, attachment and separation, self concept, transition and loss. Figure 10.1 summarises the perspectives from developmental psychology and sociology and some shared concepts.

Socialisation is taken as an example in illustrating the relationships among perspectives and disciplines. One way to show these relationships is through the invention of a dialogue. Imagine a scenario where several Scottish descendants of some rather famous theorists come together to discuss socialisation, just as the first Scottish parliament for over 300 years is about to begin its work. This account is entirely fictional!

McMaslow (humanistic developmental psychologist)
If you look at my uncle's hierarchy of needs you'll appreciate that although it doesn't specifically mention socialisation it is of great importance in reaching self-actualisation. An individual who has not acquired any ideas about how to behave in society, through the socialisation process, will have little sense of belonging to anything, probably won't even feel safe. You can't progress up the hierarchy of need towards self actualisation if you don't feel safe. An individual who hasn't been socialised into some form of family life probably won't be able to form meaningful relationships, to benefit from the school system or reach anything like his or her potential. Socialisation underpins a hierarchy of needs.

McFreud (psychodynamic psychoanalysis / developmental psychology)
I think socialisation is important too, though I'd stress that much of it takes place at an unconscious rather than a conscious level. What happens in families in the very early years of a child's life, including the ways in which children are socialised into male and female roles, how they are

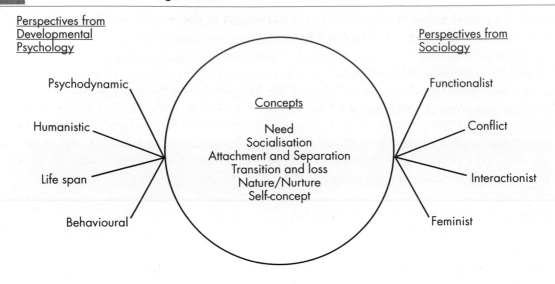

Perspectives from Developmental Psychology

Psychodynamic

Humanistic

Life span

Behavioural

Concepts

Need
Socialisation
Attachment and Separation
Transition and loss
Nature/Nurture
Self-concept

Perspectives from Sociology

Functionalist

Conflict

Interactionist

Feminist

Perspectives	Discipline	Main Theorists	Main Points
Psychodynamic	Developmental Psychology/ psychoanalysis	Sigmund Freud	Behaviour determined by experience in the early years of life
Humanistic	Developmental Psychology	Carl Rogers Abraham Maslow	Past and present equally important; need for individuals to be 'themselves'
Life Span	Developmental Psychology	Erik Erikson	Development as a life long process
Behavioural	Developmental Psychology	B. F. Skinner Albert Bandura	Development explained in terms of what a person has learned
Functionalist	Sociology	Emile Durkheim Talcot Parsons	Parts of the social system perform functions in relation to the whole
Conflict	Sociology	Karl Marx Ralph Dahrendorf	Conflict fundamental between various groups in society
Interactionist	Sociology	Max Weber George Herbert Mead	Interaction as the starting point in a study of society
Feminist	Sociology	Mary Wollstonecraft Ann Oakley	Explains the position of women in society and how they have been subordinated and oppressed

Figure 10.1 Perspectives from development psychology and sociology

toilet-trained and how they are loved, is of vital importance to the ways in which they develop psychologically later on. We are, to a large extent, our past.

McDurkheim (functionalist sociologist)

Forget the individual for a moment. I want to direct your attention away from individuals to look at society itself. Socialisation performs a vital function for society by ensuring that people absorb the culture of their society and learn about social roles. Society couldn't do without it, culture wouldn't be perpetuated without it and our institutions would fall to pieces if people didn't acquire an internalised idea of social rules, and the roles which they need to perform. Children of the future will be socialised to think of Scotland in new ways once we have the new parliament.

McErikson (lifespan developmental psychologist)

That's all very well, but you sociologists generalise too much for my liking. If you take a developmental lifespan perspective you can see exactly how socialisation applies to specific individuals. All individuals face conflicts at each stage of development and it is how they deal with these conflicts which determines whether they emerge positively or negatively into the next stage. Socialisation certainly does play a part here in resolving the conflicts which apply to each stage, especially during childhood. I have always given importance to the social context of people's lives, their families, work and relationships. Good socialisation helps children to build up trust by promoting consistent values, it helps to build autonomy and identity through encouragement in taking social roles, it can help to build initiative through encouraging responsibility. It has a most important role to play in the development of the adult towards an eventual resolution of the conflict of integrity versus despair.

McMarx (sociological conflict perspective)

The conflict of integrity versus despair – that's a good one! What about the conflict between the haves and the have nots; that's the one that seems most important to me. A lot of socialisation is a con' as it stands in the present capitalist society. People are socialised to accept a capitalist system in which power rests with the people who control the means of production and everyone else is socialised into the subordinate and accepting role of being a good industrious worker. A Scottish parliament may be a start . . . but don't forget the revolution.

McSkinner (behavioural perspective/developmental psychology)

Precisely, my dear friend McMarx, though the revolution I'm really interested in is one which enables individual people to learn, through the socialisation process and in other ways, to become balanced, happy, achieving individuals. Politics isn't really up my street, though some of my ideas, could, I suppose, have a political application. What I want to emphasise is that through a process of conditioning people can learn behaviour which it is difficult for other people to cope with. We do have to live in some harmony with one another, you know, and my theories and those of my step-father, can assist in socialising people into behaviour patterns which achieve positive results for the individual . . . and what's good for the individual is good for society, though that's a bit sociological coming from me.

McMead (symbolic interactionist sociologist)

For goodness sake – I don't agree with a single one of you. You're all barking up the wrong tree as far

as I'm concerned. My symbolic interactionist theory, which I have developed from the small beginnings made by a venerable ancestor from Chicago, nicely combines the best of sociology with the best
of developmental psychology, acknowledges the importance of socialisation in the emergence of the
self with, on the one side, 'me', an organised socialised being, and on the other side, 'I', choosing
what I'd like to do in relation to 'me'. I'm sure you understand what I'm getting at.

Mary McWollstonecraft (feminist sociologist)
I understand that you've left the woman until last, as usual, but at least I have the final word on this
subject. Socialisation is all very well. We certainly do need some means whereby we can acquire the
best of the culture of our society. But socialisation as it stands gives women a pretty raw deal. Look
at my research into socialisation. It shows that most girls in our society: play with dolls and learn to
be a good mother; play house and learn to do the housework; choose subjects at school they will be
able to use in a career which will fit around children and a male partner. Well, like my ancestors
before me, I've campaigned for years for women to have equal opportunities in all walks of life, that
was my successful slogan when I stood for election to the new Scottish parliament, and that's what
socialisation should be doing too.

> ## Activity
> Choose one other concept, or group of concepts, from the following list and develop
> imaginatively a way of looking at it from at least one psychological and one sociologi-
> cal perspective: need; attachment and separation; self concept; transition and loss;
> nature/nurture.

2. Human development and behaviour and promoting equal opportunities in a care context

The study of human development and behaviour set out in Chapters 3, 4 and 5 can be linked to
promoting equal opportunities. One way of doing this is through an exploration of what is known
as **ethnocentrism** in the psychological and sociological theories and perspectives presented. A
second way is to investigate how discrimination may affect development and behaviour.

Ethnocentrism

Ethnocentrism, a term first coined by W.G. Sumner (1906), is used to describe prejudicial
assumptions made in theorising and explaining human behaviour and aspects of society which
favour one group over others. The implication is that some, usually **our**, attitudes, customs and
behaviours are regarded as superior to others. The term is further used in criticising some theorists whose research rests upon 'narrow, parochial assumptions drawn from their own society'
(Abercrombie et al, 1984).

Although a great effort has been made in the text to avoid ethnocentrism and to give a
multi-cultural view, it is nevertheless recognised that much of the book rests upon western, British

and Scottish perspectives. The Scottish perspectives have, to a large extent, been intentional and the aim has been not to assume that this perspective applies elsewhere. The discussion of adolescence among British and Scottish young people in Chapter 3 does recognise that there are other ways of viewing adolescence, and in this sense avoids ethnocentrism. An alternative view of adolescence in Russia is presented on page 148 in Chapter 4. Lena Robinson (in Davies, 1997) draws attention to research on models of psychological **nigrescence** (i.e., the process of the psychology of becoming black) as an alternative or complement to a lot of child development research which is based largely on white middle class children. Such research has often assumed that the conclusions can be applied to all children, ignoring problems associated with black identity confusion. Care Workers need to be aware of the existence of identity confusion among many black children, of the ways in which this may affect self-image and the importance of promoting a positive black self-image in a predominantly white society. Developmental and sociological perspectives are ethnocentric to the extent that they fail to take such a need into account.

Activity

a) Look at the perspectives presented in Chapters 4 and 5 and discuss one of them in terms of the extent to which it can be seen as ethnocentric.

b) Look at Tanveer in the case study and consider how an understanding of his situation may be enhanced through taking account of ideas about nigrescence.

c) To what extent do you think that Erikson's lifespan perspective is ethnocentric? Give at least two reasons why you think it either can or cannot be applied equally to the MacDonalds and the Ahmeds in the case study.

How discrimination may affect development and behaviour

Discrimination can prevent people from playing a full part in the life of the 'society' in which they live. It **marginalises** people and in so doing limits their opportunities for development. This process of marginalisation is explained by Tossell and Webb (1991) as follows:

The overall effect of these interrelated processes of stereotyping, prejudice and stigmatising is to marginalize the victims. This means that they are prevented from taking a full part in the life of our society; they live as it were 'on the edge' or 'margin' of society. They do not share full citizenship with regard to the social, economic and political life of the community.

One way to examine the ways in which discrimination and consequent marginalisation can affect development is to revisit Maslow's hierarchy of need. The first four levels of the hierarchy are considered in turn. An activity follows relating to the remaining levels.

Physiological needs: hunger; thirst. One of the results of discrimination is often poverty or relative poverty. The poorer you are the less able you are to provide a healthy diet, to pay all of your bills. Although in Britain starvation in absolute terms is rare, poor diet and resulting poor health are not uncommon, especially among people who are marginalised. The Black Report (1980), otherwise known as *Inequalities in Health – Report of a Research Working Group*, showed how social inequality affects the growth and development of people from conception, through infancy, childhood, adolescence, adulthood and into old age, determining to a great extent the chance of health or disease and even the timing of death.

Safety needs. Discrimination does make people feel unsafe. They feel unsafe, because in general they **are** less safe than others. There has been a huge amount of media attention given in 1999 to the murder of Stephen Lawrence, a black 19 year-old. Stephen was murdered in what was almost certainly a racially motivated attack. Institutionalised racism within the Metropolitan Police Force, according to Sir William Macpherson's inquiry (1999), meant that this murder was inappropriately and insufficiently investigated, leading to a further lack of confidence in the ability of the police to protect people from racially motivated attacks. One extract from the Macpherson report illustrates this very well in referring to:

. . . the collective failure of an organisation to provide an appropriate and professional service to people because of their colour, culture or ethnic origin. It can be seen, or detected in processes, attitudes and behaviour which amounts to discrimination through unwitting prejudice, ignorance, thoughtlessness and racist stereotyping which disadvantages minority ethnic people.

Activity

How are the factors indicated above likely to lead to a feeling of being unsafe? Describe how feeling and/or being unsafe may affect growth and development. Make at least three separate points.

Belongingness and love needs / esteem needs: to affiliate with others, be accepted and belong; to achieve, be competent and gain approval and recognition. If people are discriminated against and marginalised they are deprived of a full sense of belonging to the society in which they live. This in turn affects their self esteem and self concept, vital components in emotional development. As illustration of this, Tossell and Webb use racism. They emphasise the necessity of working with children under five to counter racism before it becomes internalised and in order that the process initiated by discrimination does not proceed. They quote the CRE report 'From Cradle to School' (1989):

We know from research evidence that by the time they enter primary school, white children may well be on the road to believing they are superior to black people, black children may believe that society is not going to show them the same respect and esteem that white people receive . . . such attitudes are not innate, but learned.

Activity

Choose one form of discrimination e.g. ageism, racism, sexism, disablism. What effects upon belongingness and esteem do you think this discrimination may have?

You may have suggested:

■ feeling excluded from groups in education, work or leisure;

■ feeling uncomfortable in many social situations because of discriminatory attitudes;

■ standing less chance of belonging to a chosen work group or profession;

■ self-exclusion from situations in order to avoid the above feelings or because you feel that your safety or sense of security may be threatened.

The process described above need not be inevitable. A more positive outcome may be achieved for emotional development for those who are able, themselves or with support, to counter the negative impact of discrimination. This is illustrated in Figure 2.6, page 54.

Activity

1. Take one other level of Maslow's hierarchy of need and suggest the ways in which discrimination may affect achieving that level and the consequent impact upon development.

2. Choose a stage of development (as identified in Chapter 3, or by Erikson in Chapter 4). Write a paragraph about how development at any one stage may be affected by discrimination. Try to make at least three separate points.

3. Imagine either Nabeil Ahmed or Linda MacDonald in five years time. State three possible outcomes for either of them in each of the following circumstances: a) if they are discriminated against because of their disability or; b) if they are not discriminated against and receive positive encouragement.

3. Human development and behaviour, promoting equal opportunities in a care context and interpersonal skills for care

Why does the care worker need to understand human development and behaviour and the importance of promoting equal opportunities? How does an understanding of these assist in practising interpersonal skills for care? These are the two questions which receive some attention in this section through an examination of Annie's situation in the case study. Annie is 86 years-old and lives in a local authority residential home. Imagine that she is 'cared' for by a care worker who lacks an understanding of human development, lacks a value base or any understanding of promoting equal opportunities. How may this person respond to Annie? Do these short-comings have an impact upon her interpersonal skills? She may fail to understand or empathise with the fact that some older people may be slower to respond to requests, may have experienced cumulative losses, resulting perhaps in depression. She may also fail to understand that older people who receive stimulation, interest and respect can lead happier lives. The care worker may have incorrectly concluded that because a person is old and physically frail it isn't worth trying to encourage, stimulate and respond with empathy. She may also have failed to understand that development is possible at any stage of life and that people who are encouraged and stimulated retain their physical and mental abilities much longer than people who are subjected to 'institutional' regimes. The lack of understanding by the care worker is in itself a form of prejudice because it is based upon a stereotyped view of 'old age' instead of a realistic understanding of the potential of this stage of development. Lack of a value base or any understanding of equal opportunities may lead the care worker to be extremely insensitive to Annie's needs and to have very poor interpersonal skills.

One day Annie wandered into the staff room at the home in which she lives. A care worker was in there alone taking a tea break. 'What do you think you're doing in here? Go straight back to the lounge' shouted the care worker. An understanding of human development and behaviour would have allowed for Annie's disorientation, whilst recognising that Annie is an older adult still able to respond and to be addressed as an adult, not as a child. An understanding of equal opportunities and a value base would have enabled the care worker to appreciate that Annie should be given the same opportunities as anyone else to receive respect, to be valued as a human being. An understanding of the effects of institutionalisation would have encouraged the care worker to enhance rather than diminish Annie's self esteem and all of these things would have enhanced the care worker's own interpersonal skills.

In this one event you can draw upon information from every chapter of the book: institutionalisation in Chapters 1 and 5; equal opportunities in Chapter 2; human development and behaviour (Chapters 3, 4 and 5), the value base in Chapters 6 and 8, interpersonal skills in Chapter 6, needs and opportunities (Chapters 3, 6 and 7), and research (Chapter 9) which had an impact upon all of these ideas.

Activity

Again look at either Nabeil Ahmed or Linda MacDonald in the case study. State as many ideas as possible presented throughout the book which can be used to look at their situations and enhance their care.

4. Human development and behaviour, promoting equality in a care context and health promotion

How do all of the ideas, theories and perspectives presented earlier in the book link with health promotion? The definition of health presented at the beginning of Chapter 8 encourages you to look at the whole person. It emphasises the importance not only of genetic but also environmental factors in the promotion and maintenance of good health. This links closely with the consideration of factors which affect human development, discussed in Chapter 3. If you look back at the nature/nurture debate on page 89 you will see that many factors are interwoven to influence human development and behaviour. What are these factors? You may have mentioned genetic and socioeconomic factors, culture, gender and disability. These same factors influence health. Health promotion seeks to minimise the inequalities which exist in their distribution. The concept of **equity** is emphasised which links with discussion of **equality of opportunity** in Chapter 2. Equity in terms of health promotion means that everyone should have equality of access to, and should get the same benefit from the services. Everyone therefore should have the same opportunity to enjoy good health.

Other aspects of the value base, and particularly the concept of **empowerment**, are also relevant to health and health promotion. Empowerment means enabling service users to take control of their lives. In terms of health promotion it means that people are enabled to identify their health needs and then encouraged to develop skills to meet these needs. **Community participation** is a feature of the value base, of health promotion and of the avoidance of institutionalisation.

Activity

Choose two psychological perspectives from Chapter 4 and two sociological perspectives from Chapter 5 and discuss them in relation to health and health promotion.

In the activity above you may, for example, have taken Erikson's lifespan perspective as one perspective from psychology. Erikson emphasised that individuals need to resolve basic psychological conflicts at different stages in their lives in order to develop a **healthy** personality. This development is influenced by social and socio-cultural factors. The links between Erikson's theory and health, centre around the resolution of conflicts and a healthy personality as an important aspect of overall health. Erikson also presents the possibility of development at all stages of life, implying that if there has been poor health early in life this can be compensated for later on. This links with health promotion which also promotes a belief in change, change in individuals towards a more healthy lifestyle, which in turn may make the resolution of the conflicts of development more positive.

From sociology you may have chosen a feminist perspective. This perspective sets out to explain the position of women in society. Such a perspective in relation to health will focus upon concerns which particularly affect women and the promotion of equity of health provision. It will examine whether the location of health provision meets the needs of mothers with young children, for example; or it may focus upon links between the socialisation of women and their willingness to use health services; or it may concentrate upon links between female roles and psychological health; or upon the links between poverty, health and being a woman.

You may have chosen different perspectives from those discussed above, but whatever you chose should have enabled you to appreciate some of the links which can be made between perspectives which relate to human development and to health promotion.

CONCLUSION

And some kind of help
Is the kind of help
That helping's all about.
And some kind of help
Is the kind of help
We all can do without.

(Shel Silverstein, 1974).

By now it should be possible to distinguish between good, empowering help and poor, patronising 'help'. The above discussion has also attempted to enable you to discover links among the many threads of this book and the several subjects which you have studied. There has been an emphasis upon an holistic approach seeing both people and societies as wholes made up of interacting parts. Your development as a care worker can be carried further through gaining experience of care practice and through further training. Courses such as the HNC in Social Care or Health Care, the Diploma in Social Work, SVQs and GSVQs are all ways of enhancing your development. The foundations have been laid. It is now up to you to apply your knowledge, skills and value base to improve the quality of life of those with whom you do or will work.

SUGGESTIONS FOR FURTHER READING

At the end of a course you usually feel like a holiday. The suggested reading below should enable you to take your thinking further, whilst at the same time providing something enjoyable and reasonably undemanding to do on the beach!

Axline, V.M. (1990). *Dibs in Search of Self.* Penguin.
Brown, C. (1983). *Down all the Days.* Secker and Warburg.
Nolan, C. (1988). *Under the Eye of the Clock.* Pan.
Walker, A. (1990). *The Colour Purple.* The Women's Press.

You may also like to try works by the following Scottish authors: Liz Lochead, James Kelman, Alasdair Gray, Lewis Grassic Gibbon, George Mackay Brown, Joan Lingard, Jessie Kesson, Janice Galloway, Elspeth Davie.

Glossary

Acceptance   Taking people as they are without judging them; an absence of rejection.

Adolescence   The stage of development between childhood and adulthood, usually seen to begin with puberty and to end with responsibility and independence.

Advising   Telling others how they might act, feel or think rather than letting them decide for themselves.

Advocacy   Actively promoting and representing the cause of another; speaking on behalf of someone as if speaking *as* that person.

Ageism   Discrimination applied to or experienced by people because of their age. This term is applicable both to older and young people.

Agency   An establishment or organisation providing a service to service users.

AIDS   Acquired immune deficiency syndrome caused by the human immunodeficiency virus (HIV).

Anti-discriminatory practice   Practice which acknowledges, understands and challenges the many negative effects of discrimination.

Assessment   An exploration of service user needs as part of the process of care or health promotion, in order to enable the service user to reach a quality of life which is as good as it can be; the basis for planning.

Attitude   The way something is viewed in an evaluative way; an habitual mode of regarding anything. Attitudes affect the way people behave.

Behaviour   How people conduct themselves. The way they do things themselves and in their relationships with others.

Belief   An opinion or conviction which is held to be true, often without any sort of proof.

Body language   Non-verbal communication expressed through the position, attitude and expression of the body, or parts of the body, e.g. the way you sit, the degree of eye contact.

Care/formal care   Caring for people in society, other than self or family, in an agency whose codes of practice are dictated to and guided by legislation, policy and professional ethics.

Care plan   An agreement arising from an assessment about what needs are to be met, how they are to be achieved and how problems are to be dealt with.

Choice   Promoting choice means giving different options, real options, from which the service user can select as independently as possible.

Client   The recipient or user of a service. Although 'service user' is the term used in this book, client is still an accepted term in care practice and counselling.

Cognitive development   The gradual unfolding and increase in complexity of thought and intellectual processes during the life cycle.

Communication   Communication occurs whenever people receive and/or give messages which they regard as significant. It can be verbal, non-verbal or symbolic.

Community   A network of people who are linked, usually by sharing a geographical locality; may also refer to those linked by occupation, ethnic background and/or other factors.

Community care   Providing the services and support which people need to be able to live as independently as possible in their own homes or in 'homely' settings rather than institutions.

Confidentiality   Maintaining the right to privacy of information; not divulging personal information without consent.

Congruence   Being genuine; ensuring that your verbal and non-verbal behaviour give the same messages.

Counselling   A process which aims to help people help themselves through communication to make better choices and become better decision makers.

Culture   The way people live, lifestyles, values; can also be seen as consisting of all the messages received from society about what is good, bad, desirable, undesirable etc.

Development   Gradual unfolding; increase in complexity involving change and movement. Human development can be physical, intellectual/cognitive, emotional and social.

Deviance   Behaviour of individuals or groups that is outwith the socially defined normal limits of behaviour.

Disablism   Discrimination applied to, or experienced by people with physical or learning disabilities.

Discrimination   The process whereby some groups or individuals in society treat others less favourably than themselves, based upon prejudice and stereotypes.

Empathy   Putting yourself in someone else's shoes and attempting to imagine how he or she feels.

Empowerment   Enabling people to take control of their lives; gaining the power to make decisions and choices.

Equality of opportunity   The belief that everyone should get an equal chance to access the opportunities in society.

Ethnic group   A group with a long shared history, and a cultural tradition of its own. Other important characteristics may be common geographic origin, language, literature and religion.

Ethnocentrism   Prejudicial assumptions made in theorising and explaining human behaviour and aspects of society, which favour one or some groups over others; may lead to accounts which make false assumptions and which are biased.

Exclusion   See 'Social exclusion'.

Feminism   Sets out to explain the position of women in society; to focus attention upon how women have been subordinated and oppressed and how this can be changed.

Gay   A word used to describe someone who is homosexual; usually applied to male homosexuals.

Gender   The term used to describe socially constructed differences between men and women. Sex refers to biological differences.

Genetic   The influence of genes, which are inherited from parents and determine everything from eye colour and body shape to some illnesses, e.g. haemophilia.

Holistic care   Care which sees the whole person in a social situation and attempts to satisfy physical, intellectual, communication, emotional, cultural and social needs.

Homophobia   The fear of people who are homosexual, often displayed through discriminatory actions.

Ideology A set of beliefs and ideas that are held by a group, e.g. the ideology of the Scottish Nationalist Party or the Conservative Party.

Implementation Putting plans into effect; carrying out what has been agreed upon in the planning process.

Inclusion See 'Social inclusion'.

Incontinent Unable to retain urine and/or faeces.

Institution A part of society which has regular and routine practices, regulated by social norms.

Institutional discrimination The routine, day-to-day, ingrained discrimination which exists in any of the different institutions in society.

Institutionalisation Becoming dependent upon the routines and narrow confines of an institution resulting in such characteristics as apathy, lack of initiative and inability to make personal plans.

Keyworker A worker who is allocated to work more closely with a service user than other workers and who has a coordinating role with that service user within the agency.

Labelling Attaching a (usually negative) name to acts or conditions which then becomes a 'master status' e.g. labelling people as deviant, neurotic or difficult.

Learned helplessness A decline in the desire and ability to do things beyond what may be expected in relation to a person's state of health, usually because too much assistance is being given.

Legislation The law; Acts of Parliament.

Lesbian A woman who is homosexual.

Marginalisation Literally means to 'place at the edge' and refers to the process whereby some groups are forced to live outside the mainstream of society and denied opportunities to participate as full citizens.

Modelling Demonstrating behaviour, feelings or thoughts to others which may, if adopted, improve the quality of life for the service user.

Monitoring On-going evaluation; keeping a check on what you are doing to ensure that it meets objectives.

Nature/nurture debate Refers to dispute about whether nature (inherited characteristics) or nurture (the environment, socioeconomic factors and socialisation) determines behaviour and development.

Normalisation Affording all citizens the same rights and opportunities to develop and contribute to society in ways which are socially valued; developed predominantly as an attempt to promote the aim of integrating people with a disability fully into society.

Oppression Abuse of power by a group or an individual over a less powerful group or individual, with the effect that those less powerful are denied their rights.

Patriarchy The dominance of men over women in society.

Prejudice A strongly held negative attitude or set of attitudes based not upon fact or reason but upon irrational beliefs, lack of understanding and/or stereotypes.

Psychology The study of mind and behaviour.

Record A written account of significant information including decisions, incidents, feelings, actions and monitoring of the implementation of assessments/plans.

Relationship Being connected in some way with another; a helping relationship is characterised by empathy, genuineness and unconditional positive regard.

Residential care The provision for need in a registrable home. Under the Registered Homes Act 1984 a registrable home is one which provides board and personal care for four or more people who need such care by reason of age, disablement, past or present dependence upon alcohol or drugs or present mental disorder.

Respite care A temporary period usually spent in a supported, residential environment in order to give carers a break and/or to provide help and a change for those in need of care. It can also be used as an opportunity for assessment or re-assessment.

Role play Enacting behaviour in simulated settings or imagination.

Scapegoats Individuals or groups of people who have been inaccurately and unjustly targeted as being responsible for a problem.

Self concept A personal judgment of worthiness that is expressed in the attitudes you hold towards yourself.

Self esteem A sense of your own worth. This can be a positive or negative evaluation of yourself.

Service user One who avails him or herself of help or assistance towards fulfilling need and/or improving the quality of life; sometimes also called a client or resident.

Sexism Discrimination applied to or experienced by people on the basis of their gender.

Siblings Brothers and sisters.

Social class People in the same or similar socioeconomic circumstances. Socioeconomic differences result in differences in wealth, power and life chances.

Social exclusion The prevention of some people/groups from taking a full and valued part in society e.g. those who are marginalised because of poverty or disability.

Social inclusion Describes the idea of taking positive steps to assist and include people who have traditionally been excluded from society; includes treating everyone as a valued member of society and facilitating participation in that society.

Socialisation The process or way in which people learn the culture of their society.

Society Usually, but not always, the country or nation-state, defined in terms of language, laws, education, religion.

Sociology The study of societies and the analysis of the structure of social relationships as constituted by social interaction. No single definition is satisfactory because of the diversity of sociological perspectives.

Status Position in society or social institution; what a person is; can also mean the prestige associated with that position.

Statutory Provided by or connected with central or local government.

Stereotype A fixed, general, over-simplified and usually negative image of what a particular individual or group is like because of the possession of certain characteristics e.g. the false 'stereotypes' of all gay men being promiscuous or all people from Aberdeen being mean.

Stigma A distinguishing mark or characteristic which is both noticeable and regarded as objectionable by some individuals or groups. Stigmas have the power to spoil a person's social and personal identity.

Summarising Making statements which say briefly what you or another person has been saying; may include feedback from you.

Support Giving encouragement, help, understanding, warmth, whatever is needed, to another.

SVQ Scottish Vocational Qualification; awarded at different levels upon successful completion of a detailed assessment of practice by an approved workplace assessor.

Symbolic communication   Messages, behaviour and actions which represent something else, e.g. an unwelcoming physical environment says 'we don't care about you'.

Team   A group of people who work together to achieve the philosophy and goals of their agency.

Transitions   Changes from one life state to another which people undergo during their lives, e.g. marriage, loss of a partner, retirement.

Transsexual   A person who has made hormonal or surgical changes to their body in order to live as a member of the opposite sex, adopting a name, clothes and lifestyle of that sex.

Transvestite   A person who dresses in the clothes of the opposite gender.

Value   That which is desirable and worthy for its own sake.

Voluntary organisation   A not-for-profit, non-statutory organisation; often a charity.

References

Abbot, P. and Wallace, C. (1997). *An Introduction to Sociology: Feminist Perspectives.* 2nd edn. London: Routledge.

Abercrombie, N., Hill, S. and Turner, B. (1994). *The Penguin Dictionary of Sociology.* 3rd edn. London: Penguin Books.

Adams, G., Guillotta, T. and Montemayor, R. (1992). *Adolescent Identity Formation.* Newbury Park: Sage.

Adams, J.D., Hayes, J. and Hopson, B. (1977). *Transition: Understanding and Managing Personal Change.* London: Martin Robertson.

Alexander, M. (1995). *Painters First.* Bordon: Leader Books.

Allan, G. (1985). *Family Life: Domestic Roles and Social Organization.* London: Blackwell.

Allan, J. (1935). *Farmer's Boy,* in Maclaren, A. (1976)

Amato, P.R. (1993). 'Children's adjustment to divorce: theories, hypotheses and empirical support.' *Journal of Marriage and the Family:* 55, 23–38.

Anderson, C. and Wilkie, P. (1992). *Reflective Helping in HIV and AIDS.* Milton Keynes: Open University Press.

ASH (Action on Smoking and Health), BMA (British Medical Association) and HEA (Health Education Authority) (1988). *Two Good Reasons for a Tobacco Pricing Policy.* London: ASH/BMA/HEA.

Bamford, C. (1995). *Equal Treatment and the Law: A Guide to European Community Law in Scotland.* Edinburgh: European Commission representation in Scotland.

Bandura, A. (1965). 'Influence of model's reinforcement contingencies on the acquisition of imitative responses.' *Journal of Personality and Social Psychology* 1. 589–95.

Bandura, A., Ross, D. and Ross, S. (1963) 'Imitation of film mediated aggressive models.' *Journal of Abnormal and Social Psychology* 66. 3–11.

Barnard, A. and Burgess, T. (1996). *Sociology Explained.* Cambridge: Cambridge University Press.

Becker, H. (1963). *Outsiders: Studies in the Sociology of Deviance.* N.Y.: The Free Press.

Bee, H.L. and Mitchell, S.K. (1984). *The Developing Person.* New York: Harper and Row.

Bell, N. and Vogel, E. (1959). *A Modern Introduction to the Family.* London: Collier-Macmillan.

Biggart, A. and Furlong, A. (1996). 'Educating 'Discouraged Workers': cultural diversity in the upper secondary school.' *British Journal of Sociology of Education,* vol. 17, no. 3, p. 253–266.

Bion, W. (1968). *Experiences in Groups.* London: Tavistock.

Birren, J.E. and Fisher, L.M. (1990) 'Aging and slowing of behaviour.' *Current Theory and Research in Motivation,* 39: 1–37. Lincoln, NB: University of Nebraska Press.

Black, N. et al (1984). *Health and Disease: A Reader.* Milton Keynes: Open University Press.

Blakemore, K. and Drake, R. (1996). *Understanding Equal Opportunities Policies.* London: Prentice Hall/Harvester Wheatsheaf.

Blane, D. Brunner, E. and Wilkinson, R. (eds.) (1996). *Health and Social Organisations: towards a health policy for the 21st century.* London: Routledge.

Bottomore, T. and Ruben, M. (eds.) (1963). *Karl Marx: Selected Writings in Sociology and Social Philosophy.* Harmondsworth: Penguin.

Bowles, S. and Gintis, H. (1976). *Schooling in Capitalist America.* London: Routledge and Kegan Paul.

Bowlby, J. (1953). *Child Care and the Growth of Love.* Harmondsworth: Penguin.

Bowlby, J. (1951). *Maternal Care and Mental Health.* Geneva: World Health Organisation.

Bradshaw, J. (1972). 'The Concept of Social Need.' *New Society,* 30 March.

Breitenbach, E. (1995). *Quality through Equality: Good Practice in Equal Opportunities in Scottish Local Authorities.* Glasgow: Equal Opportunities Commission.

Bronfenbrenner, U. (1974) 'The Origins of Alienation.' *Scientific American.* 231. 53–61.

Brown, C.H. (1979). *Understanding Society.* London: John Murray.

Brown, G.M. (1995). *Beside the Ocean of Time.* London: Flamingo.

Brown, G.M. (1995). *Winter Tales.* London: Flamingo.

Brunner, E. (1996). 'The Social and biological basis of cardiovascular disease in office workers', in Blane D. et al.

Bryman, A. (1988). *Quality and Quantity in Social Research.* London: Unwin Hyman.

Burnard, P. (1989). *Teaching Interpersonal Skills.* London: Chapman and Hall.

Carlen, P. (1988). *Women, Crime and Poverty.* Milton Keynes: Open University Press.

Carstairs, V. and Morris, R. (1991). *Deprivation and Health in Scotland.* Aberdeen: Aberdeen University Press.

Chambliss, W.J. and Mankoff, M. (1976). *Whose Law? What Order?* New York: John Wiley and Sons.

Cheetham, J. (1992). *Evaluating Social Work Effectiveness.* Buckingham: Open University Press.

Clough, R. (1987). *Scandals in Residential Centres.* An unpublished report for the Wagner Committee, University of Bristol.

Commission for Racial Equality (1995). *Annual Report.* London: CRE.

Commission for Racial Equality (1997). *Annual Report.* London: CRE.

Community Care Magazine (1998). 'Deaf People from Ethnic Minorities Feel Isolated.' *Community Care,* 13–19 August, page 5.

Community Care Magazine (1998). 'Scots unclear about Children Act Legislation.' *Community Care,* 9–15 July, page 4.

Community Care Magazine (1998). 'Study Paints Picture of Isolation.' *Community Care,* 28 May–3 June, page 3.

Comte, A. (1986). *The Positive Philosophy.* London: Bell and Sons.

Cooley, C.H. (1902). *Human Nature and Social Order.* New York: Shocken.

Coser, L. and Rosenberg, B. (eds.) (1976). *Sociological Theory: a book of readings.* New York: Macmillan.

Coulshed, V. and Orme, J. (1998). *Social Work Practice.* 3rd edn. London: Macmillan.

Craib, I. (1984). *Modern Social Theory.* Brighton: Wheatsheaf Books.

Currie, E. (1989). *Life lines: politics and health 1986–88.* London: Sidgewick and Jackson.

Dahrendorf, R. (1964). 'Out of Utopia.' In Coser, L. and Rosenberg, B.

Dalrymple, J. and Burke, B. (1995). *Anti-Oppressive Practice – Social Care and the Law*. Buckingham: Open University Press.

De Beauvoir, S. (1972). *The Second Sex*. Harmondsworth: Penguin Books.

Department of Health and Social Security (1976). *Prevention and Health: Everybody's Business*. London: HMSO.

Dobash, R. and Dobash, R. (1980). *Violence against Wives*. NY: The Free Press.

Dominelli, L. (1998). *Sociology for Social Work*. London: Macmillan.

Donohue, E. (1985). *Echoes in the Hills*. Surbiton: SCA Publications.

Douglas, J.W.B. (1975). 'Early hospital admissions and later disturbances of behaviour and learning.' *Developmental Medical Child Neurology*, 17. 456–480.

Douglas, J.W.B. (1964). *The Home and the School*. London: Macgibbon and Kee.

Douglas, T. (1978). *Basic Groupwork*. London: Routledge.

Downie, R.S., Tannahill, C. and Tannahill R. (1997). *Health Promotion: Models and Values*. 2nd edn. Oxford: Oxford University Press.

Durkheim, R. (1938). *The Rules of Sociological Method*. New York: The Free Press.

Eastbank Health Promotion Centre (1997). *First Annual Report*. Glasgow: Greater Glasgow Health Board.

Edgell, S. (1980). *Middle Class Couples*. London: Allen and Unwin.

Egan, G. (1986). *The Skilled Helper*. Monterey: Brooks/Cole.

Eldridge, J.E.T. (1970). *Max Weber: the interpretation of social reality*. London: Joseph.

Engels, F. (1972). *The Origin of the Family, Private Property and The State*. London: Lawrence and Wishart.

Equal Opportunities Commission (1997). 'Making Equality Work: the Challenge for Government', *EOC Annual Report* (Scottish Extract).

Erikson, E.H. (1968). *Identity: Youth and Crisis*. New York: Norton.

Fenton, S. (1987). *Ageing Minorities: black people as they grow old in Britain*. London: Commission for Racial Equality.

Field, D. and James, N. (1993). 'Where and How People Die', in Clark, D. (ed.) *The Future of Palliative Care*. Buckingham: Open University Press.

Flanagan, C. (1996). *Applying Psychology to Early Child Development*. London: Hodder and Stoughton.

Fletcher, R. (1988). *The Family and Marriage under Attack*. London: Routledge.

Ford, J. and Sinclair, R. (1987). *Sixty Years On: Women Talk About Old Age*. London: Women's Press.

Frude, N. (1997). *Understanding Family Problems*. London: Wiley.

Furlong, A. and Cartmel, F. (1995). 'Aspirations and Opportunity Structures: 13-year-olds in areas with restricted opportunities', *British Journal of Guidance and Counselling*, vol. 23, No. 3.

Gill, A. (1999). 'Do you recognise this family?', Edinburgh: *Scotland on Sunday*. 31.1.99.

Glasgow City Council (1997). *Language Matters: A Guide to Good Practice*. Glasgow: GCC.

Glasgow University Media Group (1980). *Bad News*. London: Routledge and Kegan Paul.

Goffman, E. (1968). *Asylums*. Harmondsworth: Penguin.

Gough, E. (1959). 'Is the Family Universal? The Nayor Case' in Bell, N. and Vogel, E.

Gould, R.L. (1978). *Transformations: Growth and Change in Adult Life.* New York: Simon and Schuster.

Greer, G. (1970). *The Female Eunuch.* London: MacGibbon and Kee.

Guardian Weekly (1998). 'Girl kept in Attic.' Uncredited article. 2.7.98.

Haralambos, M. (ed.) (1966). *Sociology: A New Approach.* 3rd Edition. Ormskirk: Causeway Press.

Haralambos, M. and Holborn, M. (1995). *Sociology: Themes and Perspectives.* London: Collins Educational.

Health Education Board for Scotland (1997). *Scotland's Health at Work.*

Health Education Board for Scotland (1997). *Strategic Plan 1997 to 2000.*

Heidensohn, F. (1985). *Women and Crime.* London: Macmillan.

Heim, A. (1990). *Where Did I Put My Spectacles.* Cambridge: Allborough Press.

Heraud, B.J. (1970). *Sociology and Social Work (Perspectives and Problems).* Oxford: Pergammon Press.

Herbert, M. (1986). *Psychology for Social Workers.* Leicester: British Psychological Society Imprint.

HMSO (1987). *British Crime Survey.* London.

HMSO (1995). *Children (Scotland) Act.* London.

HMSO (1995). *Disability Discrimination Act.* London.

HMSO (1990). *National Health Service and Community Care Act.* London.

HMSO (1992). *Scotland's Health: A Challenge to Us All.* London.

HMSO (1998). *Scottish Statistical Survey.* London.

HMSO (1998). *Social Trends.* London.

HMSO (1968). *Social Work (Scotland) Act.* London.

Holmes, T.H. and Rahe, H. (1967). 'The Social Re-adjustment Rating Scale', *Journal of Psycho-Somatic Research*, 11. 213–18.

Ishii-Kuntz, M. (1990). 'Social interaction and psychological well-being: Comparison across stages of adulthood', *International Journal of Ageing and Human Development*, 30(1): 15–36.

Jones, A. (1990). *Charles Rennie Mackintosh.* London: Studio Editions.

Kahan, B. (1994). *Growing up in Groups.* London: HMSO.

Katz, J. and Sidell, M. (1994). *Easeful Death: Caring for Dying and Bereaved People.* London: Hodder and Stoughton.

Kidd-Hewitt, D. and Osborne, R. (1995). *Crime and The Media: The Post-Modern Spectacle.* London: Pluto Press.

Kinsey, R. (1993). *Policing in the City: public, police and social work.* Edinburgh: Scottish Office, Central Research Unit.

Labov, W. (1973). *The Logic of Nonstandard English* in Young, T.

Laing, R. and Esterson, A. (1970). *Sanity, Madness and the Family.* Harmondsworth: Penguin.

Lawson, T. (1991). *GCSE Sociology: A Conceptual Approach.* Chester: Checkmate Publications.

Leach, E. (1971). *A Runaway World?* London: BBC Publications.

Lewis, I. and Munn, P. (1987). *So you want to do Research*. Edinburgh: The Scottish Council for Research and Education.

McLaren, A. (1976). *Social Class in Scotland*. Edinburgh: John Donald.

McLellan, D. (1980). *Karl Marx 1818–1883. Selections in English*. London: Macmillan.

Macoby, E.E. (1980). *Social Development, Psychological Growth and the Parent Relationship*. New York: Harcourt Brace Jovanovich.

Mannheim, H. (1960). *Comparative Criminology*. London: Routledge and Kegan Paul.

Marx, K. and Engels, F. (1915). *Manifesto of the Communist Party, authorised English translation*. Chicago: C.H. Kerr.

Matthews, R. and Young, J. (1992). *Issues in Realist Criminology*. London: Sage.

Matthews, Z. (1998). 'The Outsiders', *Nursing Times*, vol. 94, no. 37: 16.9.98.

Maylor, E.A. (1994). 'Ageing and the retrieval of specialized and general Knowledge: Performance of Masterminds', *British Journal of Psychology*, 85(1).

McCurry, P. (1999), 'Wired for Work', Sutton: *Community Care Magazine* 14–20 Jan.

Mead, G.H. (1934). *Mind, Self and Society*, edited by C. Morris. Chicago: University of Chicago Press.

Meighan, R. (1981). *A Sociology of Educating*. London: Holt Rinehart.

Merton, R.K. (1968). *Social Theory and Social Structure* (enlarged edition). New York: The Free Press.

Miller, J. (1996). *Social Care Practice*. London: Hodder and Stoughton.

Mills, C.W. (1959). *The Sociological Imagination*. New York: Oxford University Press.

Montemayor, R. (1983). in Adams, G. et al.

Moonie, N. (1994). *Health and Social Care*. Oxford: Heinemann.

Moonie, N. (ed.) (1996). *Advanced Health and Social Care*. 2nd Edition. Oxford: Heinemann.

Morison, M. (1986). *Methods in Sociology*. London: Longman.

Murdock, G.P. (1949). *Social Structure*. New York: Macmillan.

Naidoo J. and Wills, J. (1997) *Health Promotion: Foundations for Practice*. London: Balliere Tindall.

Naysmith, S. (1994). 'Out in the Cold', *The Big Issue (in Scotland)*, 6. 94. 22–23.

Nelson-Jones, R. (1988). *Practical Counselling and Helping Skills*. 3rd edn. London: Cassell.

Nobbs, J., Fielding, R., Hine, B., Flemming, M. (1989). *Sociology*. 3rd edn. London: Macmillan Education Ltd.

Oakley, A. (1974). *Sociology of Housework*. Oxford: Martin Robertson.

Oakley, A. (1982). *Conventional Families* in Rapoport, R.

Oakley, A. (1985). *Sex, Gender and Society*. London: Gower/Maurice Temple Smith.

Oakley, A. (1993). *Essays on Women, Medicine and Health*. Edinburgh: Edinburgh University Press.

Oates, S. (1982). *Let the Trumpet Sound*. London: Search Press.

O'Donnell, M. (1997). *Introduction to Sociology* 4th edn. Walton-on-Thames: Nelson.

O'Donnell, M. (1993). *New Introductory Reader in Sociology*. Walton-on-Thames: Nelson.

Oldman, C. and Beresford, B. (1998). 'A Space of our Own', Haywards Heath: *Community Care Magazine*, 1–7 October 1998.

OU U205 Course Team (1985). *Birth to Old Age*. Milton Keynes: Open University Press.

Parkes, C.M. (1975). *Bereavement: Studies in Grief in Adult Life*. London: Pelican Books.

Parsons, T. (1937). *The Structure of Social Action*. New York: McGraw Hill.

Patrick, J. (1973). *A Glasgow Gang Observed*. London: Eyre Methuen.

Partridge, C. and Barnitt, R. (1987). *Research Guidelines: A Handbook for Therapists*. London: Heinemann.

Payne, G. and Abbott, P. (eds.) (1990). *The Social Mobility of Women: Beyond Male Mobility Models*. London: Falmer Press.

Payne, M. (1991). *Modern Social Work Theory*. London: Macmillan.

Peter, L. (1982). *Quotations for our Time*. London: Methuen.

Pilsbury, B. (1984). 'Doing the Month', in Black, N. et al.

Radcliffe-Brown, A. (1935). 'Structure and Function in Primitive Society', *American Anthropologist*, vol. XXXVII.

Rapoport, R. et al (eds.) (1982). *Families in Britain*. London: RKP.

Rayner, E. (1986). *Human Development*. 3rd edn. London: Unwin Hyman.

Richardson, A. (1995). *Preparation to Care*. London: Balliere Tindall.

Rogers, C. (1991). *Client-centred Therapy*. London: Constable.

Rogers, J. (1990). *Caring for People, Help at the Frontline*. Milton Keynes: Open University Press.

Rosser, R. and Harris, C. (1965). *The Family and Social Change*. London: Routledge and Kegan Paul.

Rutter, M. (1979). 'Maternal Deprivation (1972–78): New Findings, New Concepts, New Approaches', *Child Development*, 50. 283–305.

Rutter, M. (1979). *Maternal Deprivation Re-Assessed*. 2nd edn. Harmondsworth: Penguin.

Sanderson, H. et al (1997). *People, Plans and Possibilities*. Edinburgh. SHS Ltd.

Schaefer, N. (1978). *Does She Know She's There*. London: Harper and Row.

Schaie, K.W. and Labouvie-Vief, G. (1974). 'Generational versus ontogenetic components of change in adult cognitive behaviour: A fourteen year cross-sequential study', *Developmental psychology*, 1974, 10. 305–320.

Schaie, K.W. et al (1988). *Methodological Issues in Aging Research*. New York: Springer.

Scotland on Sunday (1999). 'Letter from student. (Claire Gordon, Aberdeen)', 7.2.99.

Scotsman (1998). 'Parents Hands Tied by Euro Judgement', uncredited news article, *The Scotsman* 24.9.98.

Scottish Office (1997). *Scotland's Parliament*. London: HMSO.

Scottish Office (1991). *The Patient's Charter*.

Scottish Office (1998). *Working Together for a Healthier Scotland: A Consultation Paper*. London: HMSO.

Seabrook, J. (1990). 'Law and Disorder', p. 18. *New Statesman and Society*. 5 Oct.

Shaffer, H.R. and Emerson, P.E. (1964). 'The Development of Social Attachments in Infancy', monographs of the *Society for Research in Child Development*, 29.

Sharrock, D. (1993). 'Anthony Quinn's lust for life results in 11th child at age 78', *The Guardian*, 20.8.93.

Sheridan, M. (1997). *From Birth to Five Years*. London: Routledge.

Skidmore, W. (1975). *Theoretical Thinking in Sociology*. Cambridge: Cambridge University Press.

Slater, R. (1995). *The Psychology of Growing Old*. Buckingham: Open University Press.

Smale, G., Tuson, G., Biehal, N. and Marsh, P. (1993). *Empowerment, Assessment, Care Management and the Skilled Worker*. London: HMSO.

Social Care Association (1993). *The Social Care Task*. Surbiton: SCA.

Social Care Association (1994). *An Introduction to Care Planning*. Surbiton: SCA.

Spender, D. (1983). *Invisible Women: Schooling Scandal*. London: Women's Press.

Spitz, R.A. and Wolf, K.M. (1946). 'Anaclitic Depression', *Psychoanalytic Study of the Child*, 2. 313–342.

SRC (1993). *Training Package in Residential Care*. Glasgow: SRC.

Stapleton, K. (1998). 'Signs of Improvement', *Community Care Magazine*, 30.4–6.5.98. 26–27.

Stephens, P. et al (1998). *Think Sociology*. Cheltenham: Stanley Thornes Ltd.

Strathclyde Regional Council (1991). *Strathclyde Social Trends, 1988–1995*. Glasgow: Business Information Centre.

Taylor, A. (1993). *Women Drug Users*. Oxford: Clarendon Press.

Taylor, S. and Field, D. (eds.) (1993). *Sociology of Health and Healthcare*. Oxford: Blackwell.

Thompson, K. and Tunstall, J. (1971). *Sociological Perspectives*. Middlesex: Penguin in association with The Open University Press.

Thompson, N. (1997). *Anti-Discriminatory Practice*. 2nd edn. London: Macmillan

Thomson, H. and Manuel, J. (1997). *Further Studies for Health*. London: Hodder and Stoughton.

Thomson, H. et al (1995). *Health and Social Care for Advanced GNVQ*. 2nd edn. London: Hodder and Stoughton.

Thorne, B. (1992). *Carl Rogers*. Thousand Oaks, California: Sage.

Thorpe, N. (1998). 'Scottish Women – Second Class Citizens', *The Scotsman* 20.11.98.

Tizard, B. and Hodges, J. (1968). 'The effect of early institutional rearing on the development of eight year old children', *Journal of Child Psychology and Psychiatry*, 19. 99–118.

Tossell, D. and Webb, R. (1994). *Inside the Caring Services*. 2nd edn. London: Edward Arnold.

Townsend, P., Davidson, N. (eds.) and Whitehead, M. (1992). *Inequalities in Health: The Black Report and The Health Divide*. Harmondsworth: Penguin.

Vernon, G. (video) 'Stand up the Real Glynn Vernon'.

Ward, A. (1993). *Working in Group Care*. Birmingham: Venture Press.

Ward, B. and Houghton, J. (1967). *Good Grief: exploring feelings of loss and death with over 11s and adults*. London: Cruse.

Wheal, A. in collaboration with Buchanan, A. (1994). *Answers: A Handbook for Residential and Foster Carers of Young People aged 11–18 years*. Harlow: Longman.

Williams, L. (1994). *Finding out about Society*. London: Bell and Hyman.

Willis, P. (1977). *Learning to Labour*. Farnborough: Saxon House.

Worden, J.W. (1983). *Grief Counselling and Grief Therapy*. London: Tavistock.

Young, T. (1973). *Tinker, Taylor . . . The Myth of Cultural Deprivation*. Harmondsworth: Penguin.

Young, M. and Wilmott, P. (1957). *Family and Kinship in East London*. London: RKP.

Younghusband, E. (1964). *Social Work and Social Change*. London: Allen and Unwin.

Appendix

SOCIAL CARE ASSOCIATION SCOTLAND

The Social Care Association is one of the major independent professional associations operating in the care field, both in the U.K. as a whole, with headquarters in Surbiton, and in Scotland with an office in Glasgow. Membership is not determined by qualifications; SCA welcomes care workers from all levels in residential care, day services, home care, training, inspection and registration, fieldwork, housing support and management. All members are requested to sign up to the Association's Code of Practice. The main aim of the Association is to promote high standards in care services and some key objectives are:

- to promote and maintain a high standard of training and professional practice;
- to keep in touch with individual members of the Association and other organisations, providing the opportunity for the interchange of knowledge and experience;
- to represent the views of members on matters of policy and practice;
- to improve the technical knowledge of members and others concerned with care practice by the promotion of national, regional and local meetings, lectures and discussions;
- to promote the interchange of information and opinions, research, the publication and distribution of books, papers and reports;
- to promote the welfare of staff involved in practice.

The Social Care Association in Scotland can be contacted at:
3, Strathview Park, Netherlee, Glasgow G44 3YA.
Telephone/Fax: 0141 637 6932 Web: www.socialcareassoc.com

HEATHERBANK MUSEUM OF SOCIAL WORK

The Museum, which was founded in 1975, is the only Museum of Social Work in Europe. It exists to increase public awareness of the social welfare needs of society, particularly those who are disadvantaged. The Museum has extensive book, picture, archive, journal and resource libraries which are available for use on application to the Curator. Heatherbank which is now part of Glasgow Caledonian University has a gallery situated in Cowcaddens Road in the middle of Glasgow. Continuous exhibitions are mounted here and it is open every weekday during normal hours. For further details either contact the Curator at Glasgow Caledonian University or visit the Museum Website on: http://www.lib.gcal.ac.uk/hbank/index.htm

Index

Activities, case studies and figures are not indexed

abuse 5–6, 12, 56
  protection from 226
acceptance, of service user 224
active listening 276
activities, as part of care plan 267, 283
Acts of Parliament see legislation; individual Acts
adolescence 108–116
advisory groups 60
advocacy 284, 288
anomie 207
  see also relative deprivation
anti-discriminatory practice 59–61, 74–81, 229
  see also equal opportunities; managing diversity
anticipatory socialisation 92
aspirations 263
assessment
  forms 265
  meetings 264
  of needs, in care planning 256–64
  tools, in care planning 264–7
attachment and separation 149–155
attitudes, promotion of positive health 308
attributes, of good care workers 2–3, 245

Bandura, A. 136, 145–6
behavioural perspective 136
behavioural theory 142–4
Bion's essential features of groups 291
black feminism 189
boundaries, between systems 293
Bowlby, John 149–152
breast-feeding initiative 304, 340–1

care
  anti-discriminatory practice 57–9
  changing nature of 4–7, 13
  discrimination in 55–7
  equal opportunity policies 78
  growth in demand for 14–19
  history of 4–6, 13
  providers of 3–4, 27–9
care planning
  assessment of needs 256–64
  assessment of opportunities 263–4
  good practice 224–9, 254
  relationship with providers 259
  stages 255
  tools for assessment 264–7
care plans
  features 267–8
  models 268–71
care providers
  formal 27–9
  informal 3–4
  relationships with 259
  voluntary 27–8
care work
  good practice 224–9
  monitoring and evaluation 294
  nature of work 12–13
care workers
  attributes 2–3
  essential skills 230–8, 284, 288
  knowledge of resources 259
  organisation of shifts 281
  relationships with providers 259
  relationships with service users 13, 23, 56, 215,

224–39, 247, 275–6, 282–5
  responsibility of power 11–12
  roles 246
case control studies, in epidemiology 356
case records, in research 366–8
challenging behaviour 282–3
change, managing, in health promotion 339–40
changes, lifestyle 20, 96–7, 160–2,
checklists, in assessment 265
childcare provision, and separation 152–3
childhood 106–8
  birth to two 97–102
  two to five 102–105
children
  black, identity confusion 383
  effect of divorce 154
  effects of hospitalisation 153–4
  parents' gender, and development 150
Children's (Scotland) Act 1995 71–2
choice, right to exercise 227
Citizen's Charter 317
client-centred model of health promotion 333
clients see service users
cognitive development 85
  birth to two years 99–100
  two to five years 102–3
  childhood 106
  adolescence 110–111
  adulthood 118–119
  older adult 124–5
cognitive needs, in care planning 260
Commission for Racial Equality 68
commitment, in teamwork 281
communication, effective 230–8
communication barriers 232
communication needs, meeting 259–60
community, changes in, and care 19–20
community development, in health promotion 330
confidentiality, and service user 225–6
conflict perspective 183–4
  and deviance 207–9
  and education 202–4
  and family 195–7
  and institutionalisation 215–16
content analysis 365
control theory 216
core conditions, Carl Rogers model 276
core values
  in care practice 222–3
  in health promotion 315, 318–20
counselling skills 275
covert research 358
  ethical considerations 363
crime, as deviant behaviour 206
critical incidents 282–3
cultural influences
  on access to health provision 309
  on behaviour 148
  on development 90
  effect on discrimination 50, 52
  on health 300, 305–6
cultural needs, in care planning 260
culture
  reinforcement of patriarchy 188, 198
  sociological perspective 176–7

Dahrendorf, Ralph 183–4
Data Protection Act 1998 72
data, in research 347

death
  of parent, effect 155–6
  treatment of, by society 165
Declaration of Human Rights 63
devaluation process, in disability 95
developmental psychology
  attachment and separation theory 149–55
  behavioural theory 142–4
  definition 133–4
  lifespan theory 140–2
  Maslow's Hierarchy of Needs 136–9
  overview 378–9
  perspectives 134–6
  social learning theory 145–8
deviance
  conflict view 207–9
  feminist view 210–11
  functionalist view 206–7
  interactionist view 209–10
diaries, in assessment 266
direct discrimination 41–3
disability, influence on development 94–5
Disability Discrimination Act 1995 69–71
discrimination 25–56
  against service users 55–6
  against staff 56
  challenging 59–60
  cultural 50, 52
  direct 41–3
  effect on development/behaviour 383
  effect on health provision 306–8
  indirect 43–4
  individual 47, 52
  institutional 48–50, 52
  within organisations 48
  responsibility to challenge 12, 47, 57–60
  within society 49–50
  unconscious 44–6
divorce, effect on children 154

education
  and access to health provision 311–12
  conflict view 202–4
  feminist view 204–5
  functionalist view 200–2
  interactionist view 204
  role in socialisation 92, 200
Education (Scotland) Act 1981 72
educational model of health promotion 329
Egan, Gerard 277–8
Eight Ages of Man 140–1
elder abuse 56
emotional development 85
  birth to two years 99–100
  two to five years 103–4
  childhood 106
  adolescence 111–113
  adulthood 119
  older adult 125–127
emotional needs, identifying 261
empowerment 13, 72, 227, 258, 273, 284
  in care of older people 126, 127
  through community development 330
  and disempowerment 215, 216
  and health promotion 315, 387
environment for care, good practice 291–2
epidemiology
  in health promotion 355–6
  methods 356

equal opportunities
  in care context 385–6
  policies, in care 78–9
  see also anti-discriminatory practice; managing
     diversity
Equal Pay Act 1970 65–6
equity, in health promotion 341, 387
Erikson, Erik 136, 140
ethnicity
  influences on health 305–6
  see also culture
ethnocentrism 382
European Community, legislation 64
European Convention for the Protection of Human
     Rights 65
evaluation
  of care work 294
  of health promotion 333–4
  in teamwork 281
exchange model 268
exclusion 53
  in education 72
  social 22
extended family 193

facilitators 246
family
  changing structure, effect on care 19–20
  conflict view 195–7
  extended 193
  feminist view 197–9
  functionalist view 193–5
  influences on health 300
  interactionist view 197
  nuclear 192
  socialisation 194
fathers, role in development 150
fears, of service users 263
feminist perspective 187–9
  and deviance 210–11
  and education 204–5
  and family 197–9
  and institutionalisation 216
flexibility, in teamwork 280
Freud, Sigmund 135, 140
fulfilment of potential, service users 228
functionalist perspective 181–3
  and deviance 206–7
  and education 200–2
  and family 193–5
  and institutionalisation 214–15

gender
  and access to health provision 309–11
  influence on development 93
  influence on health 304–5
  role in family 198
gender identity, development of 104
genetics
  and development 88–9
  influences on health 304–5
geographical location, and health provision 311
giftedness 262–3
good practice
  and care planning 254
  in care work 224–9
  environment 291–2
  in health promotion 315, 318–20
  teamwork 279–81
Gould's stages in personal development 159
government reports, in research 366, 368
GP contracts 320
grief and mourning 166–70
group, Bion's essential features 291
groupwork skills 288–91

handouts, questionnaires 354
health, factors affecting 300–6
Health and Safety at Work Act 1974 and 1983 316
health care, and care demands 16
health councils, local 320
health education 321–3
health prevention 323–5
health promotion 314–21
  appropriateness of messages 329, 331

and care planning 255
  elements 321–5
  evaluation of campaigns 333–4
  management skills 335–41
  models 325–6, 328–33
  related to human development 387
health protection 325
health provision, factors affecting 306–12
helping process 273–5
heredity,
  and development 88–9
  influences on health 300
holidays, for service users 283
holistic view of health 298
hospitalisation, effect on children 153–4
Hopson's model of self-esteem 162
Human Rights Act 1998 73
humanistic perspective 135–6

identification, with role models 145–6
identity, individual, development of 39
identity confusion, black children 383
imitation, in children 145–6
immunisation programmes 323
independence, developing 258, 282
indirect discrimination 43–4
individual discrimination 47, 52
individualisation 222
individualism 20–21
informal carers 3–4
institutional discrimination 48–50
institutional neurosis 213–14
institutionalisation 7–11
  conflict view 215–16
  counteraction 10–11
  feminist view 216
  functionalist view 214–15
  interactionist view 213–14
institutions, sociological perspective 177–8
intellectual development *see* cognitive development
interactionist perspective 184–6
  and deviance 209–10
  and education 204
  and family 197
  and institutionalisation 213–14
interest skills 288
interpersonal skills 230–8, 386
  advocacy 284, 288
  counselling 275
  for good care work 2–3
  see also personal qualities; skills
interviews 354–5, 357

keyworking 247
Kubler-Ross' model of grief 169

labelling, effect on behaviour 209–10
language use
  appropriate 236–7
  and attitudes to service users 45–6
learned helplessness 126
legislation 63–74
  Acts of Parliament 41, 48, 65–73, 316–17, 332
  effect on health provision 312
  for health promotion 316–17, 320
  in health protection 325
  for improved care services 30
  limitations 73
  protective, effect on demand for care 18
liberal feminism 188
life events 160–1
life experiences, sympathising with 23
life skills 288
life story books 283–4
lifespan perspective 136
lifespan theory 140–2
lifestyle, changes 20, 160–2
  due to health promotion 339–40
  unexpected, and development 96–7
listening skills 235, 276
longevity, factors contributing to 15–19
longitudinal research 359
loss 119, 163–70

management skills, in health promotion 335–41
managing diversity 80

Manual Handling Operations Regulations Act
     1992 316
marginalisation 22, 53, 383–4
  and crime 208
marital breakdown, effect on children 154
marketing model of health promotion 330–1
Marx, Karl 183, 207
marxist feminism 189
Maslow, Abraham 135
Maslow's Hierarchy of Needs 136–9, 383–4
maternal deprivation 150–1, 152
Mead, George Herbert 185–6
media
  challenging prejudice 40
  contribution to prejudice 36–7
  coverage of campaigns 73
  in health promotion 323, 329
  programmes for minority groups 58
  role in socialisation 93
  as secondary source 365
medical model of health promotion 328
minority groups, health factors 300–6
models
  exchange 268
  Egan's three stage skills 277–8
  Erikson's Eight Ages of Man 140–1
  Gould's stages in personal development 159
  health promotion 325–6, 328–33
  Hopson's model of self esteem 162
  Kubler-Ross model of grief 169
  Maslow's Hierarchy of Needs 136–9, 383–4
  person centred planning 268–9
  Rogers core conditions 276
  Tannahill's model of health promotion 325–6
  Worden's 'four tasks of mourning' 166–7
monitoring of care work 294
'mortification of self ' 213, 215, 216
mothers, role in development 150
mourning 166–70
multistage random sampling 351

National Disability Council 70
nature/nurture debate 89, 134
needs, examining in care planning 256–62
negotiation, in teamwork 280
networks, individual 280
NHS and Community Care Act 1990 55, 317, 332
non-random sampling 351
non-verbal communication 231, 235–6, 261
normalisation 260
not-for-profit organisations 29
nuclear family 192

Oakley, Ann 188, 198, 199, 305
observation
  in assessment 265–6
  in research 358–9
occupational classes 180, 300
official statistics 364
open questions 276
operant conditioning 142
opportunities, assessment 263–4
organisations, discrimination within 48

paraphrasing, in listening 276
parental responsibilities 71
parenthood, development through 120
parents, role in development 150
partnership, in teamwork 280–1
Patient's Charter 317
peer groups, and development 108, 114
person centred planning 268–71
personal development and change 159
personal qualities
  in care work 241–5
  see also interpersonal skills; skills
perspectives
  developmental psychology 134–6
  sociology 180–9
physical development 85
  birth to two years 98
  two to five years 102
  childhood 106
  adolescence 110
  adulthood 117–118
  older adult 124

physical needs
  assessment 258
  meeting 282
PIES (physical, intellectual/cognitive, emotional, social) 85
pilot studies, in research 352
play, in development 104, 106, 108
political model of health promotion 332
politics, need for awareness 23–7
postal questionnaires 354
poverty, effect on demand for care 17–18
power
  abuse of 56, 215
  responsibility of 11–12
  see also empowerment
pregnancy and childbirth, effect on emotional development 117
prejudice 35–41
  challenging 40–1
  history 37–8
  see also discrimination
presentation, research 370
presentation skills 341–3
pressure groups 61
primary data 347
primary socialisation 91
principles of good practice *see* good practice
privacy, of service user 225
private sector, service providers 29
professional skills 288
project work, management 336–7
protection, of service user 226
psychodynamic perspective 135
psychology, branches 133
punishments, in socialisation 147

qualitative research data 347, 357–9
quantitative research data 347, 349–357
questioning, in assessment 265–6
questionnaires 352–5
quota sampling 350–1

Race Relations Act 1976 67–9
radical feminism 188
random sampling 349
randomised control trials
  in epidemiology 356–7
  ethical considerations 363
records and reports 292–3
reflective responding 276
relationships
  factors affecting caring 230–1
  with care providers 259
  of intimacy, in support 120
  with service users
    abuse of power 56, 215
    acceptance 224
    advocacy 284, 288
    challenging behaviour 282–3
    contributing to self esteem 222
    empathy 282, 284
    ensuring quality of life 228
    giving right to choose 227
    individual 13
    keyworking 247
    listening skills 235, 276
    Roget's core conditions 276
    communication skills 230–8
    sympathetic response 23
    using counselling skills 275
    working on life story books 283–4
relative deprivation 208
  see also anomie

reliability in research 352
religion, role in socialisation 93
research
  epidemiology 355–6
  ethical considerations 363
  presentation 370
  process of 346
  qualitative 347, 357–9
  quantitative 347, 349–57
  questionnaires 352–5
  sampling methods 349–52
  secondary sources 347, 363–8
  topics 347–8
resources for service users 259
rewards, in socialisation 147
rights, individual 63, 65
risk taking, importance of 227, 283
Rogers, Carl 135, 276
role and status 178–9
role models, in development 146
roles, of care workers 245–7

sampling methods 349–52
Scotland, incidence of poor health 299, 301, 332
Scottish Parliament, accessibility 75
scrapbooks, in assessment 266
secondary socialisation 92–3
secondary sources, in research 347, 363–8
self-actualisation 137–9
self-awareness, and discrimination 58
self concept 155, 261
  development of 106, 112, 119
self esteem 157–8
  contribution of care worker 222
  importance for older people 125–6
self image 155–7
separation 149–155
  conflict in adolescence 113
service users 11
  acceptance of 224
  aspirations 263
  cognitive needs 260
  communication needs 259–60
  confidentiality 225–6
  contribution to evaluation 294
  discrimination against 55–6
  emotional needs 261
  empowerment 13, 72, 337, 227, 258, 273, 284
  fears 263
  fulfilment of potential 228
  holidays 283
  image 29
  independence 258, 282
  meeting physical needs 282
  poor treatment of 5–6, 12, 56
  privacy 225
  protection 226
  reaction to life experiences 23
  right of choice 227
  social needs 261
  social welfare 223
  spiritual needs 261
Sex Discrimination Act 1975 41, 48, 65–7
sexual harassment 42
sexuality, in development of self 113
shift organisation, to meet service users needs 281
sincerity, in relationships 233
skills
  groupwork 288–91
  life, interest and professional 288
  presentation, in health promotion 341–3
  for unstructured interviews 357–8
  see also interpersonal skills; personal qualities

Skinner, B. F. 136, 142
social action theory 186–7
social class 179–80
  and access to health provision 309
  influence on health 300–4
  occupational classes 180, 300
social development 85
  birth to two years 100–102
  two to five years 104
  childhood 108
  adolescence 114–116
  adulthood 120–1
  older adult 127–8
social exclusion 22
social expectations 148
social learning theory 145–8
social needs, fulfilling 261
social welfare, of service users 223
socialisation 36, 50, 145–8
  anticipatory 92
  from different perspectives 379–82
  through education 200
  by family 194
  influence on development 90–2
society
  'institutionalised' discrimination 49–50
  sociological perspective 176
socio-economic influences
  on access to health provision 309
  on development 89
  on health 300–4
sociology
  and developmental psychology 379
  effect on care practice 174
spiritual needs, fulfilling 262
statutory service providers 27–8
stereotypes, and prejudice 35–6, 44
stratified random sampling, 350
stress 119
structured interview questionnaires 354–5
subcultures 208, 210
summarising, in listening 276
support, in emotional crises 119, 120
support groups 60
surveys, in epidemiology 356

Tannahill's model of health promotion 325–6
teamwork 279–81
telephone questionnaires 355
three stage skills model 277–8
time management 335–6
total institutions 213
  see also institutions; institutionalisation
transition 119
  and loss 163–170

unconscious discrimination 44–6
understanding, skill of 232
United Nations 63
unstructured interviews 357

validity, in research 352
value base 221
values, in care practice 222–3
verbal communication 231, 261
voluntary service providers 27–8

warmth, in relationships 231
Weber, Max 186–7
Worden's 'four tasks of mourning' 166–7
work, emotional and social roles of 121–2
workplaces, health promotion 316–17
World Health Organisation 298, 315